Mastering United States
Government Information

Mastering United States Government Information

SOURCES AND SERVICES

Christopher C. Brown

LIBRARIES
UNLIMITED®

An Imprint of ABC-CLIO, LLC
Santa Barbara, California • Denver, Colorado

Library of Congress Cataloging-in-Publication Data

Names: Brown, Christopher C., 1953- author.
Title: Mastering United States government information : sources and
    services / Christopher C. Brown.
Description: Santa Barbara, California : Libraries Unlimited, [2020] |
    Includes bibliographical references and index.
Identifiers: LCCN 2019059474 (print) | LCCN 2019059475 (ebook) | ISBN
    9781440872501 (paperback ; acid-free paper) | ISBN 9781440872518 (ebook)
Subjects: LCSH: Government information—United States. | Electronic
    government information—United States. | Government Web sites—United
    States. | Government information agencies—United States. | Government
    publications—Bibliography—Methodology. | Government
    information—United States—Problems, exercises, etc.
Classification: LCC ZA5055.U6 B76 2020 (print) | LCC ZA5055.U6 (ebook) |
    DDC 025.17/340973—dc23
LC record available at https://lccn.loc.gov/2019059474
LC ebook record available at https://lccn.loc.gov/2019059475

ISBN: 978-1-4408-7250-1 (paperback)
        978-1-4408-7251-8 (ebook)

24 23 22 21 20   1 2 3 4 5

This book is also available as an eBook.

Libraries Unlimited
An Imprint of ABC-CLIO, LLC

ABC-CLIO, LLC
147 Castilian Drive
Santa Barbara, California 93117
www.abc-clio.com

This book is printed on acid-free paper ∞

Manufactured in the United States of America

Contents

CHAPTER 4

CHAPTER 12

Foreword

I admit it that I'm a total government documents nerd. While others are soaking up the latest from Neil Gaiman or rereading *Pride and Prejudice* for the 20th time, I like nothing better than curling up with a good book born of a deep dive into government documents. The footnotes are just as intriguing as the text, for it is in them that I discover the documents and records that form the basis of the world that we government information librarians know and love.

Chris Brown's new text demonstrates that he is a government documents nerd par excellence. I've been a government documents librarian for 20 years, and like Chris, I teach a class on the subject for the Library and Information Science Program at my university. Reading *Mastering United States Government Information: Sources and Services* put me on notice that, geek though I may be, there is still a great deal that I don't know about federal government information.

If one needs proof of the value of librarians, it can be found here. Chris previously demonstrated his own mastery of using search engines in his book *Harnessing the Power of Google: What Every Researcher Should Know.* Now, he shows us how to apply those strategies to locate government information. But the book doesn't stop there. *Mastering* doesn't just tell you the *what*; it also explains the *why* of how government information is organized and made available so the reader can develop a conceptual understanding of the structures and flows of government information.

Chris's long experience as a government documents librarian shows through his intricate explication of the arcane world of the federal government, from regulations and laws to patents and data. He combines a wide variety of source material with his own research findings. Government information changes so rapidly that one cannot hope to adequately describe how to find it using mere lists of resources. Chris knows this and has responded by emphasizing concepts, strategies, and tools.

His passion for helping users find government information is evident on every page. The breadth and depth of his expertise is obvious in the astonishing detail he provides surrounding Congressional publications and the legislative process. While you may not conclude, as did John Godfrey Saxe, that "laws, like sausages, cease to inspire respect in proportion as we know how they are made," you will surely respect *Mastering*'s demystification of the inner workings of that august body.

Helpful appendixes cover the SuDocs classification scheme, years and sessions of Congress, abbreviations, foreign government domains, correspondence between the U.S. Code and the *Code of Federal Regulations*, and major databases for federal government information. Abundant illustrations, charts, graphs, and tables will please readers who need to see, as well as read about, relationships and concepts. Exercises reinforce the material presented in each chapter. The final chapter on citing government documents contains numerous examples that will be of use to neophytes and veterans alike.

A host of long-serving government documents librarians have retired in the past decade and have been replaced by new talent. Many of these old-timers (if you will forgive the term) have been able to train their replacements, but for those situations where no direct transfer was possible, *Mastering United States Government Information: Sources and Services* may represent a sort of "brain dump" of the collected wisdom of many years in the weeds with federal documents. This volume will turn any librarian into a confident searcher and user of government information. It rightly takes its place beside the classic works of Boyd and Rips, Schmeckebier, Sears and Moody, Morehead, and Hartnett, Sevetson and Forte.

Gwen Sinclair
Chair, Government Documents & Maps Department
University of Hawaiʻi at Mānoa Library

Introduction

This book is apolitical, and yet it is filled with political themes. The publications of a nation nearly 250 years old contain lofty policies, as well as failed ones. It is hoped that the material contained in these chapters will guide librarians, journalists, researchers, students, and curious citizens through the maze of resources that comprise what we call government information.

I have had a passion for helping others discover government information for most of my library-related life. It all goes back to the first time I learned how to research legislative histories, and I didn't really get it. I took that research seminar three years in a row before I finally understood how to effectively research the background of public laws. My goal since then has been to make it easier for students and researchers to understand the process more quickly than I did. That interest continued when I was hired as a reference librarian at the University of Denver. I was given several choices for area of emphasis. Without blinking, I chose government information. One of the benefits was attending annual and (at that time) semi-annual Federal Depository Library Conferences in the Washington, D.C., area and in other parts of the country. Libraries pay a lot of money to maintain depository library collections, so it is a small consolation that the government pays for these conferences. Few conferences are as helpful and informative for the profession.

Finding information from the federal government has never been particularly easy. In the early days of the Republic there was little form or structure, and nobody had access to anything. Today, we have the internet at our fingertips, but the size of government is beyond what anyone can imagine (Figure I.1).

While some would argue that the government is too big, others wish for more government programs. Either way, we need guides that explain how government information is produced, disseminated, and discovered as we

Figure I.1   Federal budget receipts in millions of dollars.
Source: Office of Management and Budget, 2019.

approach the third decade of web-based discovery. But this is not enough; we also need to understand the tools of the past, since many of them still have value today as we search for obscure publications.

I have been teaching classes on government information in the University of Denver Library School program since 2003 and have taught the class over a dozen times. The course was supposed to be taught on a three-year rotation, but students kept demanding it, and it has been offered almost every year. Although most of the students will not go on to be government information librarians, I'm sure they will incorporate what they learned into whatever aspect of the information profession they find themselves in. This book is dedicated to them.

ORGANIZATION

Government information is complex. In an effort to organize this book, some resources that could be mentioned under executive agencies are in the statistical chapter. The index should help locating resources.

I have arranged the book in much the same way I have taught the class. Originally, the government information class at the University of Denver was a three-credit class, but most of the time, it has been a two-credit class. That means that I have to spend time on the most important topics. In particular, I opt to focus on the areas in which most of the questions from patrons, students, and the public come from, namely legislation and statistics.

The book focuses on the government entities that publish the information and not so much on topics like education, health, or business. You will find each of these topics interwoven throughout the book in topics such as the executive branch agencies, census tools, and regulations. I find that the questions that come my way fall into patterns. A high percentage of questions revolve around the legislative process. For this reason, two chapters are devoted to legislative history research. So many questions involve statistics that I devote an entire chapter to how to think about statistics generally, and three chapters to how to understand the census and how to mine this data for users.

You will notice that this book does not have individual chapters on many topical areas such as education, business, and agriculture. Instead, the focus is on the difficult skill sets that are necessary to access and understand government information (functions of congressional publication, researching legislative histories, understanding publication patterns of presidential issuances, cross-walking from legislation to regulations, etc.). Those topical areas are highlighted in chapter 6, covering executive branch resources.

LINKS TO ONLINE CONTENT

I give URLs to specific titles or publications when necessary to get to an exact publication. Often, URLs are simply too long to render attractively in print. In those cases, I suggest a Google search that will inevitably lead to the document.

But I am introducing two conventions in this work that have not been used before. I am doing this so that not quite as many long, ugly URLs are included in the text, to make it easier for you, the reader, to quickly get to the resource to which I am referring, and to make this work relevant for a longer period of time (in other words, to minimize the inevitable "link rot" that occurs when web citations go bad).

The first new convention is using Google to point to a publication. Examples in the text include the following:

site:state.gov Status Foreign Relations of the United States

site:gao.gov "rapid dna"

Google: *FDLP superintendent of documents scheme*

The italicized words in these cases show the terms to be typed into Google (or another web search engine, such as Bing) to get to the results. Many government web sites notoriously rearrange their web content often (the State Department being one of the worst offenders). If I merely have a static URL, the usefulness of this book will likely be truncated. In the second case above, I purposely use "straight quotes" rather than "curly quotes" to denote phrase searching, a helpful search convention that forces words to be a single term, increasing the relevancy of the results. In some cases, where it may not be clear that I am suggesting a Google search, I overtly preface the search terms with "Google:" so that the reference to a suggested search is clear.

The Google search phrase, entered in italics, serves two purposes; it should ultimately lead you to the publications to which I refer, and it teaches you the recommended method for doing deep searches for government publications.

The second convention I introduce throughout the book is heavy integration of reference to HathiTrust digital repository content. Many references are made to content within the HathiTrust (HT). Each of these reference points to full-text availability with HathiTrust. I find it helpful to point to specific records within the repository, so that users can easily locate materials. In the book, you will see "See HT record 010111371." This refers to a specific record ID within the HathiTrust collection. These records can be accessed in two ways: (1) simply put the number in the HathiTrust search box (making sure that the catalog search option is selected rather than full text); or (2) append the HT record ID number to this URL stem: https://catalog.hathitrust.org/Record/, like this: https://catalog.hathitrust.org/Record/010111371. By referring the HT records in this way, we avoid ugly and long URLs in these cases. At times, however, reference to a specific page within a document needs to be referenced. In these cases, long HT URLs are unavoidable. This use of HathiTrust works perfectly in the context of U.S. government information, since it is generally freely available. This convention would not work in contexts where copyright restrictions existed.

The Internet Archive (text archive) is also referenced throughout the book. Although it does not contain as many U.S. government publications as HathiTrust does, when present, the works are more easily browsed and can be fully downloaded. If you find a publication in HathiTrust, you may want to also search the title in the Internet Archive to see if it shows up. You will then have more options available for reading, printing, and downloading. HathiTrust usually follows the accepted cataloging practice of cataloging a serial title, and then attaching individual records to the title. The Internet Archive, on the other hand, generally catalogs each individual serial issue, making it difficult to pull all the issues together under a single serial title. So HathiTrust makes it easier to locate content, while the Internet Archive makes it easier to use the content.

The Government Printing Office became the Government Publishing Office in December 2014 (P.L. 113–235, Division H; 128 Stat. 2130, 2537). Throughout the book, if the primary emphasis is on older materials, I will refer to the GPO as the Government Printing Office. If, however, emphasis is on current practices, I will refer to the Government Publishing Office. This saves the time of having to continually explain the name change.

EXERCISES

I envision that some will use this book in government information courses. Because of that, I have included exercises at the end of each chapter.

REFERENCE

Office of Management and Budget. 2019. "Historical Tables." Accessed August 12, 2019. https://www.whitehouse.gov/omb/historical-tables/.

1

The Shape of United States Government Information

Information comes at us nearly every minute via our smartphones. Some of it comes from friends updating us on their activities and their "likes"; other information comes in the form of automatic notifications from apps we forgot we had. Then there are the ads, pushed at us by companies demanding our attention and our dollars. Information is valuable: by it we can be persuaded to spend our money, and by knowing what our preferences are, companies can both offer us more ways to spend it and leverage our preferences to persuade others to do the same.

Our founding fathers couldn't have envisioned the information-rich world in which we now live, but they did understand the value of knowing what government entities are doing and that an informed citizenry is preferable over the alternative. To understand our present context of government information, we need to understand our historic past. After all, we might have had a country where all government information was viewed as a commodity, where only those who can afford to pay can have access.

EARLY FOUNDERS AND ACCESS TO GOVERNMENT INFORMATION

One of the most treasured values of the United States of America is the firm commitment to open and free access to government information. When our country was formed, we were rebelling against a monarchy and a system of government that laid many burdens upon its people. It is easy to find many statements among our early founders regarding the desire to have this new country be one in which citizens have free and easy access to what their government is doing. This ethic permeates our nation's history and is still strongly with us today.

From the early days, efforts were made to distribute documents far and wide to ensure that citizens knew what their government was doing. In 1813, legislation was passed that sent copies of the Journals of Congress to select universities and historical societies (3 Stat. 140). In 1895, we saw the first glimpses of a systematized depository distribution program. From then until 1962, all depository libraries received the same print distributions. But with the Depository Library Act of 1962 (P.L. 87-579, 76 Stat. 352, 44 U.S.C. ch. 19), regional depository libraries were designated to receive all items distributed through the program, and selective depository libraries were allowed to designate which items they wanted to receive to best serve local clientele.

This foundational emphasis on free and open access to information, when in the current context of worldwide internet access, has created a wealth of information—so much information, in fact, that few know how to deal with it. If you ask students today if they feel comfortable using search engines to find anything they want, they will generally answer in the affirmative. But when asked to find specific regulations, comments from a presidential press conference, or a technical report on bridge stress, they usually have difficulty navigating the online landscape. It's one thing to be able to put a few words in a search engine; it's quite another to understand the underlying file types, data sets, and information portals that contain this information and that are, very often, opaque to Google crawling.

CHALLENGES TO FREE ACCESS

Many forces seek to restrict this free access. In some cases, access to government information is not truly free. It's understandable that commercial interests need to make profits to exist. As examples of this, commercial publishers have largely taken over publication of court cases, and the Commerce Department charges money for certain of its documents, albeit on a cost-recovery basis. But for the most part, information in this country is free, even though citizens must be ever-vigilant to protect this right for future generations.

Even though the early founders had free public access to government information in mind, many forces pull in the opposite direction. On the international level, the United Nations used to charge money for many of its information products. In recent years, fortunately, that trend has been reversing. Now the UN treaties databases and other major UN websites are freely available. Foreign countries often have closed portals to their laws. U.S. states do not always abide by the same principles as the federal government. Freedom of information laws are becoming more well-known and practiced around the world, but this is still evolving, and there are many nations with restrictions (Banisar 2010). The United Nations' E-Government Survey and its E-Government Development Index seek to track individual nations' use of information technologies to promote access and inclusion of its people (UN 2019). The Sunlight Foundation's Web Integrity Project monitors federal websites for content changes and removal of information (Sunlight Foundation 2019).

Another challenge is classification of information. National security demands that certain types of information be kept from nefarious interests that desire to harm our national interests. In addition to national security, there are personal security concerns. Recently, several publications that had been distributed far and wide to depository libraries were recalled by the Government Publishing Office because they contained social security numbers and other personal information.

Then there's the challenge of fugitive documents—documents that never become properly recognized, cataloged, preserved, and entered into the national memory of publications. This is the old "if a tree falls in the forest" problem. If information is posted on the internet, but nobody captures the document for archival preservation or for indexing/cataloging purposes (by GPO and other entities), does it really exist? We get into this more in chapter 2.

GOVERNMENT DOCUMENTS OR GOVERNMENT INFORMATION?

There is great ambiguity in the term "government documents." Many depository libraries have historically called their depository units the "government documents" collection. Yet this term can be used to denote the following:

- Government publications issued by an official government agency (federal, state, or local) for public distribution. These may be in the form of books, reports, statistical databases, or sets of regulations, to mention just a few examples.

- Private issuances related to a legal matter. These may include judicial orders, injunctions, findings, or many other matters that may be sealed for privacy purposes.
- Government records with retention schedules. Typically, government records are maintained by the National Archives and Records Administration (NARA).
- Classified or secret government information that can only be released by court order, executive order, FOIA request, or timed release (as in a retention schedule).

Given this ambiguity, it is no wonder that many people now prefer the terms government publications or government information over government documents, although these terms are subject to ambiguities of their own. In this book, I use the term government information or government publications to refer to the first of the bulleted options above—the freely available government issuances, whether in print, microformat (microfiche, microfilm, or microopaque), online website or PDF file, or database format. In the past, these were issued by any of the three branches of government, often, but not always, through the auspices of the Government Printing Office. These are the kinds of physical publications housed in depository libraries across the United States and usually cataloged in library catalog records (although many large depository libraries still have vast amounts of uncataloged publications). The National Academy of Public Administration (NAPA 2013) estimated that there were approximately 2.3 million items in the Federal Depository Library Program, with up to one third of them having never been cataloged.

WHAT DO USERS WANT?

What kinds of government information are users seeking? We can answer this question in several ways.

- Analytics.usa.gov. Just take a minute and visit analytics.usa.gov. You will get a "live" window into what government websites people are visiting now, in the past seven days, and in the past 30 days. This site is informative and addicting.
- Ourdocuments.gov. Cosponsored by the National Archives and Record Administration (NARA), ourdocuments.gov has "The People's Vote" section, where people have voted for the most influential documents in U.S. history. This is another addicting website.

- University of Denver Click-Through Project. I know which documents users in my library use. I did a little study of a period of 10 years, where I tracked document "click throughs" from the university's library catalog to online publications. You can check it out in Brown (2011).

There is no single answer to what users want. Users want their questions answered, and "e-government" is a huge part of that. Students and scholars often want congressional hearings. Scientists and engineers need technical reports, sometimes older ones. GIS data and mapping tools are continually growing in importance. The legal community needs quick access to authenticated regulations, statutes, codes, and cases.

THE FORMATS OF GOVERNMENT INFORMATION

In simpler times, all government information was disseminated in print format. The advantage of print is that it doesn't need to be updated and migrated to the latest format, as digital content does. The disadvantage is that it eventually disintegrates, some types of paper more than others. Another obvious down side is that you need to find a library where the physical document exists in order to examine it. The shelves of libraries around the country are filled with paper documents. More than ever, libraries are feeling a space crunch, and there is a major push to withdraw print materials from depository libraries. There are several reasons for this: (1) there is so much print government information, (2) physical collections are receiving less and less use, (3) much (but certainly not all) of this content is available online, and (4) libraries want to use the shelf space for other purposes.

Microformats were something like the "internet of the past." GPO began issuing documents in microfiche in the 1970s (GPO 2016). Microfilm/microfiche could be duplicated relatively inexpensively and, thus, provided access to valuable materials without having to actually own the print versions. Libraries without much money or shelf space could purchase microfiche or microfilm and have access to resources that were previously held only in larger libraries. Microformats were relatively inexpensive to produce, utilized a fraction of the space of print, and enabled dissemination of rare materials to a broader audience (thus the similarities to today's internet access). Many initiatives capitalized on microformat dissemination, especially microfiche. Examples of this included the ERIC fiche project (see chapter 6), the Department of Energy fiche distribution project that began in the 1970 and was later folded into the DOE's former Information Bridge database (now OSTI.gov), and the fiche from the NASA technical reports. During the 1980s until the 2000s, microfiche was a popular distribution format for many depository libraries. Much of this content can be found online now, but not enough to just push fiche cabinets into a dumpster. The format has the advantage of stability (as long as it is one of the stable fiche formats), but it can be difficult to file in fiche drawers and cabinets, and it is easy for fiche to be misfiled and lost forever.

Today's government information is usually published online in formats familiar to all. Documents in Adobe's popular portable document format (PDF) are most common. Occasionally, a publication will appear in Microsoft Word format (.doc or .docx), and other formats can be found as well, such as e-book formats like MOBI or EPUB. Government information also comes in the form of online databases, some coming from agencies themselves, and others coming from the Government Publishing Office.

Older electronic publications were issued on floppy discs, CD-ROMs or DVD-ROMs. Occasionally these materials (often referred to as "tangible electronic formats") contained proprietary formats and even required proprietary software that ran on now-obsolete computer systems. Examples of this are the CD-ROM discs from the 1990s that contained census data. The data has largely been migrated to newer systems or is available via commercial vendors. The ever-growing popularity of government data, such as that hosted on data.gov, opens up many other electronic formats.

The access and preservation mission of depository libraries is complicated by the proliferation of nonbook formats over time. Examples included floppy discs of various sizes, videos (VHS), and kits (multiple material types combined together). Occasionally, tangible media contain software programs that were intended to retrieve the data on the media.

But before this proliferation of online content with its many formats, there were print publications. For most of our nation's history, the print format ruled. Daily publication of the print proceedings of Congress, now called the *Congressional Record*, documented the goings on of the House and Senate. Annual reports of executive branch agencies dealt with budgets, programs, and plans of these agencies.

Then there is the issue of language. While the majority language of the United States is English, selected documents have been made available in other languages. Not surprisingly, Spanish is the most popular of the foreign languages. But documents have also appeared in well over 100 languages. You can see the list for yourself by going to the advanced search feature of Catalog of Government Publications (catalog.gpo.gov). Hundreds of Braille editions are regularly published, particularly from the Social Security Administration, National Park Service, Department of Education, and Library of Congress.

DOCUMENT TOPICS

What topics are covered within government publications? Perhaps we should ask the converse: What topics are not covered? Documents librarians often say that almost any question can be turned into a government documents question. There are several ways to show the diversity of topics. One would be to see what the Government Publishing Office portal (Govinfo.gov) includes. However, GPO's mission does not extend to all government agencies. Even so, by going to Govinfo.gov and performing a few searches, you will quickly discover a wide breadth of information.

If you are considering accesses to government web content, then analytics.usa.gov is the place to look. This site is a USA.gov version of what Google analytics does for the web generally. But with analytics.usa.gov, you can get a sense of what government information is important to people at a given point in time. Looking at the top downloads, it is clear that e-government (downloadable forms) is most important. The scope of the analytics is only executive branch and military sites. It mostly overlooks the legislative and judicial branches.

If we think about information the way it is divided up in the academic world—science and engineering, social sciences, and the humanities—the humanities topics are not well represented. What is strong is content in the sciences and engineering, and medicine. Social sciences are strong when one considers all the public policy issues surrounding legislation and judicial information. Aside from attempts to place percentages on large swaths of content, it is difficult to find a topic that is not somehow addressed in government publications.

DOCUMENT TYPES

Government issuances span the spectrum from official publications to ephemeral brochures. A high percentage of publications are considered serial publications, since they are issued on a regular (or sometimes irregular) basis. Table 1.1 shows some examples from the print world and from the online realm of government publications of various types.

It may not be obvious from Table 1.1, but some of these document types are sets of bound volumes that occupy hundreds of shelves (e.g., the *Congressional Record*), whereas others are single slips of paper (e.g., some treaties, fact sheets, or brochures). This presents a challenge for depository libraries opting to shelve these materials. Do they just shelve all these materials together and hope that the little slips of paper don't get lost? Do they buy "Princeton files" and keep them on the shelves in hopes that things will stay together? Do they take large sets out and shelve them in another part of the library—for example, taking materials out of the superintendent of documents call number order and placing them in the Library of Congress classification section of the library?

Table 1.1   Types of government documents with examples

Document Type	Title and Access Information
Annual Reports	Office of Surface Mining annual report. SuDocs: I 71.1: http://purl.access.gpo.gov/GPO/LPS1323.
Brochures	Visitor Guide, Great Sand Dunes National Park and Preserve. SuDocs: I 29.21/2:G 79/. https://purl.fdlp.gov /GPO/gpo92831.
Budgets	The Budget of the United States Government. OCLC: 932137. SuDocs: PREX 2.8: http://purl.access.gpo.gov /GPO/LPS43689.
Census Data	Income and poverty in the United States. SuDocs: C 3.186/41-2: http://purl.fdlp.gov/GPO/gpo65616.
Codes	United States Code. OCLC: 2368380. SuDocs: Y 1.2/5: http://purl.access.gpo.gov/GPO/LPS2873.
Comic Books	Browse the Government Comics Collection from the University of Nebraska: https://mediacommons.unl .edu/luna/.
Directories	Biographical Directory of the United States Congress, 1774–1989. SuDocs: Y 1.1/3:100-34; Y 1.1/2: SERIAL 13849/ HT 001950338.
Fact Sheets	Fact sheet. Other Tobaccos. OCLC: 43455620. SuDocs: A 112.15: T 55/ HT 007417350.
Forms	Schedule A (Form 1040), itemized deductions. OCLC: 671488468. SuDocs: T 22.51:1040/SCH.A/FORM/ http://purl.fdlp.gov/GPO/gpo255.
Handbooks and Manuals	United States Government Manual. OCLC: 1788884. SuDocs: AE 2.108/2: HT 009815800.
Hearings (Congressional Testimony)	Immigration Reorganization and Improvement Act of 1999: hearing before the Subcommittee on Immigration and Claims of the Committee on the Judiciary, House of Representatives, One Hundred Sixth Congress, first session, on H.R. 2528, July 29, 1999. Note: this hearing is not included in Govinfo .gov. SuDocs: Y 4.J 89/1:106/76. HT 011341362.
Historical Works	Seven Firefights in Vietnam / United States Army, Office of the Chief of Military History. SuDocs: D 114.2:V 67 http://purl.access.gpo.gov/GPO/LPS73516.
Maps	Summer motor vehicle use map. White River National Forest. Aspen—Sopris Ranger District, Colorado. SuDocs: A 13.28:W 58/17/. http://purl.fdlp .gov/GPO/gpo86955.
Patents	Search http://patft.uspto.gov for examples.

Table 1.1   (continued)

Document Type	Title and Access Information
Presidential Speeches	*Public Papers of the Presidents of the United States.* SuDocs: AE 2.114: http://purl.access.gpo.gov/GPO /LPS4752.
Proceedings and Debates	*Congressional Record* [Permanent ed.]. OCLC: 5058415. SuDocs: X. http://purl.access.gpo.gov/GPO /LPS76447.
Regulations	*Federal Register.* SuDocs: AE 2.106: http://purl.access .gpo.gov/GPO/LPS1756.
Reports (Congressional)	Spurring Private Aerospace Competitiveness and Entrepreneurship Act of 2015: Report Together with Minority. SuDocs: Y 1.1/8:114-119. http://purl.fdlp.gov /GPO/gpo57640.
Statistical Compendia	Statistical Abstract of the United States. SuDocs: C 3.134/7: HT 007911858, 000533311.
Statutes	Patient Protection and Affordable Care Act. SuDocs: AE 2.110:111-148 http://purl.access.gpo.gov/GPO /LPS124425.
Technical Reports	Modeling Natural Gas Regulatory Proposals Using the Project Independence Evaluation System. SuDocs: E 3.26/3:1 https://www.osti.gov/biblio/6276017.
Treaties	Investment Guaranties: Agreement between the United States of America and Bulgaria, Signed at Sofia June 7, 1991. OCLC: 34342224; SuDocs: S 9.10:11500 HT 102195821.
Vital Records	Vital Statistics of the United States. SuDocs: HE 20.6210: http://purl.access.gpo.gov/GPO/LPS25040.

ORGANIZATION OF GOVERNMENT/ORGANIZATION OF PUBLICATIONS

At the outset, it is important to understand the complex structure of the U.S. federal government. There is no better resource for doing this than the *United States Government Manual.* Published annually since 1935 by various entities of the federal government, the manual lists every government entity for all three branches of government, legislative, judicial, and executive. It is considered the "official handbook" of the U.S. government.

The United States Government Manual. Washington, DC: Office of the Federal Register: 1935–. (GS 4.109: and AE 2.108/2:) (HT 009815800). Title varies: *United States Government Organization Manual*, 1949–1972.

Although the government manual is archived on the GPO website (https:// www.govinfo.gov/app/collection/GOVMAN), the current, interactive version is much easier to use at https://www.usgovernmentmanual.gov/. The historical versions of this resource, together with the *Guide to U.S. Government Publications* (OCLC 1795366), are critical to understanding changes to government entities over time. The manual is available on Govinfo.gov back to 1995, but issues back to 1935 are available by searching the title in the Internet Archive and HathiTrust.

Each government entry is accompanied by reference to the creating act or order. For example, "The Federal Maritime Commission was established by Reorganization Plan No. 7 of 1961 (46 U.S.C. 301–307), effective August 12, 1961." A special section of the manual tracks the history of agency organizational changes with reference to statutes and executive orders. Also, organizational charts assist in understanding hierarchical relationships.

The current edition of the *U.S. Government Manual* pointed to on Govinfo.gov is at this URL: https://www.usgovernmentmanual.gov/. I find that this interface is not very user-friendly, is difficult to navigate, and makes it nearly impossible to find organizational charts. The print versions are much easier to navigate. The PDF versions of recent volumes are merely all the HTML pages pieced together into a nearly incompressible format. I recommend using a version in the Internet Archive instead (https://archive .org/details/unitedstatesgove01unit).

Another official resource that many find helpful in the task of organizing the federal government is *Codes for the Identification of Federal and Federally Assisted Organizations*, an organizational coding standard to be used for physical and computer access to federal facilities by employees and contractors. This NIST publication is available at https://nvlpubs.nist.gov /nistpubs/SpecialPublications/NIST.SP.800-87r2.pdf. Most people reading this book would not be interested in the codes themselves but would be interested in the detail with which organizations are detailed and how they are related to each other. As an example of how this work might be helpful, see Table 1.2. An excerpt from the Department of Education is shown.

Those seeking to make web pages of government agencies and not wanting to omit any subagency would want to consult both the *Government Manual* and the NIST codes document mentioned above to ensure that nothing is omitted.

SUPERINTENDENT OF DOCUMENTS CLASSIFICATION SYSTEM

Most library users are quite familiar with subject-based classification systems such as the Library of Congress or the Dewey Decimal schemes.

Table 1.2   Example of Department of Education codes from the NIST publication

Code	Organization
9100	EDUCATION, Department of
9101	Immediate Office of the Secretary of Education
9102	Office of the Deputy Secretary of Education
9103	Office of the General Counsel
9104	Office of Inspector General
9105	Office of Management
9106	Office of the Chief Financial Officer
9107	Office of Legislation and Congressional Affairs
9108	Office of the Under Secretary
9109	Office of Communications and Outreach
9110	Office of Planning, Evaluation and Program Development
9111	Office for Civil Rights
9115	Office of the Chief Information Officer
9121	Office of English Language Acquisition
9131	Federal Student Aid
9132	Immediate Office of the Director of Education Sciences
9135	National Center for Education Research
9136	National Center for Special Education Research
9137	National Center for Educational Evaluation and Regional Assistance
9138	National Center for Education Statistics
9139	Institute of Education Sciences
9146	Office of Elementary and Secondary Education

These popular systems are subject-based, meaning that the logical arrangement is based on subjects or topics, ordered in a logical and hierarchical manner. But U.S. federal publications in recent years are famously cataloged by a provenance-based system, the Superintendent of Documents Classification System (abbreviated SuDocs). Developed between 1891 and 1897 by the young librarian Adelaide Hasse, the system is easily recognizable, with its generally pneumonic letters, together with dashes, slashes, and colons (Nelson and Richardson 1986). The Government Publishing Office distributes documents to depository libraries with the SuDocs classification numbers already assigned, something that saves libraries that choose to use the system an enormous amount of time.

Depository libraries are not required to use the system. It's just that in past decades, so many documents were received by regional or large selective libraries that keeping the documents in a separate SuDocs collection saved cataloging time and made inventory work more efficient. Often, however, smaller libraries elect to integrate government publications into their existing classification schemes, usually the Dewey Decimal Classification system (DDC) or the Library of Congress Classification system (LC).

To quickly see how the Superintendent of Documents classification system works in real life, I can point the reader to a crude tool I made several years ago to help users navigate the documents shelves at the University of Denver library. In reality, I think that very few library users actually use the tool. It seems only to be used in classes when I am teaching about the SuDocs system. This is especially the case since 2011, when the University of Denver moved all tangible documents to offsite storage. With not one government publication from the SuDocs collection in the on-campus library stacks, how does one replicate a browsing experience? The tool attempts to accomplish that task. Originally designed for an Innovative Interfaces Millennium/Sierra integrated library system, the entire tool needed to be revised in 2016 to accommodate the switch to an ExLibris Alma/Primo system.

The tool can be viewed at https://libguides.du.edu/BrowseDocs. Browsing the tool, one observes the obvious pneumonic device inherent in the assignment of stems: most of the stem assignments are shortcuts to the agency name, making the SuDocs classification the easiest of systems to commit to memory. For example, A for Agriculture, C for Commerce, D for Defense, and so forth. Toward the end of the alphabet, things fall apart, with Y being used for Congress. I always joke with my students that this actually makes sense, since we often ask "Y" is Congress doing that? To be clearer, X is used for the *Congressional Record* and congressional journals Y contains the major divisions of Y1 for House and Senate bills, reports and documents; Y 3 for congressional commission publications; Y 4 for congressional hearings and committee prints; and Z is used to retrospectively refer to the publications of the Continental Congress.

The provenance-based system would work well if government agencies were never reorganized. But clearly, this is not the case. Just take a look at the *Guide to U.S. Government Publications* (commonly referred to as "Andriot") to see the hundreds of changes that have occurred. Most agencies change over time, with the SuDocs numbers, and often even the stems under which they are organized, changing along with them. Since a very high percent of publications can be considered serial publications, this becomes problematic. Libraries are left with three choices.

1. Leave the documents under the classification to which they are assigned,

DIFFERENCES BETWEEN SUBJECT-BASED AND PROVENANCE-BASED SYSTEMS

To illustrate the differences between classifying materials in a provenance-based system like SuDocs and a subject-based system like the Library of Congress classification system, consider Table 1.3.

Table 1.3   Differences in classification between SuDocs and LC classification using climate change documents as examples

Title	SuDocs Classification and Publishing Agency	Library of Congress Classification and Broad Subject
Assessing potential climate change pressures across the conterminous United States: mapping plant hardiness zones, heat zones, growing degree days, and cumulative drought severity throughout this century	A 13.78/3:NRS-9 Forest Service	QC 981.8.C5 Climatology
Coral reef resilience to climate change in Guam in 2016	C 55.13/2:CRCP 29 National Oceanic and Atmospheric Administration	QH 541.5.C7 Ecology
An abrupt climate change scenario and its implications for United States national security	D 1.2:C 61 Department of Defense	QC 981.8.C5 Climatology
Climate change indicators in the United States (October 2016)	EP 1.2:C 61/20 Environmental Protection Agency	QC 903.2.U6 Climatology
Climate change: observations on the potential role of carbon offsets in climate change legislation: testimony before the Subcommittee on Energy and Environment	GA 1.5/2:GAO-09-456 T Government Accountability Office	QC 903.2.U6 Climatology
Cultural resources climate change strategy	I 29.2:C 61/5 National Park Service	QC 902.9 Climatology
Climate projections based on emissions scenarios for long-lived and short-lived radiatively active gases and aerosols	PREX 23.2:EM 6 Executive Office of the President	QC 882.42 Climatology

Notice that in Table 1.3, documents on the same topic, climate change, have been published by a wide variety of government agencies. Thus, each of them is assigned a SuDocs stem corresponding to that agency. However, most of these publications, under the Library of Congress classification system, would be shelved very near each other in the QC classification.

With a subject-based system, users would see like materials shelved together, whether the publication was from a commercial publisher or a government agency. This puts less strain on the users. With a provenance-based system, users have to do more legwork, but they see the work of individual governmental agencies and can appreciate the distinctiveness of these publications.

Arguably, the SuDocs system puts much more strain on the library user. But when depository libraries were receiving many more materials in print that they are now, it was impractical for them to take the time and expense to classify all government publications into another system like LC, especially when one considers that the shipping list coming from GPO told them what the SuDocs number is when the materials arrive. This is why in most larger depository libraries, government publications are shelved in a separate area in a SuDocs arrangement. Small depositories may be more likely to spend the time to classify materials into a subject-based system to save the users' time and to make government publications more accessible.

2. Use the original classification, and

3. Use the latest (most recent) classification.

When libraries opt to use either option one or three above, they generally leave markers of some kind in the stacks (often called "dummy boards"), notifying users that they have holdings under that SuDocs number that are shelved in a different location. With modern online catalogs doing much of the "heavy lifting," other libraries do not bother to follow this practice.

Let's use the *Annual Report of the Governor of the Panama Canal.* This serial publication was published from 1915 to 1951, but the underlying agencies changed several times, as Table 1.4 shows.

The same thing can be seen with more familiar publications. To get greater clarity on this, we need some examples (Table 1.5).

Hundreds of these changes can be seen in the Agency Class Chronology within the *Guide to U.S. Government Publications.*

A SuDocs number generally consists of three parts: the author symbol (which is usually pneumonic), a series designation, and a document number or "Cutter" number of some kind. (Charles Ammi Cutter originally

Table 1.4   SuDocs changes over time with the *Annual Report of the Governor of the Panama Canal*

Years	Agency	SuDocs
1915–1947	War Department	W 79.1:
1948	Military Establishment	M 115.1:
1949	Defense Department	D 113.1:
1950–1951	Canal Zone	PaC 1.1:

Table 1.5   SuDocs changes within two federal agencies over time

Agency Hierarchy	Years	SuDocs
Education Office		
Independent Dept. until 1869, then Interior Dept., Education Bureau.	1867–1929	I 16
Dept. of the Interior, Office of Education.	1929–1939	I 16
Federal Security Agency, Office of Education.	1939–1969	FS 5
Dept. of Health and Human Services, Office of Education.	1970–1972	HE 5
Dept. of Health and Human Services, Education Division, Office of Education.	1972–1979	HE 19.100
Dept. of Education.	1979–	ED 1
Soil Conservation Service		
Dept. of the Interior. Soil Erosion Service.	1933–1935	I 30
Dept. of Agriculture. Soil Conservation Service.	1935–1942	A 57
Dept. of Agriculture. Agricultural Conservation and Adjustment Administration. Soil Conservation Service.	1942	A76.200
Dept. of Agriculture. Food Production Administration. Soil Conservation Service.	1942–1943	A 79.200
Administration of Food Production and Distribution. Soil Conservation Service.	1943–1944	A 80.2000
Dept. of Agriculture. War Food Administration (independent agency). Soil Conservation Service	1944–1945	A 80.500
Dept. of Agriculture. Soil Conservation Service.	1945–	A 57

devised a system of letters and numbers to provide an alphabetical book arrangement.) Let's look at some simple examples.

C 3.134:932

> C—SuDocs designation for the Commerce Department
>
> 3—Subclassification for the Census Bureau, organized under the Commerce Department.
>
> .134—Series designation for the serial title *Statistical Abstract of the United States*
>
> :932—Year of the issue. Notice that in the twentieth century, a three-digit system was used (nobody had considered the Y2K era!). Beginning in 2000, four-digit designations became necessary.

HE 1.2:R 11

> HE—SuDocs designation for the Department of Health and Human Services
>
> 1—Subclassification for the Department proper.
>
> .2—General publications of the Department.
>
> :R 11—Cutter designation for the title *Racial, Ethnic, and Sex Enrollment Data from Institutions of Higher Education.*

There are many nuances to the SuDocs classification system. Originally the four series designations were incorporated into the system:

.1 Annual Reports

.2 General Publications

.3 Bulletins

.4 Circulars

These four series have been used fairly consistently over the years. As time went by, additional designations were assigned, but they have not been used as regularly:

.5 Laws

.6 Regulations, rules, and instructions

.7 Press releases

.8 Handbooks, manuals, and guides

.9 Bibliographies and lists of publications

.10 Directories

.11 Maps and charts

.12 Posters

.13 Forms

.14 Addresses

More information on the intricacies of the SuDocs classification system can be found on the FDLP website (Google: *FDLP superintendent of documents scheme*).

This little lesson in the Superintendent of Documents classification system will not be necessary for most users, since they will prefer to retrieve online materials whenever possible. But we should all keep in mind the immense time and effort librarians of past generations have invested in making print government information accessible. Libraries will be around with print resources for generations to come, and it is helpful to know something of the ways these collections tend to be organized.

GOVERNMENT PUBLICATIONS, PRINT COLLECTIONS, AND ONLINE ACCESS

Years ago, being a designated depository library was considered prestigious. "Federal Depository Library status is a great honor. It is seen by most libraries as a unique and very valuable asset" (GPO 1986). Today, many libraries are seeing declining usage statistics and can't withdraw documents fast enough. At the same time, nobody wants these documents to completely disappear, so numerous digitization efforts continue to provide access to as much content as possible. Much discussion continues as to who can keep what in terms of historic government publications. Do all regional libraries need to keep everything? Can there be shared regionals to focus on selected SuDocs stems to the exclusion of others?

Collection development for government publications in the print era brought great honor for being a depository library. In this not-so-much print electronic era, prestige is not the issue; it is economizing space. The online era tempts us with the ease of linking to online government content, but the subtle danger exists that this content may be volatile. It may not even be there tomorrow.

What is missing from all of these discussions is an authoritative checklist of publications. There was the 1911 checklist and others that came later. But there has never been an authoritative checklist of all government publications emanating from the federal government. Given all that has been said so far about fugitive documents from the print era and digital fugitives, we can begin to understand why this is the case. Nevertheless, effort should be made for an ongoing, continually updated, checklist of documents. In addition, this list should link out to libraries that hold these materials. The Association of Southeastern Research Libraries is taking strides at a database of inventories of depository libraries in their region (Swanbeck and Harris 2012), but this inventory is not open to non-member libraries. University of North Texas Libraries continues to maintain the U.S. Congressional Serial Set Inventory (UNT 2014). At least that is a start, but a comprehensive checklist of documents, together with a linked inventory of library holdings, is how we can get some kind of control over what publications exist in all formats and what libraries own them.

COMPETENCIES OF GOVERNMENT INFORMATION PROFESSIONALS

As you can tell by perusing the table of contents of this book, the government information professional dabbles in many areas. Skills span all academic categories, from the humanities (history, art, architecture, printing) to social sciences (politics and policy, social work and psychology, law and legislation, business and economics), and science and engineering (aerospace, agriculture, wildlife, ecology and environment), and standards, to mention just a few areas. The competencies required at various times include the skills listed in Table 1.6.

USING GOOGLE TO FIND GOVERNMENT INFORMATION

When web-based search engines first arrived on the scene in the mid-1990s and early 2000s, they transformed the way users search for information. When the Google search engine became popular, it took the search engine concept to new realms. While web content was often created with little helpful metadata, Google looked to those who excelled at creating superb metadata: librarians and publishers. Leveraging that knowledge, Google Scholar was born. By making the radical step of approaching university libraries and offering to scan their materials, index the full text, and use the metadata for access, Google Books came into being. The partner libraries realized that they needed a kind of insurance program to protect their interests, and the HathiTrust was initiated. All of this points out the ascendancy of Google and how they pushed passed the competition. Today, worldwide desktop market share of Google, compared with Bing, Yahoo!, Baidu, and Yandex RU, is over 88 percent (Stat-Counter 2019).

Table 1.6   Selected knowledge skills required of government information librarians

Skill Area	Explanation
Bibliography	Historic documents and documentation
Budgets and Financial Statements	OMB vs. CBO processes; budgets vs. expenditures
Case Law	Appellate process; finding cases
Census and Demography	Knowledge of census types; survey types; all the various kinds of census reports
Economic Census and Businesses	NAICS vs. SIC codes; surveys
Environmental Conservation	Soil surveys; environmental treaties
Legislative Histories	History of laws from introduction as a bill to signing into law by the President.
Mapping and GIS	Traditional maps, legends; latitude/longitude, current GPS software products
Medicine and Health	PubMed database searching
Patents	Patent classification system, patent claims
Regulatory Law	Knowledge of rulemaking process
Statistics and Data	Over 100 federal agencies issue major statistical series
Statutory Law	Converting from session laws to codifications
Technical Reports	From many agencies including EPA, OSTI, NASA, and many others

Testing Government Database Exposure in Google

One noticeable feature of Google is the extent to which, over the years, they have been able to access the content of many government database records that were previously unavailable to search engines. A simple way to test this is to go to a government database and perform a search. Find a record within that government database, and then see if that record can be pulled up through a Google search. Table 1.7 shows results of some of these tests. If the test failed, this means that the government database is not exposed to Google searching. But if the record is found in Google (success), then Google searching would be an alternative way to access the data.

Of course, many databases don't lend themselves at all to search engine exposure. Numerical data sets, consisting of scientific measurements, weather data, and so forth, would not be able to be contributed to Google

Table 1.7   Openness of selected databases to Google searching

Government Website	Testing Site Presence in Google	Results of Test
Catalog.gpo.gov	*site:catalog.gpo.gov "Immigration Reorganization and Improvement Act of 1999"*	Failed in Google
Govinfo.gov	*site:govinfo.gov "76 FR 62213—Endangered and Threatened Wildlife and Plants"*	Success in Google
Pubmed ncbi.nlm.nih.gov/pubmed	*site:ncbi.nlm.nih.gov "Rhinocerebral Mucormycosis: A Prospective Analysis of an Effective Treatment Protocol"*	Success
Federalregister.gov	*site:federalregister.gov "Raisins Produced From Grapes Grown in California; Increased Assessment Rate"*	Success
Catalog.archives.gov	*site:catalog.archives.gov "Correspondence Relating to Rivers and Harbors, 1923–1942"*	Failed
	site:catalog.archives.gov "Applications for Seaman's Protection Certificates, 1916–1940"	Success
Trademark database	*site:tsdr.uspto.gov "DEMPSTER DUMPSTER"*	Failed
Patent database (PatFT)	*site:patft.uspto.gov D853,385*	Failed
ERIC eric.ed.gov	*site:eric.ed.gov "Government Publications and Gray Literature in Turkey"*	Success
PubAg pubag.nal.usda.gov	*site:pubag.nal.usda.gov "Excretion patterns of Campylobacter jejuni by dairy cows"*	Success
EPA NEPIS nepis.epa.gov	*site:nepis.epa.gov Bibliography of References Used in the Climate Change, Wildlife, and Wildlands Case Studies*	Success
National Map viewer.nationalmap.gov	Not possible	Failed
SEC EDGAR	*site:sec.gov "MICROSOFT CORPORATION FORM 10-K for the Fiscal Year Ended June 30, 2018"*	Success
Gao.gov	*site:gao.gov Information on Nuclear Exports Controlled by U.S.-EURATOM Agreement*	Success
Crsreports.congress.gov	*site:crsreports.congress.gov Mongolia IF10926*	Success

content. But it is amazing how much more content is available today than has been in the past.

While it's true that not everything is on the internet, a tremendous amount of government information is. I'm talking about:

- Documents originally published in print or microfiche, but are now scanned in PDF format,
- Data sets that are searchable and browsable, and
- Integrating tools that can bridge the gap between issuances and current state of laws.

Records in Library Catalogs

The fact that massive amounts of government publication tonnage are now online has not gone unnoticed by library directors. They covet space. When they realize that well over 50 percent of what is in government microfiche cabinets is in government databases and that much of the printed materials are already present in HathiTrust, they wonder why shelves can't immediately be cleared. They often need to be reminded that depository libraries do not own the materials on their shelves; they are the property of the U.S government. Libraries cannot just toss out government publications received through the depository library program (FDLP 2018).

Although a high percentage of government information is online, libraries have not done a good job of notifying users. An example is library catalog records that have been diligently added over the decades. When these records were originally added, either through copy cataloging, original cataloging, or vendor record loads, librarians likely did not make a note that the materials existed somewhere online. I was continually frustrated with that fact and spent many years adding URLs to print and fiche catalog records. I often did this with automated processes, downloading massive amounts of records, finding matches in government databases, writing the URLs to the appropriate catalog record fields, and then importing the catalog records back into the catalog. I felt good about doing this, as users were now on notice that the obscure NASA technical report that they wanted was available in inconvenient microfiche format, as well as online via the NASA Technical Reports Server. The point is that depository libraries often have so many records in their catalogs for fiche formats that there are not enough resources to tell users that these documents may also be online so that users can avoid trying to use old fashioned microfiche readers.

When I see a user approach our microform viewing machines in the library, I try to assist them (without being too nosy). I ask them the title they are trying to use. Often, if it is a government information title, I will take a minute to see if the content is on the web somewhere, either in a government database or in an institutional repository. I don't like to see people suffer with microfiche.

Domain Searching

I observe most people searching Google with simple searches, rather than doing any kind of power searching. There is a problem with this approach. While Google does a superb job of relevance ranking (that's why they are billionaires, and I am not!), you cannot access many of the records retrieved in the search. For example, if I search Google for *environmental impact rocky flats*, I get "about 10,300,000 results" (July 12, 2019). Of those results, Google will only let me see about 400 of them. Sometimes it might be more, other times less, but never more than 1,000 results. What are the chances that the things you want are in that top part of the result set? Google does some pretty good result ranking, but there is a good chance that you will want to see what is in the other 10 million results. The easiest workaround for this is to do domain-specific searching. By this, I mean using Google commands to return results only from specified websites. If we want our search for *environmental impact rocky flats* to come only from the U.S. Environmental Protection Agency, then we could limit results to that site like this: *environmental impact rocky flats site:epa.gov.* Now instead of over 10 million results, I get "about 9,400" results—still more than Google will let me view, but much better.

In order to be effective at domain searching, we have to know what internet domains are generally and how they apply to government information. In general, the .gov internet domain is used for federal government sites, but there are many notable exceptions to this. Not all federal government agencies use the .gov internet domain. Examples of exceptions include those in Table 1.8.

As of September 2019, there were 5,851 registered .gov domains and 208 .mil domains (https://domainnamestat.com/statistics/tldtype/generic), although not all the .gov domains are federal, as we will see in chapter 16. Occasionally a federal entity or quasifederal entity uses a .com, .org, .edu, or .us domain.

Although far from scientific, I can illustrate this point with a study I did in 2004 with the University of Denver (DU) online library catalog. DU had been a federal depository library since 1909 and has cataloging records for most online government publications. After extracting all government URLs from catalog records for government publications, I did a little analysis. Here is what I found: .gov (87.15 percent); .edu (4.09 percent); .org (2.87 percent); .com (2.41 percent); .net (2.00 percent); .mil (1.17 percent); .us

Table 1.8   U.S. government information on top-level domains other than .gov (selected sites)

Domain	Examples
.com domain	United States Postal Service: usps.com; Army recruitment—goarmy.com; Navy recruitment—navy.com; Air Force recruitment—airforce.com; Marines recruitment—marines.com
.mil domain	All military sites. Example: Defense Technical Information Center (DTIC): dtic.mil
.us domain	U.S. Forest Service: fs.fed.us
.org domain	United States Institute of Peace: usip.org [signed into law by President Reagan, P.L. 98-525, Title XVII].
.edu domain	National Defense University: ndu.edu

(0.20 percent); and numeric IP addresses (0.10 percent). Most, but not all, government publications emanate from a .gov internet domain (Brown 2004).

In 2003 the .gov domain that was previously restricted only to federal government entities as defined in the *United States Government Manual* was expanded to include state, local, and Native Sovereign Nations (see 68 FR 15089 [March 28, 2003], 81 FR 23494 [April 21, 2016] and 41 CFR Part 102–173). While opening up the .gov domain registration to U.S. state and local enti-

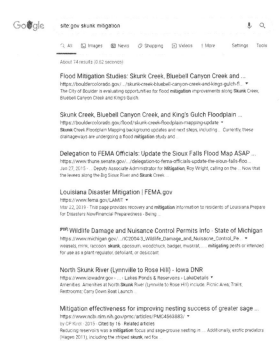

Figure 1.1 Mixture of federal, state, and local results in a *site:gov* search

ties was a generous move, it wreaked havoc with internet searching. Now when doing general .gov domain searches, we see federal, state, and local content all mixed together, as shown in Figure 1.1.

Notice the federal (fema.gov, nih.gov, senate.gov), state (michigan.gov, iowadnr.gov), and local (bouldercolorado.gov) results from the *site:gov* search. The workaround for this is to be more specific. If we are only interested in federal agency information, then we need to find which federal agencies would likely have the information we need. Before doing our specific internet search, we need to do preliminary research into which government entities care about the topic and search by their respective internet domains.

We need to find out which government entities care about skunks. [Note: the only reason I am searching for skunks here is that as I was walking to the library this morning, I encountered a skunk on the sidewalk—and quickly crossed to the other side of the street!] My task here is to make a brief list of federal sites that have skunk information. I need to overlook all the state and local results and focus on federal. So I search Google like this: *site:gov skunks*.

My list includes the following federal entities:

- fws.gov Fish and Wildlife Service
- nps.gov National Park Service
- ncbi.nlm.nih.gov [PubMed]
- cdc.gov Centers for Disease Control and Prevention
- fs.usda.gov Forest Service
- itis.gov White House Subcommittee on Biodiversity and Ecosystem Dynamics, originally referred to as the Interagency Taxonomic Information System
- loc.gov Library of Congress
- nsa.gov National Security Agency
- energy.gov Department of Energy

Some of these results can be omitted, since they refer to single, unrelated resources (loc.gov, energy.gov). I also generally look past PubMed references (ncbi.nlm.nih.gov), since they refer to peer-reviewed journal articles and not government information.

Now that I have a working list of "who cares" of government entities, I can re-execute my Google searches.

- *site:fws.gov skunk mitigation*
- *site:nps.gov skunk mitigation*
- *site:cdc.gov skunk mitigation*
- *site:fs.usda.gov skunk mitigation*

I now get more focused results, still sometimes more than Google will allow me to view, but much better than the general Google search before the domain limitation.

File Type Searching

Another way to escape Google's viewing restriction of 1,000 results or fewer is to limit by file type. File type or file format may be more familiar to those who use Windows-based computers. Although Macintosh and Windows computers have the option of concealing file type extensions, those that opt to see the extensions are familiar with these common three-letter extensions after file names: Adobe Acrobat (.pdf), Microsoft Word (.doc or .docx), Microsoft Excel (.xls or .xlsx), Microsoft PowerPoint (.ppt or .pptx), and generic text file (.txt). Limiting by these commons file types with Google's syntax is most helpful in isolating research-related content. Very often substantive reports, studies, articles are posted on the web in Adobe Acrobat or .pdf format. Using syntax similar to site-specific searching, we can restrict results to .pdf format like this: *filetype:pdf.* The Microsoft file types mentioned above have two versions, the older version without the final "x," and the newer file types with the "x." Both need to be searched on their own.

It is also possible to search by less common file types such as WordPerfect (.wpd), Lotus AmiPro (.ami), generic rich text format (.rtf), Apple Keynote presentation (.key), and so forth.

Table 1.9 summarizes these three most important power-searching strategies.

USA.gov provides a useful interface for browsing and searching federal government information. It is especially useful for navigating the complex agencies within the three branches of government. It gives assistance in navigating government programs and opportunities. One of the weaknesses of USA.gov, however, is its inability to separate out state or local websites from federal ones. This is not the fault of the search engine. Rather, it is a result of the expansion of the .gov domain in 2003 to allow state and local government entities to register and use the .gov domain for their purposes.

Google Web is especially strong in searching for government information and publications. The first step in searching is to determine which

Table 1.9   Commonly used power-searching strategies

Search Type	Description	Examples
Phrase searching	Searches a phrase as a literal string of characters	"united states" "human rights"
Site-specific searching	Searches within a specified internet domain	*site:census.gov* *site:state.co.us*
File-type searching	Searches for a specified file type	*filetype:pdf* *filetype:doc*

federal agencies are likely to have the desired information and what their internet domains are. Then it's a matter of doing site-specific searching in Google to find the information.

Applying file-type searching to our skunk problem, we can limit results to more substantial documents:

- *site:fws.gov skunk mitigation filetype:pdf*
- *site:fws.gov skunk mitigation filetype:docx*
- *site:nps.gov skunk mitigation filetype:pdf*
- *site:cdc.gov skunk mitigation filetype:pdf*
- *site:fs.usda.gov skunk mitigation filetype:doc*

Direct versus Indirect Google Searching

As we saw in Table 1.7, although there is a lot of government information visible to direct Google searches, there are many databases that are not adequately exposed. For these, we need a different approach to searching. We need to employ indirect Google searching. Here is an example of a direct Google search: *water rights in Colorado*

But an indirect Google search might look like this (Figure 1.2):

Rather than "going for the gold"—that is, attempting to search for the precise result you ultimately want to arrive at, you search broadly, hoping to find a resource like a data set, database, or web portal of some kind that will lead you to the direct answer. Database types that are not likely to

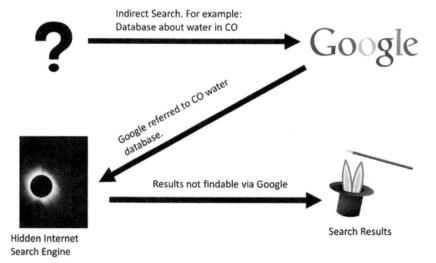

Figure 1.2 Indirect Google search model

work well with direct Google searching include statistical, numerical, mapping, and scientific databases. Textual resources, on the other hand, have a better chance of being exposed to Google and those providing results in direct search queries. Even so, it is advisable to employ indirect searching here as well. Even though textual material may be findable via a direct Google search, those results may not be high enough within the results listing to do you any good.

More help on searching for government information in search engines can be found in *Harnessing the Power of Google: What Every Researcher Should Know* (Brown 2017).

HATHITRUST, INTERNET ARCHIVE, AND GOVERNMENT PUBLICATIONS

HathiTrust (https://www.hathitrust.org/) has become one of the most important places to access historic federal publications. The project began in 2008 as a collaboration with what is now the Big Ten Academic Alliance and the University of California system. It arose out of the Google Books scanning project as a way to preserve digital content. Many government publications have made their way into the Google Books project, but not as many of them are actually freely accessible. They should be, since nearly all of them are free of copyright. It's just that nobody at Google is there to ensure that all the U.S. federal documents are completely viewable or downloadable. In fact, a very high percentage of government information is locked down as if it were under copyright protection. Next time you find a government publication in Google Books that you cannot access, try going to that same title in the HathiTrust archive. You will likely find it there in fully viewable mode.

Downloading government information from HathiTrust is another matter. Only HathiTrust member libraries are able to download entire documents, although downloads of one page at a time are possible. If it is important for you to download the entire document, you might try the same title in the Internet Archive text archive (https://archive.org/details /texts). There are not nearly as many government publications there, but when they do appear, many more viewing and downloading options are available.

The reason HathiTrust works so well with government information is that it is more carefully curated. The stated goal of HathiTrust in relation to federal documents is to "build a comprehensive HathiTrust digital collection of federal documents distributed in print format by the Government Publishing Office as part of the Federal Depository Library Program." HathiTrust's three-fold goals include building a comprehensive digital

Figure 1.3 Google Books search for a serial publication

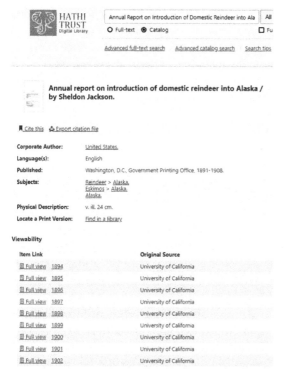

Figure 1.4   Serial title in HathiTrust. Courtesy of HathiTrust (HT 007925130).

collection, enduring access, and collaboration within a community of stakeholders committed to identifying, cataloging, digitizing, organizing, preserving, hosting, and providing access to U.S. federal documents. As of July 1, 2019, the federal documents within HathiTrust were comprised of 542,731 bibliographic records and 1,353,343 "digital objects," which can be considered equivalent to individual documents (serial issues, annual publication, individual monographs, etc.) (HathiTrust 2019).

HathiTrust, unlike Google Books, catalogs serials correctly. This is important to know, because Google Books treats each serial issue as a separate entity. Let's take the *Annual Report on Introduction of Domestic Reindeer into Alaska* as an example. This publication ran from 1891 through 1908. Figure 1.3 shows the results of a Google Books search of that title.

That same title in HathiTrust shows titles with individual serial issues attached to the record (Figure 1.4).

Figure 1.5 Government Serials in the Internet Archive. *Source:* Internet Archive. Used with permission.

One of the advantages of HathiTrust's cataloging methods is that you can search OCLC accession numbers in the search interface and retrieve the results efficiently.

The Internet Archive text archive catalogs serial issues independently, but at least they pattern together at the top, and they are easy to navigate (Figure 1.5).

The interesting thing about document curation in HathiTrust is that we find full-view documents of newer documents and not just those from before January 1, 1923, the date before which all content can be considered in the public domain (https://www.copyright.gov/circs/circ15a.pdf). In 1998, the Sonny Bono Copyright Term Extension Act (P.L. 105-298, 112 Stat. 2827, 17 U.S.C. 101 note) extended the duration of copyright from 75 years to 95 years. This meant that beginning on January 1, 2019, and every year after that, another year could be added to what could be considered public domain. For digital collections that are not closely curated, it is doubtful that changes would come about very quickly. But for HathiTrust, a closely curated collection, we could expect changes very quickly. In the case of government publications, we don't need to think about copyright cutoff dates, since documents from 1923 to the present are fully viewable, unlike materials under copyright (see Figure 1.6).

It should be noted that this same publication is found in Google Books, but with "No preview" noted.

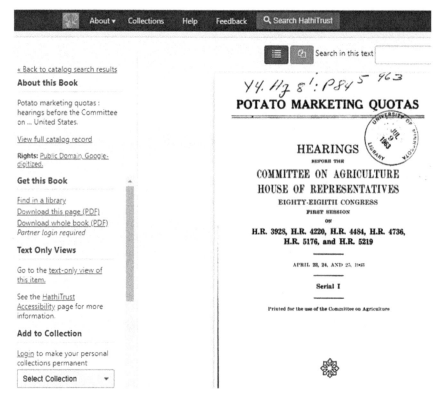

Figure 1.6   Congressional hearing from 1963 in HathiTrust. Government items in HathiTrust are free of copyright restrictions. Courtesy of HathiTrust (HT 102456043).

HathiTrust has its limitations. For example, many documents were distributed to depository libraries in microfiche format. Since these were not released in paper format, they were not in the scope of the Google Books scanning project and, thus, were not contributed to the HathiTrust collection. In many cases, there is a good chance that these have been digitized by other initiatives that a Google search would uncover.

EXERCISES

1. Find the website for the parent agency of the Voice of America. Using the internet domain of this agency, find the most recent annual report and give the URL.

2. Find a serial record for the title *Statistical Abstract of the United States* in a library catalog (preferably a larger library's, such as a large public library

system or an academic library). Now do the same search in HathiTrust (hathitrust.org). And again, do the same search in the Internet Archive (archive .org). What differences did you notice in the way individual years of *Statistical Abstract* are presented?

REFERENCES

Banisar, David. 2010. "Freedom of Information around the World 2006: A Global Survey of Access to Government Information Laws." SSRN. Accessed December 12, 2019. https://papers.ssrn.com/sol3/papers.cfm?abstract_id=1707336.

Brown, Christopher C. 2004. "Knowing Where They're Going: Statistics for Online Government Document Access through the OPAC." *Online Information Review* 28, no. 6: 396–409. DOI: 10.1108/14684520410570526.

Brown, Christopher C. 2011. "Knowing Where They Went: Six Years of Online Access Statistics via the Online Catalog for Federal Government Information." *College and Research Libraries* 72, no. 1: 43–61. Accessed December 12, 2019. https://crl.acrl.org/index.php/crl/article/view/16131.

Brown, Christopher C. 2017. *Harnessing the Power of Google: What Every Researcher Should Know.* Santa Barbara, CA: Libraries Unlimited.

FDLP (Federal Depository Library Program). 2018. "Legal Requirements and Program Regulations of the Federal Depository Library Program." Accessed December 12, 2019. https://purl.fdlp.gov/GPO/gpo89707.

GPO (Government Printing Office). 1986. *The Designation Procedure for Federal Depository Libraries: A Handbook for Senators, Representatives and Other Officials Who Are Empowered to Designate Federal Depository Libraries.* Washington, DC: GPO Library Programs Service. HT 011411150.

GPO (Government Publishing Office). 2016. *Keeping America Informed, the U.S. Government Publishing Office: A Legacy of Service to the Nation.* Revised ed. Washington, DC: GPO. Accessed December 12, 2019. http://purl.fdlp .gov/GPO/gpo71799.

HathiTrust. 2019. "HathiTrust U.S. Federal Government Documents Program." Accessed September 29, 2019. https://www.hathitrust.org/usgovdocs.

NAPA (National Academy of Public Administration). 2013. "Rebooting the Government Printing Office: Keeping America Informed in the Digital Age." Washington, DC, January 2013. Accessed December 12, 2019. http://purl .fdlp.gov/GPO/gpo34038.

Nelson, Gail K., and John V. Richardson Jr. 1986. "Adelaide Hasse and the Early History of the U.S. Superintendent of Documents Classification Scheme." *Government Publications Review* 13, no. 1 (1986): 79–96.

StatCounter. 2019. "Worldwide Desktop Market Share of Leading Search Engines from January 2010 to April 2019." Chart. May 17, 2019. Statista database.

Sunlight Foundation. 2019. "Web Integrity Project." Accessed September 29, 2019. https://sunlightfoundation.com/web-integrity-project/.

Swanbeck, Jan and Winston Harris. 2012. "Automating the Federal Documents Disposition Process." *DttP: Documents to the People* (Summer): 25–33.

United Nations. 2019. "UN E-Government Knowledgebase." Accessed September 29, 2019. https://publicadministration.un.org/egovkb/en-us/data/compare -countries.

UNT (University of North Texas Libraries). 2014. "U.S. Congressional Serial Set Inventory." Accessed September 29, 2019. https://digital.library.unt.edu /govdocs/ssi/.

2

Federal Information Dissemination

What is known today as the Federal Depository Library Program (FDLP) has its origins in the early history of our country. During the Constitutional Convention of 1787, James Wilson stated, "The people have a right to know what their Agents are doing or have done, and it should not be in the option of the Legislature to conceal their proceedings" (Farrand 1911, 260). Many subsequent acts passed into law support that sentiment. It is not enough to publish what our representatives are doing; those publications must be disseminated far and wide so that citizens in every corner of the country can have access to the information.

The Government Publishing Office's (GPO) excellent work *Keeping America Informed* (GPO 2016a) documents the birth and evolution of printing in the early days of the republic. What I want to accomplish here is a broad-stroke view of the phases of information dissemination from the early days until now. Broadly speaking, there are three major eras of government information dissemination. Each of these initiatives is monumental and is ongoing to this day. These eras demonstrate a resolve to get information into the hands of citizens.

FIRST ERA: EARLY PRINTING AND THE
U.S. CONGRESSIONAL SERIAL SET

I have already mentioned early efforts at ensuring that government information is disseminated throughout the country. Individual act of Congress were small but important steps in this process.

The period of the first fourteen Congresses was a bit chaotic. There were roughly a dozen private printers. The state of early printing is clearly set forth by August A. Imholtz, Jr., as he names each private printer for the early House and Senate journals. This resulted in a lack of a uniform numbering system for the documents, meaning they are difficult to track and cite. Also, there was no method for ensuring that documents were distributed, no uniform size, and no editorial control (Imholtz 2003).

Background of the Serial Set

These early problems were among the many motivations behind what is perhaps the most important record of government publications throughout our history—the *U.S. Congressional Serial Set*. This huge set now comprises nearly 16,000 volumes. The vulnerability of federal documents to destruction was highlighted when the British destroyed the Capitol building in 1814. This was just one of the factors behind the motivation to begin the *U.S. Congressional Serial Set* in the 15th Congress in 1817. Of course, there were documents before 1817, but it was the congressional action in creating the Serial Set that marks the beginning of this first era. It was sometimes called the Congressional Series or the "sheep-bound set" because of its original binding in sheep skin. Bound volumes were issued and numbered "serially," one after another. The idea was to bind the documents together for easier distribution to libraries across the states. It was this strategy, still in place today, that first systematically distributed documents to the states.

Libraries that have the old sheep-bound volumes will attest to the fact that the bindings did not withstand the test of time. Holding these old volumes today makes hands and clothes brown and dusty with a dirt that is difficult to remove. Handling them leaves your hands brown, as the leather falls into pieces.

The order to produce the Serial Set was a House Order from December 8, 1813, contained in the *Journal of the House of Representatives* (Figure 2.1).

Fortunately, the notion that the pages be consecutively paged was not carried through. The current legal authority for publication of the Serial Set can be found at 44 U.S.C. §§ 701, 719, and 738. Each independent document found in the Serial Set is separately paged. This means that many bound volumes of the Serial Set are "bound-with" volumes. Larger depository libraries have many "bound-with" publications in their collections, creating massive challenges for catalogers and the systems used to catalog them.

American State Papers

On motion of Mr. Pickering,
Ordered, That henceforward all messages and communications from the President of the United States, all letters and reports from the several departments of the government, all motions and resolutions offered for the consideration of the House, all reports of committees of the House, and all other papers, which, in the usual course of proceeding, or by special order of the House, shall be printed in octavo fold, and separately from the journals, shall have their pages numbered in one continued series of numbers, commencing and terminating with each session.

Figure 2.1   Journal of the House of Representatives, 13th Congress, Second Session, p. 20. Courtesy of HathiTrust. https://babel.hathitrust.org/cgi/pt?id=njp.32101065268771;view=1up;seq=26.

To deal with the problem of documents from the 1st through the 14th Congresses, the *American State Papers* were authorized by a resolution in 1833 and an act in 1858. The *American State Papers* is a retrospective republication of about 6,280 numbered publications of mostly congressional materials, with some executive materials as well. Of these documents, only about 4,100 cover the first fourteen Congresses; the rest cover the years overlapping the early Serial Set publications (Imholtz 2008). They were published in 38 folio-sized volumes. So as not to conflict with the numbering system already in place for the Serial Set, which began with number one in the 15th Congress, the American State Papers were assigned numbers preceded by zero (FDLP 2017). Thus, the volumes are numbered 01, 02, 03, and so forth.

- Foreign Relations: Six volumes. Volumes 01–06 (512 documents)
- Indian Affairs: Two volumes. Volumes 07–08 (257 documents)
- Finance: Five volumes. Volumes 09–013 (938 documents)
- Commerce and Navigation: Two volumes. Volumes 014–015 (270 documents)
- Military Affairs: Seven volumes. Volumes 016–022 (808 documents)
- Naval Affairs: Four volumes. Volumes 023–026 (652 documents)
- Post Office Department: One volume. Volume 027 (131 documents)
- Public Lands: Eight volumes. Volume 028–035 (1,611 documents)
- Claims: One volume. Volume 036 (628 documents)
- Miscellaneous: Two volumes. Volumes 037–038 (547 documents)

Since the *State Papers* were published from 1832 through 1861, many depository libraries have these volumes in print. Digital versions are available through the American Memory project of the Library of Congress (https://memory.loc.gov/ammem/amlaw/lwsplink.html), as well as selected volumes in the HathiTrust (HT 009727010) and the Internet Archive.

Contents of the Serial Set

To give an idea of what comprises the Serial Set, we can look at how the Readex Serial Set database has analyzed the publication categories for materials from 1817to 1994 as follows:

- Annual Reports (13,211)
- Congressional Journals (378)
- Congressional Rules and Procedural Materials (11,600)
- Contested Election Materials (1,115)
- Court of Claims Reports (295)
- Executive Department Publications (47,906)
- Hearings (1,249)
- Impeachment Materials (96)
- Index to Documents and Reports (1895–) (58)
- Legislative Report—Private Bills (136,262)
- Legislative Report—Public Bills (1,098,541)
- Memorials and Petitions (9,406)
- Monographs (2,845)
- Motions and Resolutions (5,265)
- Names Lists (12,881)
- Presidential Communications and Messages (18,148)
- Public Document Catalogs (1893–) (24)
- Sessional Volume Indexes (1817–1895) (2,383)
- Sessional Volume Tables of Documents (408)
- Treaties and Conventions (1,057)

As for the categories of numbered materials in the Serial Set, they are as follows:

- Senate or House Documents—May include reports of executive agencies or departments, some of which may be required filings. Sometimes committee prints are also ordered to be printed as documents for larger distribution. Often, historical tomes are issued as documents.

- Senate Treaty Documents—Texts of treaties submitted for ratification by the Senate from the President. Prior to the 97th Congress (1981), these were known as Senate Executive Documents.

- Senate or House Reports—Senate reports related to proposed legislation or findings on matters under investigation.

- Senate Executive Reports—reports on treaties from the Senate Committee on Foreign Relations or nomination reports from other Senate committees.

Numbering of the Serial Set

John G. Ames, of the Documents Division of the Department of the Interior, devised the serial numbering system. Serial number 1 would be assigned to the first volume of the 15th Congress in 1817 (FDLP 2017).

The easiest way to see the numbering of the Serial Set is to visit the University of North Texas Library's Serial Set Inventory project (https://digital .library.unt.edu/govdocs/ssi/). This not only shows which volume numbers are associated with which Congress but it also provides insight into the contents of each volume. Perusing this list, you will notice that each volume is an integer, with some exceptions. Occasionally a multivolume set is given a breakdown such as this: 7470-1, 7470-2, 7470-3, and 7470-4 (for four volumes of the *Foreign Relations of the United States* series included in the Serial Set).

With a project this huge, there were bound to be exceptions to the consecutive numbering system. Virginia Saunders and August A. Imholtz, Jr., note these exceptions in their article "U.S. Congressional Serial Set: Assigned Serial Numbers Not Used," published in the official newsletter of the FDLP (Saunders and Imholtz 1998).

Intellectual Access to the Serial Set

For most of its lifespan the *Congressional Serial Set* has been underutilized. The reason for this is simple: it is a massive set with inadequate intellectual access tools. By this I mean a lack of indexing. If a library creates a record to keep track of all their print volumes (such as OCLC 3888071; HT 003051567), then they have wonderful inventory control and lousy intellectual access. Individual analytical cataloging is lost. If, on the other hand, each report or document is individually cataloged, then greater access is achieved, but nobody can easily see which Serial Set volume numbers can be found on the shelves. Many libraries with massive collections do it both ways. To further complicate matters, there have been many microfiche initiatives over the years, and many depositories have these holdings as well.

Digitization and the capability of full-text searching of the Serial Set in the past few decades have opened up new and exciting avenues of research. The Document Catalog and the Monthly Catalog did not adequately index the contents of the Serial Set. For example, the Document Catalog gives the title for S. Rpt. 3290 from the 59th Congress (1906) as "Report from Committee on Claims, Amending by Substitute S. 1751, to Revive and Amend Act for Collection of Abandoned Property and Act Amendatory." But by today's standards, the title would be "Claims under Captured and Abandoned Property Act. May 2, 1906.—Ordered to be printed." While this might not seem like a big deal, it can create a great deal of confusion when trying to identify documents and to distinguish one from another. It was this imprecision that was employed when the *CIS US Serial Set Index* was initially published.

Even with its imperfections the *CIS US Serial Set Index* (published in print from 1975 to 1986) was a major advancement in intellectual access to the Serial Set. But the real advancement came with digitization of the entire Serial Set by Readex and ProQuest. Now Hein is digitizing it as well. Researchers who do not have access to libraries with any of these commercial subscriptions may still be able to access the full text via the HathiTrust or the Internet Archive, although that is a much more cumbersome task.

Several older bibliographies deserve to be mentioned. These cover the years just before the Document Catalog and the Monthly Catalog, including publications issued in the Serial Set. The works by Poore and Ames, mentioned in greater detail later in this chapter under "General Tools and Finding Aids," will be helpful if you don't have access to the *CIS Index*. Of greater help may be *Tables of and Annotated Index to the Congressional Series of United States Public Documents*, also detailed below.

The *CIS Index* was not published until 1977. Earlier scholars had to deal with the tedious task of going through the above-mentioned sources. It could be that the Serial Set's design is its downfall. Suzanne DeLong (1996) suggests that most researchers are not aware of the Serial Set, and, thus, it accounts for a minimal amount of usage.

Series within Series

The Serial Set is a complex compilation of materials. Some items stand alone rather than in any series. Others are items in a series that pop up in seemingly random volumes of the set. It is common to see executive branch materials appear in the Serial Set, depending on the year. Some annual reports appear in the Serial Set, and then in other years, the reports

Table 2.1   Selected Serial Set volumes from 1882 showing complexities of serials within the Serial Set. (Based upon University of North Texas U.S. Congressional Serial Set Inventory https://digital.library.unt.edu/govdocs/ssi/)

Vol. No.	Contents	Description
2088	Senate Reports	Senate Reports
2089	House Journal, 47th Congress, 2nd Session	Journal of the House of Representatives of the United States. (HT 002137422). [serial]
2090	State of the Union address; Foreign relations, 1882	Papers relating to the foreign relations of the United States/ transmitted to Congress with the annual message of the President (HT 008584696). [serial]
2091–2096	Annual report of Secretary of War, 1882, v. 1–4	Annual report of the Secretary of War. (HT 000078451).
2097	Annual report of Secretary of Navy, 1882	Annual report of the Secretary of the Navy. (HT 012202882).
2098	Annual report of Postmaster General, 1882	Annual report of the Postmaster General. (HT 000518137). [serial]
2099	Annual report of Secretary of Interior, 1882 #1/12 Annual report of Commissioner of General Land Office, 1882	Annual report of the Secretary of the Interior. HT 004761459). [serial]; Annual report of the Commissioner of the General Land Office to the Secretary of the Interior. (HT 001719265). [serial]
2100	Reports accompanying annual report of Secretary of Interior	
2101	Annual report of Director of Geological Survey, 1882	Annual report of the United States Geological Survey to the Secretary of the Interior. (HT 001719636). [serial]
2102	Annual report of Commissioner of Education, 1882	Annual report of the Commissioner of Education. (HT 011683193).

for the same serial are not included. Some of the complexities of the Serial Set are seen in Table 2.1, which shows consecutive volumes from 1882.

These complexities make cataloging and providing access to content a challenge. In a sense you have many "bound-withs" and complex series within series. Very rarely do libraries have the time and resources to catalog a serial that appears within the Serial Set. A library may have a record for the *Annual Report of the Postmaster General* but may not note that it owns the 1882 issue that is contained in Serial 2098. Another complicating factor is that differences sometimes exist between the department edition (issued independently of the Serial Set) and the document edition (issued as part of the Serial Set). Several noteworthy titles have historically been published as both department editions and document editions, including the *Budget of the United States*; *Economic Report of the President*; *Security and Exchange Annual Report*; and the *Corps of Engineers Report* (GPO 1994).

Many executive branch annual reports appear in the Serial Set. This is particularly the case from 1861 through 1957. Since the late 1950s, this practice was ceased, and only congressional reports and documents appear in the set. As an example of an annual report that was sometimes included in the Serial Set, the *Annual Report of the Secretary of War* is generally included within the Serial Set, with the exception of the years 1920–1941.

Let's look at the complexities of the Serial Set in a yet different way. The *U.S. Army Register* through time has been issued as a House Document but was also issued as department editions in SuDocs classification for the War Department (W 3.11: 1935–1947), the Military Establishment (M 108.8: 1948–1949), and the Defense Department (D 102.9: 1950–recent). It is common for good cataloging records to make note of when government publications were also issued in the Serial Set. In this case, if we look at HT 002138335, we see a note: "Issued also 1896– in the congressional series as House documents." This is the cue of its presence in the Serial Set. Table 2.2 shows that the *Army Register* can be found in two places, in the "congressional series" as House Documents, and in the department editions issued with Superintendent of Documents classification numbers.

There are many serials or series within the Serial Set that are noteworthy. Among them are:

Constitution of the United States of America: Analysis and Interpretation: Annotations of Cases Decided by the Supreme Court of the United States. Serial 11592, S. Doc. 82-170 (1952); Serial 12558, S. Doc. 88-39 (1963), Serial 12980, S. Doc. 92-82 (1972), Serial 13611, S. Doc. 99-16 (1985), as well as many supplements in intervening years.

Biographical Directory of the United States Congress. Title varies. Biographical Directory of the American Congress 1774–1927 (Serial 8732, H. Doc. 69-783); Biographical Directory of the American Congress, 1774–1949. The Continental Congress, from September 5, 1774 to October 21, 1788 and the Congress of the United States from the first to the Eightieth Congress, from March 4, 1789 to January 3, 1949, inclusive. (Serial 11414, H. Doc. 81-607); Biographical directory of the American Congress 1774–1961 (Serial 12108, H. Doc. 85-442); Biographical

Table 2.2   U.S. Army Register, 1935–1953, found in the Serial Set and in the SuDocs classification

Year	House Doc. No.	Serial Set Vol.	SuDocs
1935	H.Doc. 74-36	9945	W 3.11:935
1936	H.Doc. 74-341	10042	W 3.11:936
1937	H.Doc. 75-31	10136	W 3.11:937
1938	H.Doc. 75-401	10185	W 3.11:938
1939	H.Doc. 76-31	10361	W 3.11:939
1940	H.Doc. 76-484	10408	W 3.11:940
1941	H.Doc. 77-30	10608	W 3.11:941
1942	H.Doc. 77-530	10709	W 3.11:942
1943	H.Doc. 78-28	10809	W 3.11:943
1944	H.Doc. 78-427	10892	W 3.11:944
1945	H.Doc. 79-28	10979	W 3.11:945
1946	H.Doc. 79-544	11071	W 3.11:946
1947	H.Doc. 80-20	11167	M 108.8:947
1948	H.Doc. 80-530	11257; 11258	M 108.8:948
1949	H.Doc. 81-330	11336	D 102.9:949
1950	H.Doc. 81-406	11439	D 102.9:950
1951	H.Doc. 82-29	11535	D 102.9:951
1952	H.Doc. 82-297	11624	D 102.9:952
1953	H.Doc. 83-27	11704; 11705	D 102.9:953

Directory of the American Congress, 1774–1971. The Continental Congress, from September 5, 1774 to October 21, 1788 and the Congress of the United States from the First through the Ninety-First Congress, from March 4, 1789 to January 3, 1971, inclusive (Serial 12938, H. Doc. 92-8); Biographical Directory of the United States Congress, 1774–1989. Bicentennial edition. The Continental Congress, from September 5, 1774 to October 21, 1788 and the Congress of the United States from the First through the One Hundredth Congresses, from March 4, 1789 to January 3, 1989, inclusive (Serial 13849, H. Doc. 100-34).

Without going into as much detail, other titles include *The War of the Rebellion: A Compilation of the Official Records of the Union and Confederate Armies*; Census reports from the Seventh through the Eleventh Census; *Statistical Abstract of the United States* (1879–1976) as numbered House Documents; *Congressional Directory* (1882–1933) as numbered

House Documents; House and Senate Procedure Manuals (from 1896 to present); and Budget of the United States Government (from1923 to current) as numbered House Documents.

An easy way to discover these many series that run through the Serial Set is to search the library catalog of any medium to large depository library or the OCLC bibliographic database (WorldCat). It has long been the practice of catalogers to note when materials appear in the Serial Set by making a public-displayed note something along these lines: "Some volumes issued in the congressional series as Senate or House documents" or "Published also in the Congressional series." With this in mind, just search the notes field of a large online catalog for a note such as, "Congressional series."

Tangible Serial Set Collections

Regional depository libraries and larger selective depositories tend to have substantial Serial Set holdings, but no library has a complete collection. Usually libraries will not have print copies fully cataloged, so a phone call to the depository coordinator is the best advice. Many libraries house their Serial Set collections in offsite storage for preservation reasons (temperature and optimal storage conditions), as well as security (taking valuable volumes out of open stacks keeps them away from razor blades). It should be noted that GPO stopped distributing print copies of the Serial Set to selective depositories in 1997, so don't expect selectives to have any physical volumes after those years.

In this digital era, why would anyone want physical copies of the Serial Set? I regularly get calls from historians who want actual physical maps. Even the best digital projects will not satisfy researchers who need the greatest level of detail.

Hints on Free Online Access to the Serial Set

The commercial tools (Readex, ProQuest, and HeinOnline) admittedly make searching the Serial Set much easier. But you can still do excellent research if you don't have access to these. In order to find things easily, you need to determine the Serial Set volume number your material is in. Once you have that number, you can likely find it easily within HathiTrust (HT 006228203) or in Govinfo.gov if it is from the mid-1990s to the present.

Numerical Lists and Other Print Finding Aids to the Serial Set

If you don't have access to the commercial finding aids to the Serial Set mentioned below, you will need to use the print tools that are available.

The "numerical lists" are a convenient way to locate a Serial Set volume number when you already know the House or Senate Report or Document Number. Fortunately, these older volumes are online through the HathiTrust or Internet Archive.

GPO has an online version of the Numerical Lists covering the 85th

NUMERICAL LISTS

Of the Reports and Documents of the 74th Congress, 2d Session

SENATE REPORTS

No.		Vol.; serial
776.	Methods and practices for safety of life at sea, pts. 2–4. [See note, p. 62]	A; 9990
944.	Investigation of munitions industry, pts. 3–7. [See note, p. 61]	1–5; 9983–7
1156.	Deportation of criminals, etc., pt. 2. [See note, p. 61]	6; 9988
1251.	Annual leave for Government employees, pt. 2. [See note, p. 61]	6; 9988
1252.	Sick leave for Government employees, pt. 2. [See note, p. 61]	6; 9988
1462.	Inspection, control, and regulation of steam boilers and unfired pressure vessels in D. C.	6; 9988
1463.	Revoking or suspending motor-vehicle operator's license of nonresident person in D. C. for any sufficient cause	6; 9988

Figure 2.2   Example from the Numerical Lists for determining Serial Set volume number when Senate Report number is known

Congress (1957) to recent (https://www.govinfo.gov/help/serial-set). The Law Librarian's Society of Washington, D.C., has a most useful guide for Serial Set volumes from the 91st Congress, Second Session (1970) to recent years for which the final Serial Set volumes have been issued (https://www.llsdc.org/serial-set-volumes-guide).

As Figure 2.2 illustrates, when a document or report number is known, it is an easy lookup to determine which volume number to consult within the Serial Set.

The numerical lists will help you locate volumes, but they do not provide any content analysis of the Serial Set. For that, you can consult *Tables of and Annotated Index to the Congressional Series of United States Public Documents*. It provides the numerical list function, and, in the second half of the work, it provides subject indexing (at least up to the 52nd Congress, Second Session, 1892). The Document Catalog and the Monthly Catalog continue subject analysis of Serial Set contents for later years.

However, the most helpful print finding aid for analyzing contents of the Serial Set is the *CIS US Serial Set Index*. This includes an index of subjects, names, and organizations mentioned in the series, including the *American State Papers*. This series evolved into what is now ProQuest Congressional.

Below is the complete bibliographic information for the resources mentioned above.

Congressional Information Service. *CIS US Serial Set Index*. Washington, DC: Congressional Information Service, 1975–1998. 4 volumes in 58.

Index to the subjects of the documents and reports and to the committees, senators, and representatives presenting them. (13 volumes.) 1896–1907. Washington, DC: U.S. GPO. (SuDocs GP 3.7; HT 008607122, 008607123).

Index to the Reports and Documents of the ... Congress ... with Numerical Lists and Schedule of Volumes (30 volumes.) 1909–1933. (SuDocs: GP 3.7; HT 008607122).

Numerical Lists and Schedule of Volumes of the Reports and Documents of the ... Congress ... Session, compiled under the direction of the Superintendent of Documents. 1934–1982. Washington, DC: U.S. GPO. (SuDocs: GP 3.7/2; HT 001719813).

Tables of and Annotated Index to the Congressional Series of United States Public Documents. Washington, DC: GPO, 1902. (HT 001168029; also available via Internet Archive: https://archive.org/details/tables andannota00docugoog/)

Commercial Online Versions of the Serial Set

ProQuest Serial Set

The ProQuest online version can trace its roots back to the indexing originally produced by Congressional Information Service (CIS), beginning in the late 1960s. CIS had already been indexing contemporary congressional publications through its index, titled *CIS Annual*. The CIS U.S. Serial Set Index was a retrospective indexing of the Serial Set from its beginnings in the 15th Congress and also included the *American State Papers*. Indexing for this set was done not by actually examining the Serial Set volumes themselves, but by taking document titles from sources such as the Numerical Lists. These short titles served their purpose over the years, but they would not suffice as legitimate titles according to modern cataloging rules. The CIS indexing project was sold to LexisNexis, which then published the CIS index products as databases. LexisNexis Congressional, where the optional content lived, eventually scanned the Serial Set volumes, while preserving the brief titles from the CIS project.

In 2010, the LexisNexis Congressional content was sold to ProQuest. They renamed the product ProQuest Congressional, preserving the CIS indexing and the LexisNexis document scans. When the Readex database records were compared with the ProQuest database records, the title metadata differed in many cases. Readex had titles garnered directly from the volumes themselves, rather than just from numerical lists of volumes. After some time, ProQuest updated its product so that its titles were corrected to match cataloging standards, as Readex had done.

Readex Serial Set

August A. Imholtz, Jr., one of the developers of the *CIS US Serial Set Index*, went on to work for Readex to do his life work all over again, seeking to develop a version of the Serial Set with superior metadata. The CIS project relied primarily on Monthly Catalog entries, and, thus, the titles in the print edition were abbreviated and not up to cataloging standards. The Readex Serial Set is a work of art, with indexing unlike that of most other bibliographic databases.

Unlike the ProQuest Serial Set (included within ProQuest Congressional), which folds the *American State Papers* within the Serial Set interface, the Readex Serial Set separates out the *American State Papers* as a separate database. Although most users will simply search the Readex database using the search box, browsing is available by Congress, Standing Committee, Publication Category, Act, Location, and Subject. Perhaps most stunning is browsing by "person." This is not merely persons who authored materials (as a standard index would accomplish); it is an index to all individuals mentioned within the Serial Set. What other product indexes like that? None.

Although the Readex version has, by far, the best metadata, the ProQuest version is easier to use when it comes to searching and saving full text PDFs.

HeinOnline Serial Set

Newer content contains HeinOnline's PDFs. Older content points to full text within the HathiTrust. Unlike the ProQuest and Readex products, the Hein product is still being developed as of this writing.

There are strengths and weaknesses to each of the online versions. Law schools generally prefer the ProQuest version because it more seamlessly integrates with other Lexis products. The Readex set has superior indexing, as noted above. But the interface can be a bit more challenging to navigate. The ProQuest version has the advantage of integrating the *American State Papers*, the Serial Set proper, and the Executive Branch Documents into a single interface, placing less strain on the user having to know the history of what is included and what is not included in the Serial Set over time.

SECOND ERA: THE FEDERAL DEPOSITORY LIBRARY PROGRAM

Although the roots of the Federal Depository Library Program can be traced back to the Printing Act of 1895 (28 Stat. 601, ch. 23), the current shape of the program was most affected by the Act of 1962 (P.L. 87-579, 76 Stat. 352). This act established regional depository libraries throughout the states and selective libraries administratively related to the regional libraries of the state.

Decades after the 1962 Act, the law is showing its age. Numerous attempts have been made to modernize the program, most recently in the 115th Congress and the FDLP Modernization Act of 2018 (H.R. 5305). Unfortunately, the bill died at the end of the 115th Congress. The current law, written in the pre-internet days, is completely based on a print culture. Online distribution, access, and preservation need to be written into the depository law, as do structural considerations with the program itself.

The FDLP has an interesting and colorful history. Table 2.3 attempts to highlight some of the more interesting developments leading over three centuries. Links to online content are provides, generally from the HathiTrust, to make reading the primary documents easier.

Table 2.3   Highlights from the Depository Library Program History (Based upon McGarr (2000))

Year	Action	Online Reference
1813	Act of 1813; J. Res. No. 1 (3 Stat. 140)	HT 011571265, vol. 3, p. 140
	Authorized distribution of one copy of House and Senate Journals to select university and state libraries and historical institutions.	
1819	March 3, 1819; J. Res. No. 6 (3 Stat. 538)	HT 011571265, vol. 3, p. 538
	Resolution regarding printing of congressional bills and resolutions.	
1852	Printing Act of 1852 (10 Stat. 30, ch. 91)	HT 012153241, vol. 10, p. 30
	Appointed a Superintendent of Public Printing within the Department of the Interior.	
1857	January 28, 1857; J. Res. No. 5 (11 Stat. 253)	HT 012153241, vol. 11, p. 253
	Shifted responsibility for depository distribution to Secretary of the Interior, who also was authorized to designate depository libraries.	
1858	March 20, 1858; J. Res. No. 5 (11 Stat. 368)	HT 012153241, vol. 11, p. 368
	Representatives authorized to designate a depository from own district.	
1859	February 5, 1859 (11 Stat. 379, ch. 22)	HT 012153241, vol. 11, p. 379
	Authorized each senator to assign one depository in own state.	
1860	Printing Act of June 23, 1860; Joint Resolution No. 25 (12 Stat. 117)	HT 012153241, vol. 12, p. 117
	Established Government Printing Office (GPO) in the legislative branch to consolidate Congressional printing; authorized superintendent of public printing to administer a government printing program.	
1861	March 4, 1861	
	Government Printing Office and President Abraham Lincoln inaugurated on same day.	

Table 2.3   (continued)

Year	Action	Online Reference
1869	March 3, 1869 (15 Stat. 283, 292, ch. 121)	HT 012153241, vol. 12, p. 292

Appropriations Act established a superintendent of documents within Department of the Interior.

| 1876 | July 31, 1876 (19 Stat. 102, 105, ch. 246) | HT 012153241, vol. 19, p. 105 |

Title of superintendent of public printing changed to public printer.

| 1887 | J. Res. No. 16, March 3, 1887 (24 Stat. 647) | HT 012153241, vol. 24, p. 647 |

Establishes a geological depository program to distribute geological survey publications. Program discontinued in 1924.

| 1895 | Printing Act of 1895 (28 Stat. 601, ch. 23) | HT 012153241, vol. 28, p. 601 |

Transferred superintendent of documents from the Department of the Interior to the Government Printing Office. Also created Official Gazette Depository Libraries (p. 621), otherwise known as patent depositories.

| 1907 | March 1, 1907 (34 Stat. 1012, 1014, ch. 2284) | HT 012153241, vol. 34, p. 1014 |

Land grant colleges added to depository system.

| 1947 | First biennial survey of depository libraries conducted. | |

| 1962 | Depository Library Act of 1962 (P.L. 87-579, 76 Stat. 352) | HT 007401279, vol. 76, p. 352 |

Increased to two the number of depository libraries permitted per congressional district.

- Added libraries from independent Federal agencies
- Authorized establishment of regional depositories
- Provided for distribution of non-GPO publications

1972	Highest appellate courts of the states added to system (P.L. 92-368, 86 Stat. 507).	HT 007401279, vol. 86, p. 507
1977	More than 1,200 libraries in depository library system; JCP authorized GPO to distribute microfiche to depository libraries.	
1978	Law libraries added to system (P.L. 95-261, 92 Stat. 199).	HT 007401279, vol. 92, pt. 1, p. 199
1988	First CD-ROMs distributed to depository libraries.	

(continued)

Table 2.3   (continued)

Year	Action	Online Reference
1993	Government Printing Office Electronic Information Access Enhancement Act of 1993 enacted (P.L. 103-40, 107 Stat. 112) "GPO Access Law."	HT 007401279, vol. 107, pt. q, p. 112
1994	GPO Access service launched; available by subscription, free to depositories.	
1995	Centennial year of Federal Depository Library Program; GPO Access free to all users.	
1996	GPO releases *Study to Identify Measures Necessary for a Successful Transition to a More Electronic Federal Depository Library Program*; outlines a transition to a predominantly electronic depository library program in 5 to 7 years.	HT 003093271
1998	GPO releases *Managing the FDLP Electronic Collection: A Policy and Planning Document.*	HT 003531675
2008	First digital signatures on PDFs for content authenticity.	*site:fdlp.gov digital signatures authentication*
2009	FDsys went live, replacing GPO Access.	
2014	GPO name changed to Government Publishing Office. Title "Public Printer" changed to "Director of the Government Publishing Office." (P.L. 113-235, Division H (2014), 128 Stat. 2130, 2535)	https://www.govinfo.gov/app /details/PLAW-113publ235/, p. 2535
2015	National Plan for Access to Government Information.	*site:fdlp.gov national plan access*
2016	Govinfo.gov went live in beta version.	
2018	FDLP eXchange launched. Provides depository libraries an expedited Needs & Offers process.	*site:fdlp.gov fdlp exchange*
2018	FDsys retired as Govinfo.gov goes into full release.	

More detailed histories of the GPO and the FDLP can be found in:

100 GPO Years: 1861–1961: A History of United States Public Printing. 2010. Sesquicentennial edition. Washington, DC: U.S. Government Printing Office. http://purl.access.gpo.gov/GPO/LPS126616.

Keeping America Informed: The U.S. Government Publishing Office: A Legacy of Service to the Nation, 1861–2016. 2016. Revised ed. Washington, DC: U.S. Government Publishing Office. http://purl.fdlp.gov/GPO /gpo71799.

Selective and Regional Depository Libraries

One of the most important concepts to grasp about the depository library program is the role of regional depository libraries in relation to selective depositories. The purpose of this book is not to serve as a manual for depository libraries. For that, please see *Legal Requirements and Program Regulations* (FDLP 2018a). In short, selective depositories may withdraw materials only after first offering them to their regional library or libraries, and then they may offer them to other depositories in their region or nationally. GPO has recently initiated "FDLP eXchange" to encourage depositories to offer materials to other depositories so that materials can be housed in libraries that are interested in preserving tangible copies of federal publications.

Regional libraries serve a crucial role in preserving tangible materials for their region. No regional has all materials—not even close. The redundancy within the program is designed to ensure that there are multiple copies in various geographic locations for both access and preservation purposes. Depository libraries are essential in preserving tangible collections of government publications. One reason for this is that GPO has no tangible collection. There is no government publications library housed at GPO offices in Washington, D.C. Historically they added items to the Monthly Catalog but distributed all copies to depository libraries without keeping copies for themselves. Thus, the online MOCAT is the only instance of a library catalog that describes the holdings of nothing.

Most depository libraries are academic libraries, but not all of them are. Even though the number of public libraries that are depositories is continuing to shrink, they still make up the second-largest category. Table 2.4 breaks down the depository library system by type of library.

Although there are a limited number of regional depository libraries throughout the country, there are still many medium- to large-sized academic libraries with substantial tangible holdings of government publications. Whether these institutions are publicly funded or private institutions,

Table 2.4   Categories of Depository Libraries

Academic Libraries, General	618
Academic Libraries, Community College	53
Academic Law Libraries	143
Federal Agency Libraries	35
Federal Court Libraries	10
Public Libraries	178
Service Academies	4
Highest State Court Libraries	35
State Libraries	39
Special Libraries (nine are public law libraries)	14
Total	**1,129**

Source: Federal Depository Library Directory. Numbers as of March 14, 2019.

if they are depository libraries, they are open to the public, even if everything else on campus is open only to the closed campus community. That's part of the deal. To be a depository library, they must serve the general public. After all, the "deposited" documents are the property of the federal government, and not of the library itself.

As of July 1, 2019, there were still 46 regional libraries remaining in the depository library program. Table 2.5 lists them.

Outdated Mandate

For years, the underlying laws that govern the GPO have been outdated. Nobody argues with that. In 1994, the General Accounting Office (the former name of the present Government Accountability Office) stated, "For all practical purposes, the framework of laws and regulations used to manage many aspects of government publishing has become outdated" (GAO 1994). The 2013 National Academy of Public Administration report on the GPO acknowledged that "GPO's statute is outdated and precedes current technology" (NAPA 2013). At the same time, GPO has been able to introduce new technologies, services, and products.

Some amendments to Title 44 have succeeded, while others have failed. Some of the failed attempts include the following:

- 1991 saw the introduction of H.R. 2772, the GPO Wide Information Network for Data Online Act of 1991. The bill would have folded online government information products under the purview of the GPO at no cost to the user (Cornwell et al. 1993). Might we have seen

Table 2.5   Regional Libraries within the Federal Depository Library Program

Institution Name	City	State
Auburn University at Montgomery Library	Montgomery	Alabama
University of Alabama, Amelia Gayle Gorgas Library	Tuscaloosa	Alabama
Arizona State Library, Archives & Public Records	Phoenix	Arizona
Arkansas State Library	Little Rock	Arkansas
California State Library	Sacramento	California
University of Colorado, Boulder, Norlin Library	Boulder	Colorado
Connecticut State Library	Hartford	Connecticut
University of Florida, George A. Smathers Libraries	Gainesville	Florida
University of Georgia, Map and Government Information Library	Athens	Georgia
University of Hawaii at Manoa Library	Honolulu	Hawaii
University of Idaho Library	Moscow	Idaho
Illinois State Library	Springfield	Illinois
Indiana State Library	Indianapolis	Indiana
University of Iowa, Main Library	Iowa City	Iowa
University of Kansas Libraries	Lawrence	Kansas
University of Kentucky, William T. Young Library	Lexington	Kentucky
Louisiana State University, Baton Rouge, Troy H. Middleton Library	Baton Rouge	Louisiana
Louisiana Tech University, Prescott Memorial Library	Ruston	Louisiana
University of Maine, Orono, Raymond H. Fogler Library	Orono	Maine
University of Maryland, College Park, McKeldin Library	College Park	Maryland
Boston Public Library	Boston	Massachusetts
University of Minnesota, Government Publications Library	Minneapolis	Minnesota
University of Mississippi, J. D. Williams Library	University	Mississippi
University of Missouri Libraries	Columbia	Missouri

(continued)

Table 2.5   (continued)

Institution Name	City	State
University of Montana, Mansfield Library	Missoula	Montana
University of Nebraska, Lincoln, Don L. Love Memorial Library	Lincoln	Nebraska
Newark Public Library	Newark	New Jersey
University of New Mexico, University Libraries	Albuquerque	New Mexico
New York State Library	Albany	New York
University of North Carolina at Chapel Hill, Davis Library	Chapel Hill	North Carolina
North Dakota State University Libraries	Fargo	North Dakota
University of North Dakota, Chester Fritz Library	Grand Forks	North Dakota
State Library of Ohio	Columbus	Ohio
Oklahoma State University, Edmon Low Library	Stillwater	Oklahoma
State Library of Oregon	Salem	Oregon
State Library of Pennsylvania	Harrisburg	Pennsylvania
University of South Carolina, Columbia, Thomas Cooper Library	Columbia	South Carolina
University of Memphis, McWherter Library	Memphis	Tennessee
Texas State Library and Archives Commission	Austin	Texas
Texas Tech University Library	Lubbock	Texas
Utah State University, Merrill Cazier Library	Logan	Utah
University of Virginia, Alderman Library	Charlottesville	Virginia
WA Office of the Secretary of State, Washington State Library	Tumwater	Washington
West Virginia University, Downtown Campus Library	Morgantown	West Virginia
University of Wisconsin, Madison, Memorial Library	Madison	Wisconsin
Milwaukee Public Library	Milwaukee	Wisconsin

a world where users don't have to pay for products like NTIS reports or PACER documents had this bill passed? The bill got no further than being introduced in the House.

- Another attempt at GPO reform took place in the 105th Congress in 1998. S 2288, "A bill to provide for the reform and continuing legislative oversight of the production, procurement, dissemination, and permanent public access of the Government's publications," was well-supported by GPO staff, but lacked congressional support and enough time for passage (GPO 2016a).

- FDLP Modernization Act of 2018 (H.R.5305—115th Congress). If passed, the bill would have required federal agencies and the GPO to work more closely together to ensure that more content is captured (i.e., fewer fugitive documents), and it would have authorized further digitization and preservation initiatives. The bill did not advance past the House of Representatives.

Now the successes:

- Government Printing Office Electronic Information Access Enhancement Act of 1993 (P.L. 103-40, 107 Stat. 112). This Act laid the groundwork for the highly successful GPO Access database. Now it is two generations ago, with the intervening FDsys database and the current Govinfo.gov system now in place.
- P.L. 113-235, Division H (2014); 128 Stat. 2130, 2535–Consolidated and Further Continuing Appropriations Act, 2015 did little to amend Title 44 other than to change the title of the Public Printer of the United States to the Director of the Government Publishing Office and to change the office from the Government Printing Office to the Government Publishing Office.

It's obvious that many Title 44 changes are necessary and will likely come about at some point. In the meantime, GPO and the FDLP continue to provide free public access, as required by 44 U.S.C. § 1911: "Depository libraries shall make Government publications available for the free use of the general public." Yet there is no provision in Title 44 to provide funds to depository libraries. They are on their own.

Leaving the Program

Equally as important, there are government information professionals in each of these libraries who are always willing to help members of the public find, use, and understand the publications, regardless of format. Even though much of the information is online somewhere, it isn't always easy or convenient to use it that way. The government information librarian or staff member will do whatever humanly possible to provide access that works for the user.

The unfortunate reality is that the number of depository libraries is slowly declining. Despite efforts by GPO to communicate the value of

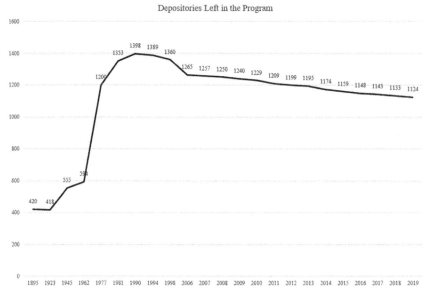

Figure 2.3 Most data from GPO Annual Reports. Early years from McGarr (2000). Data for 2010, 2012–14, and 2019 are the author's numbers derived from searches of the Federal Depository Library Directory in May or June of that year.

being a depository library, the occasional addition of new tribal, public, and academic libraries and the recent thrust to encourage electronic-only depository libraries, the numbers are declining, which means that the number of government information experts is diminishing, as Figure 2.3 shows.

THIRD ERA: ONLINE DISSEMINATION

The Government Printing Office Electronic Information Access Enhancement Act of 1993 (P.L. 103-40, 107 Stat. 112) was arguably the most important change to Title 44 since the Depository Library Act of 1962 (P.L. 87-579, 76 Stat. 352). This resulted in the release of GPO's first online information service, GPO Access in 1994. The web was in its infancy, and, originally GPO access was only available via subscription, while being freely available in depository libraries. But by December 1995, it was freely available to the public. Even though widely used, the database was built upon Wide Area Information Server (WAIS) technology and limped along for many years. In 2004, GPO announced the development of a new retrieval and preservation system to replace GPO Access, FDsys. By 2009, the new Federal Digital System had been released. The system included digitally signed documents that GPO had been gradually rolling out since 2006. These authentication measures went a long way to ensuring that digital government publications could be fully accepted in courts of law and would be yet another step toward public acceptance of the new format. By late 2010, FDsys had fully replaced GPO Access and was GPO's system of record. In 2016, GPO launched a beta version of the new Govinfo website. The new site was more mobile-friendly and had more options for browsing content (GPO 2016a). In January 2018, Govinfo.gov was fully released, and by December of that year, FDsys was history.

The depository program itself has seen its extensive network of tangible distribution evolve into the digital age. From July 1976, when the first machine-readable cataloging (MARC) records had been created for the Monthly Catalog of Government Publications until 2019, over 97 percent of items identified for distribution by the GPO are available in electronic format. This had effects on the depository program itself, as some libraries dropped out of the program altogether. GPO continually struggles with ways to convince libraries of the value of remaining in the program. It also struggles with convincing government agencies to fully follow the law requiring agencies to provide GPO with the content they generate.

The online dissemination age requires us to be aware of several technical aspects that are germane to the online world in a unique way.

PURLs—Persistent Uniform Resource Locators

We all know what URLs are—Uniform Resource Locators, the web addresses that serve as pointers to websites, documents, or databases. The idea behind PURLs is to ensure that users are taken to the current location of the resource and not to an expired link. As we are aware, there is a substantial percentage of "link rot." There are numerous reasons for U.S. government information to disappear. For one, government agencies are not libraries and do not have the permanent access mandate that is so important to those in the depository community. They are all about current information. Superseded documents are usually taken down. Outdated information is removed, especially medical and legal information, so that the public is not confused by what is current versus what is historical information. This is why the Government Publishing Office takes very seriously the capture, cataloging, and archiving of documents it discovers on government websites. Another reason content goes dark is a change of administration. Elections do have consequences, and one of these is that content supportive of a previous administration is scrubbed. That is the reason the End-of-Term Archive was created (see below under "Fugitive Documents").

The Government Publishing Office uses PURLs when cataloging to provide enduring access to resources. PURLs are a redirection technology. When a user clicks on a PURL, the PURL server redirects the user to the current URL. If the URL has changed, the URL can be changed on the PURL server to direct the user to the new location. If, however, the content has disappeared from the government website, the PURL server can point to an archived copy of the document. Since 1998, GPO has been using PURLs and archiving the content it catalogs to the extent possible.

GPO PURLs have changed their format over the years. Older PURLS may look like this (with #### standing for unique PURL identifiers): http://purl.access.gpo.gov/GPO/LPS#### OR http://purl.fdlp.gov/GPO/FDLP####. But current PURLS look like this: https://purl.fdlp.gov/GPO/gpo#### (notice the current use of the https standard).

You will see all these forms still in use today. There are currently about 240,000 PURLs in existence. If you are curious and want to view the content archived by the FDLP in conjunction with the PURL project, it can be found in the Federal Depository Library Program Web Archive: https://archive-it.org/home/FDLPwebarchive.

Consider how depository libraries receive their catalog records. They may receive them through GPO (there are several ways to do this), or they may pay for a record service such as Marcive and load GPO records on a periodic basis. If each record for an electronic resource has a URL (rather than a PURL), then if and when a government URL goes bad, it goes bad for every library that has loaded that record into its catalog. But if a PURL is used instead of a mere URL, when a government URL has been discovered to be bad, GPO can amend the place the PURL points to, thus repairing the link in all the catalogs around the country. Brilliant idea!—except that it doesn't exactly always work that well. In an ideal world, GPO would have the time and resources to wake up each day and check each of the 240,000 extant PURLs to ensure that each of them is working. But they don't do that. Instead, when a document information professional notices a defective PURL, they notify GPO, and the link is fixed for everyone within a matter of days.

Authentication

In 2016, GPO released its National Plan for Access to U.S. Government Information (2016b). The five guiding principles of this plan were:

- Principle 1: The public has the right of access to government information.
- Principle 2: Government has the obligation to disseminate and provide broad public access to its information.

- Principle 3: Government has an obligation to guarantee the authenticity and integrity of its information.

- Principle 4: Government has an obligation to preserve its information.

- Principle 5: Government information created or compiled by government employees or at government expense should remain in the public domain.

Authenticity of government information has always been important. It doesn't matter if you agree with what the government says or not, the point is that documents coming from the government have a stamp of "officialness" to them. When we see the title page of a print resource that says "Government Printing Office," we immediately know that this is an authentic government publication.

But in the online world, do we really know anything with absolute assurance? We all regularly receive emails suggesting that they are from government entities. Upon close inspection, the emails don't come from .gov domains, use irregular grammar and spelling, and have other strange aspects. Most people don't fall for these scams, but some do.

The legal community has been understandably reluctant to rush headlong into the digital age. After all, how do we know that documents submitted to courts or other official authorities in digital format have not been altered in some way? At least print resources have undergone some kind of vetting through established publishing houses. GPO has an answer for this problem. Since 2008, GPO has been authenticating various kinds of publications (GPO 2011). GPO is a "trusted steward" in the chain of provenance between government content authors and users of government information. To verify the integrity of the content, cryptographic technologies are employed. Behind the scenes, cryptographic hash values are encoded in the metadata. If any digital content is altered, added, or omitted, it will fail the test. GPO provides the tools for all these tests to take place. This is what gives users and the legal system confidence to know that a PDF passed along via email is unchanged and authentic and contains valid content.

These authenticated publications can be widely found in Govinfo.gov, GPO's official dissemination platform. Publications that have been authenticated have the eagle logo with the words "authenticated U.S. Government Information" on the top left-hand side of the initial page of the document (Figure 2.4). In addition, when opening the document in Adobe Acrobat, a signature panel can be seen, declaring the authenticity of the publication.

The certification states that the document has not been modified since it was certified. But when something has been tampered with, here is what happens (see Figure 2.5).

Figure 2.4   GPO authentication mark and signature panel

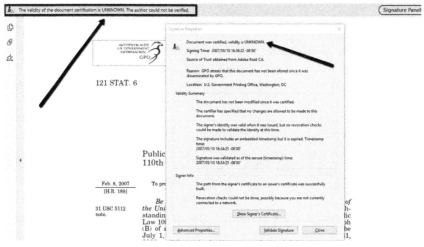

Figure 2.5   GPO signature panel showing that validity is unknown

In this case, something failed in the validation process. This document did not pass the test and should not be trusted. Want to see this signature failure in action for yourself? Download this file to your computer, open it in Adobe Reader, and check the signature for yourself: https://bit.ly/30FipGm.

Preservation

Not only do we need to consider how to keep online content in perpetuity, we also need to consider how to migrate it so that can always be accessible. Think about it this way: do you really think that the PDF file format will exist in 100 years? If not, then what will replace it, and what will we do with the tens of millions of online publications currently in that format? These are very different considerations than in the tangible world. With print publications, the concern is preservation of paper.

Consider too the scans that have already been done of government publications. Often the scans done by Google have fingers in the pages (see Figure 2.6).

Sometimes the scans are less than perfect (Figure 2.7).

In the rush to digitize content and place it on the web, many compromises have been made and shortcuts taken. We

The National Topographic Map Series also includes other special-purpose maps which are prepared from standard quadrangles but do not follow the standard quadrangle format.

Paper size E-W N-S width length (inches)	Quadrangle area (square miles)
¹ 22×27	49 to 70
29½×32¼	71
¹ 17×21	197 to 282
² 18×21	207 to 281
⁴ 34×22	4,580 to 8,669
	73,734 to 102,759
27×27	

Figure 2.6 Example of a finger in a Google scan of a government publication. Courtesy of Hathi-Trust: https://babel.hathitrust.org/cgi/pt?id=uc1.ax 0003628443&view=1up&seq=11.

must be careful not to let tangible content disappear while relying on often imperfect digitized content.

As libraries rush headlong into the digital age, depository libraries are discarding an increasing number of print copies. Sure, there are procedures in place, such as the newly created Depository Selection Information Management System (DSIMS) tool for item selection and FDLP eXchange for needs and offers. It is left to regional depositories to ensure that enough tangible copies exist throughout the country to allow selectives to withdraw items without fear of creating gaps in national holdings.

On December 28, 2018, GPO became the first organization in the United States and the second organization in the world to achieve ISO 16363:2012 certification as a trusted digital repository. What this means is that GPO has demonstrated that its repository is able to ensure the access, viability, security, usability, and discoverability of its content for the long term, according to industry best practices (FDLP 2018b). This means that data stored in Govinfo.gov is as secure as can be by today's standards and best practices.

But GPO cannot do all digital preservation by itself. Digital access stewards contract to provide permanent public access to selected digital

Figure 2.7   Defective scan for a government publication from Google Books. Google and the Google logo are registered trademarks of Google Inc., used with permission.

content hosted at their institution. The Preservation Stewardship Program, an outgrowth of the National Plan, enlists depository libraries as partners in the task of preservation of tangible content. As of September 2019, there were 61 partnerships noted (Google: *site:fdlp.gov partnerships*). Most of the projects are for high-profile titles, such as *U.S. Statutes at Large*; *Federal Register*; *Code of Federal Regulations*; *Public Papers of the Presidents*; *Congressional Record* (and previous titles); and the Official Gazette of the Patent Office. Some have very narrow scopes, such as publications of the 101st Airborne Division. Others are ambitious in scope: congressional hearings, EPA publications, Department of State publications, and the entire Congressional Serial Set (FDLP 2012b).

Obviously, there is much more that needs to be done in terms of scanning existing tangible documents (often called "legacy content"), whether the original is in paper or microformat. There are many challenges for this endeavor that differ from the challenges of preserving born digital content. Original pages may be in bound volumes, which may require destructive scanning to get the best image quality. Some paper is very thin and bleed-through issues can occur with printing on the back sides of pages. File sizes from legacy scans are much larger than with born digital files. Adding optical character recognition (OCR) to the files multiplies the file size many times.

Dissemination

Local Online Catalogs

Depository libraries select the items that best suit the needs of the local community. A regional depository library has a comprehensive collection profile, whereas a public library may choose materials focused on their states, consumer issues, and basic legislative materials. Libraries generally acquire catalog records in some kind of automated distribution method, perhaps through the GPO's Cataloging Record Distribution Program (Google: *site:fdlp.gov cataloging record distribution*) or through a vendor such as Marcive or OCLC.

While your local selective depository may suit your needs in most cases, searching catalog records of regional depository libraries has many benefits. Often regionals catalog with a great deal of detail, providing analytical access to complex publications.

Basic Collection

The FDLP has defined a "basic collection" of titles that all depository libraries must make available for immediate use. All depositories will feature these titles in their online catalogs, and most will also have print versions. Searching the Catalog of Government Publications will retrieve all the titles (https://bit.ly/2P4gbPs).

Secondary Sources

Depository libraries are distinguished by their primary sources. Sometimes the most efficient way to get to these resources is by using secondary sources. Depositories are encouraged to acquire print and online resources that assist with this. You will find these secondary sources mentioned throughout this book in the relevant places. One example of secondary sources is the digital Serial Set tools from Readex, ProQuest, and HeinOnline. Without the superb indexing and browsing capabilities provided by these products, we would be lost in a 16,000-volume heap.

Fugitive Documents

The federal government is always changing. With changing presidential administrations adding (and occasionally eliminating) government agencies, we need powerful tools to keep track of all of this. Here are some important initiatives to assist us.

Print Fugitive Documents

Fugitive documents are not a new phenomenon. With the publication of the first issue of what became known as the Monthly Catalog in 1895, acknowledgment was made that omissions were inevitable.

> It is essentially desired that omissions be promptly pointed out, in order that the missing titles may be printed in the next monthly issue. There are about one hundred and twenty Departments, bureaus, and offices of the Government that publish the public documents of the United States, and even with the courteous cooperation that has been almost uniformly extended to me it is a task of some magnitude to gather all the publications from so many sources. If the task had been completely accomplished, and there were no omissions from the first Monthly Catalogue, it would be almost miraculous. As this is not the age of miracles, some omissions will doubtless be detected, but I am hopeful that they will be neither numerous nor important. (F. A. Crandall, Superintendent of Documents. Monthly Catalogue, January 1895)

As early as 1896, in the report of the Superintendent of Documents, fugitive documents were acknowledged as an issue to be dealt with (https:// babel.hathitrust.org/cgi/pt?id=uc1.b3032148;view=1up;seq=71).

An important study on fugitive documents was included in the hearing, *Title 44, U.S. Code—Proposals for Revision* (HT 011343797). Appendix 3C of that hearing is the study "Fugitive Documents: Scope of the Problem" (1997). That study concluded that "more than 50 percent of all tangible Government information that it produces is not being made available to the Federal Depository Library Program."

One attempt at reigning in the many fugitive documents and nondepository publications was the Documents Expediting Project (DocEx). Spanning from 1946 to 2004, this program, operated out of the Library of Congress, was a true collaborative effort involving libraries, library associations, the Library of Congress and other federal agencies, and the Superintendent of Documents. These documents, not distributed through the depository program, were distributed to member depository libraries for inclusion in their local collections. Many of these items were submitted to the Monthly Catalog for inclusion in the official record, and many have been preserved through the HathiTrust (Sinclair 2019).

Online Fugitive Documents

Fugitive documents persist in the electronic age to an even greater extent than they did in the print era. Fugitive documents, in the online context, are government publications that had not been discovered and captured by the GPO's cataloging and archiving programs. That these documents exist in great numbers has been demonstrated by comparing the results of the End-of-Term Archive web crawls with documents actually distributed through the FDLP. In the 2008 EOT crawl, there were 160 million distinct URLs identified, compared with 10,200 items distributed through the FDLP that year (Jacobs 2014). We can safely assume that most of these 160 million URLs are not documents worthy of preservation. Many will be ephemeral web pages, press releases, announcement of events, administrative pages, and so forth. But even if we assume that only 1 percent of this content is a publication, that means that there are a lot of fugitives out there.

In 2006, GPO undertook an experiment in web harvesting (FDLP 2012a). Two private companies were tasked with harvesting content from the Environmental Protection Agency and were to employ technologies to determine which of the harvested materials fell into the scope of the FDLP. In other words, they would be able to find both materials that had already been identified and cataloged and discover fugitive publications as well. Each company did three separate crawls over a six-month period and refined their harvesting rules and instructions before the next crawl. The results were startling. One company found 83,229 documents determined to be in-scope of the program, and the other company discovered 239,478. The bottom line is that government agencies produce a huge amount of fugitive content, and it will likely disappear without anyone noticing that it ever existed.

Government Archiving

Some government agencies create their own archived websites. The Commerce Department has archived content available dating back to 2001. The State Department, through the Department of State Foreign Affairs Network (DOSFAN) project, a partnership with the Federal Depository Library Program (https://purl.fdlp.gov/GPO/gpo109353), provides archived content from 1990 to 1997. Additional State Department archived content can be found by searching Google for *State Department archive websites*. Other agencies that provide selective archiving include the Department of Education.

White House websites are considered presidential records. For this reason, the National Archives has been archiving presidential web content since 1994, with the Clinton administration (*site:archives.gov archived Presidential White House websites*). For example, the Obama White House content is available here: https://obamawhitehouse.archives.gov/. George W. Bush's content is available at https://georgewbush-whitehouse.archives.gov/.

Wayback Machine

The Wayback Machine, one of many components of archive.org, works extremely well for vanished government content. Governments, the federal government included, are constantly reorganizing their websites to make them better. At the same time, those who may have cited content previously available at a particular web address may find that the content has disappeared. This happened to me as I was preparing the section of this book on census geographies. I was wanting to cite this URL https://www.census.gov /geo/maps-data/data/tallies/national_geo_tallies.html. If you try the URL now, you will see that it redirects to a different page. The redirection is helpful, but it does not actually point to the content that previously existed at the URL in question. To see the content that originally existed, we need to use the Internet Archive's Wayback Machine (Figure 2.8).

From this, we can see previous dates when the content had been archived by the Wayback Machine (Figure 2.9).

There is enough information here for us to track the current URL for the same content. By searching *site:census.gov "national geographic tallies,"* we are able to see that the current URL for the same content is currently available at https://www.census.gov/geographies/reference-files/time-series/geo /tallies.html. Had the same content truly disappeared, we could have pointed to the version in the Wayback Machine.

End-of-Term Archive

The goal of the End-of-Term Archive (http://eotarchive.cdlib.org/) is to archive federal government information every four years. The idea is to capture government websites as presidential administrations change, even if it will be a second term. Begun in 2008 with the changeover from George W.

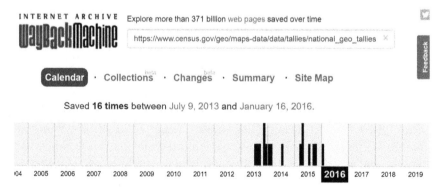

Figure 2.8 Example of using Wayback Machine to retrieve original content. *Source:* Internet Archive.

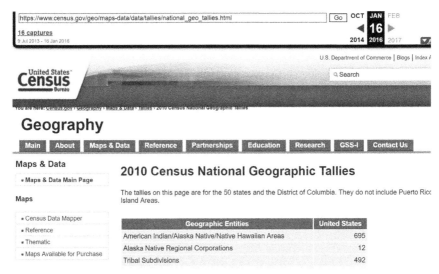

Figure 2.9   Wayback Machine used to access content removed from government servers. *Source:* Internet Archive Wayback Machine.

Bush to Barack Obama, the project has been resurrected at each subsequent four-year interval to capture more sites. The idea is that as new administrations come, the previous content is taken down. The list of collaborators is impressive, including the Internet Archive, the Library of Congress, the Government Publishing Office, California Digital Library, University of North Texas Libraries, Stanford University Libraries, and George Washington University. The project has been increasing capacity, having captured 3,305 websites from the 2008 crawl, and 53,324 sites from the 2016 crawl.

The online era continues to be an exciting one, as well as a learning experience for government information librarians, GPO, and library vendors. Advances have included permanent URLs—the PURL program—although there are few things permanent about the PURLs. It's kind of like the *Wizard of Oz.* Things happen as long as someone is behind the curtain. GPO does not have sufficient funding to truly maintain PURLs. What should happen is a system that daily notices PURLs that are bad and an automated way to either update the URL in the PURL database or to notify a GPO cataloger of the situation. Since that does not happen, it is left up to vigilant documents librarians to notify GPO to make changes, which they are ever so willing to do.

SUMMING UP THE THREE ERAS

What should be evident by now is that the U.S. government has been serious about getting government information into the hands of citizens. With all the misfires, fugitives, and struggling to keep up with

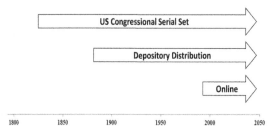

Figure 2.10   Three eras of U.S. government information dissemination

current technologies, it remains clear that GPO is committed to keeping the United States informed.

Figure 2.10 shows the overlapping coverage of the three eras described above. What will the future hold?

GENERAL TOOLS AND FINDING AIDS

This section will first present the quickest ways to solve most government documents inquiries. This initial approach will solve the vast majority of questions about publication titles, whether they are online or not, and how to locate them in libraries. The second part of the chapter will focus on the more difficult questions, which many government publication questions seem to be.

Catalog of Government Publications (CGP)

The online Catalog of Government Publications (CGP) is the online continuation of the print Monthly Catalog of Government Publications that started in 1895 (see further discussion under "Print Tools, below). In July 1976, electronic records were produced in addition to the print Monthly Catalog, but by December 2004, the print version had ceased to exist. The current CGP is the official version of what was once the print catalog. The current online version uses an ExLibris Aleph interface that libraries use for their integrated library systems, including their online catalogs. But the significant distinction in the case of this GPO tool is that, unlike other libraries using the Aleph interface, GPO does not have a physical library, and never has had one. This presents unique challenges when cataloging new editions or government serials.

Since GPO is the official cataloging authority, they assign authoritative SuDocs classifications numbers as well as permanent URLs (PURLs) to records for new materials. To the extent possible, GPO archives the online content when cataloging the materials. This backup system is essential for the inevitable takedown of documents by the agency that hosted them online. In a sense, we can't get upset with agencies for taking down documents, since they have no mission to preserve information in perpetuity.

After all, preservation is the mission of libraries. There are cases when GPO is not able to capture and preserve online content. These cases include online databases, which cannot be captured, since they entail the use of a complete interface that is dependent on sophisticated software of the time, as well as all the content contained within the database.

Not only is GPO adding records for new publications into the CGP, they are also seriously adding older records as well. As previously noted, GPO never kept the print publications that they cataloged and distributed to depository libraries. But they did keep track of things in a "shelflist." The GPO Historic Shelflist is gradually being added to the CGP. These are electronic version of GPO's physical card catalog from the 1870s to October 1992. According to GPO, the historic shelflist contains:

• Over one million 3x5 cards arranged in Superintendent of Documents (SuDoc) order;

• Bibliographic information for U.S. Government documents from all three branches of the government in a variety of formats, including monographs, maps, serials, microfiche, and posters;

• Cards representing documents that were distributed to libraries in the Federal Depository Library Program (FDLP) and documents that were not distributed but were required by the Cataloging and Indexing Program, as required by U.S.C. Title 44;

• An estimated 455,000 OCLC cards that were produced by GPO through OCLC beginning in July 1976; and

• An extensive collection of bibliographic information but not a complete inventory of publications distributed through the FDLP (GPO 2012).

As of early 2019, 75 percent of this transcription process had been completed, with over 200,000 of these records added to the CGP. One thing we need to keep in mind, however, is that these catalog records are not a true cataloging with item in hand, as one currently does in the cataloging process. Rather, it is a transcription of catalog records from a time when a cataloger did have the item in hand. As such, there may be differences between records for the same item in the OCLC database (GPO 2019).

WorldCat Bibliographic Database

OCLC's WorldCat database is the largest bibliographic database in the world. There are two versions of this database. One is a subscription service currently available on the FirstSearch platform. Most academic libraries and many public libraries make this database available to users. Since the WorldCat database is a union catalog of 72,000 libraries around the world, it contains a wide variety of cataloging practices and duplication of records. No quest for government information would be complete without searching it, although it does not always have SuDocs numbers or local holdings information.

The other interface to WorldCat is through the freely available World-Cat (https://www.worldcat.org/). All records from the subscription World-Cat are represented in the free version, but not all bibliographic fields are viewable. Fields such as note fields (5xx), earlier title (780), and later title (785) for serials cannot be seen. This is a big problem when doing the challenging research that is usually necessary for finding complex government serial publications.

Govinfo.gov

The Government Publishing Office has a long history as a leader in providing digital access to government content. The Government Printing Office Electronic Information Access Enhancement Act of 1993 (P.L. 103-40, 107 Stat. 112) laid the groundwork for the highly successful GPO Access database. When GPO Access needed a remake, FDsys was released and was a tremendous improvement. Govinfo.gov was launched as a beta release in February 2016 and fully replaced FDsys in December 2018.

This is the first place to go for certain major publications when the official full text is needed. When you search the database, you are not just searching metadata, as you do when searching a local library catalog or the CGP. You are searching the full text of publications, sometimes referred to as "deep searching." Results are returned quickly, allowing quick limiting with the facets on the left side. If you know you are looking for something in the *Federal Register*, for example, just put your search into the Govinfo search box. There is no need to preselect the source publication. The system also allows for efficient browsing of content, since that is sometimes the easiest way to access known content. Citation search is another feature that works quite well. A summary of useful general government information online tools is in Table 2.6.

Finding Older Publications

Much has been written in previous generations about the print finding aids to locating government publications. Morehead (1999) has helpfully pointed out the shortcomings in Poor's work and that, while the successor work by Ames is better, it is still far from completely adequate. He also noted that the 1909 Checklist never came out with volume two, which was

Table 2.6   General online tools useful in locating government information

General Online Tools	Comments
Catalog of Government Publications (CGP)	Use when searching for any government publication, especially from July 1976 onward. Retrieves all formats, print, fiche, and online. Does not deep search anything.
Govinfo.gov	Use when searching congressional publications and selected Executive Branch publications. Deep searching of content.
HathiTrust	Best to do independent verification of title, etc. first in a tool like WorldCat. Then, with good cataloging information, search HT. Catalogs serials in the same way OCLC does. Deep searching is possible, but catalog metadata search is more effective for known items.
Internet Archive (e-Books and Texts)	Catalogs individual serial issues; not grouped as series or serial titles. Deep searching is possible, but catalog metadata search is more effective for known items.
WorldCat	Use as a last resort when trying to verify the existence of a government publication. Searching of metadata only.

to provide the subject access to volume one. It is best, if one is fortunate enough to have access, to make up for these deficiencies by searching first in the ProQuest Executive Branch Documents (an add-on module within ProQuest Congressional). That, combined with the Serial Set (also contained within ProQuest Congressional), covers a vast swath of publications from 1789 through 1948 (ProQuest is continually updating the years of content within the Executive Branch module). As a cross-check and update of years on that, ProQuest again has their online version of the Monthly Catalog (1895–1976). These sets of tools take all the rough edges away from the deficiencies of the print tools I will mention below.

In this section, we will look at general finding aids, including catalogs, checklists, classification guides, specialized bibliographies, and manuals that help with general government information questions. This presentation will be format independent. Some of the materials originated in print but are also available either in HathiTrust, the internet archive, or have a new life of their own in an independent, searchable database.

These print tools are mentioned not because they are the best starting points today, with all the fine online resources available to all and the vendor tools available to institutions that can afford them, but for the following reasons:

- Documents librarians that own these tools in their libraries should ensure that they retain these valuable finding aids.
- Online tools are often incomplete or experience failures. Having access to print resources often assists in these cases.
- There are fugitive documents that were only discovered long after they were published. This holds true both for the print realm and the digital era.
- Many publications are issued in serial format, and indexing most of these is not a priority.

For these reasons, we need to cover many kinds of finding aids, from print indexes and catalogs to online databases.

Poore, Benjamin Perley. 1885. *A Descriptive Catalogue of the Government Publications of the United States, September 5, 1774–March 4, 1881.* Washington, DC: GPO. S. Misc. Doc. 67, 48th Congress, 2nd Session, Serial Set Vol. No. 2171 Session Vol. No. 2. HT 001168028. It has a subject index that is defective (Freidel 1974).

Ames, John G. 1905. *Comprehensive Index to the Publications of the United States Government, 1881–1893*, by John G. Ames, Chief of Document Division, Department of the Interior. 2 vols. Washington, DC: U.S. Dept. of the Interior, Division of Documents: U.S. GPO. SuDocs: I 15.2:In 2/2/. H. Doc. 754 pts. 1 and 2, 58th Congress, 2nd Session, Serial Set Vols. No. 4745 and 4746. HT 001168031. Complete coverage for the years it covers, but it does not have complete coverage of departmental documents (executive branch documents). It is arranged by subject with an excellent analysis of periodicals within the Serial Set.

Checklist of United States Public Documents, 1789–1909: Congressional to Close of Sixtieth Congress, Departmental to End of Calendar Year 1909. Compiled under the direction of the Superintendent of Documents. 3rd ed., rev. and enl. Washington, DC: G.P.O., 1911. (GP 3.2:C 41/2). (HT 001168034, 102499857, 000205838). This was an attempt to list all government documents and even to retrospectively assign them the SuDocs numbers they never had when they were originally published. Also available via the University of North Texas Digital Library (https://digital.library.unt.edu/ark:/67531/metadc1029/).

The Document Catalogue and the Monthly Catalog

One of the results of the Printing Act of 1895 was the creation of two publications to give information about government publications. The

Document Catalogue was initially the more serious of the two serials, giving precise bibliographic information. The other publication, initially serving more like a sales catalog, was the Monthly Catalog of Government Publications and, originally bore the title, Catalogue of Publications of the Government of the United States. When it was first published, Superintendent of Documents Francis A. Crandall said,

> It is considered that the Monthly Catalogue is an ephemeral publication, not intended primarily for the use of librarians. It is the chief medium this office will have for reaching the general public. (Crandall 1895, 3)

The Document Catalogue was intended to be used by librarians and was to be a comprehensive index and permanent record of publications. The Document Catalogue's full title is Catalog of the Public Documents of the . . . Congress and of all Departments of the Government of the United States. Mandated by the Printing Act of 1895 to be a comprehensive index, this work was strong in its bibliographic features. It covers 1893–1940 in 25 volumes.

Catalogue of the Public Documents of the . . . Congress and of all Departments of the Government of the United States for the period from . . . to . . . 1895–1940. Washington, DC: Government Printing Office. (GP 3.6:). (HT 001719811; 100074648; 010423301 [incomplete holdings]). Also contained within the Serial Set.

The Monthly Catalog of Government Publications (MOCAT)

Also having its genesis in the Printing Act of 1895, this serial publication started out more as a trade publication, listing what the government was printing, with less emphasis on bibliographic description than the Document Catalogue. As time went on, the Monthly Catalog became better at bibliographic description, and the Document Catalogue went away. ProQuest has the entire run of the old MOCAT available in database format by subscription. If you can afford it, it sure beats searching all those many volumes and cumulations. (HT 100699859; 101715677 [incomplete holdings]). (SuDocs: GP 3.8).

Because of many title changes, it takes many cataloging records to represent the Monthly Catalog over the years:

Catalogue of United States Public Documents: issued monthly by the Superintendent of Documents. Washington, DC: GPO: 1895–1907. 25 volumes. (GP 3.8:). GPO is digitizing this. (HT 010688747).

Monthly Catalogue, United States Public Documents: issued by the Superintendent of Documents. Washington, DC: GPO: 1907–1933. (HT 010688347).

Monthly Catalog, United States Public Documents: issued by the Superintendent of Documents. Washington, DC: GPO: 1933–1939. (HT 009049770).

United States Government Publications Monthly Catalog: issued by the Superintendent of Documents. Washington, DC: U.S. GPO: 1940–1951. (GP 3.8:). (HT 010690843).

Monthly Catalog of United States Government Publications: issued by the Superintendent of Documents. Washington, DC: U.S. GPO, 1951–. (HT 009049771)

Most larger depository libraries will still have rather complete holdings of these print volumes, if that is what you desire. The difficulty of going through multiple volumes of the print MOCAT has been mitigated in recent generations by several tools. First of all, the Monthly Catalog itself issued various cumulative indexes over the years, so that at least each and every annual index or monthly issue index would not need to be consulted. But commercial publishers came to the rescue in the 1970s with some helpful tools. It should be noted that GPO is currently in the process of digitizing all issues of MOCAT back to 1895.

The Checklist of U.S. Public Documents, 1789–1976 [microform] was one such resource. Known at the time as "Checklist '76," this was a microfilm edition of the GPO shelflist cards that existed at that time. Some of the items described on the cards were never distributed to depository libraries, making this resource a valuable one when trying to hunt down obscure fugitive documents. A companion publication, the Cumulative Title Index to United States Public Documents, 1789–1976 is a multivolume print work that will be easier to locate and use than Checklist '76 would be. One weakness of this project is that it omits any work without an assigned SuDocs number. This rules out all congressional reports, documents, and other Serial Set publications, since SuDocs numbers were not assigned to items appearing in the Serial Set.

Cumulative Title Index to United States Public Documents, 1789–1976. Compiled by Daniel W. Lester, Sandra K. Faull, and Lorraine E. Lester. 16 v. Arlington, VA: United States Historical Documents Institute.

Cumulated indexes save a lot of time when trying to find older government publications. A helpful 15-volume set from Carrollton Press covers the years 1900–1971.

Cumulative Subject Index to the Monthly Catalog of United States Government Publications, 1900–1971. Washington, DC Carrollton Press. 15 v.

The subscription database, U.S. Documents Masterfile: 1774–2018 from Paratext is a continually updated guide to federal, state, local, and international public documents.

Other tools include the following:

Guide to U.S. Government Publications (Andriot)

This publication comes out annually, but you really only need to get it updated every four to five years. This unique research tool presents all documents series, arranged in SuDocs order, through the years. Nothing else does what Andriot does in showing the provenance of government serials and the changes in SuDocs classification. This is not a listing of document titles, but of series and SuDocs stems.

Guide to U.S. Government Publications. McLean, VA: Documents Index; Detroit, MI: Thomson Gale, 1973–. Published annually. Commonly known as "Andriot."

Finding Aids for Government Reports

Throughout the colorful political history of the United States, there have been congressional investigations, oversight reports, and congressional hearings, many of which had popular names associated with them. The Meese Report on pornography, the 9/11 Commission Report, the Warren Commission Report, and the Starr Report are some of the headliners of past years. These reports, often mentioned in the popular press with no attribution, can be extremely challenging to find, especially several generations after they were originally published. The following resources will help in the quest for elusive government reports.

Bernier, Bernard A. Jr., and Katherine F. Gould. 1984. *Popular Names of U.S. Government Reports: A Catalog.* 4th ed. Washington, DC: Library of Congress. (HT 000390229). The Pop Names Database Project from Indiana University provides access to a PDF version of this work (but note that the PDF texts from this project are not "OCR-ed").

Bengtson, Marjorie. "Popular Names of U.S. Government Reports: A Supplement." *Illinois Libraries* 69 (September 1987): 472–477.

Bengtson, Marjorie. "Popular Names of U.S. Government Reports: Second Supplement." *Illinois Libraries* 75 (April 1993): 161–165.

Bookheim, Louis W. 2017. *Reports of U.S. Presidential Commissions and Other Advisory Bodies: A Bibliographic Listing.* Getzville, NY: Hein.

Also available online via the HeinOnline database, where the full text of most reports is also viewable.

Graf, Jeff and Lou Malcomb. "Identifying Unidentified U.S. Government Reports." *Journal of Government Information* 21 (1994): 105–128.

U.S. Library of Congress. Division of Bibliography. 1930. *Federal Commissions, Committees, and Boards.* 71st Cong., 2nd sess., S. Doc. 71–174, Serial 9214.

Wolanin, Thomas R. *Presidential Advisory Commissions: Truman to Nixon.* Madison, WI: University of Wisconsin Press, 1975.

Zink, Steven. *Guide to the Presidential Advisory Commissions, 1973–1984.* Alexandria, VA: Chadwyck-Healey, 1987.

Online Tools: Free and Subscription

The databases, index, finding aids, and full-text services providing access to government information can be confusing and overwhelming. In the coming chapters, specific databases will be covered. But in an effort to provide a quick general overview. Table 2.7 shows freely available and subscription products for locating government materials generally, and then for each of the three branches of government.

GovDoc-L

Government information libraries have among the most helpful librarians anywhere. Their shared passion for free access to information motivates them to assist others in need of assistance. Joining this list, or asking someone who is already a member of the list, can be one of the quickest ways to get an answer to a difficult reference question. One need not be an official government information librarian or associated with the FDLP to

Table 2.7   Summary of federal online resources both free and fee-based (likely to be found in large depository libraries)

General Finding Aids	
Freely Available Resources	*Fee-Based Products*
Catalog of Government Publications (1995 to present with selected older coverage)	ProQuest Monthly Catalog (1895–present)
WorldCat (http://www.worldcat.org/)	WorldCat (FirstSearch)
MetaLib (http://metalib.gpo.gov/)	Public Documents Masterfile

Table 2.7   (continued)

Legislative Branch Materials

Freely Available Resources	*Fee-Based Products*
Govinfo.gov (https://www.govinfo.gov/)	ProQuest Congressional (Serial Set, all hearings, Cong. Rec. and more)
Congress.gov (http://www.congress.gov/)	
HathiTrust (http://www.hathitrust.org/)	ProQuest Legislative Insight (Legislative histories, historic to present)
Internet Archive (http://archive.org /details/texts)	
American Memory (http://memory.loc .gov/)	Readex U.S. Congressional Serial Set
Google Books (http://books.google.com/)	

Executive Branch Materials

Freely Available Resources	*Fee-Based Products*
Govinfo.gov (https://www.govinfo.gov/)	HeinOnline (Presidential materials)
HathiTrust (http://www.hathitrust.org/)	LLMC Digital (Agency annual reports)
Internet Archive (http://archive.org /details/texts)	
Google Books (http://books.google.com/)	ProQuest Executive Branch Documents
Internet search by site restriction (*site:doc.gov economic statistics*)	

Judicial Branch Materials

Freely Available Resources	*Fee-Based Products*
Govinfo.gov (https://www.govinfo.gov/)	HeinOnline
U.S. Courts (http://www.uscourts.gov/)	Westlaw Campus Research
FindLaw (http://www.findlaw.com/)	Nexis Uni
Internet search by site restriction (*site:state.co.us court*)	Pacer (http://www.pacer.gov/)

Statistical Materials

Freely Available Resources	*Fee-Based Products*
Fedstats.gov	ProQuest Statistical Insight
Census.gov	Social Explorer
Data.census.gov	PolicyMap
FRASER (fraser.stlouisfed.org)	SimplyAnalytics

Technical Reports

Freely Available Resources	*Fee-Based Products*
NTIS (https://ntrl.ntis.gov/NTRL/)	NTIS (via various commercial vendors)
TRAIL Project (http://www .technicalreports.org/)	
SciTech Connect (http://www.osti.gov /scitech/)	

join. The main URL for this mail distribution list is http://govdoc-l.org/. You will find instructions for joining the list and subscription options. Hundreds of documents professionals monitor this list daily, and it is usual not to get a response on the same day. A browsable and searchable GovDoc-L archive is also available by searching Google: *govdoc-l archives.*

REFERENCES

Cornwell, Gary, Ridley R. Kessler Jr, Duncan Aldrich, Thomas K. Andersen, Stephen M. Hayes, Jack Sulzer, and Susan Tulis. 1993. "Problems and Issues Affecting the US Depository Library Program and the GPO: The Librarians' Manifesto." *Government Publications Review* 20, no. 2: 121–140.

Crandall, Francis A. 1895. *Monthly Catalog of U.S. Government Publications* (January): 3.

DeLong, Suzanne. 1996. "What Is in the United States Serial Set?" *Journal of Government Information* 23, no. 2: 123–135.

Farrand, Max, ed. 1911. *The Records of the Federal Convention of 1787.* Vol. 2. New Haven, CT: Yale University Press, p. 260.

FDLP (Federal Depository Library Program). 2012a. "Environmental Protection Agency (EPA) Web Publication Harvesting Pilot Project." Updated July 13, 2016. Accessed August 26, 2019. https://www.fdlp.gov/about-fdlp/23-projects/132-epa-harvesting.

FDLP (Federal Depository Library Program). 2012b. "Partnerships." Updated July 2, 2019. Accessed August 26, 2019. https://www.fdlp.gov/about-the-fdlp/partnerships.

FDLP (Federal Depository Library Program). 2017. "U.S. Congressional Serial Set: What It Is and Its History." Updated December 20, 2017. Accessed August 26, 2019. https://www.fdlp.gov/about-fdlp/mission-history/u-s-congressional-serial-set-what-it-is-and-its-history.

FDLP (Federal Depository Library Program). 2018a. "Legal Requirements and Program Regulations of the Federal Depository Library Program." Accessed August 26, 2019. https://purl.fdlp.gov/GPO/gpo89707.

FDLP (Federal Depository Library Program). 2018b. "Trusted Digital Repository ISO 16363:2012 Audit and Certification." Updated May 28, 2019. Accessed August 14, 2019. https://www.fdlp.gov/preservation/trusted-digital-repository-iso-16363-2012-audit-and-certification.

Freidel, Frank Burt. 1974. *Harvard Guide to American History.* Cambridge, MA: Harvard University Press.

"Fugitive Documents: Scope of the Problem." 1997. In United States Congress. Senate. Committee on Rules and Administration. *Title 44, U.S. Code—Proposals for Revision: Hearings before the Committee on Rules and Administration, United States Senate, One Hundred Fifth Congress, First Session . . . April 24, May 8, and May 22, 1997* Appendix 3C, 353–58. Also appears in

Congressional Record, May 22, 1997, vol. 143, Extension of Remarks, E1045–E1046. SuDocs: Y 4.R 86/2:S.HRG.105-139; HT 011343797.

GAO (General Accounting Office). 1994. "Government Printing: Legal and Regulatory Framework is Outdated for New Technological Environment." GAO Report, April 1994. Accessed September 29, 2019. https://www.gao.gov /assets/220/219439.pdf.

GPO (Government Printing Office). 1994. *Report of the Serial Set Study Group*. Submitted to the Public Printer, October 7, 1994. Accessed December 12, 2019. http://purl.fdlp.gov/GPO/gpo67453.

GPO (Government Printing Office). 2011. *Authenticity of Electronic Federal Government Publications*. Washington, DC: U.S. Accessed December 12, 2019. Government Printing Office. http://purl.fdlp.gov/GPO/gpo9376.

GPO (Government Printing Office). 2012. "GPO Historic Shelflist." Updated July 23, 2014. Accessed August 1, 2019. https://www.fdlp.gov/project-list/gpo -historic-shelflist.

GPO (Government Publishing Office). 2016a. *Keeping America Informed: The U.S. Government Publishing Office: A Legacy of Service to the Nation 1861–2016*. Revised ed. Washington, DC: GPO. Accessed December 12, 2019. http:// purl.fdlp.gov/GPO/gpo71799.

GPO (Government Publishing Office). 2016b. "National Plan for Access to U.S. Government Information: A Framework for a User-Centric Service Approach to Permanent Public Access." February 2016. Google: *site:fdlp.gov national plan access filetype:pdf*.

GPO (Government Publishing Office). 2019. "Historic Shelflist Transcription Update." Accessed August 1, 2019. https://www.fdlp.gov/news-and-events /3957-historic-shelflist-transcription-update.

Imholtz, August A., Jr. 2003. "The Printing and Distribution of the Serial Set: Preliminary Contribution to the 19th Century Congressional Publishing." *DttP: Documents to the People* 31, no. 1: 8–19.

Imholtz, August A., Jr. 2008. "The American State Papers: The Incomplete Story, or What Was Selected and What Was Omitted." *DttP: Documents to the People* 36, no. 1: 18–22.

Jacobs, James A. 2014. "Born-Digital U.S. Federal Government Information: Preservation and Access." Prepared for the Center for Research Libraries Global Resources Collections Forum, March 17, 2014. *site:crl.edu borndigital federal government*.

McGarr, Sheila M. 2000. "Snapshots of the FDLP." Updated February 23, 2016. Accessed December 12, 2019. https://www.fdlp.gov/about-fdlp/mission -history/2500-snapshots-of-the-fdlp-august-2000.

Morehead, Joe. 1999. *Introduction to United States Government Information Sources*. 6th ed. Westport, CT: Libraries Unlimited.

NAPA (National Academy of Public Administration). 2013. *Rebooting the Government Printing Office: Keeping America Informed in the Digital Age*. Washington, DC, January 2013. Accessed December 12, 2019. http://purl.fdlp .gov/GPO/gpo34038.

Saunders, Virginia, and August A. Imholtz, Jr. 1998. "U.S. Congressional Serial Set: Assigned Serial Numbers Not Used." *Administrative Notes Technical Supplement* 5, no. 11: 1–19. (SuDocs GP 3.16/3-3:5/11). Accessed September 29, 2019. https://digital.library.unt.edu/ark:/67531/metadc463527/.

Sinclair, Gwen. 2019. "The Documents Expediting Project, 1946–2019." *DttP: Documents to the People* (Summer): 8–15. Accessed September 29, 2019. https://journals.ala.org/index.php/dttp/article/view/7032/9565.

3

Legislative Branch Information Sources

The legislative branch publishes a vast amount of materials, from its daily *Journals* and *Congressional Record* to all the reports; documents; hearings; committee prints; and numerous other publications of committees, subcommittees, commissions, and boards. The Government Publishing Office is under the legislative branch, giving it more stability than if it were an executive branch agency, subject to changes of administrations and the mood of the times.

Perhaps the publication that comes to mind first for many people is the voluminous *Congressional Record*, the official debates of both houses of Congress. From the perspective of a depository library, the most circulated materials from the print realm are congressional hearings. At least 20 percent of that which is checked out of government documents collections are hearings, and that same percentage holds for clicks to online hearings from the library catalog (Brown 2011).

While the SuDocs classification system uses many letters to represent all the executive branch agency publications, congressional publications are confined to X and Y (and Z if you consider the Continental Congress). Table 3.1 provides details.

The 2019 prepared testimony of acting Deputy Director of the GPO Herbert H. Jackson, Jr., on the scope of GPO's publications for the Legislative Branch, summarizes the familiar and less commonly known publications.

Table 3.1   Selected congressional publications within the Superintendent of Documents classification system

SuDocs Stem	Publication	Notes
X	*Congressional Record*	
XJH	House Journal	Beginning in 1953. Before that time, they are in the Serial Set (1818–1952).
XJS	Senate Journal	Beginning in 1953. Before that time, they are in the Serial Set (1818–1952).
Y 1	House and Senate Reports, Documents, Bills, and General Publications	Y 1.4 is used for House and Senate Bills, in microfiche in many libraries.
Y 3	Commissions, Committees, and Boards	Many of these no longer exist. Use *Guide to U.S. Government Publications* to see specific SuDocs stems.
Y 4	Hearings, Committee Prints, Publications	Hearing and Prints are interfiled.
Y 6	Impeachment Proceedings	
Y 7	Memorial Addresses	
Y 10	Congressional Budget Office	
Z	Continental Congress	1774–1788

For the Clerk of the House, the Secretary of the Senate, and the committees of the House and the Senate, GPO publishes the documents and publications required by the legislative and oversight processes of Congress in digital and tangible formats. This includes the daily *Congressional Record*, bills, reports, legislative calendars, hearings, committee prints, and documents, as well as stationery, franked envelopes, memorials and condolence books, programs and invitations, phone books, and the other products needed to conduct the business of Congress. We produce all the printing work required every four years by the Joint Congressional Committee on Inaugural Ceremonies. We also detail expert staff to support the publishing requirements of House and Senate committees and congressional offices such as the House and Senate Offices of Legislative Counsel. We work with Congress to ensure the provision of these services under any circumstances, including emergency weather and other conditions. (Jackson 2019)

LISTEN TO THE PARLIAMENTARIANS

How our laws are made is a complicated process, with rules and procedures differing in the House and Senate. For those who may need a refresher in basic civics, or who may be relatively new immigrants to the United States, I recommend "I'm Just a Bill," a video short that was part of the Disney-produced children's television series *Schoolhouse Rock!* that aired in 1976. The DVD is available in some libraries, and a YouTube search will find perhaps less-than-legal clips of this three-minute feature (*site: youtube.com i'm just a bill*).

Those needing a more thorough treatment should consult the true authorities in these matters, the parliamentarians of the House and the Senate. If anyone should know the rules, it would be these folks. A helpful CRS report provides background information on these offices (CRS 2018d).

Occasionally, each respective parliamentarian issued a document detailing the procedures of their respective chambers. The iteratively published *How Our Laws Are Made* (House Parliamentarian) and *Enactment of a Law* (Senate Parliamentarian) are chief among the many instructional materials contained within the Serial Set covering the operations of the House and Senate.

We don't have time or space to explain the complexities of the legislative law-making processes and how they differ between the House of Representatives and the Senate. However, it is useful to point you to sources that can explain the process. Covering the House of Representatives, *How Our Laws Are Made* has been published as a House Document in over 20 editions in the Serial Set going back to 1953. The most recent version was updated in 2007.

U.S. Congress. House. *How Our Laws Are Made*, revised and updated by John V. Sullivan, Parliamentarian, U.S. House of Representatives. H. Doc. 110-49. July 24, 2007. (HT 005862787). Available at: http://purl .access.gpo.gov/GPO/LPS103851.

To learn how the House conducts its business, the exhaustive rules of House procedure are contained in the *Precedents of the United States House of Representatives* and its previous titles (see https://www.govinfo .gov/collection/precedents-of-the-house).

On the Senate side, *Enactment of a Law* formerly appeared in the Serial Set (S. Doc. 96-15 [1979]; S. Doc. 94-152 [1975]; S. Doc. 90-35 [1967]; S. Doc. 730155 [1934]). The most recent edition, from 1997, authored by Senate parliamentarian Robert B. Dove, is not contained in the Serial Set, but is a separate publication (http://purl.access.gpo.gov/GPO/LPS56394).

Riddick's Senate Procedure contains the exhaustive, current practices of the U.S. Senate. It was also issued in the Serial Set (http://purl.access.gpo .gov/GPO/LPS29146) and is searchable via a special GPO site at https:// www.riddick.gpo.gov/.

OUR AMERICAN GOVERNMENT

The House Document titled *Our American Government* presents a basic civics lesson in Q and A format (Google: *H. Doc. 108-94*; HT 003885550). Some of the answers are very specific and detailed explanations of the workings of all three branches of government. This book emphasizes finding and using the publications connected with lawmaking, not the rules and procedures that lawmakers follow. This makes it particularly useful for those of us attempting to follow the machinations of our government, and it may be a helpful to review the process, as outlined in Figure 3.1.

BILLS AND RESOLUTIONS

Bills are draft forms of legislation, used to initiate the lawmaking process for most legislation. The typical enabling language at the beginning of a bill is: "Be it enacted by the Senate and the House of Representatives of the United States of America in Congress assembled." This practice has been followed since 1871, when it was prescribed by statute (Revised Statutes, Sections 7–9; U.S. Code. Title 1, § 101–105).

Most bills don't make it all the way to becoming law. The nongovernmental website Govtrack.us provides a historical statistical analysis of bills and resolutions that have been introduced and how far they got in the legislative process. In recent years, only 3 to 6 percent of bills introduced made it all the way to becoming enacted law. In the 115th Congress (2017–2018) for example, 13,556 bills or resolutions were introduced, but only 443 (3 percent) became law (GovTrack 2019).

Different Types of Bills and Resolutions

Bills may originate in either the House or the Senate; however, all bills for raising revenue must originate in the House (Constitution, Article I, Section 7). By tradition, appropriation bills originate in the House. There are two types of bills, public and private, which, if passed, become public laws or private laws respectively. House Bills are designated as "H.R." and

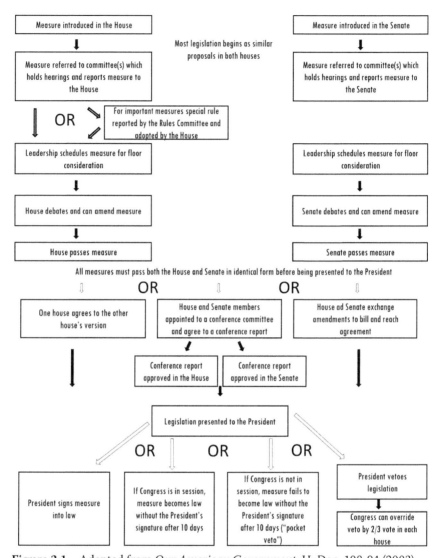

Figure 3.1   Adapted from *Our American Government*, H. Doc. 108-94 (2003)

Senate simply as "S." A public bill affects the public generally. A private bill is often used for immigration and naturalization matters and for claims against the United States. The easiest way to get a sense of the nature of private laws is simply to browse them using Congress.gov (https://www .congress.gov/private-laws/).

Resolutions are of three types, simple, concurrent, and joint. Simple resolutions are designated as "H. Res." followed by a number in the House, and "S. Res." in the Senate. They concern rules, operations, or opinions. They do not carry the force of law. Search Congress.gov like this: *"h res"* or *"s res"* [be sure to use the quotation marks], and you will see the most recent simple resolutions.

Concurrent resolutions, "H. Con. Res." and "S. Con. Res," are used for matters affecting both Houses of Congress, are not usually presented to the president for signature, and are used for expressing facts or sentiments of Congress. These might be used to set the time for the adjournment of Congress, to congratulate another country on the anniversary of its independence, or to establish the annual congressional budget resolution regarding spending goals for the next fiscal year. Searching Congress.gov using the abbreviated forms in quotes will retrieve examples of concurrent resolutions.

Joint resolutions are introduced in either the House or the Senate, and there is no real difference between them and bills. They are abbreviated as "H.J. Res." and "S.J. Res." and can be easily located in Congress.gov, using the same search techniques noted above. There is one major, noteworthy difference with joint resolutions, however. It takes a joint resolution to introduce an amendment to the Constitution.

When a joint resolution amending the Constitution is approved by two-thirds of both Houses, it is not presented to the president for approval. Rather, such a joint resolution is sent directly to the archivist of the United States for submission to the several states, where ratification by the legislatures of three-fourths of the states within the period of time prescribed in the joint resolution is necessary for the amendment to become part of the Constitution (*How Our Laws Are Made*, H. Doc. 110-49). Except for joint resolutions of proposed amendments to the Constitution, they became law in the same way as bills (U.S. Senate 2002).

The Twenty-Sixth Amendment, introduced in the Senate in 1971 as S.J. Res. 7 and H.J. Res. 223 in the House and took only one hundred days from introduction in Congress to ratification by the states, extended the national voting age to 18. Presently on the federal level, amendments to the Constitution are extremely rare. With some states however, they happen all the time. See chapter 16 on state government research for further discussion.

Most prevalent uses for types of bills and resolutions (Source: CRS 2010):

Bills (H.R. or S.)

- Authorization or reauthorization of federal policies, programs, and activities
- Amendment of existing law (sometimes also by joint resolution)
- Establishment of federal departments and agencies, or alteration of their structure
- Revenue (tax) legislation (originates in House only)

- Regular annual general appropriations
- Supplemental appropriations (sometimes also by joint resolution)
- Reconciliation bill (alters spending authority pursuant to instructions in a congressional budget resolution)
- Private bill (provides specified benefits to named individuals)

Joint Resolutions (S.J. Res. or H.J. Res.)

- "Incidental, inferior, or unusual purposes of legislation" (House Manual, section 397)
- Proposed constitutional amendment (requires two-thirds vote in each house)
- Declaration of war
- Continuing resolution (extends appropriations for specified purposes until regular appropriations are enacted)
- Transfer of appropriations
- Adjustment of debt limit
- Abrogation of treaty
- Alteration of date for convening of Congress
- Resolution of disapproval or approval (of specified executive action pursuant to a statute making a contingent delegation of authority)
- Extension of expiration or reporting dates under existing law (e.g., date for President to submit budget)
- Congratulations, condolences, welcomes, thanks, and so forth (also by simple or concurrent resolution)
- Recognition of and support for commemorative periods (House Rule XII, clause 5, prohibits measures that actually establish commemorative periods)

Concurrent Resolutions (S. Con. Res. or H. Con. Res.)

- Congressional budget resolution (sets targets for spending and revenue, procedurally enforceable against subsequent legislation; may set instructions to committees for reconciliation bill)
- Adjournment sine die
- Recess of either or both houses of more than three days
- Providing for a joint session of Congress
- Creation of a joint committee
- Correction of conference reports or enrolled bills
- Request for return of measures presented to the president

- "Sense of Congress" resolution (expresses "fact, principles, opinions, and purposes of the two houses," House Manual, section 396. "Sense of Congress" provisions may also appear in lawmaking measures)

Simple Resolutions (H.Res. or S.Res.)
- Adoption or amendment of chamber rules
- Special rule (for considering a measure) or other "order of business resolution" (House)
- Establishment of a standing order (principally Senate)
- Privileges of the House resolution (principally House; to secure a chamber's rights, safety, dignity, or integrity of proceedings, House Rule IX)
- "Blue slip resolution" (House; returns a Senate tax measure as violating House privilege to originate revenue measures)
- Personal privilege of individual member
- Disposition of contest to a member's election
- Expulsion of a member (requires two-thirds vote)
- Censure or other discipline of a member
- Citation for contempt of Congress
- Authorization of response to subpoena by members or employees
- Resolution of ratification (advice and consent to treaty; Senate)
- Election of committee members or chamber officers
- Committee funding
- Expenditures from chamber's contingent fund (e.g., printing House and Senate documents, also by concurrent resolution)
- Creation of a special or select committee (e.g., investigating committee)
- Resolution of inquiry (requests factual information from executive branch; principally House)
- Providing notifications to the other house, president, and so forth
- Request for other house to return a measure (for technical corrections)
- Discharge of committee from a measure, nomination, or treaty (Senate)
- Instructions to conferees already appointed (Senate)
- Establishment of, requests for establishment of, or recognition of and support for, commemorative periods (principally Senate)
- "Sense of the Senate" or "sense of the House" resolution (expresses fact, principles, opinions, or purposes of one house, House Manual, section 395; such provisions may also appear in lawmaking measures)

Either a bill or a joint resolution can become a public law. For example, the bill H.R. 430 in the 116th Congress eventually became the TANF Extension Act of 2019, P.L. 116-4 (133 Stat. 9). But H.J. Res. 28, also in the 116th Congress, became Further Additional Continuing Appropriations Act, 2019 (P.L. 116-5, 133 Stat. 10).

Getting the Full Text of Bills and Resolutions

For the text of bills and resolutions from 1989 (101st Congress) to the present, Congress.gov is the place to go. It has not always been easy to acquire the full text of older bills and resolutions. Massive print volumes were occasionally kept in depository libraries, and later, fiche cabinets were filled with endless bill filings. But researching the various version of bills was extremely tedious. You can also get bills from the 103rd Congress (1993–1994) through Govinfo.gov, but most will find Congress.gov a bit easier to navigate.

Two ProQuest products now make the work of finding all versions of older bills much easier. *ProQuest Congressional* has an add-on module for "Digital U.S. Bills and Resolutions, 1789–Present." This contains all bill versions, whether they were connected with public laws or not. *ProQuest Legislative Insight* contains all bill versions that were part of legislative histories—in other words, legislation that went on to become law.

Govinfo.gov uses about 80 designations for "common" versions of bills (https://www.govinfo.gov/help/bills). Reading these designations is enough to make heads spin. To make better sense of this, it is best to search for bills in Congress.gov. For the current congressional session, the current status is shown. It is always possible that while Congress is in session, the status could change. Congress.gov makes very timely updates to bill status. For prior Congresses, the bill status is final—frozen in time.

DISTINGUISHING STATE BILLS FROM FEDERAL BILLS

It is relatively easy to tell the difference between citations to state bills and U.S. federal legislation. Federal bills have the abbreviated format H.R. and S., respectively, for a bill from the House of Representatives and from the Senate. Most state general assemblies will have the bill format H.B. and S.B. (or HB and SB) as their abbreviations for bills. Federal resolutions have the format S. Res. and H. Res., and state formats for resolutions vary widely. Nebraska, having only one legislative chamber (the technical term is a "unicameral legislature"), uses LB for legislative bill and LR for legislative resolution.

Importantly, Congress.gov also provides Congressional Budget Office (CBO) cost estimates and Congressional Research Service (CRS) bill summaries within the detailed bill information.

Bill Tracking Services

Some bill tracking services are subscription based, and others are topical, or issue based. As for comprehensive, freely available services, GovTrack.us (https://www.govtrack.us/) not only allows users to track federal legislation, it also provides voting records all the way back to 1789. Users can sign up for alerts for major legislative activity, upcoming legislation, new laws, new bills and resolutions, and bill summaries. GovTrack.us is not affiliated with any government and receives revenues through advertising and crowdfunding.

Law school students have access to bill tracking through Lexis and Westlaw, and academic libraries typically have access to the academic versions of these tools, Nexis Uni and Westlaw Campus Research, respectively.

Congress.gov has several bill tracking features. If you know the bill number or sponsor, then you can view up-to-date events related to that bill. Suppose you want to see all the legislation that California Senator Kamala Harris sponsored that went on to become law. Follow these steps: (1) In Congress.gov, select Members from the pulldown menu, and type Harris in the search box. (2) Click on Senator Kamala D. Harris. (3) From the navigation tools on the left, select Sponsored Legislation (or Cosponsored Legislation). (4) Under Status of Legislation, select Became Law. The same type of research can be done for other members of the House or Senate, back to the 93rd Congress (1973–1974).

Browsing by "policy area" is a major research capability of Congress.gov. This capability can be difficult to locate on the site. It can be found under Browse → Legislation by Subject and Policy Area → Policy Areas. Or it may be easier to go to this direct link: https://www.congress.gov/browse /policyarea/. Once you click on a policy area (subject), you can then navigate by Status of Legislation to see how far various bills and resolutions have gone through the legislative process. This feature works for all Congresses back to the 93rd Congress (1973–1974).

Roll-call votes can be found under bills and resolutions where numbered votes were taken, but they can also be browsed back to the 101st Congress (1989–1990) at: https://www.congress.gov/roll-call-votes.

Congress.gov is a major enhancement over its predecessor, thomas.loc .gov. Browsing and searching can also be done by committee, subcommittee, sponsor, cosponsor, and political party—all the way back to the 93rd Congress (1973–1974).

HOUSE AND SENATE JOURNALS

The House and Senate both maintain Journals, as required by the Constitution (Article I, Section 5). The Journals do not contain debates but merely the bare parliamentary proceedings. There are differences between House and Senate Journal practices. The Senate maintains a legislative journal and an executive journal. The executive journal is published annually and contains proceedings related to treaties and nominations. When there are impeachment proceedings (when the Senate sits as a court of impeachment for any kind of impeachment), a separate journal of proceedings is maintained. The House Journal contains a minimum amount of information.

Interestingly, the Journal has limited distribution in print and is not available for purchase from the Government Publishing Office (44 U.S.C. § 713).

The 1st to 43rd Congress House and Senate Journals are available via the Library of Congress's American Memory project.

- House Journal: https://memory.loc.gov/ammem/amlaw/lwhjlink.html
- Senate Journal: https://memory.loc.gov/ammem/amlaw/lwsjlink.html
- Senate Executive Journal: https://memory.loc.gov/ammem/amlaw /lwejlink.html

The early years of the House and Senate Journals are contained in the Serial Set. Beginning in 1953, they were published as separate publications, now classed as XJH (*House Journal*) and XJS (*Senate Journal*) in the SuDocs classification system. HathiTrust also has selected issues of the House Journal (HT 002137422, 100884583), Senate Journal (HT 003930921), and the Senate Executive Journal (HT 001300805, 100884660, 011482983).

Govinfo.gov has House and Senate Journals for selected recent years, but not the current ones. As of this writing, from 1992 to recent were covered for the House, and from 2004 to recent for the Senate. It should be noted that the *Congressional Record* Daily Edition, in the daily digest section, performs a function similar to the Journals in that they chronicle the daily actions of both chambers.

PROCEEDINGS AND DEBATES OF CONGRESS

There was nothing in the Constitution or in the early years of the U.S. government that required that the workings of Congress be open (Pasley 2004). The requirement was that results of congressional actions (laws that had passed) be published. In these early days that meant publication in various newspapers around the country.

Let's briefly look at the early debates of Congress in the years before the now familiar *Congressional Record.*

Early Debates

Since 1873, congressional proceedings have been published in the *Congressional Record.* Before that there were three earlier titles, listed below. I have also included the *Journal of the Continental Congress* for completeness.

Commercial publishers produced the proceedings of Congress from the earliest days, before the birth of government printing in 1861.

Journals of the Continental Congress (1774–1789)

Although technically out-of-scope for the United States, the *Journals of the Continental Congress* are included here for historical completeness.

Journals of the Continental Congress, 1774–1789. Edited from the original records in the Library of Congress. 34 vols. Washington, DC: GPO, 1904-37. (HT 006771172, 003917207).

Debates and Proceedings in the Congress of the United States (1789–1824)

Informally known as the Annals of Congress, they are more formally known as the *Debates and Proceedings in the Congress of the United States,* covering the First Congress through the first session of the 18th Congress, from 1789 to 1824. The Annals were not published during the congressional sessions but were compiled between 1834 and 1856, using the best records available, primarily newspaper accounts. Speeches are paraphrased rather than presented verbatim, but the record of debate is more complete than that available from the House and Senate Journals.

The Debates and Proceedings in the Congress of the United States. 22 vols. Washington, DC: Gales and Seaton, 1834–1856. (HT 001719524, 100187247, 008688952).

Register of Debates in Congress (1824–1837)

This series in not a verbatim account of proceedings but, rather, provides a summary of the debates and incidents. It was published by a commercial publisher, Gales and Seaton, and overlaps from 1833 to 1837 with the *Congressional Globe* (Twenty-Third Congress, First Session through Twenty-Fifth Congress, First Session; 1833–1837).

Register of Debates in Congress: Comprising the Leading Debates and Incidents of the . . . Session of the . . . Congress. 1824–1837. Permanent ed. 14 vols. Washington, DC: Printed and published by Gales & Seaton. (HT 008688491, 001719525).

Congressional Globe (1833–1873)

The first five volumes of the Globe (23rd Congress, First Session through 25th Congress, First Session, 1833–1837) overlap with the Register of Debates. Initially, the Globe contained a "condensed report" or abstract rather than a verbatim report of the debates and proceedings. With the 32nd Congress (1851), however, the Globe began to provide something approaching verbatim transcription.

The Congressional Globe, 1833–1873 [Permanent ed.]. Washington, DC: Blair & Rives. 46 vols.

The *Annals*, the *Register of Debates*, and the *Congressional Globe* are all available through the Library of Congress American Memory project (*site:memory.loc.gov annals debates globe*). Some users may find it more convenient to access this content via HeinOnline, with its powerful searching, browsing, and downloading capabilities.

What Is in the *Congressional Record*?

Since 1873, the title for the debates and proceedings of Congress has been the *Congressional Record*. The Record is a "substantially verbatim account" of remarks made by Representatives and Senators on the floor of the House and Senate. Included in it are a record of all bills, resolutions, proposed motions, debates, and roll-call votes (U.S. Senate 2015).

The current proceedings are not always an exact transcription of what is spoken on the floor of Congress. Practice has varied over the years, but members of Congress have been allowed to edit their spoken words before publication in the proceedings.

Much has been written about the colorful history of the House and the Senate and how things are recorded in the *Congressional Record*. Congressional theatrics occasionally make headlines. In 2013, Texas senator Ted Cruz took to the floor of the Senate and talked for a massive 21-hour filibuster to show discontent with the Patient Protection and Affordable Care Act (ObamaCare), 159 Cong. Rec. 14143; 159 Cong. Rec. Daily S6701 (September 24, 2013). At page 14175 (S6732 in the Daily edition), he read Dr. Seuss's

Green Eggs and Ham. (Perhaps the quickest way to look up the citations above for yourself is to use the citation look-up feature in Govinfo.gov.)

Senator Strom Thurmond takes the prize for the longest filibuster, when he spoke for 24 hours and 18 minutes concerning the Civil Rights Act of 1957 (103 Cong. Rec. 16263 [1957]). Note: You can use the Govinfo.gov to browse to this citation; at present the interface does not allow you to locate this with a citation search. HeinOnline will allow you to search by citation and to find the text immediately.

All drama aside, the most important thing to know and understand is that there are two editions of the *Congressional Record*, detailed below.

The *Congressional Record*: Daily Edition versus Permanent Edition

There are two versions of the *Congressional Record*. This has created great confusion over the years. Differences in pagination and omitted content are the biggest issues. The Bluebook recommends citing the bound (permanent) edition whenever possible. However, since there is a several-year time lag in producing the permanent edition, this is often not possible. The HeinOnline interface (if you are fortunate enough to have access to it) has a "Congressional Record Daily to Bound Locator" tool for easy cross-walking from the daily edition to the permanent bound edition.

> *Congressional Record: Proceedings and Debates of the . . . Congress* [Permanent edition]. 1873–present. http://purl.access.gpo.gov/GPO/LPS76447 OCLC: 5058415. (HT 008885968). A separate collection for the *Congressional Record Index* is available on Govinfo.gov.

Neither the daily edition nor the permanent edition is always an exact verbatim account of the words spoken in the House or Senate. For the daily edition, a member may decide to withhold remarks subject to revision. Withheld remarks were published later in the appendix of the daily edition. They would appear in the permanent edition in the proper place. Because of these editing anomalies, it is possible for reporters to publish quotes in newspapers that may not match what the *Congressional Record* recorded (Schmeckebier and Eastin 1969).

At times, there have been differences between the daily edition and the permanent edition. Let's compare the two editions. According to Congress .gov, the Patient Protection and Affordable Care Act was originally introduced in 2009 by Rep. Charles Rangel as "H.R. 3590. A bill to amend the Internal Revenue Code of 1986 to modify the first-time homebuyers credit in the case of members of the Armed Forces and certain other Federal employees, and for other purposes; to the Committee on Ways and Means."

Here is that page from the *Congressional Record* (Daily) in Figure 3.2.

Figure 3.3 shows how things change when published in the Bound Edition.

We immediately notice several differences between the bound and the daily editions.

Figure 3.2   *Congressional Record* (Daily Edition)

1. The pagination is different. The Daily Edition gives the page as H9729, but the Bound Edition has 22007, with no reference to House (H) or Senate (S) pagination.

2. The Bound Edition has volume and part information in the page header (Vol. 155, Pt. 16). This information is lacking from the Daily Edition.

Figure 3.3   *Congressional Record* (Bound Edition) (Some material elided from page.)

Other changes can also be made in the bound edition, such as edits, revisions, or rearrangement of text. You would think it would be an easy thing to cross-walk from the Daily Edition to the Permanent Edition, but this is not always the case. The reason is that PDF documents are susceptible to many fails. Line breaks, hyphenated words, hyphenated words with line breaks, multiple columns, tables and charts, orientation changes (portrait/ landscape), image captions, table titles, paginated headers/footers, and running titles in headers are just a few reasons for unexpected underlying text anomalies. Less is more when it comes to searching for full text in PDFs.

Notice that in the excerpt from the Monthly Catalog for one of the parts of the permanent edition, differences are noted between the daily edition and the permanent edition to aid the reader (Figure 3.4).

Now let's discuss the arrangement of the daily edition of the *Congressional Record*. Starting with volume 113 (the 90th Congress, 1967), the

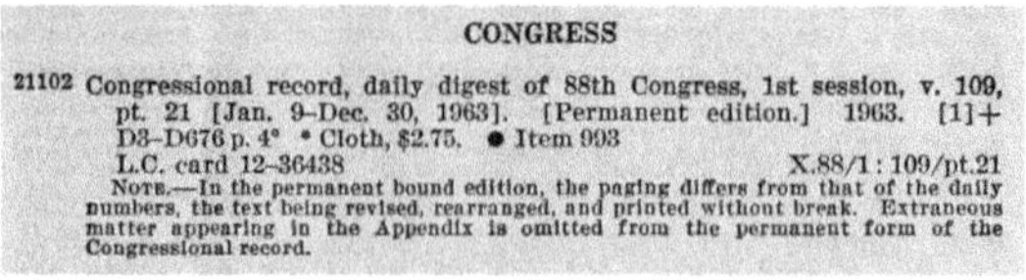

CONGRESS

21102 Congressional record, daily digest of 88th Congress, 1st session, v. 109, pt. 21 [Jan. 9–Dec. 30, 1963]. [Permanent edition.] 1963. [1]+D3–D676 p. 4° • Cloth, $2.75. ● Item 993
L.C. card 12–36438 X.88/1 : 109/pt.21
NOTE.—In the permanent bound edition, the paging differs from that of the daily numbers, the text being revised, rearranged, and printed without break. Extraneous matter appearing in the Appendix is omitted from the permanent form of the Congressional record.

Figure 3.4 Entry from *Monthly Catalog of U.S. Government Publications*, December 1964. *Source:* Internet Archive.

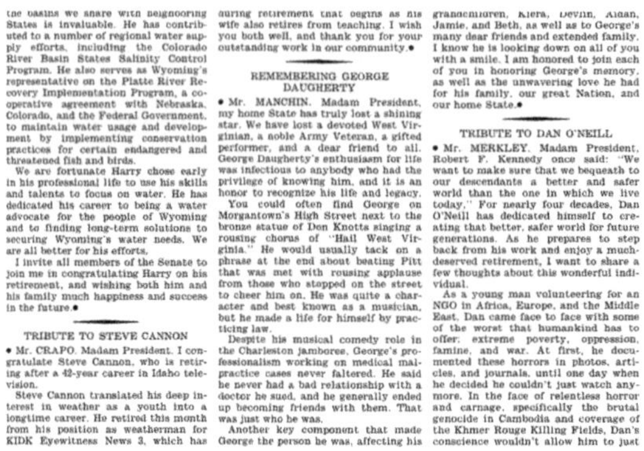

the basins we share with neighboring States is invaluable. He has contributed to a number of regional water supply efforts, including the Colorado River Basin States Salinity Control Program. He also serves as Wyoming's representative on the Platte River Recovery Implementation Program, a cooperative agreement with Nebraska, Colorado, and the Federal Government, to maintain water usage and development by implementing conservation practices for certain endangered and threatened fish and birds.

We are fortunate Harry chose early in his professional life to use his skills and talents to focus on water. He has dedicated his career to being a water advocate for the people of Wyoming and to finding long-term solutions to securing Wyoming's water needs. We are all better for his efforts.

I invite all members of the Senate to join me in congratulating Harry on his retirement, and wishing both him and his family much happiness and success in the future.•

TRIBUTE TO STEVE CANNON

• Mr. CRAPO. Madam President, I congratulate Steve Cannon, who is retiring after a 42-year career in Idaho television.

Steve Cannon translated his deep interest in weather as a youth into a longtime career. He retired this month from his position as weatherman for KIDK Eyewitness News 3, which has during retirement that begins as his wife also retires from teaching. I wish you both well, and thank you for your outstanding work in our community.•

REMEMBERING GEORGE DAUGHERTY

• Mr. MANCHIN. Madam President, my home State has truly lost a shining star. We have lost a devoted West Virginian, a noble Army Veteran, a gifted performer, and a dear friend to all. George Daugherty's enthusiasm for life was infectious to anybody who had the privilege of knowing him, and it is an honor to recognize his life and legacy.

You could often find George on Morgantown's High Street next to the bronze statue of Don Knotts singing a rousing chorus of "Hail West Virginia." He would usually tack on a phrase at the end about beating Pitt that was met with rousing applause from those who stopped on the street to cheer him on. He was quite a character and best known as a musician, but he made a life for himself by practicing law.

Despite his musical comedy role in the Charleston jamboree, George's professionalism working on medical malpractice cases never faltered. He said he never had a bad relationship with a doctor he sued, and he generally ended up becoming friends with them. That was just who he was.

Another key component that made George the person he was, affecting his grandchildren, Kiera, Devlin, Aidan, Jamie, and Beth, as well as to George's many dear friends and extended family. I know he is looking down on all of you with a smile. I am honored to join each of you in honoring George's memory, as well as the unwavering love he had for his family, our great Nation, and our home State.•

TRIBUTE TO DAN O'NEILL

• Mr. MERKLEY. Madam President, Robert F. Kennedy once said: "We want to make sure that we bequeath to our descendants a better and safer world than the one in which we live today." For nearly four decades, Dan O'Neill has dedicated himself to creating that better, safer world for future generations. As he prepares to step back from his work and enjoy a much-deserved retirement, I want to share a few thoughts about this wonderful individual.

As a young man volunteering for an NGO in Africa, Europe, and the Middle East, Dan came face to face with some of the worst that humankind has to offer: extreme poverty, oppression, famine, and war. At first, he documented these horrors in photos, articles, and journals, until one day when he decided he couldn't just watch anymore. In the face of relentless horror and carnage, specifically the brutal genocide in Cambodia and coverage of the Khmer Rouge Killing Fields, Dan's conscience wouldn't allow him to just

Figure 3.5 Example of bullets representing extensions of remarks in the Senate section of the *Congressional Record*, March 12, 2019, S1790

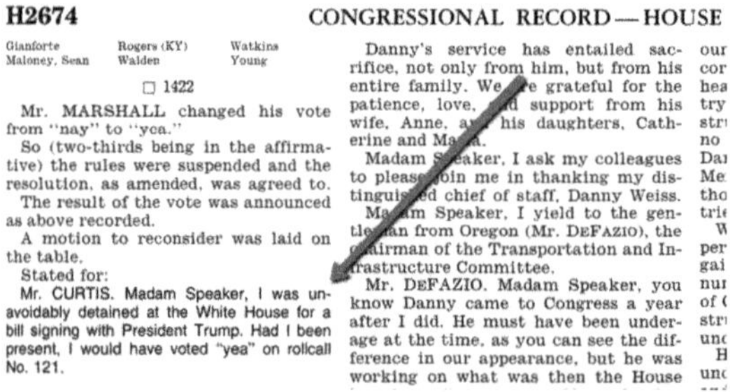

H2674 CONGRESSIONAL RECORD—HOUSE

Gianforte Rogers (KY) Watkins
Maloney, Sean Walden Young

□ 1422

Mr. MARSHALL changed his vote from "nay" to "yea."

So (two-thirds being in the affirmative) the rules were suspended and the resolution, as amended, was agreed to.

The result of the vote was announced as above recorded.

A motion to reconsider was laid on the table.

Stated for:

Mr. CURTIS. Madam Speaker, I was unavoidably detained at the White House for a bill signing with President Trump. Had I been present, I would have voted "yea" on rollcall No. 121.

Danny's service has entailed sacrifice, not only from him, but from his entire family. We [illegible]e grateful for the patience, love, [illegible]d support from his wife, Anne, a[illegible] his daughters, Catherine and Ma[illegible]a.

Madam S[illegible]eaker, I ask my colleagues to please [illegible]oin me in thanking my distingui[illegible]d chief of staff, Danny Weiss.

Ma[illegible]m Speaker, I yield to the gentle[illegible]an from Oregon (Mr. DEFAZIO), the [illegible]irman of the Transportation and In[illegible]rastructure Committee.

Mr. DEFAZIO. Madam Speaker, you know Danny came to Congress a year after I did. He must have been underage at the time, as you can see the difference in our appearance, but he was working on what was then the House

Figure 3.6 Sans serif typeface denoting inserted or appended words in the House in the H section pages

"SHED" page numbering practice began. There are four sections, with page numbers beginning with letters S, H, E, and D. These stand for Senate, House, Extension of Remarks, and Daily Digest respectively. Each of these lettered sections continues the page numbering from the previous issue of the daily edition. Generally, the House pages are first, but an acronym of HSED is not as easy to remember.

S and H—Senate and House pages. House floor transcripts of debates and remarks, notice of bills introduced, roll-call votes, and other features. The Senate places any additional statements not spoken on the floor in the S pages with a bullet (•) denoting the additional words in the S section (Figure 3.5). When House members want to insert text not spoken on the floor, they may optionally be included with a sans-serif font in the H section. Figure 3.6 illustrates this. Note that the E section is also used by the House for additional remarks.

E—Extensions of Remarks. Includes tributes, statements, and other information that supplements statements made on the congressional floor.

This section is only used by House members, not Senate members. A sans-serif font is used to denote words that were not spoken on the floor by a House member. A serif font in the Extensions section means that the words were actually spoken on the floor.

D—Daily Digest. This serves as a table of contents and index for the daily edition. It includes highlights of the day's actions, a summary for each house, including measures introduced, reported, passed, or under consideration. Specific House and Senate page numbers are given. Also included are a list of committee meetings held that day and scheduled for the following day, the next scheduled meeting day for each chamber, and a list of Extensions of Remarks included in that issue

The Govinfo.gov interface allows for sophisticated searching and concatenating of URLs for specific segments of the *Congressional Record*. Rather than detailing them here, just go to https://www.govinfo.gov/help/crec to see them for yourself.

The helpful House Document *Our American Government* (H. Doc. 108-94) informs us that "since 1979 in the House and 1986 in the Senate, floor sessions have been televised. Videotape copies of House and Senate Chamber activities are preserved and available for research use at the Library of Congress and at the National Archives." Via the C-SPAN Video Library (https://www.c-span.org/about/videoLibrary/), C-SPAN (House) and C-SPAN2 (Senate) provide coverage of congressional sessions, as well as selected committees going back several years. C-SPAN's Congressional Chronicle serves as an index to these recordings (http://www.c-spanvideo .org/videoLibrary/aboutCC.php). In addition to C-SPAN, the Senate website provides archived floor proceedings, which are available back to 2012 at https://www.senate.gov/floor/.

Résumé of Congressional Activity

Beginning in 1947, at the end of each session of Congress, a "Résumé of Congressional Activity" is published in the *Congressional Record*. The résumé consists of two tables: (1) all legislative business transacted by the Senate and House, and (2) an accounting for all nominations submitted to the Senate by the president of the Senate for confirmation. This one- or two-page document is a handy summary of the session, including days in session, time in session, pages of proceedings in each house, number of extensions of remarks in each house (the Senate often has none), measures passed by bill/resolution type, yea and nay votes, and disposition of executive nominations. The Senate website has a link to all résumés from present back to 1947 (*site:senate.gov resume of congressional activity*).

Searching the *Congressional Record*

Although Govinfo.gov has a search function, often the full text of resources such as the *Congressional Record* do not uncover the desired results. It is advisable to also do your full-text search in the Congress.gov version of the *Congressional Record*: https://www.congress.gov/congressional-record.

The *Congressional Record* is also available via ProQuest Congressional and HeinOnline, where sophisticated searches can be employed for greater precision in locating desired materials.

Congressional Record Index

Don't underestimate the value of an index. We are so accustomed to full-text keyword searching that we rarely consider consulting an index. But we should, especially in the case of the *Congressional Record*. An index normalizes words and terms and brings together like concepts that otherwise would be difficult to find.

Often, even a full-text search using Govinfo.gov does not retrieve what you are looking for. In these cases, the *Congressional Record Index* can work quite well.

REPORTS AND DOCUMENTS

When we discuss congressional reports and documents, we use the terms report and document as technical terms, not as generic words. The reports and documents are formally and orderly numbered, and they appear in the Serial Set. They all typically have a header that includes the Congress and Session information, whether it is a House of Senate issuance, and then the report of document number. House and Senate Reports tend to nearly always have this kind of format, whereas House and Senate Documents do not always have the format shown in Figure 3.7.

Reports

Congressional reports are some of the most valuable publications of both Houses of Congress, as can be seen below under the description of the four main types of committee reports (CRS 2014):

- Reports that accompany a legislative measure. These are valuable because they provide explanations from the committee of the measure and arguments as to why the measure should be approved by the entire chamber. This is perhaps the best primary source for legislative intent.

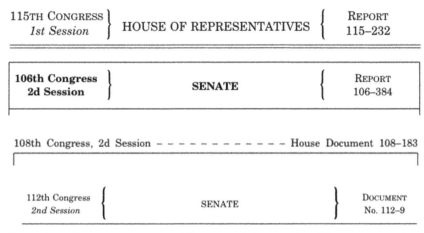

Figure 3.7 Typical Congressional Report and Congressional Document headers

Many of these reports may also contain minority viewpoints, which are also valuable in understanding the opposing viewpoints. Congressional reports conveying legislative intent are dealt with in more detail in the following chapter.

- Oversight or investigative reports. When committees evaluate a federal agency's performance concerning alleged government waste, inefficiency, or wrongdoing, they generally issue a report. Example: *Report of the Senate Select Committee on Intelligence committee study of the Central Intelligence Agency's Detention and Interrogation Program*. H. Rpt. 113-288. http://purl.fdlp.gov/GPO/gpo53958.

- Conference reports. When the House and Senate both pass a piece of legislation, a conference committee is created to resolve any disagreements in language or amendments. At the completion of this work, the committee releases a conference report that presents the formal legislative language to which the conference has agreed ("Conference Reports and Joint Explanatory Statements." CRS Report, June 11, 2015. 98–382). Example: *Energy Policy Act of 2005: Conference Report (to accompany H.R. 6)*. H. Rpt. 109-190.http://purl.access.gpo.gov/GPO/LPS62846.

- Committee activity reports. All House committees and most Senate committees are required to submit reports detailing their activities. These reports summarize a committee's legislation and oversight responsibilities, as well as delineate any hearings they have had on waste, fraud, abuse, or mismanagement (CRS 2018a). Example: *Activity Report of the Committee on Energy and Commerce of the U.S. House of Representatives for the One Hundred Twelfth Congress Together with Minority Views*. H. Rpt. 112-746 (*site:govinfo.gov H. Rept. 112-746*).

Notice that in Figure 4.1 (in the next chapter), there is a box drawn around congressional reports and documents. This is to point out that both reports and documents are eventually cumulated into the Congressional Serial Set. This is of no concern for recent publications, since they will be most easily found in Govinfo.gov. But for older reports and documents, knowing this is essential, since one of the Serial Set finding aids may be required to locate these older publications.

Reports from recent Congresses can most easily be found in Govinfo .gov. If a library has catalog records for congressional reports, they can usually be very quickly located by doing a keyword search on the report number. If you were trying to find House Report 112-746 in a large academic library catalog, doing a keyword search for *114-539* is distinctive enough that the report can easily be gleaned from the results page. The URL should quickly get you to the report.

Recent House and Senate Reports connected with legislation can easily be viewed in one place by using Congress.gov's browse features. Follow this path: Congress.gov → Browse → [Select Congress] → Committees → Select House Reports or Senate Reports. You will see House Report numbers, the report title, and the bill number that the report accompanies. Obviously, you will need to know the bill number in advance, but this is a very fast and efficient way of browsing reports that contain the information of why bills were introduced (legislative intent).

Older congressional reports are most easily accessed through one of the online Serial Set tools (Readex, ProQuest, or HeinOnline). If you don't have access to these, numerical listings of reports by Congress can be found using the Numerical Lists (see discussion in chapter 2). Many indexing tools exist in print that provide access by number and subject to these reports. Users needing a detailed listing of these resources should consult Schmeckebier and Eastin (1969).

Documents

Congressional documents, like congressional reports, are included in the Serial Set. Recent documents are most easily found using the freely available Govinfo.gov interface. Documents are generally not important to the legislative history research process. Communications from the president to Congress, including veto actions, can be communicated via congressional documents. Documents are often used to publish miscellaneous congressional publications. A common type of document is the tribute document, commonly issued as a Senate Document when a senator retires. CONAN, the *Constitution of the United States Annotated*, is issued as a Senate Document. House Documents often deal with national emergencies, foreign relations, emergency funding, messages from the president (such as the State of the Union message, veto messages, transmittal messages, and presidential agendas (such as a message for tax relief). House and Senate Executive Documents are another category of documents used for reports made to Congress by the executive branch. Up until 1981, Senate Executive Documents were used for treaty text submitted to the Senate for ratification by the president. From 1981 onward, these documents are called Senate Treaty Documents. The House and Senate Miscellaneous Documents contains all the other publications, except those ordered by Congress.

Selected notable historical Senate Documents include the following:

Robert C. Byrd. *The Senate, 1789–1989.* Four volumes (S. Doc. 100-20; Serial 13723-13724; HT 002983380).

Bob Dole. 1989. *Historical Almanac of the United States Senate* (S. Doc. 100-35; Serial 13850; HTG 100888133).

Mark O. Hatfield and Wendy Wolff. *Vice Presidents of the United States, 1789–1993* (S. Doc. 104-26; Serial 14332; HT 003150715; see also Govinfo.gov).

U.S. Congress. Senate. 1998. *Minutes of the Senate Democratic Conference: Fifty-Eighth through Eighty-Eighth Congresses, 1903–1964* (S. Doc. 105-20; Serial 14457; HT 007425411).

U.S. Congress. Senate. 1999. *Minutes of the Senate Republican Conference: Sixty-Second Congress through Eighty-Eighth Congress, 1911–1964* (Doc. 105-19; Serial 14456; HT 007425413).

U.S. Congress. Senate. 1997. *A History of the United States Senate Republican Policy Committee, 1947–1997* (S. Doc. 105-5; Serial 14391).

Also published as Congressional documents are *the Constitution of the United States of America: Analysis and Interpretation* (often abbreviated as CONAN), and supplements (S. Doc. 106-8; S. Doc. 106-27; S. Doc. 112-9; S. Doc. 108-19; S. Doc. 115-8); *Biographical Directory of the United States Congress* (H. Doc. 108-222); and *Our American Government* (H. Doc. 106-216; H. Doc. 108-94).

HEARINGS

Hearings contain transcripts of testimony given before committees or subcommittees of the two houses of Congress. They may be about proposed legislation, concerning oversight or investigation of an agency or an issue, or may be hearings considering a confirmation to an appointed office. Unlike the *Congressional Record*, which is published on the next government day, hearings are often not printed for months after testimony was given (CRS 2014).

Hearings are of great interest to the public at large. I know this because I have done statistical studies on documents usage, both of print and online resources, at the University of Denver. The study was done by capturing usage statistics from clicks on URLs from government documents records within the library online catalog. The highest used SuDocs stem of all was the Y 4s (the congressional hearings). After six years of statistics from my click-through project, I found that 20.56 percent of URLs clicked for government publications in the local library catalog were for hearings. This was in complete agreement with years of circulation statistics for tangible documents as well (Brown 2011). The study continued through mid-2014, and the same usage trends for hearings persisted. Users want hearings!

Congressional hearings are of various types: legislative hearings, oversight hearings, investigative hearings, and confirmation hearings (CRS 2018d). Typically, hearings take place on Capitol Hill, but, occasionally, they are held in other locations, such as in a committee member's district or state or at a site related to the subject of the hearing. These remote location hearings are called field hearings. For example, a field hearing was held in February 2014 in Charleston, West Virginia, to investigate the Elk River chemical spill that took place on January 9, leaving nearly 300,000 residents without access to drinking water. The House Committee on Transportation and Infrastructure conducted the hearing at the Kanawha County Courthouse in Charleston.

Hearings are often of more interest to academics and public policy wonks than they are to attorneys. Although they can be extremely interesting, they do not generally contain information that contributes to legislative intent. Thus, they are not part of the formal legislative history. In determining legislative intent, it is more important to look at congressional debate in the *Congressional Record* or legislative background information that is found in many congressional reports than it is to examine oral testimony or submitted materials from hearings.

Hearings contain not only edited transcription of oral testimony given before the committees, but also materials submitted by those testifying. These materials may be particularly interesting. Occasionally these materials are copyrighted and present problems for free public access to information.

Occasionally movie stars or other celebrities make the news because they testify in hearings. Among the many to have done so include the following:

Comedian Stephen Colbert testified at the hearing titled *Protecting America's Harvest*, Sept. 24, 2010. (SuDocs: Y 4.J 89/1:111-150), (HT 102387434).

Elmo the Muppet testified in support of music education. In the hearing, he is formally listed as "Elmo Monster, Sesame Street Muppet," and, when he spoke, the transcribed testimony introduces him as "Mr. Monster." Hearing title: *Departments of Labor, Health and Human Services, Education, and Related Agencies Appropriations for 2003*, pages 342–350. (SuDocs: Y 4.AP 6/1:L 11/2003/PT.7A). (HT 100832784, pt. 7A). Julia Roberts testified on Rett Syndrome in the same hearing as Elmo (above), pages 1129–45.

Many other celebrities have testified over the years. If you are interested, you can use your preferred search engine to see if one of your favorites has ever been involved in a hearing.

Now let's look at the four types of hearings a little more in depth (CRS 2018e).

Legislative Hearings

Hearings put a spotlight on legislation for the congressional committee, the public, the press, and other stakeholders. Very often legislative hearings are the first formal committee action so that members can hear the strengths and weaknesses of the proposal from executive branch agencies, representatives of relevant industries, and the general public. Hearings are a way for the public to observe what is going on surrounding legislation, but they are in no way required. That is likely why they are not listed at the end of public laws and are not even mentioned in Congress.gov. The real work of the committee is the formal markup work of the committee (CRS 2018c). Yet hearings are extremely popular with the general public. For this reason, hearings are included in the old Congressional Information Service print indexes, the online version of the CIS indexes within the ProQuest Congressional database, and in ProQuest Legislative Insight.

As examples of legislative hearings, in the 115th Congress, the Weather Research and Forecasting Innovation Act of 2017 was passed (Pub. L 115-25, 131 Stat. 91). There were no hearings connected with this legislation in the 115th Congress, but ProQuest Legislative Insight lists one hearing from the 112th Congress, one two-part hearing from the 113th Congress, and two hearings from the 114th Congress that are informally linked to this topic.

To Observe and Protect: How NOAA Procures Data for Weather Forecasting: Hearing before the Subcommittee on Energy and Environment, Committee on Science, Space, and Technology, House of Representatives, One Hundred Twelfth Congress, second session, Wednesday, March 28, 2012. http://purl.fdlp.gov/GPO/gpo34559.

Restoring U.S. Leadership in Weather Forecasting. Part I, Thursday, May 23, 2013: Hearing before the Subcommittee on Environment, Committee on Science, Space, and Technology, House of Representatives, One Hundred Thirteenth Congress, First Session. http://purl.fdlp.gov/GPO/gpo41034.

Restoring U.S. Leadership in Weather Forecasting. Part II, June 26, 2013: Hearing before the Subcommittee on Environment, Committee on Science, Space, and Technology, House of Representatives, One Hundred Thirteenth Congress, First Session. http://purl.fdlp.gov/GPO/gpo41034.

Bridging the Gap: America's Weather Satellites and Weather Forecasting: Joint Hearing before the Subcommittee on Environment & Subcommittee on Oversight, Committee on Science, Space, and Technology, House of Representatives, One Hundred Fourteenth Congress, First Session, February 12, 2015. http://purl.fdlp.gov/GPO/gpo61241.

Weathering the Storm: How can We Better Communicate Weather to Enhance Commerce and Safety?: Hearing before the Committee on Commerce, Science, and Transportation, United States Senate, One Hundred Fourteenth Congress, First Session, April 22, 2015. http://purl.fdlp.gov/GPO/gpo63096.

This illustrates the reality that public policy issues commonly span several sessions of Congress and points to the great value in tools like ProQuest Legislative Insight.

Oversight Hearings

Oversight hearings are similar to legislative hearings in that they, too, have a formal purpose and follow similar procedures: to gather relevant information for the committee's work (CRS 2008).

Examples of oversight hearings include:

Oversight of the Federal Trade Commission: Hearing before the Committee on Commerce, Science, and Transportation, United States Senate, One Hundred Fourteenth Congress, Second Session, September 27, 2016. http://purl.fdlp.gov/GPO/gpo81143.

Ensuring Government Transparency through FOIA Reform: Hearing before the Subcommittee on Government Operations of the Committee on Oversight and Government Reform, House of Representatives, One Hundred Fourteenth Congress, First Session, February 27, 2015. http://purl.fdlp.gov/GPO/gpo58762.

Investigative Hearings

In the 110th Congress, there were alleged irregularities surrounding Roll Call Vote 814 (http://clerk.house.gov/evs/2007/roll814.xml) in August 2007. This resulted in a two-day investigative hearing on the matter in May 2008.

Investigative Hearing Regarding Roll Call 814, Day 1: Hearing before the Select Committee to Investigate the Voting Irregularities of August 2, 2007, House of Representatives, One Hundred Tenth Congress, Second Session, May 13, 2008, Washington, DC. http://purl.access.gpo.gov /GPO/LPS109874.

Investigative Hearing Regarding Roll Call 814, Day 2: Hearing before the Select Committee to Investigate the Voting Irregularities of August 2, 2007, House of Representatives, One Hundred Tenth Congress, Second Session, May 14, 2008, Washington, DC. http://purl.access.gpo.gov /GPO/LPS108357.

The partisan divisions were noted in the press coverage (Allen 2008).

Confirmation Hearings

There are those occasions when confirmation hearings reach a fever pitch and the entire country is fixed upon live coverage. Such was the case in the confirmation hearings for Brett Kavanaugh to become an associate justice of the Supreme Court, held from September 4–6 and 27–28, 2018.

Nongovernment affiliated commercial transcription services play a role in providing these unofficial transcripts. Two such services are CQ-Roll Call, Inc. (formerly Federal News Service before December 2014) and Bloomberg Government. In the ProQuest Congressional database, these hearing transcripts come up under the facet "Hearings Pre-Published." In some cases, both the prepublished and the published versions of hearing can be found within ProQuest Congressional. On occasion, transcripts of House or Senate hearings can be found in reports or documents of the respective chamber.

Senate hearings from the 98th Congress and forward have a numbering system. For example, S. Hrg. 102-487 and S. Hrg. 116-27. These are generally reflected in their corresponding SuDocs numbers: Y 4.J 89/2:S.hrg.102-487 and Y 4.G 74/9:S.HRG.116-27, respectively. The House does not number its hearings.

Most hearings are published from six to twelve months after the hearing is held, but this is completely up to the discretion of the individual committees. Transcripts of unpublished hearings are submitted to the National Archives. The release dates differ for each house. For the Senate, unpublished hearings transcripts can be released after 20 years, for the

House it is 30 years. But sometimes, for national security reasons, they are kept at NARA for 50 or more years (ProQuest 2012).The ProQuest Congressional database has a module for unpublished hearings, as well as for recent hearing transcripts, which, although unofficial, can provide some kind of access to recently held hearings before the official GPO version becomes available. Some hearings are never published at all.

The C-SPAN Video Library contains not only video of full House and Senate proceedings but also coverage of selected hearings of committees (https://www.c-span.org/congress/).

Locating Hearings Generally

Where can we find information about congressional hearings? The *Congressional Record* Daily Edition has a section on committee meetings. This section mentions hearings and whether they were closed or open. This can be a tedious way to track down hearings.

Another way to track hearings within the past few years is to search the committee's website. Look for the committee calendar or a dedicated page for hearings. Unfortunately, the published legislative calendars generally make no mention of hearings.

The CIS indexes are the best resources for tracking down hearings of any type, whether published or unpublished. This content is completely online via the ProQuest Congressional database.

Locating Hearings Connected to Legislation

An easy way to track down hearings connected with legislation is to first look in congressional reports, since hearings will usually be noted in reports other than conference reports. As an example, H.R. 3375 from the 116th Congress is a bill called "Stopping Bad Robocalls Act." As of July 25, 2019, the measure had been received in the Senate, but a committee report had been published, H. Rept. 116-173. Going to that report, we notice from the contents that committee hearings are mentioned on page 12. This states that a hearing was held on April 30, 2019, titled *Legislating to Stop the Onslaught of Annoying Robocalls* in the House Committee on Energy and Commerce, Subcommittee on Communications and Technology. As of August 6, 2019, there is no sign of this hearing in the CGP or in Govinfo .gov. On the subcommittee website, however, we see most of the elements from the hearing in an unofficial form. There is a summary of the proceedings, opening statements, transcription of witness testimony from various witnesses, and a 2-hour, 47-minute video of the hearing.

The most efficient way to locate hearings with legislation that is not as recent as the above is to use ProQuest Legislative Insight. This will only give hearings related to bills that became law, and not to legislation that didn't become public law. For that, you would need to consult ProQuest Congressional. Legislative Insight not only mentions hearings from the Congress in which the bill became law but also from previous Congresses. This acknowledges the fact that public policy issues often take several years to be passed into law.

COMMITTEE PRINTS

Although not as frequently published as committee hearings are, committees also publish other kinds of information in what are referred to as "committee prints." These include a variety of publications, such as committee rules, committee and subcommittee membership lists, draft legislation, reports on policy issues of interest to the committee, or historical works on the history of a matter (CRS 2014).

Committee prints are sometimes connected to specific pieces of legislation but usually are not. They can be valuable research tomes that serve as background works for members of Congress as they draft legislation, analyze budgets and expenditures, and provide oversight. They are often authored by congressional staff who may be lawyers or researchers and can be excellent background research on various topics. It is not uncommon for a committee print to be identical to a CRS Report. Here are some examples showing the research value of committee prints.

United States. Congress. Senate. Committee on Homeland Security and Governmental Affairs. Permanent Subcommittee on Investigations. *Combatting the Opioid Epidemic: A Review of Anti-abuse Efforts in Medicare and Private Health Insurance Systems.* Washington, DC: GPO, 2017. S.PRT.114-29. SuDocs: Y 4.G 74/9:S.PRT.114–29. https://purl.fdlp.gov/GPO/gpo76648

United States. Congress. Senate. Committee on Finance. *An Examination of Foster Care in the United States and the Use of Privatization.* Washington, DC: GPO, 2017. S.PRT.115–18. SuDocs: Y 4.F 49:S.PRT.115-18. https://purl.fdlp.gov/GPO/gpo85978.

United States. Congress. House. Committee on Science and Technology. Subcommittee on Space Science and Applications. *Space Activities of the United States, Soviet Union, and Other Launching Countries/Organizations, 1957–1983: Report.* Washington, DC: GPO, 1984. SuDocs: Y 4.Sci 2:98-Y. (HT 006748242).

United States. Congress. Senate. Committee on Foreign Relations. *China's Impact on Korean Peninsula Unification and Questions for the Senate: A Minority Staff Report Prepared for the Use of the Committee on Foreign Relations.* Washington, DC: GPO, 2012. S.PRT.112–44. SuDocs: Y 4.F 76/2:S.PRT.112–44. http://purl.fdlp.gov/GPO/gpo33775.

In depository libraries, they are interfiled with congressional hearings in the Y 4 SuDocs classification, which is an arrangement that is based on the first meaningful letter in the name of the House or Senate committee.

The *Guide to U.S. Government Publications* (Andriot), mentioned in chapter 2, is the best place to find a comprehensive, historical listing of SuDocs stems for House and Senate Committees. If you were to walk the stacks of a larger depository library, within the Y 4s, you would find hearings and committee prints interfiled, since they all come from their respective House or Senate Committees.

Examples:

Astronauts and Cosmonauts Biographical and Statistical Data: Report (1994). (HT 008524067).

An Examination of Foster Care in the United States and the Use of Privatization (2017) (https://purl.fdlp.gov/GPO/gpo85978).

Final Report of the Task Force on Combating Terrorist and Foreign Fighter Travel (2015) (http://purl.fdlp.gov/GPO/gpo62413).

Were Relevant Documents Withheld from the Congressional Committees Investigating the Iran-Contra Affair? (1989). (HT 008516673).

A Compendium of Laws and Rules of the Congressional Budget Process (2015) (http://purl.fdlp.gov/GPO/gpo61921).

Most committee prints are independent publications that are not connected with legislation. ProQuest Legislative Insight lists committee prints that it deems connected with legislation. Here are a few examples.

In connection with P.L. 99-335 (100 Stat. 514), the Federal Employees' Retirement System Act of 1986, several committee prints were published. One was titled *Civil Service Retirement System: History, Provisions, and Financing* (HT 011343659). This provides an excellent historical overview of the historical development of the civil service retirement and disability system, tracing it back to the Pendleton Act of 1883.

Associated with P.L. 91-510 (84 Stat. 1140), the Legislative Reorganization Act of 1970 was a committee print published in a previous Congress, Budget Process in the Federal Government (HT 001340381). It covers the federal budget cycle, with charts showing the major steps in the budget process, preparation, and execution of the federal budget, and several relevant Bureau of the Budget internal publications are attached to the document.

PUBLIC LAWS

After a bill (or a resolution for a law) passes both houses of Congress, it is sent to the president for signature. If it is signed, it becomes law. Public laws (as well as private laws) are initially issued as "slip laws" (also known as session laws) a few days after enactment. These are unbound and are printed on one or several pages of paper (in addition to now being issued online). They are eventually bound together in consecutive order in the *United States Statutes at Large* (abbreviated Stat.). Laws enacted during and after 1957 are cited by public law number (ex.: P.L. 115-3). Laws enacted before 1957 are cited by the date of enactment of the law and the Statutes at Large chapter number assigned to it (ex: 49 Stat. 28, Chap: 15).

Although the current title of the bound statutes is *United States Statutes at Large*, it underwent quite a few title changes over time. OCLC record number 426275236 contains an extensive title history, which will be of interest to those researching very early statutes.

> TITLE HISTORY: The public statutes at large of the United States of America: from the organization of the government in 1789, to March 3, 1845, v. 1–8; The statutes at large and treaties of the United States of America from . . . , v. 9-v. 11 (Dec. 1, 1845 to Mar. 3, 1851—Dec. 3, 1855 to Mar. 3, 1859); The statutes at large, treaties and proclamations of the United States of America from . . . , v. 12-v. 15 (Dec. 5, 1859 to Mar. 3, 1863—Dec. 1867 to Mar. 1869); The statutes at large and proclamations of the United States of America from . . , v. 16-v. 17 (Dec. 1869 to Mar. 1871—Mar. 1871 to Mar. 1873); The statutes at large of the United States from . . . , v. 18, pt. 3-v. 49, pt. 2 (Dec. 1873 to Mar. 1875—Jan. 1935 to June 1936); *United States Statutes at Large*, v. 50, pt. 1 (1937).

Most of these volumes are freely available through the Library of Congress (http://purl.access.gpo.gov/GPO/LPS52578); HathiTrust (HT 011571265), as well as other records; and the Internet Archive.

A helpful listing of all public laws from 1789 to present can be found on the House Office of the Law Revision Counsel United States Code site. Known as the "Table III Tool," the table serves as a listing of all Statutes at Large volumes, since they contain all the public laws that had been classified into the U.S. Code at the time. Links to a digital version of the public laws are provided below. There are three ways to access this tool:

- by year: https://uscode.house.gov/table3/table3years.htm
- by Congress: https://uscode.house.gov/table3/table3congresses.htm
- by *U.S. Statutes at Large* volume number: https://uscode.house.gov/table3/table3statutesatlarge.htm

This may well be the quickest way to link out to historic public laws (and it's completely free!).

PRIVATE LAWS

Mentioned briefly in this chapter under bills, private laws are also acts of Congress but are done on behalf of an individual, not the general public. Private legislation is based on the idea that general law cannot cover all situations equitably and that sometimes Congress must address these unique situations. This concept is rooted in the right "to petition the government for a redress of grievances," as guaranteed by the First Amendment to the Constitution. The majority of private laws have to do with immigration matters, with second place going to a broad variety of claims against the government. At one time, issuances of private laws were common, but recently, they have become extremely rare (CRS 2015).

One thing is obvious as you browse through the listing of private laws via Congress.gov (https://www.congress.gov/private-laws/), and that is that there are very few private laws being passed in recent Congresses compared with older Congresses. Between 1973 and 2017 (93rd–115th Congresses), 838 private laws have been enacted (Table 3.2).

UNITED STATES CODE

Where *United States Statutes at Large* is the sequential grouping of session laws, without regard for topic but merely in the order in which they were passed into law, the United States Code (abbreviated U.S.C.) is "a consolidation and codification by subject matter of the general and permanent laws of the United States." Perhaps the easiest way to browse the Code is through the House Office of the Law Revision Counsel (http://uscode.house.gov/), or simply Google: *house us code.* This resource is updated more than 30 times per year and is more current than the print annual supplements to the U.S. Code. It is most helpful in answering background questions about the Code, especially for non-attorneys. Refer to the FAQ section (http://uscode.house.gov/faq.xhtml) to get background information on the distinctions between positive law titles versus nonpositive law titles of the Code, what laws are not included in the Code (such as appropriation laws and temporary laws, such as the naming of a post office), and updating practices performed by the Law Revision Counsel.

The point of accessing the U.S. Code in the legislative research process is to see where the various parts of a public law have been codified or placed within the Code. This is not always easy, since complex laws may be spread over multiple parts of the Code. Commercial products, such as ProQuest Legislative Insight, make this task easy. Here is an example of where the Energy Policy Act of 2005 (P.L. 109-58) has been added to the Code (Figure 3.8).

Table 3.2   Enactments of private laws, 1973–2018

Congress (Years)	Number of Private Laws Enacted
93rd Congress (1973–1974)	123
94th Congress (1975–1976)	141
95th Congress (1977–1978)	170
96th Congress (1979–1980)	123
97th Congress (1981–1982)	56
98th Congress (1983–1984)	54
99th Congress (1985–1986)	24
100th Congress (1987–1988)	48
101st Congress (1989–1990)	16
102nd Congress (1991–1992)	20
103rd Congress (1993–1994)	8
104th Congress (1995–1996)	4
105th Congress (1997–1998)	10
106th Congress (1999–2000)	24
107th Congress (2001–2002)	6
108th Congress (2003–2004)	6
109th Congress (2005–2006)	1
110th Congress (2007–2008)	0
111th Congress (2009–2010)	2
112th Congress (2011–2012)	1
113th Congress (2013–2014)	0
114th Congress (2015–2016)	0
115th Congress (2017–2018)	1

Source: Congress.gov.

There are other freely available sources that tell where public laws were placed within the Code. The simplest place to look is on the first page of the public law, right after the short title (Figure 3.9).

Using the link to the U.S. Code mentioned above, we can browse to the relevant section, as seen in Figure 3.10.

In the uscode.house.gov table of contents, you will see that the last section is "Popular Names and Tables." Under that, you will see "Table III: Statutes at Large," which shows where each public law has been placed in the Code. This table is over 3,000 pages in length, since it shows where every statute from 1789 to recent years has been codified (Figure 3.11).

UNITED STATES CODE CLASSIFICATION TABLE—CONTINUED
109th Congress, 1st Session NA

Public Law			United States Code		
Number	Section	119 Stat.	Title	Section	Description
109-55	301	588	2	8	
109-56	1(a), (b)	591	21	823	
109-56	1(c)	591	21	823	nt new
109-57	1(a)	592	21	801	nt new
109-57	1(b)	592	21	953	
109-58	1(a)	594	42	15801	nt new
109-58	2	604	42	15801	new
109-58	101(a)	605	42	8259a	new
109-58	101(c)	606	2	1815	repealed
109-58	102(a)(1)	606	42	8253	
109-58	102(a)(2)	606	42	8253	nt new
109-58	102(b)-(e)	607	42	8253	
109-58	102(f)	607	42	8256	
109-58	102(g)	608	42	8258	
109-58	102(h)	608	42	8258b	
109-58	103	608	42	8253	
109-58	104(a)	609	42	8259b	new
109-58	105(a)	611	42	8287	
109-58	105(b)	611	42	8287	nt new
109-58	106	611	42	15811	new
109-58	107	612	42	15812	new
109-58	108(a)	612	42	6966	new
109-58	109	614	42	6834	
109-58	110(a)	615	15	260a	
109-58	110(b)	615	15	260a	nt new
109-58	110(c), (d)	615	15	260a	nt new
109-58	111	615	42	15813	new
109-58	121(a)	616	42	8621	
109-58	121(b)	616	42	8630	new
109-58	121(c)	616	42	8630	nt new
109-58	122(a)	616	42	6872	
109-58	122(b)	616	42	6862	
109-58	123(a)	616	42	6322	
109-58	123(b)	616	42	6324	new
109-58	123(c)	617	42	6325	
109-58	124	617	42	15821	new
109-58	125	618	42	15822	new
109-58	126	618	42	15823	new

Figure 3.8 References to placement of P.L. 109-58 within the U.S. Code, showing only page 16 of the table. The list goes on through page 28! *Source:* http://uscode.house.gov/classification/tbl109pl_1st.pdf.

119 STAT. 594   PUBLIC LAW 109-58—AUG. 8, 2005

Public Law 109-58
109th Congress

An Act

Aug. 8, 2005
[H.R. 6]

To ensure jobs for our future with secure, affordable, and reliable energy.

Be it enacted by the Senate and House of Representatives of the United States of America in Congress assembled,

Energy Policy Act
of 2005.
42 USC 15801
note.

SECTION 1. SHORT TITLE; TABLE OF CONTENTS.

(a) SHORT TITLE.—This Act may be cited as the "Energy Policy Act of 2005".

(b) TABLE OF CONTENTS.—The table of contents for this Act is as follows:

Figure 3.9 First page of P.L. 109-58, showing note where codification of Act is discussed in the U.S. Code

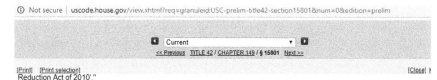

Reduction Act of 2010'."

SHORT TITLE OF 2007 AMENDMENT

Pub. L. 110–69, title V, §5001, Aug. 9, 2007, 121 Stat. 600, provided that: "This title [enacting subchapter XVII of this chapter and sections 7381g to 7381r of this title, amending sections 7381a, 7381d, 7381e, and 16311 of this title, and enacting provisions set out as a note under section 7381g of this title] may be cited as the 'Protecting America's Competitive Edge Through Energy Act' or the 'PACE–Energy Act'."

SHORT TITLE OF 2006 AMENDMENT

Pub. L. 109–375, §1, Dec. 1, 2006, 120 Stat. 2656, provided that: "This Act [amending section 15855 of this title] may be cited as the 'Sierra National Forest Land Exchange Act of 2006'."

SHORT TITLE

Pub. L. 109–58, §1(a), Aug. 8, 2005, 119 Stat. 594, provided that: "This Act [see Tables for classification] may be cited as the 'Energy Policy Act of 2005'."

Pub. L. 109–58, title IV, §431, Aug. 8, 2005, 119 Stat. 760, provided that: "This subtitle [subtitle D (§§431–438) of title IV of Pub. L. 109–58, enacting part C (§15991) of subchapter IV of this chapter, amending sections 201, 202a, 203, and 207 of Title 30, Mineral Lands and Mining, and enacting provisions set out as a note under section 201 of Title 30] may be cited as the 'Coal Leasing Amendments Act of 2005'."

Pub. L. 109–58, title V, §501, Aug. 8, 2005, 119 Stat. 763, provided that: "This title [enacting subchapter V of this chapter, section 7144e of this title, and chapter 37 (§3501 et seq.) of Title 25, Indians, amending section 5315 of Title 5, Government Organization and Employees, and section 4132 of Title 25, and enacting provisions set out as a note under section 3501 of Title 25] may be cited as the 'Indian Tribal Energy Development and Self-Determination Act of 2005'."

Pub. L. 109–58, title VIII, §801, Aug. 8, 2005, 119 Stat. 844, provided that: "This title [enacting subchapter VIII of this chapter] may be cited as the 'Spark M. Matsunaga Hydrogen Act of 2005'."

Pub. L. 109–58, title IX, §901, Aug. 8, 2005, 119 Stat. 856, provided that: "This title [enacting subchapter IX of this chapter, amending sections 8101 and 8102 of Title 7, Agriculture, and section 5523 of Title 15, Commerce and Trade, enacting provisions set out as notes under section 8102 of Title 7 and section 2001 of Title 30, Mineral Lands and Mining, amending provisions set out as notes under section 8101 of Title 7, and section 1902 of Title 30] may be cited as the 'Energy Research, Development, Demonstration, and Commercial Application Act of 2005'."

Figure 3.10   Excerpt of text of U.S. Code from http://uscode.house.gov/ showing summary notes reflecting placement of P.L. 109-58 within the Code

This is the same as the information provided by ProQuest Legislative Insight, but it is freely available. In some ways, it is easier to use, since it provides a crosswalk from sections of the public law to specific sections of the Code.

Beyond 50 Titles

For years, we have discussed "the 50 titles of the U.S. Code," but that has recently been changed by the House Office of the Law Revision Counsel. This is

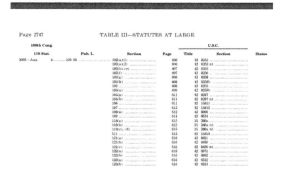

Figure 3.11   Placement of P.L. 109-58 in the U.S. Code according to U.S. Code, Table III: *Statutes at Large*

necessary because of the difficult task of incorporating new laws, repealed laws, transfers, and obsolete laws into an old structure that is increasingly inadequate and difficult to deal with. As of July 2019, the Office states that, officially, there are 54 titles, but they are not yet finished attempting to reorganize the Code. Here is a recommended Google search to follow the latest development on this reclassification project: *site:uscode.house.gov reclassification.*

Title 51—National and Commercial Space Programs—P.L. 111-314

Title 52—Voting and Elections [from Titles 2 and 42]—was an editorial reclassification. See http://uscode.house.gov/editorialreclassification /t52/index.html.

Title 53—[originally designated for Small Business, but on August 28, 2017, it was reassigned to Title 57]

Title 54—National Park Service and Related Programs—P.L. 113-287

Title 55—Environment—various bills from 2009 onward

Title 56—Wildlife

Title 57—Small Business [See: http://uscode.house.gov/codification/t57 /index.html]

U.S. Code in Time

The House Office of the Law Revision Counsel's version of the U.S. Code shows the current version of the code, unless otherwise noted with a list of "Pending Updates." From the same pulldown menu, it is possible to go back to previous versions of the Code on an annual basis. Since the full printed version of the U.S. Code is published every six years, with annual updates in intervening years, users can select which version they want to see, with no ambiguity how current each rollback would be.

This is the view of possible rollbacks as of July 2019 (Table 3.3).

Law libraries are the old-fashioned way to access superseded codes. They need to keep old codifications so that lawyers can use them for legal purposes, but historians can also benefit from accessing the old dusty books as well.

U.S. Code Appendices

Classification Tables

The classification tables at the end of the U.S. Code are often overlooked but are extremely useful. Public law sections are correlated with locations in the U.S. Code. You can get this list sorted either by public law number

Table 3.3   Rollback dates available through the uscode.house.gov site

Current
2012 Ed. and Supplement V (1/12/2018)
2012 Ed. and Supplement IV (1/6/2017)
2012 Ed. and Supplement III (1/3/2016)
2012 Ed. and Supplement II (1/15/2015)
2012 Ed. and Supplement I (1/16/2014)
2012 Main Ed (1/15/2013)
2006 Ed. and Supplement V (1/3/2012)
2006 Ed. and Supplement IV (1/7/2011)
2006 Ed. and Supplement III (2/1/2010)
2006 Ed. and Supplement II (1/5/2009)
2006 Ed. and Supplement I (1/8/2008)
2006 Main Ed. (1/3/2007)
2000 Ed. and Supplement V (1/2/2006)
2000 Ed. and Supplement IV (1/3/2005)
2000 Ed. and Supplement III (1/19/2004)
2000 Ed. and Supplement II (1/6/2003)
2000 Ed. and Supplement I (1/22/2002)
2000 Main Ed. (1/2/2001)
1994 Ed. and Supplement V (1/25/2000)
1994 Ed. and Supplement IV (1/5/1999)
1994 Ed. and Supplement III (1/26/1998)
1994 Ed. and Supplement II (1/26/1997)
1994 Ed. and Supplement I (1/16/1996)
1996 Main Ed. (1/4/1995)

or by the order in the U.S. Code. This is useful for those doing very exacting research (Google: *site:house.gov classification tables*).

Popular Name Tool

Since many official titles of law are very long, the popular name tool is useful, giving not just the popular name, but also links to the public laws (hosted on the Office of Law Revision site) and to references in the U.S. Code. The easiest way to use this tool is to click on the PDF link, open it in Adobe Acrobat, and search away. Browsing it in the HTML interface is a bit difficult. For example, if you wanted to find the citation to the GPO

Electronic Information Access Enhancement Act of 1993, just search (without using the GPO acronym) and you will find the public law number, the date of enactment, the Statutes at Large citation, and where it is placed in the U.S. Code (Google: *site:house.gov popular name tool*).

Table III Tool: Statutes at Large

This tool contains information about every public law from 1789 onward. It is organized by Statutes at Large citation, and links out to the full text of the public laws from Statutes at Large. This may well be the easiest way to access public laws when you have a Statutes at Large citation. It tells where it was classified in the Code and the current status (eliminated, repealed, etc.). If nothing else, this serves as an exhaustive listing of every public law by year (Google: *site:house.gov Table III statutes*).

There are also Table I and Table II tools, but they relate to minute details of positive law reclassification and reclassification of the Revised Statutes of 1878 and are too much "in the weeds" for discussion here.

Tables IV, V, and VI are also very useful, especially in light of the discussion of presidential issuances in the chapter 5.

- Table IV Executive Orders in the U.S. Code (*site:house.gov table IV executive orders*)
- Table V Proclamations in the U.S. Code (*site:house.gov table V proclamations*)
- Table VI Reorganization Plans in the U.S. Code (*site:house.gov table VI reorganization plans*)

Statute Compilations

These compilations are produced by the House Office of the Law Revision Counsel. These are useful in two situations: the public law doesn't appear in the Code because of the way the codification process worked, or the law is not in a positive law title, meaning that the Code itself is not the final authority. In these situations, these PDFs, even though unofficial, are very helpful. They are relatively up-to-date, but are not as current as the House Office of the Law Revision Counsel (Google: *site:house.gov statute compilations*).

Commercial Versions of the U.S. Code

You will often see citations to U.S.C.S. or U.S.C.A. in legal citations or policy papers. These are the two commercial versions of the United States

---

LEGISLATIVE RESEARCH PATHS

When someone tells me that he or she is researching a certain law, my first question usually is, "Are you researching the law as passed, or as amended?" In other words, I'm asking if the researcher wants to see the thinking of the members of the House and Senate in the days of consideration of the bill versions, or whether he or she wants to study the law as it stands today.

For example, if a researcher is looking for Title IX concerning sex discrimination, that could mean the current state of the law, as instantiated in the United States Code, in this case 20 U.S.C. ch. 38 § 1681 et seq. (the law as amended). But if he or she was doing research for a class that required a look at the original Act as passed by Congress and all the arguments that were made in the years up until the original passage of the Act, then I would direct the researcher to the Education Amendments of 1972 (P.L. 92-318, 86 Stat. 235) (the law as passed). We would then look at the *Congressional Record*, congressional reports, and other document relevant to the legislative history of this Act.

Code (U.S.C.). United States Code Service (U.S.C.S.) is published by Lexis, and United States Code Annotated (U.S.C.A.) is published by West. The print versions of both publications contain pocket parts and pamphlets updated regularly and inserted in the back of the respective bound volumes. They are essential in the legal community for both updating the Code for currency, as well as integrating into the vast existing legal publication systems. For example, U.S.C.A. has the West key number system throughout the code to integrate with the controlled vocabulary West has used for many years. These publications have been necessary for many years, given the publication schedule of the print U.S.C. (published in full only every six years, with annual supplements).

Individual researchers and attorneys have their preferences for either the West or the Lexis versions of the Code. Yet, when the dust has settled, many researchers value the annotations, tables, and permanent value of the official U.S. Code published by the GPO.

CONFUSING NOMENCLATURE

Words such as "title" and "section" are regularly tossed around without regard for the varying definitions that can be associated with a given usage. For example, title may refer to a title of the U.S. Code, a section of a Public Law as contained in *United States Statutes at Large*, or a title of a monographic publication. Title IX actually refers to Title IX of the Education

Act Amendments of 1972. Title VII often refers to the Equal Employment Opportunity section of the Civil Rights Act of 1964. Section 8 is actually part of the Housing Act of 1937 (42 U.S.C. § 1437f). Title X usually refers to the Family Planning Services and Population Research Act of 1970, which is Title X of the Public Health Service Act [42 U.S.C. 300 et seq.], also known as the "Gag Rule."

The media and the general public throw these terms around, often not knowing precisely what they actually refer to. In many cases search engines will help to know what the "title" and "section" reference are referring to. It is advisable to do this background research at the outset of any legal research questions, so that you are sure you are travelling down the right track.

ADDITIONAL CONGRESSIONAL PUBLICATIONS

House and Senate Journals

Journals are the official records of their respective houses. Article I, Section 5 of the Constitution states that "each House shall keep a Journal of its Proceedings, and from time to time publish the same, excepting such Parts as may in their Judgment require Secrecy."

The Journal does not contain transcripts of debates but, rather, is a listing of actions ("minutes of floor actions"), including titles of introduced legislation, results of votes, presidential veto messages, and other matters the House or Senate decide to include (CRS 2018b).

Historic House and Senate Journals are available online through the Library of Congress American Memory project (*site:loc.gov "journals of congress"*). They can also be found in HathiTrust: House (HT 002137422, 100884583); Senate (HT 100884660); and Senate Executive Journal (HT 001300805). Recent years for both House and Senate Journals can be found in Govinfo.gov. These are like "year in review" volumes, with bills and resolutions listed together with votes. In depository libraries. House Journals are shelved at SuDocs XJH and Senate Journals at XJS.

Legislative Calendars

Committee calendars are comprehensive records of their actions in a summary format. They usually contain committee rules, membership, and subcommittees. Also provided is a brief legislative history of each measure referred to, lists of hearings, and conference reports. Other committee publications are listed as well. All House and Senate committees, except the House and Senate Ethics and Appropriations committees (and the House Administration Committee since the 103rd Congress), publish calendars. There is nothing that requires the publication of calendars; it has just been their practice for over 50 years. Most calendars are published at the end of each session of Congress. The information is cumulative, so the final calendar for each Congress identifies all activities of a given committee. But these final calendars are often not available in printed form for several months after the conclusion of a Congress (CRS 2014).

Govinfo.gov is the source for House and Senate calendars. Browsing by date, you will find the full text of an entire day's PDF or PDFs for each of the individual sections. To get a feel for the calendar and its functions, it is best to click on just the top-most document under each respective legislative day. That will give you all the sections in a single document, as shown in Figure 3.12.

Congressional calendars are useful for tracking the workings of current congressional machinations. Given that the House and Senate are quite different in the rules they follow and how things are placed on their respective calendars, it can be quite interesting from a political science perspective to study the placement of bills on calendars with respect to majority party control.

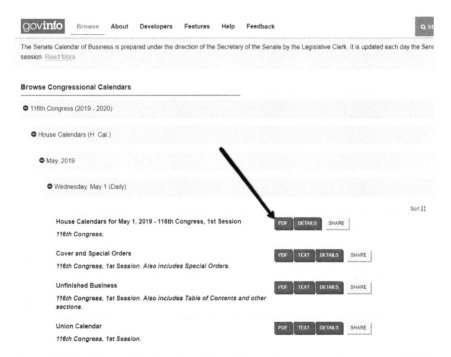

Figure 3.12   House Calendar from Govinfo.gov, showing top document with full text of entire calendar. Remaining documents are for individual sections of the day's calendar.

In addition, Congress.gov has a "Calendars and Schedules" resource page that is incredibly helpful. Use Google to find the current URL (*site:congress.gov "calendars and schedules"*).

House and Senate calendars are available on the Govinfo.gov site back to 104th Congress (1995–1996) and selected congressional committee calendars (called Legislative Calendars on Govinfo.gov) are available back to the 101st Congress, but committee coverage is extremely spotty.

Congressional Directories

Print directories of members of Congress have been long-standing tools in reference collections. They are still published, but for current directory functions, Congress.gov is the quickest, most up-to-date, and most convenient resource. The online directory can be found on the lower half of the initial page of the website. Selecting a member of the House or Senate immediately displays legislation they have sponsored or cosponsored. All members from 1993 to present are shown, whether they are currently serving or not.

Unofficial directories had been published in one form or another since the first Congress (HT 004448314, 008686653). The official directory of the U.S. Congress is the *Congressional Directory*, sometimes titled *Official Congressional Directory* (GP 3.22/2:228/) and was published in print from 1887 onward, sometimes annually, other times biennially (HT 007395434, 008885064, 003917021). The 105th Congress (1997–1998) online publications are available via Govinfo.gov (*site:govinfo.gov congressional directory*).

The most recent edition of the *Biographical Directory of the United States Congress* covers from 1789 to recent. Older editions of the directory appear in the Serial Set, with titles such as *Biographical Directory of the United States Congress* and *Biographical Directory of the American Congress*. Searching HathiTrust by the title also brings up individual editions of the directory.

The *Congressional Pictorial Directory* is in Govinfo.gov back to the 105th Congress (1997) (*site:govinfo.gov congressional pictorial directory*; HT 000535816).

Congressional Commission Publications (Y 3)

Congressional commissions issue important reports and miscellaneous publications. Since these materials are not connected to legislation, they are not indexed in resources such as ProQuest Congressional. Example of these commissions include:

National Advisory Committee for Aeronautics (1915–1958) (SuDocs: Y 3.N 21/5)

Committee on Public Information (1917–1919) (SuDocs: Y 3.P 96/3)

White House Conference on Handicapped Individuals (1976) (SuDocs: Y 3.W 58/18)

Selective Service System (1948–) (SuDocs: Y 3.Se 4)

Nuclear Regulatory Commission (1975–) SuDocs: Y 3.N 88)

The easiest way to understand to history of these many commissions is to consult the *Guide to U.S. Government Publications* ("Andriot"), mentioned in chapter 2.

CONGRESSIONAL RESEARCH SERVICE (CRS) REPORTS

Congressional Research Service is one of the investigative arms of Congress, providing comprehensive research and analysis on legislative and oversight issues. It responds to questions from representatives and senators in an attempt to clarify policy issues. It is organizationally under the Library of Congress, having been signed into law by President Woodrow Wilson in 1914 (38 Stat. 454, 463, ch. 141). Authors of CRS reports are often research analysts or attorneys.

These are among the first places anyone doing research on virtually any public policy topic imaginable should look. Here is a sampling of recent titles:

Blockchain and International Trade (IF10810)

Covert Action and Clandestine Activities of the Intelligence Community: Selected Congressional Notification Requirements in Brief (R45191)

The Emoluments Clauses of the U.S. Constitution (IF11086)

Haiti's Political and Economic Conditions (R45034)

Improving Intercity Passenger Rail Service in the United States (R45783)

Location of Medication-Assisted Treatment for Opioid Addiction: In Brief (R45782)

Mexico's Immigration Control Efforts (IF10215)

National Park Service Appropriations: Ten-Year Trends (R42757)

Off-Label Use of Prescription Drugs (R45792)

Poland: Background and U.S. Relations (R45784)

The Temporary Assistance for Needy Families (TANF) Block Grant: Responses to Frequently Asked Questions (RL32760)

U.S.-China Relations (IF10119)

Variable Renewable Energy: An Introduction (IF11257)

These are excellent for students because they tend to be clearly written and are replete with statistical data. (Think about it: CRS Reports have to be clear so that even members of Congress can understand them!)

Since CRS Reports have historically been authored primarily for members of Congress, they have not been part of the depository library program. It had often been difficult to access them or even to know what had been published. That changed in 2018, with the passage of the Consolidated Appropriations Act, 2018 (P.L. 115-141, 132 Stat. 348). Section 154 of the Act, Equal Access to Congressional Research Service Reports, charges the Librarian of Congress with setting up a public website where CRS Reports can be searchable, sortable, and downloadable, even in bulk form. On September 18, 2018, Crsreports.congress.gov was launched. Even though the content is still being built out, the features are stunning. Links to PDF files, as well as notations of previous versions of the documents are clearly available.

For example, the title Navy Force Structure and Shipbuilding Plans: Background and Issues for Congress (RL32665) defaults to the most recent version (in this case, version 260, July 21, 2019). But links backward to version 249 (July 31, 2018) and every version in between are provided as well. As you can see, sometimes versions are updated frequently—even on the same day (https://crsreports.congress.gov/product/details?prodcode= RL32665).

Penny Hill Press has, for years, been the place to purchase print CRS reports. Even in this day of web access, it is still in business, claiming to have all CRS reports issued since 1995. ProQuest offers an add-on module to ProQuest Congressional called the ProQuest Congressional Research Digital Collection (CRDC). Most unclassified CRS reports from 1916 to present are available.

In 2018, Congress passed a law (P.L. 115-141, Division I—Legislative Branch Appropriations Act 2018, Sec. 154, Equal Access to Congressional Research Service Reports). Resulting from this law, the CRS reports database is quite stunning in several respects. The results default to the most recent version of a report, and the interface clearly shows previous versions of the same CRS reports. This is extremely important when trying to ensure that you are viewing the most recently updated version, something that is not so easy to do when performing a Google search or when searching other CRS report archives. This service is just starting out, but it is sure to grow in size, as coverage extends to previous years and as older versions are added to current titles. Table 3.4 summarizes freely available CRS report sites.

GOVERNMENT ACCOUNTABILITY OFFICE REPORTS

Established in 1921 as an independent, nonpartisan agency, then called the General Accounting Office (Budget Accounting Act of 1921, P.L. 67-13,

Table 3.4   Free Sources of CRS Reports

Project Name	Comments / URL
Congress.gov	Best source for most recent CRS reports. Links to prior versions of same report.
	https://crsreports.congress.gov/
University of North Texas Digital Library	Over 41,000 reports.
	https://digital.library.unt.edu/explore/collections /CRSR/browse/
Federation of American Scientists	Topical arrangement.
	https://fas.org/sgp/crs/
Archive-It (Stanford University, Social Sciences Resource Group)	Captures and archives the index pages of sites that post CRS reports, including State Dept. FAS, Embassies, and selected international organizations.
	https://www.archive-it.org/collections/1078
Everycrsreport.com	Claims to have over 15,000 reports.
	https://www.everycrsreport.com/
Various House or Senate Websites	Members of Congress often post CRS reports on their official sites. Example searches: *site:house.gov crs report*; *site:senate.gov crs report*.

42 Stat. 20, ch. 18), the GAO was renamed the Government Accountability Office in 2005 (GAO Human Capital Reform Act of 2004 [P.L. 108-271, 118 Stat. 811]), preserving the acronym. GAO reports are sometimes related to legislative topics and can show the outcomes and highlight successes or failures of policies. The searchable GAO database (gao.gov) is particularly strong because it searches the full text of all GAO reports included in it. It serves Congress in its role as an audit institution. Over 100 years of reports can be found in the database.

When searching the database, you are searching not just metadata but also deep searching the full text of documents. It is also quite effective to use Google to search for GAO publications (*site:gao.gov [your topic]*).

CONGRESSIONAL BUDGET OFFICE MATERIALS

The Congressional Budget Office was established by the Congressional Budget and Impoundment Control Act of 1974 (P.L. 93-344, 88 Stat. 297). This Act also gives Congress increased oversight of the federal budget. The CBO produces cost estimates for selected bills. These cost estimates can be searched at https://www.cbo.gov/cost-estimates. They are also linked to from within individual bills on the Congress.gov site, making them easy to locate in the legislative research process.

COMMITTEE AND SUBCOMMITTEE MEMBERSHIPS

Committee members of each House of Congress are generally listed at the beginning of committee hearings and occasionally in reports (in the context of committee votes). Committee constituency can often be found in the *Congressional Record* or in the Journals, especially the House Journal, but this is a much more difficult task.

However, there are times when you want a directory of all committee assignments for a particular session of Congress. Congress.gov has some nice features, like "Committee Name History" that provides names of committees and how they evolved over the years—back to the 1800s. When it comes to committee members themselves, only the current House and Senate members are listed—no historical listing by committee. We need additional help to find these names. Fortunately, that help comes in the form of congressional publications, as well as third-party publishers.

Committee and subcommittee memberships can generally be found for the Senate back to the 1990s in a Senate publication (S. Pub.) under this PURL: http://purl.fdlp.gov/GPO/gpo8662. Finding the official list of House committee assignments is more challenging. You will need to rely on the Wayback Machine for this. Search for clerk.house.gov (https://web.archive.org/web/*/clerk.house.gov). Then look under various dates for the link to "official list of standing committees," "list of members with committee assignments," or similar terms. You will then find a PDF with committees and committee members. (Note: this is a good example of a series of fugitive documents!)

The best help for committee memberships comes from a commercial publisher. The following titles from Congressional Quarterly will assist in finding membership of congressional committees from 1789 through 1992.

Canon, David T, Garrison Nelson, and Charles Stewart III. *Committees in the U.S. Congress, 1789–1946*. Washington, DC: CQ Press. 2002. 4 v.

Nelson, Garrison and Clark H. Bensen. *Committees in the U.S. Congress, 1947–1992*. Washington, DC: Congressional Quarterly, 1993–94. 2v.

Congress.gov has links to current congressional committee work (https://www.congress.gov/committees). A separate page contains committee name histories (https://www.congress.gov/help/field-values/current-committees).

CONGRESS.GOV

Congress.gov is among the most stunning new tools to come out in several years. For those who have been around awhile, this is the replacement of the Library of Congress' Thomas website—Thomas.loc.gov, which was retired on July 5, 2016 (Congress.gov 2014).

Here are just a few of the things you can do with Congress.gov:

* Find how many bills became law by Congress member.
* Find how many pieces of legislation have been sponsored by your representatives.
* See what the House of Senate is doing on their respective floors today.
* See what nominations have been recently received from the president.
* Monitor treaty actions that have been sent to the Senate.
* See remarks in the *Congressional Record* by your representatives.
* Get roll call votes for all bills and resolutions back to the 101st Congress (1989-1990).
* View calendars and committee schedules for House and Senate committees.
* View bills that have been presented to the president and are awaiting signature.
* View text of bills that were received for the record today.
* View a ranking, by Congress, of who has sponsored the most legislation.
* See communications to the Senate or the House from the president or from agencies transmitting official notifications.
* See chronological list, by Congress, of all nominations.
* Browse all congressional actions by date.
* View Congress days in session graphically by calendar view.
* Browse legislation by popular titles and short titles by Congress.
* Browse the *Congressional Record* by date.
* Browse Committees of the U.S. Congress, with links to activities.
* Browse legislation by policy area (subject).
* Browse treaty documents by topic.

It can easily be argued that Congress.gov is better at many tasks than fee-based products such as Lexis or Westlaw.

COMMERCIAL GUIDES TO CONGRESS

Congressional Quarterly's Guide to Congress. 1st ed, 1971; 2nd ed. 1976; 3rd ed. 1982; 4th ed. 1991; 5th ed. 2000 (2 vols); 6th ed. 2008; 7th ed. 2013. Thousand Oaks, CA: CQ Press; London: SAGE. Provides an institutional history of Congress.

CQ's Politics in America. Washington, DC: CQ Press. Biennial (published every two years). Available online.

National Journal. Washington, DC: Government Research Corp. Weekly. 1969–. Title varies, *National Journal Reports* (1973–1975). Became National Journal Daily in 2010.

CQ Weekly Report / Congressional Quarterly Weekly Report / CQ Weekly / CQ / CQ Magazine. Title varies. Thousand Oaks, CA: CQ Press. Weekly magazine and website. Issues back to the 1950s.

EXERCISES

1. Use your favorite search engine to find the names of celebrities who have testified before Congress. Now use your sleuthing skills to find this testimony in the congressional hearing. [Hint: ProQuest Congressional will be the easiest way to do this.]

2. Why was the Smith-Lever Act of 1914 needed? [Hint: Use ProQuest Legislative Insight to look for congressional reports.]

3. Which recent president has had the most vetoes? [Hint: do a null search in Congress.gov, then limit.]

4. Provide the information as requested for Public Law No: 107-201 = _____ Stat. _____

   Short title:

   Codified at: _____

5. Short title: National Wildlife Refuge System Improvement Act of 1997

   Public Law No.: _____ – _____ = _____ Stat. _____

   Codified at: _____

6. Using Congress.gov, your local online catalog, or PQ Legislative Insight, provide legislative history information for the Tsunami Warning and Education Act. [This shows how you can do legislative history research with free resources.]

   a) Provide "Major Actions."

   b) Locate a hearing related to this bill and give the SuDocs number.

   c) Find a Congressional Report and give:

   Report number:

SuDocs number:

Serial set number:

d) This became Public Law ____ – ____ = ____ Stat. ____

3) This law is codified at:

e) Why was this law needed?

7. A student is researching the Fallen Hero Survivor Benefit Fairness Act of 2001. Using ProQuest Congressional or ProQuest Legislative Insight suggest:

   a) the congressional report providing the legislative intent of the act. H. Rpt. ____ – ____

   b) SuDocs number of this report:

   c) Serial Set number where this report is found.

   d) Why was this Act needed? [from the above report]

   e) What is the Public Law number of this Act?

   f) Where is it found in Statutes at Large?

   g) Where is it codified in the US Code?

8. Do a legislative history on any Public Law between 1995 and 2005. Your Public Law must meet these criteria: it must have at least one relevant hearing, and it must have at least one Senate or House Report. Your legislative history should include all relevant materials: House or Senate Reports or Documents, Hearings, Committee Prints, Congressional Debate, and comments from the president, if available. Be sure to include SuDocs numbers or Serial Set numbers (as appropriate). You don't have to find the actual documents; just identify the relevant parts of the legislative history. [Use ProQuest Legislative Insight or ProQuest Congressional if you have access to either of these resources. If you don't have access, use freely available resources.]

9. Considering the public law you selected in question 8, what parts of this legislative history could have been found using Congress.gov? What parts could not be found using Congress.gov?

10. A famous bear named "Smokey" turned 75 years old in 2019. Is his name "Smokey the Bear" or "Smokey Bear"?

   a) Using Congress.gov, ProQuest Congressional, and other tools mentioned in the text, make an argument as to which is the proper name for this famous bear.

   b) Do newspapers over the years generally get the name right?

   c) Extra credit: skip ahead to the chapter on intellectual property. Do a search of the trademark database to support your answer.

REFERENCES

Allen, Jared. 2008. "GOP 'Stolen Vote' Investigators say Dems' Explanations 'Implausible.'" *The Hill.* Accessed August 14, 2019. https://thehill.com

/homenews/news/15010-gop-stolen-vote-investigators-say-dems -explanations-implausible.

Brown, Christopher C. 2011. "Knowing Where They Went: Six Years of Online Access Statistics via the Online Catalog for Federal Government Information." *College and Research Libraries.* 72, no. 1: 43–61. Accessed December 12, 2019. https://crl.acrl.org/index.php/crl/article/view/16131.

Congress.gov. 2014. "About Congress.gov." Accessed July 22, 2019. https://www .congress.gov/about.

CRS (Congressional Research Service). 2008. "House Committee Organization and Process: A Brief Overview." RS20465. Updated April 21, 2008. Accessed December 12, 2019. https://crsreports.congress.gov/product/pdf /RS/RS20465.

CRS (Congressional Research Service). 2010. "Bills and Resolutions: Examples of How Each Kind is Used." Report No. 98-706. Updated December 2, 2010. Accessed December 12, 2019. https://crsreports.congress.gov/product/pdf /RS/98-706.

CRS (Congressional Research Service). 2014. "Publications of Congressional Committees: A Summary." Report No. 98-673. Updated May 21, 2014. Accessed December 12, 2019. https://crsreports.congress.gov/product/pdf /RS/98-673.

CRS (Congressional Research Service). 2015. "Procedural Analysis of Private Laws Enacted: 1986–2015." RS22450. Updated August 31, 2015. Accessed December 12, 2019. https://crsreports.congress.gov/product/pdf/RS /RS22450.

CRS (Congressional Research Service). 2018a. "Guide to Committee Activity Reports: Purpose, Rules, and Contents." CRS Report, February 15, 2018. R45104. Accessed December 12, 2019. https://crsreports.congress.gov /product/pdf/R/R45104.

CRS (Congressional Research Service). 2018b. "The House Journal: Origin, Purpose, and Approval." Report No. R45209. Updated May 31, 2018. Accessed December 12, 2019. https://crsreports.congress.gov/product/pdf/R/R45209.

CRS (Congressional Research Service). 2018c. "Introduction to the Legislative Process in the U.S. Congress" R42843. Updated November 15, 2018. Accessed December 12, 2019. https://crsreports.congress.gov/product/pdf /R/R42843.

CRS (Congressional Research Service). 2018d. "The Office of the Parliamentarian in the House and Senate." Report No. RS20544. Updated November 28, 2018. Accessed December 12, 2019. https://crsreports.congress.gov /product/pdf/RS/RS20544.

CRS (Congressional Research Service). 2018e. "Types of Committee Hearings." CRS Report, 98-317. Updated November 15, 2018. Accessed December 12, 2019. https://crsreports.congress.gov/product/pdf/RS/98-317.

GovTrack. 2019. "Statistics and Historical Comparison." Accessed July 5, 2019. https://www.govtrack.us/congress/bills/statistics.

Jackson, Herbert H., Jr. 2019. "Prepared Statement before the Subcommittee on Legislative Branch Committee on Appropriations, U.S. House of

Representatives on GPO's Appropriations Request for FY 2020." February 27, 2019. Accessed December 12, 2019. https://www.gpo.gov/docs/default -source/congressional-relations-pdf-files/testimonies/247-794_po29_gpo _jackson-house-prepared-statement_2_2019_new.pdf.

Pasley, Jeffrey L. 2004. "Democracy, Gentility, and Lobbying in the Early U.S. Congress." In Julian E. Zelizer, ed., *The American Congress: The Building of Democracy*. Boston, MA: Houghton Mifflin Company, pp. 38–52.

ProQuest. 2012. "ProQuest Congressional Help—Committee Hearings." Accessed August 14, 2019. https://congressional.proquest.com/help/congressional /committeehearingspt_cpt.html.

Schmeckebier, Laurence F., and Roy B. Eastin. 1969. *Government Publications and Their Use*. 2nd revised ed. Washington, DC: Brookings Institution.

U.S. Senate. 2002. "Types of Legislation." Accessed August 23, 2019. https://www .senate.gov/legislative/common/briefing/leg_laws_acts.htm.

U.S. Senate. 2015. "Congressional Records." Accessed August 23, 2019. https:// www.senate.gov/legislative/congrecord.htm.

4

Legislative History Research

RESEARCHING THE DOCUMENT TRAIL

Having briefly touched upon how laws are made, we need to focus on the aspect of lawmaking that is accessible to the researcher, the document trail that is left behind. Figure 4.1 is intended to show the document trail left behind as legislation works its way through the system. The elements between the bill and the public law are not intended to show any order; they are just to group like document types together.

People do legislative history research for many reasons. Here are a few of them.

- To attempt to understand ambiguities in legislation
- To discover what motivated lawmakers to pass a piece of legislation (legislative intent)
- To understand where legislation fits into the history of a public policy issue
- To understand successes or failures of outcomes of legislation
- To understand the social or cultural influences on legislation within a particular slice of time

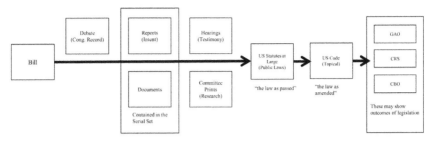

Figure 4.1   Document trail of legislation (Not intended to show chronology)

SOURCES OF LEGISLATIVE HISTORIES

Let's be clear on what we are doing when we approach legislative history research. We are researching the background of bills that have become law (public laws). We are not researching bills or resolutions that died somewhere in the process. In most cases, we don't have to reinvent the wheel. There are existing resources that tell us where these documents behind the legislative history are. We can use "hooks"—numbers or, in some cases, titles with which to more quickly locate these materials.

Legislative histories do not immediately show up, however. The comprehensive ones covering hearings and other items may take several months to wind up in the places we mention below.

Endnotes to Public Laws

One of the "poor man's" secrets is that on the back of recent public laws (in an endnote), there is an abbreviated legislative history. Beginning with the 94th Congress in 1975, a brief legislative history was appended at the end of all public laws (slip law and Statutes at Large versions). Elements present in these brief legislative histories include major *Congressional Record* citations, congressional reports, and presidential remarks (Figure 4.2).

Congress.gov

The first place to look for the most basic materials on legislative history is Congress.gov. By clicking "All Actions" for a bill or resolution, you will see a reverse chronological presentation with

LEGISLATIVE HISTORY—H.R. 6:
HOUSE REPORTS: No. 109–190 (Comm. of Conference).
CONGRESSIONAL RECORD, Vol. 151 (2005):
    Apr. 20, 21, considered and passed House.
    June 14–16, 20–23, 28, considered and passed Senate, amended.
    July 28, House agreed to conference report.
    July 29, Senate agreed to conference report.
WEEKLY COMPILATION OF PRESIDENTIAL DOCUMENTS, Vol. 41 (2005):
    Aug. 8, Presidential remarks and statement.

Figure 4.2   Legislative history at end of P.L. 109-58, 119 Stat. 594, 1143, Energy Policy Act of 2005

dates, actions, and links to the *Congressional Record*, including roll call votes. This is usually updated a day or two after a bill is signed into law. What you will find in Congress.gov are the bills or resolutions (all versions of bills or resolutions), the votes on the bills in the House or Senate, congressional reports with numbers of the reports, whether or not there was congressional debate in the House or Senate, with dates the debate took place, and the public law itself in text and PDF format. The PDF of the public law (the slip law) will itself contain the brief legislative history, noting report numbers and dates of congressional debate. You would then need to go the *Congressional Record* for that date to read the debate (Govinfo.gov is as fast a tool as any for this). Remember that there is a many-year delay in publishing the permanent-bound *Congressional Record*, so you will need to view the daily edition. What Congress.gov will not do for you is give references to hearings. You will need to consult with ProQuest Legislative Insight for that. Otherwise you could go to the House or Senate Committee's website to see if hearings were held. Often, you will find hearings from previous sessions of Congress, even if there has been a change of party control in the chamber.

History of Bills in Govinfo.gov

Although titled History of Bills, this website includes all types of bills and resolutions from the 98th Congress (1983–1984) to recent (*site:govinfo .gov history of bills*). This resource is useful when trying to determine when additional sponsors or cosponsors signed on to legislation (with links to the *Congressional Record* pages). This format is not as informative as the Congress.gov, but some may find this useful.

ProQuest Legislative Insight

If several months have passed since passage, you will want to look for the legislative history in ProQuest's Legislative Insight. This subscription database is available in most medium to large depository libraries. Although you will not be able to access this tool remotely if you are not affiliated with that library, you will be able to walk in to the library and use the database onsite. Legislative Insight will give you everything related to the legislative history: every bill version, every *Congressional Record* citation, all congressional reports of all types, conference reports and the more substantive reports on various topics within the legislation, all related congressional hearings, any related congressional documents, any related committee prints, presidential signing statements, and the full text of the public law itself.

Also included are references to the codification in the U.S. Code. For bills, debate, reports, documents, committee prints, and hearings, any relevant documents in previous Congresses will be included as well. This is because many pieces of legislation take more than two years to pass and need to be reintroduced in subsequent Congresses. Reasons include political ones; lack of interest on the part of lawmakers; and the fact that many policy issues take time to develop research, public interest, and motivation on the part of members of Congress. This makes Legislative Insight one of the most valuable go-to resources for doing legislative history research. The intention is for ProQuest to include nearly every law from the 1st Congress onward. They have a long way to go, but they presently have at least one legislative history from every Congress, and they are gradually filling in the gaps. As you can imagine, it takes considerable time and research effort to complete the early laws.

A word needs to be said here about ProQuest Congressional and their legislative history module. ProQuest Congressional is built on the print *Congressional Information Service (CIS) Annual Index*. The Annual Index was later purchased by LexisNexis and made available online via Lexis-Nexis Congressional. In 2010, the CIS content and LexisNexis interfaces to the CIS content were purchased by ProQuest, and that's how we got to ProQuest Congressional. One of the important component parts of the *CIS Annual Index* was its legislative history component. This subset compiles all the congressional publications that are connected to all bills that were passed into law. The Annual Index included all publications, but, importantly, the legislative history index included only those connected to public law. But Legislative Insight is a vast improvement over the legislative histories in the ProQuest Congressional legislative history index.

Compiled Legislative Histories

Many works have been published that document the broad legislative histories of important acts, and the research will save much time by consulting these. However, the tools available today, particularly ProQuest Legislative Insight, are the first ones to think of when doing legislative history research.

Reams, Bernard D., Jr., comp. 1994. *Federal Legislative Histories: An Annotated Bibliography and Index to Officially Published Sources.* Westport, CT: Greenwood Press.

HeinOnline (subscription) contains many of these compiled legislative history works in its U.S. Federal Legislative History Library.

BILLS AND RESOLUTIONS IN THE LEGISLATIVE PROCESS

The text of bills and resolutions can sometimes be helpful in the legislative history process, although I rarely spend much time with this. Researching various bill versions is important if you are researching amendments, bills that have been through many changes, or where a turn of the phrase is perhaps important. But for most students engaged in public policy research, I guide them directly to congressional reports.

CONGRESSIONAL DEBATE IN THE LEGISLATIVE PROCESS

At times, congressional debate as found in the *Congressional Record* (or its preceding titles for older legislation) can shed light on proposed legislation, thus providing a window into the thought of the times when passage was being considered. However, floor debate is considered less persuasive than arguments contained in the congressional committee reports (Costello 1989).

As an example of this, congressional debate concerning the Metric Conversion Act of 1975 (which became P.L. 94-168, 89 Stat. 1007) can be found in the *Congressional Record* (121 Cong. Rec. 27683). Here, Representative James Quillen of Tennessee argues the merits of Congress supporting a changeover from the English to the metric system as national policy. Arguments include shame (the United States is the only industrialized country that has not officially adopted the metric system), long-term economic benefits (increased volume of international trade), and the fact that the United States already has the metric system in some aspects of business and engineering. It is informative, especially to historians and social scientists, to examine the rhetoric used by the original sponsors of legislation.

For recent legislation, Congress.gov provides links to debate in the *Congressional Record*. For information about consideration and voting on bills, both the index and the "Daily Digest" section of the *Congressional Record* bound edition can be consulted. Using Govinfo.gov's digitized version of the bound *Congressional Record*, these volumes are typically the last two volumes for a given year.

Let's look at a case study of congressional debate informing the legislative history of a bill. On the back of the slip law for the Energy Policy Act of 2005 (P.L. 109-58, 119 Stat. 594) (see Figure 4.2 above), we see that there was mention of congressional debate on several dates. If we look at the comments from April 20, 2005 (151 Cong. Rec. 7072), we read this:

> Mr. DEFAZIO. Mr. Speaker, I have nothing against classics. I drove a 1968 Barracuda to work today. But I am looking at hybrids because of the high cost of gas and to get a little more efficient.

The Republicans are offering us a classic energy bill today, firmly rooted in the 1950s: no improvements in efficiency, no investment in energy-efficient technologies, no breakthroughs. Even worse, $8 billion of subsidies to the oil and gas industry. Well, heck, they need it. That was only the quarterly profit of ExxonMobil gouging people at the pump last quarter. They want to give us more of the same.

The President's own energy information administration says this bill will, quote, have only negligible impact on production, consumption and imports of oil. In fact, they said it will probably increase the price of gasoline by 3 cents per gallon. I guess that is to pay for the new subsidies to the suffering oil and gas industry.

That is an energy policy for the 21st century?

Congressional debate may or may not get us to why a bill was considered, but it often points out the contentious nature of policy issues, the personalities behind the policies, and can provide some entertaining quotes.

CONGRESSIONAL REPORTS AND LEGISLATIVE INTENT

While it may be quite time consuming to find relevant text within the *Congressional Record* regarding the legislative intent of legislation, it is extremely easy with congressional reports. As covered in chapter 3, congressional reports are of four main types: legislative reports, oversight or investigative reports, conference reports, and committee activity reports (CRS 2014).

Legislative reports accompany a legislative measure when it is reported for action in the House or Senate. Sometimes the "need for legislation" section is at the beginning of the report. Other times, it follows the text of the bill. Often, the background and need for legislation sections of congressional reports summarize and explain the bill in a much clearer fashion than any of the media coverage has. It is generally considered that committee legislative reports are the most reliable and persuasive elements of legislative history. These reports constitute nearly 50 percent of Supreme Court references to legislative history materials (Costello 1989).

I often go to either House or Senate reports surrounding legislation in situations where the user is not asking for legislative history. The background sections in these reports are often so succinct and well-written that they can be used in basic undergraduate papers. The student gets the benefit of clear language surrounding the topic and a primary source to include in the bibliography. Targeting congressional reports is usually much easier than trying to find clear explanation of a public policy issue in the media coverage.

Example 1: P.L. 114-51 (129 Stat. 494) is the E-Warranty Act of 2015. The law was intended to modernize the warranty requirements for consumer products by displaying the terms of the warranties on the internet. There was both a House Report (H. Rpt. 114-243) and a Senate Report (S. Rpt. 114-77) on the topic. The House report clearly presents rationale for the Act under the heading "Background and Need for Legislation." The Senate report uses the heading "Background and Needs." Both make the same points. Under the then-current rules, manufacturers would not satisfy the warranty requirements by only posting warranty information online. This Act seeks to modernize the warranty notice rules. Both reports can be retrieved by searching Govinfo.gov: *"e-warranty act of 2015"*.

Example 2: P.L. 114-198 (133 Stat. 695) is the Comprehensive Addiction and Recovery Act of 2016. There are several relevant congressional reports from the 114th Congress that address the opioid crisis. Among them is House Report 114-539, *Comprehensive Opioid Abuse Reduction Act of 2016*, which was a related title in the history of the development of the final legislation. The "Background and Need for the Legislation" section defines the term "opioid" and lists the common names of natural and synthetic forms of the drug. In four paragraphs, the effects of the drugs, enforcement efforts, and proposed grant program to address the problem are clearly discussed. The report can be viewed in Govinfo.gov at: http://purl .fdlp.gov/GPO/gpo67829.

PRESIDENTIAL SIGNING STATEMENTS

Presidential signing statements are often merely ceremonial pronouncements made at the time of signing legislation into law. They have been relatively rare in the early years of the country but had become common by the 1950s. President Reagan expanded the signing statement to make assertions of presidential authority and intent, a practice that has continued, more or less, in subsequent administrations. Thus, they become part of the legislative history of laws. The CRS Report "Presidential Signing Statements: Constitutional and Institutional Implications" (Halstead 2007) provides a detailed history through much of the George W. Bush administration.

These statements typically show up in the *Compilation of Presidential Documents*, later cumulated in the *Public Papers of the Presidents*. Another resource helpful in researching presidential signing statements is coherentbabble.com (http://www.coherentbabble.com/). In addition, the American Presidency Project has several sections covering signing statements (*site:presidency.ucsb.edu signing statements*).

OUTCOME STUDIES AND LEGISLATIVE HISTORIES

Even though the formal legislative history ends when the president signs a bill or resolution into law, it is helpful for researchers to study the impact after passage. Obviously, there are numerous secondary sources that do this, but we will stick with government publications here. The publications of three investigative arms of Congress are helpful at this point: Congressional Research Service (under the Library of Congress), the Government Accountability Office, and the Congressional Budget Office.

REVIEW OF LEGISLATIVE HISTORY RESEARCH

Having covered the document trail of legislation, let's review a typical research process for basic history of legislation. Table 4.1 shows each publication relevant to the process, with comments on their significance.

LEGISLATIVE HISTORY CASE STUDIES

We have reviewed congressional publication types (chapter 3). We just finished covering how to use the relevant publications in legislative history

Table 4.1   Use of publications in legislative histories

Publication	Interest and Use in Legislative History Research
Bill	Make sure you have the enrolled bill number and text. Sometimes previous bill versions, or the corresponding bill in the other house may be of interest.
Debate	This isn't usually of interest, but if you have time, it may be entertaining.
Reports	Conference reports, even though they appear in the brief legislative history at the end of public laws, aren't usually very interesting. You want to go for House or Senate reports that contain background, need for legislation, or similar headings.
Hearings	Hearings are not referenced in the formal legislative history, but are usually of great interest to public policy research. Don't limit your search to the current Congress; look for similar hearings on the topic from antecedent Congresses.
Committee Prints	It is unusual to find committee prints directly related to legislation, but sometimes you will find ones that give a comprehensive history of the topic of the bill. These are invaluable.
Public Law	The law "as passed." This will be the historical text of the law as originally passed by both Houses of Congress and signed into law by the President.
U.S. Code	The law "as amended." This is the current state of the law as placed in the relevant sections of the codification of laws.
Signing Statements	Often contain presidential reservations as to how the law will or will not be enforced.

research. Let's now take a few public laws and see what can be derived from a legislative history and also derive what was motivating passage of the acts, what the public policy drivers were, and what the outcomes of the legislation were.

Legislative History Case Study 1: Rapid DNA Act of 2017

Bill Versions and Text

To begin with, we need a "hook" to the enacted bill number or the public law number. Searching this title in Congress.gov informs us that the bill number is H.R. 510 (115th Congress) and the public law number is P.L. 115-50 (131 Stat. 1001).

The bill's sponsors and cosponsors are available in Congress.gov by clicking the cosponsors tab. Related bills (usually identical or closely connected bills in the other House of Congress) are found in another tab through the interface.

Full text of this bill, both the (ugly) text version and an official PDF version are linked to from within Congress.gov. But you could also get all versions of the bill from Govinfo.gov. Search: "H.R. 510," then limit to 2017. "H.R. 510 (ENR)" stands for the enrolled version. You will see many other versions as well. To even begin to understand the 80 bill version and status abbreviations, you will need to go here: https://www.govinfo.gov/help /bills, or Google: *site:govinfo.gov bill versions help.*

There were no roll call votes in connection with this bill, since actions were agreed to by voice votes or unanimous consent.

Full text of all bill versions can also be found in ProQuest Congressional (with the full text bills being an optional add-on that many larger depository libraries may have) and ProQuest Legislative Insight.

Congressional Debate

Within Congress.gov and navigating to "All Actions," we see that there was congressional debate for 40 minutes on May 16, 2017. The way Congress.gov denoted "DEBATE" makes this a quicker way to get to more substantive comments than we can even through ProQuest Legislative Insight. Using Govinfo.gov, we can read the debate in the *Congressional Record* (daily edition) on that date. On page H4204, we read these comments from Mr. Goodlatte:

> With Rapid DNA technology, it is possible to test the DNA of arrestees as soon as they are in custody and determine within hours whether they match the DNA profile from a crime scene or from other earlier crimes.

This technology would also enable police to check the Federal DNA database to see if an arrestee matches the DNA profile from previous crimes for which a DNA sample exists but no known suspect has been identified.

Rather than waiting weeks for a DNA sample to be processed and risk releasing a suspect back into the public to potentially reoffend, creating new victims, police will be able to determine at initial booking if the suspect is a person of interest in other crimes.

This bill will provide important tools for law enforcement.

Mr. Sensenbrenner, the bill's sponsor, adds his comments, among which is:

There is only one problem with Rapid DNA technology: Federal law. Our law, written in 1994 when DNA technology was still in its infancy, prohibits the use of Rapid DNA technology in booking stations. (Vol. CR H4205, May, 16, 2017)

We are now beginning to see the rationale behind this bill.

Congressional Reports

Now let's move on the congressional reports. Congress.gov notes that there was one report, a House Report from the Committee on the Judiciary, held May 11, 2017 (H. Rept. 115-117). We could have also discovered this report number from the endnote of the Public Law itself. From Congress.gov, we can click through to that report and view the PDF full text hosted on the Congress.gov website. Alternatively, we could also have found this report on Govinfo.gov. Pulling up the report, the first thing we notice is that the content of the report has headings for "purpose and summary" and "background and need for legislation." The summary is to the point: "H.R. 510 will establish a system for integration of Rapid DNA instruments for use by law enforcement to reduce violent crime and reduce the current DNA analysis backlog."

Now for the need for this legislation. First, it is noted that a previous act, the DNA Identification Act of 1994, authorized the FBI to compile DNA information into a database called the Combined DNA Index System (CODIS), with only accredited state labs allowed to do testing. At that time, DNA testing took many days or weeks before results could be known. Technology advancement now enables results to be known in a matter of hours. But the 1994 Act only allowed state labs to use this technology. Currently, booking stations have to send off results to accredited state labs and wait a long period of time. H.R. 510 would change the current law to allow local booking agencies to have access to the database for quicker turnaround times in order to eliminate potential suspects and capture those who have committed the crimes.

Having access to this legislative intent statement from congressional committees themselves makes this primary source content much more valuable than newspaper accounts and can clear up any ambiguities.

Congressional Hearings

As noted previously, Congress.gov makes no mention of congressional hearings. ProQuest Legislative Insight is the easiest way to discover if any hearings were held in conjunction with this bill. If you don't have access to Legislative Insight, you will need to look to other sources. Let's look for the hearing on the committee's website. This was a House bill and, according to Congress.gov, was first considered by the House Committee on the Judiciary (*site:house.gov judiciary committee hearings*). We note that we are looking for hearings within May 2017. We don't see anything clearly related to this bill on the House Judiciary website. It is at this point that Legislative Insight really shines. It informs us that no hearings were connected to this legislation from the 115th Congress, but in a previous Congress, the 114th Congress, the House Judiciary Committee held a hearing on June 18, 2015, titled *Rapid DNA Act* (SuDocs Y 4.J 89/1:114-25). This is confirmed by the House Report, mentioned above, which tells us that no hearings were held on H.R. 510, but hearings were held on a nearly identical bill, H.R. 320 from the previous Congress, on June 18, 2015.

To further confirm things, we go to the Catalog of Government Publications at catalog.gpo.gov. There, we discover a catalog record for this hearing, with a PURL in one of the catalog records. We could also have gone directly to Govinfo.gov and found the PDF of the hearing there. So how does this hearing inform our legislative history research?

The hearing's table of contents reveals that the committee heard from three witnesses and that their oral testimony and prepared statements have been included in the published hearing. Two additional prepared statements from representatives are also included, as are materials submitted for the record.

How does this hearing help in our research? Here are some points:

- Cases that show criminals arrested for older crimes were tested after a recent arrest;
- CODIS statistics: how many installations of CODIS and how many investigative leads generated;
- Costs of Rapid DNA devices and costs per test;
- Standards used and rigor employed in DNA testing; and
- Supportive statement of a rape survivor as anecdotal support.

These are at least a few ways in which a hearing can support legislative history research.

Public Law and U.S. Code

The public law itself (P.L. 115-50, 131 Stat. 1001) is easily found using Govinfo.gov, or from within the Congress.gov interface. Under the short title on the slip law (or in 131 Stat. 1001), you can see where this law is codified in the U.S. Code—42 U.S.C. 13701 note. Although you can navigate to the U.S. Code using Govinfo.gov, it is rather cumbersome. By going to the House Office of the Law Revision Counsel site (Google: *site:house .gov us code*), you can quickly navigate to that section, knowing that this is an updated version of the Code, and any amendments in the past few days having been incorporated into it (although unofficial). When we go to that site in the U.S. Code, we are informed that the section has been reclassified to 34 U.S.C. § 12101. Going to that section on the House U.S. Code site, we find our codified law. A bit complicated, but it works!

GAO/CRS/CBO Reports

Let's check Government Accountability Office Reports first. We can use the search engine provided on the gao.gov site, or search Google (*site:gao .gov "rapid dna"*). Although some of the results are too old and are irrelevant, a GAO report from May 21, 2019 (https://www.gao.gov/assets/700 /697791.pdf) informs us that Rapid DNA technology is being used to identify victims and family members in cases of disasters.

Searching Congressional Research Service reports via crsreports .congress.gov, we discover one relevant report, *DNA Testing in Criminal Justice: Background, Current Law, and Grants* (R41800), updated January 24, 2018. This 16-page report updates things since passage of the Act two years before, discussing topics such as quality control of DNA profiles, DNA backlog, quality assurance and proficiency testing standards, and postconviction DNA testing. All of these are excellent public policy outcome topics related to passage of P.L. 115-150.

Although the Congressional Budget Office does not have any reports about Rapid DNA after passage of the law, searching Google for *site:cbo .gov "rapid dna"* reveals the original cost estimate for H.R. 510.

There we have a rather thorough legislative history search, suitable for a college student to write an excellent paper, filled with primary governmental sources.

Legislative History Case Study 2: Check Clearing for the 21st Century Act

Let's try another one, this time the Check Clearing for the 21st Century Act (P.L. 108-100, 117 Stat. 1177, October 23, 2003). The short title in the Public Law states that the title may be cited as the "Check Clearing for the 21st Century Act" or the "Check 21 Act."

Bill Versions and Text

The enacted bill was 108 H.R. 1474. But we notice from the "All Actions" page in Congress.gov that the Senate had their own version of the bill, S. 1334, the Check Truncation Act of 2003, which they preferred over the House version. Texts of bills can be found within Congress.gov, with links to both the (ugly) text version and an official PDF version. Full text of all bill versions can also be found in ProQuest Congressional (with the full text bills being an optional add-on that many larger depository libraries may have) and ProQuest Legislative Insight.

The bill was sponsored by Rep. Melissa A. Hart and had 32 cosponsors.

Roll call votes are also plainly noted within Congress.gov. In this case "Roll no. 246" was taken on June 5, 2003, with a link out to a listing of the yeas and nays broken down by person and cross-tabulated by political party. This is not the official version from the *Congressional Record*. In the permanent edition, it can be found at 149 Cong. Rec. 13889 (2003) (Roll no. 246). In the daily edition it can be found at 149 Cong. Rec. H5022 (daily ed. June 5, 2003) (Roll no. 246). Remember that you cite to the permanent edition if possible.

Congressional Debate

The brief legislative history in the endnote of the Public Law gives four dates in the *Congressional Record*:

June 5, considered and passed House.

June 26, considered and passed Senate, amended, in lieu of S. 1334.

Oct. 8, House agreed to conference report.

Oct. 15, Senate agreed to conference report

But Congress.gov provides greater detail as to what happened on each of these dates. To save time, we'll go with Congess.gov. We'll look at what took place on June 5, 2003 by following the link to the *Congressional Record* for the discussion on that date (149 no. 82 CR H 5001, June 5, 2003).

Ms. Hart provided a lengthy discussion of the problems with the existing system of check clearing, the inordinate about of time to clear checks, and the advantages of digital check imaging. Points are well made and very clear. Anyone writing a paper would have no problem quickly picking up the points and making a case for the legislation. Objections to the bill are anticipated and addressed within the discussion.

Congress.gov also links out to the October 8 discussion of the conference report. It alluded to concerns that the Federal Reserve and the Treasury Department had relating to "currency collateralization and compensating balances." We will want to look for those concerns as we continue our document hunt.

Congressional Reports

Again, the endnote of the Public Law alerts us to three congressional reports:

HOUSE REPORTS: Nos. 108–132 (Comm. on Financial Services) and 108–291 (Comm. of Conference).

SENATE REPORTS: No. 108–79 accompanying S. 1334 (Comm. on Banking, Housing, and Urban Affairs).

The two House reports are linked to from within the Congress.gov "all actions" page for H.R. 1474, but the Senate report is not. This is because the Senate report was issued in conjunction with a parallel Senate bill, S. 1334, and if we were to go to the Congress.gov page for that bill, we would find a link to that report. But an easier way to get to the report is to simply type *108-79* into Govinfo.gov and navigate to Senate reports to get the PDF of that report.

Let's begin with the Senate report, S. Rpt. 108-79. Under "Purpose of the Legislation," the first paragraph discusses current law (at that time) and how banks must physically return original checks in order to receive payment, unless they have an agreement with another bank to engage in electronic transactions. But with over 15,000 banks and similar institutions, obtaining agreements on a large scale is unworkable. The second paragraph discusses the merits of the Check 21 Act.

Under the hearings heading of the Senate report, we note that the [Senate] Banking Committee held a hearing on April 3, 2003. It is important to note this, since Congress.gov will not tell us that.

Let's now look at the two House reports. We are looking for H. Rpt. 108-132, and if you type *108-132* into Govinfo.gov, the report shows up in the early search results. The "Purpose and Summary" provides a summary spanning about five paragraphs. The "Background and Need for Legislation" section begins with a useful statistic: "42.5 billion checks are processed in the United States every year." The context of the events of September 11, 2011 and the halting of air traffic, with the subsequent stalling of the U.S. payment system are introduced into the discussion.

Under the "Hearings" heading of this House report, it is noted that a House Subcommittee on Financial Institutions and Consumer Credit held a hearing on April 8, 2003. Again, we need to note that hearing as well, since Congress.gov is of no help on this.

Congressional Hearings

We made note of two hearings from the Senate and House reports, one from the Senate, held on April 3, 2003, and the other from the House, held on April 8, 2003. Those hearings are likely too old to still be posted on the committee websites, so we can look for them in Govinfo.gov. If we search *"Check Clearing for the 21st Century"* [search term enclosed in quotes] we see four hearings, two of which are the ones we are looking for.

In the two hearings, there is discussion of consumer protections under the new law. These appear to be at least some of the concerns expressed by the Federal Reserve. It is quite time-consuming to read through the entire hearings, since they do not have the format that congressional reports have. with clear headings that scream, "Here—read this section." But opening up a PDF hearing in Adobe Acrobat and doing an advanced search for relevant terms can make navigating a complex hearing a bit easier.

Looking at the legislative history for this Act in ProQuest Legislative Insight confirms the research we have done so far on hearings: there were only two hearings in the 108th Congress on this topic. What Legislative Insight excels at is bringing in antecedent Congresses, since most legislation is not completed in the two-year span of the two sessions of a numbered Congress. In this case, there was a hearing in the 107th Congress with the title *H.R. 5414—The Check Clearing for the 21st Century Act.* This was one of the titles retrieved when we searched Govinfo.gov for hearings. We were lucky in that case; it doesn't always work out that way. Legislative Insight is really an invaluable research tool that power researchers cannot live without.

Public Law and U.S. Code

Public Law 108-100 can be most easily located using Govinfo.gov and simple searching *108-100* in the search box. This retrieves the authenticated, official version. Another way to navigate to the public law is to search the statutory compilation (*United States Statutes at Large*). That is easily retrieved using the "citation" feature within Govinfo.gov. You just need to know that the citation is 117 Stat. 1177, October 23, 2003.

In the margin of the public law, you will see the short title, and under that, you will see where to find this law in the U.S. Code. In this case it reads, "12 USC 5001 note." You can most easily navigate to this by again using the Govinfo.gov citation feature. There, you can choose which version of the Code you want to see, whether it is the version in and around 2003 or the current version. To see the unofficial but up-to-date version of the Code, use the House Office of the Law Revision Counsel site (uscode.house.gov— or Google: *house us code*). You can easily browse to the citation, and you will see any changes that may have been incorporated into the law.

Presidential Signing Statement

President George W. Bush signed H.R. 1474 into law on October 28, 2003, and it then became P.L. 108-100 (117 Stat. 1177). This is getting ahead of ourselves, since presidential issuances are covered in chapter 5, but we can find the signing statement in numerous places. It was first issued in the *Weekly Compilation of Presidential Documents* (39 Weekly Comp. Pres. Doc. 1485) and when the *Public Papers of the Presidents* came out several years later, it was published there as well (2003 Pub. Papers 1409). *The Bluebook* states that one should cite to the Public Papers, rather than the Weekly Compilation, if available.

Now, as for the content of the signing statement itself, President Bush states how his executive branch will interpret a specific section of the law:

> Section 16(b) of the Act purports to require executive branch officials to submit to the Congress recommendations for legislative action. The executive branch shall construe section 16(b) in a manner consistent with the President's authority under the Recommendations Clause of the Constitution to submit for the consideration of the Congress such measures as the President shall judge necessary or expedient.

The text of this signing statement can also be found in the American Presidency Project (Google: *site:presidency.ucsb.edu signing statements*).

GAO/CRS/CBO Reports

Legislative Insight notes two CRS publications relevant to this topic. One of these is from November 8, 2003, just shortly after passage of the Act, and the other is from September 30, 2010, long after the Act had been in effect. Neither of these are available via Crsreports.congress.gov at the time of this writing, but PDFs of both are linked to from Legislative Insight.

The 2003 CRS Report (RL31591) presents a summary of the issues that is arguably even clearer than that presented in the congressional reports, hearings, or debate. Several illustrations and tables illustrate the flow of transactions, since this is a very complex issue. Remember: the primary audience of CRS Reports are members of Congress, so things must be spelled out very clearly. We, as members of the general public, are looking over their shoulders with these reports, which were not originally intended for us as the audience.

Apart from Legislative Insight, searching Google for *site:gao.gov Check Clearing for the 21st Century* proves to be beneficial. A GAO report from 2008, five years after passage of the act, provides their analysis of the legislative outcomes. Among the findings:

- Check truncation has not yet resulted in overall gains in economic efficiency for the Federal Reserve or for a sample of banks, while Federal Reserve and bank officials expect efficiencies in the future.

- Most bank consumers seem to have accepted changes to their checking accounts from check truncation.

- To the extent that banks have employed check truncation, bank consumers have realized benefits and costs relating to faster processing and access to account information (GAO 2008).

Now for the Congressional Budget Office. Searching Google: *site:cbo.gov check clearing* leads us to CBO's original cost estimate for H.R. 1474 from May 2003. Other documents show up in the search results as well and may help with general background information.

There we have our legislative history of P.L. 108-100.

Legislative History Case Study 3: Emergency Daylight-Saving Time Energy Conservation Act of 1973

Our first task is to get some "hooks," the numbers that will help us navigate the documents. Doing a general Google search, we see that the Public Law number is 93-182, and the Statutes at Large citation is 87 Stat. 707, with the bill number H.R. 11324 (93rd Congress), December 15, 1973. Of course, we will want to double check as we go through our research, since mistakes can and do happen with unofficial sites on the web.

We are endeavoring on a legislative history of a topic that has many public laws preceding it, and many others that came after it. We are just looking at events that led up to the passage of this Act and what the cultural and historical situation was at the time.

The first year for which Congress.gov contains legislative actions is 1973. As a result, there are no links out to the full text of bills, reports, or

Congressional Record content. We can use the information for reference purposes but will need to use our knowledge of other resources to get the text of the documents. Congress.gov confirms the information we got from our initial Google search.

Bill Versions and Text

Although bill text is often contained in the *Congressional Record* and in congressional reports, we must look elsewhere to get the enrolled version of H.R. 11324. The two places to most easily get bill text are ProQuest Congressional (with the congressional bills add-on module) or ProQuest Legislative Insight. Most larger depository libraries will likely have access to either or both of these products, and you should be able to walk in and search the databases at no charge.

Congress.gov provides us with the names of the sponsor and cosponsors. If the legislation had been from an older session of Congress, we would have needed to use ProQuest Congressional, ProQuest Legislative Insight, or go to the *Congressional Record* itself to find sponsorship.

Congressional Debate

ProQuest Legislative Insight provides references to references in the *Congressional Record* for when the bill was reported in the House and when it was placed on the Senate calendar, with direct links to the unofficial full text. It has extensive references to related bills from the House and Senate in the same session of Congress. Congress.gov has none of that, likely because early versions of the database didn't include that information. GPO has published all of the *Congressional Record* online, so you could use that, but it takes a very long time to open the PDF from the scanned version, and the optical character recognition (OCR) of the volumes may not be perfect. A better alternative, if you have access, is HeinOnline in their U.S. Congressional Documents library. This is the quickest way to access the content for this bill.

Congressional Reports

Now we want to get to the heart of the issue with congressional reports, where we will look for legislative intent. From Congress.gov, we learn of H. Rept. 93-643. There was also a conference report, H. Rept. 93-709, but that will be of lesser interest to us, since it will bring together House and Senate final language. There was a companion bill in the Senate (S. 2702). If we search Congress.gov for that bill from 1973, we learn of a Senate report, S. Rpt. 93-504. Each of these three reports are also mentioned in ProQuest Legislative Insight.

Let's look at House Report 93-643. The report is not linked to from Congress.gov. It is too early for Govinfo,gov. Searching the Catalog of Government Publications (catalog.gpo.gov), we learn that the title of the report is "Daylight Saving Time Act of 1973: Report from Committee on Interstate and Foreign Commerce to Accompany H.R. 11324." Since congressional reports are contained in the U.S. *Congressional Serial Set* (see Figure 4.1 above), we could locate it via the three commercial sources for the Serial Set: Readex, ProQuest, or HeinOnline. But those are all subscription resources.

Let's assume that we want to go to a depository library to get our hands on an actual copy of the report. We will need to know the Serial Set volume number. Using the Law Librarians' Society of Washington, D.C.'s Schedule of Volumes of the U.S. *Congressional Serial Set*, 1970 to Current (https:// www.llsdc.org/serial-set-volumes-guide, or Google: *serial set schedule of volumes*) and click on 1973, we learn that the volume number is 13020-6. Now we have the information we need to head off to a large depository library (but call first to ensure that they have the volume you need!). With a great deal of pain, this report can be found in the HathiTrust (HT 009989679 No. 13020-6).

From the report, the "Purpose" section states that the bill would provide for a two-year trial period of daylight-saving time. The "Background" section contains a history lesson on all the previous daylight-saving acts, from the Standard Time Act in 1918 through to the Uniform Time Act of 1966. Under the "Need for Legislation" section, we learn that this bill is "part of the emergency legislative program requested of the Congress by President Nixon on November 8, 1973." Among the justifications for passage in the section are the oil shortage, avoiding confusion (having to change the time two times per year), and reducing crime (by having people return home from work during daylight).

The other congressional reports would be just as interesting to go through.

Congressional Hearings

ProQuest Legislative Insight suggests that there were three hearings in conjunction with this legislation, two published and one unpublished. One of the valuable advantages of Legislative Insight is the inclusion of unpublished hearings. The unpublished hearing has the less-than-memorable title, "H.R. 11324, H.R. 11010, and H.R. 5463." It is a "stenographic transcript" from the House Committee on Rules that contains some interesting points germane to the topic.

The other two published hearings can also be found using OCLC's WorldCat database. With a search like *daylight saving time hearing** and a limit to 1973, you can get the titles and SuDocs numbers for these hearings. Both hearings can be found in the HathiTrust (HT 003214550, 003214106).

Committee Prints

There is a committee print issued in conjunction with this legislation. From Legislative Insight, we find a reference to the "Uniform Time Act of 1966 and Other Related Acts and Background Information, for Hearings on H.R. 11324 and Similar Bills Relating to Year-Round Daylight Saving Time" (SuDocs: Y 4.In 8/4:T 48/4). This contains the full text of previous related laws and a summary of daylight-saving time and exceptions to it from 1918 onward. It is a helpful addition to the discussion.

Public Law and U.S. Code

The quickest (and free) way to get access to the public law is by going to Govinfo.gov citations section and searching *U.S. Statutes at Large* for this citation (87 Stat. 707). That is the law "as passed."

Of course, this law does not stand today, since it was a two-year temporary measure.

Because this is an older statute, the codification citation to the U.S. Code is not noted in the margin. However, Legislative Insight tells us that it was codified at 15 U.S.C. § 260a. To see the law "as amended"—in other words, as it stands today, we need to go to the House Office of the Law Revision Counsel site. Navigating to the citation in 15 U.S.C. noted above, we read this about the status of P.L. 93-182 (87 Stat. 707):

> Emergency Daylight Saving Time Energy Conservation
>   P.L. 93–182, Dec. 15, 1973, 87 Stat. 707, as amended by P.L. 93-434, Oct. 5, 1974, 88 Stat. 1209, enacted the Emergency Daylight Saving Time Energy Conservation Act of 1973, which extended daylight saving time. The act was effective at 2 a.m. on the fourth Sunday which occurred after Dec. 15, 1973 and terminated at 2 a.m. on the last Sunday of April 1975.

The text of the current law appears above that note.

If you need the official version of the U.S. Code, you can use Govinfo .gov to get the U.S. Code (published every six years) with its annual supplements. Not a joy to use!

Presidential Signing Statement

As noted in Legislative Insight, President Nixon's signing statement was made on December 15, 1973. This can be found in the *Weekly Compilation of Presidential Documents* (9:50 Weekly Comp. Pres. Doc. 1462). As of this writing, the Compilation is not available via Govinfo.gov. It is available via HathiTrust (HT 000519783).

Since the *Public Papers of the Presidents* has been published for the Nixon years, it is best to cite to it instead of the Weekly Compilation. The Public Papers can be found on Govinfo.gov, but it is slow to pull up the older volumes. Use it if you must. Faster access is through HeinOnline (1973 Pub. Papers 1014).

GAO/CRS/CBO Reports

Many CRS reports have been published over the years on daylight saving time. Crsreports.congress.gov has a report (R45208), updated July 18, 2019, that gives a history of daylight-saving legislation from 1918 to the present. However, the relatively new database doesn't provide access all the way back to the beginning of these reports (to 1916). ProQuest Congressional's add-on Congressional Research Digital Collection (CRDC) collection has all the CRS reports that are not classified. One such report, "Daylight Saving Time—Background and Legislative Analysis," from August 12, 1974, provides a viewpoint from shortly after passage of P.L. 93-182. ProQuest Congressional CRS Reports has other reports related to the topic as well.

EXERCISES

1. Using Congress.gov, go to any session of Congress and limit the results to "Status of Legislation" = "Became Law." You can do a "null" search in Congress.gov to see all results that meet that criterion. Now pick a law and go through the steps for producing a legislative history. Try to pick a law that is not too long or too short. Be sure to look for legislative intent in the congressional reports.

2. Do you have a building in your hometown named after someone—perhaps a post office building? Do a little research to discover when the building was dedicated to this person and whether it was an act of Congress that initiated this action. Find that legislation and read about the background of the person.

3. There was great controversy in 1953 concerning the statehood of Ohio. Apparently, procedures had not been properly followed way back in 1802 and 1803, and, technically, Ohio had never been officially admitted to the Union. There was activity in both Houses of Congress in 1953. Supply relevant report numbers, the public law number, and give a brief summary of the legislative intent of this act.

REFERENCES

Congressional Research Service. 2014. "Publications of Congressional Committees: A Summary." Report No. 98-673. Updated May 21, 2014. Accessed January 14, 2020. https://crsreports.congress.gov/product/pdf/RS/98-673.

Costello, George A. 1989. "Sources of Legislative History as Aids to Statutory Construction." Congressional Research Service Report 89-86 A. January 27, 1989.

GAO (Government Accountability Office). 2008. "Check 21 Act: Most Customers Have Accepted and Banks Are Progressing toward Full Adoption of Check Truncation." Accessed July 29, 2019. https://www.gao.gov/assets/290/282975.pdf.

Halstead, T. J. 2007. "Presidential Signing Statements: Constitutional and Institutional Implications." Congressional Research Service Report RL33667. September 17, 2007.

5

Documents of the Presidency

Presidential documents are often of great interest to the general public. The White House website is often the best and first place to go for speeches and issuances that just happened. After that, we need to rely on official sources of publication as described in this chapter.

Under the SuDocs classification system, the PR classification is used to organize publications from presidents. The 1909 Checklist retrospectively imputes PR stems to prior presidents, even though the system didn't exist when the documents were first available. Theoretically, the PR SuDocs classification is used to organize presidents from the first president (George Washington, PR 1) to the current president (Donald J. Trump, PR 45). But in practice, most depository libraries don't begin using this system until the presidency of Franklin D. Roosevelt (PR 32). Since he was elected president four times and served from 1933 until his death in office in 1945, we can see the impact of the New Deal and wartime drama as it played out through documents under the PR classification.

Much reorganization of the U.S. government came out of the FDR years. One of those outcomes was the creation, in 1939, of the Executive Office of the President. The SuDocs stem for this is PREX, often rendered as PrEx. Under the executive office is the Office of the Vice President (with its own SuDocs class, PRVP), the Council of Economic Advisors (PREX 6), the Council on Environmental Quality (PREX 14), the National Security Council (PREX 3), the Office of Management and Budget (PREX 2), the

Office of National Drug Control Policy (PREX 26), the Office of Policy Development (PREX 15), the Office of Science and Technology Policy (PREX 23), and the United States Trade Representative (PREX 9), among others.

PRESIDENTIAL ISSUANCES

Presidential issuances is a broad term used to cover executive orders, presidential proclamations, determinations, memoranda, administrative orders, and other kinds of issuances. The interesting thing about presidential issuances is that they tend to appear in multiple sources. This is attestation of their importance and the speed with which the public desires access.

Several publications are crucial to tracking presidential matters. These include the *Federal Register, Code of Federal Regulations*, Title 3, and *Compilation of Presidential Documents*. The *Public Papers of the Presidents* does not contain the text of the issuances, as the sources just mentioned do, but an appendix at the end of each volume contains a listing of "Presidential Documents Published in the *Federal Register.*" This is a helpful listing of executive orders, proclamations, and other issuances with references to *Federal Register* volumes and page numbers for quick access.

Executive Orders

The executive order is an extremely powerful tool in the hands of the chief executive. It has much the same power as an act of Congress, becoming part of the U.S. Code on occasion (see chapter 3). Executive orders have been used to establish policy, reorganize government agencies, change regulations, and affect how legislation is interpreted and implemented. National emergencies are typically declared via executive orders. It has been observed that presidents tend to go on an EO issuing spree at the beginning of their terms of service, and then again at the end, especially when party control of the White House will change to the other party (Mayer 1999).

Executive orders are one of the most common types of presidential documents. From the time of President Washington until the end of 2018, there had been over 15,000 EOs (American Presidency Project 2019). EOs began with Washington, but the practice of numbering EOs didn't begin until 1907, when the State Department initiated the practice, starting the numbering with the second administration of Theodore Roosevelt in 1905. They then imputed numbers back to 1862. Many EOs fell through the cracks, and as additional executive orders were discovered, a letter was inserted within the numbering rather than renumbering the entire series. For example, according to the NARA disposition table, EO 7709-A, "Abolishing the National Emergency Council," signed September 16, 1937 (2 FR 2195, September 21, 1937), was inserted after EO 7709 (which was not published in the *Federal Register*). Clifford Lord's two-volume work on Executive Orders provides a more complete historical explanation of the numbered and the unnumbered orders (Lord 1944, 1979).

It is interesting to study EO output by president and to note the average number of EOs per year. Table 5.1 shows output from FDR through the second year of the Trump administration.

Executive orders often appear in the U.S. Code. Table IV in the back of the bound volume of the U.S. Code shows where EOs have been placed in the Code. This can be easily viewed in the online version from the Office of

Table 5.1   Executive order output by president from FDR through Trump (December 2018). Adapted from American Presidency Project.

President	Total Orders	Avg/Year	Years in Office	EO Number Range
Franklin D. Roosevelt	3,721	307	12.12	6071–9537
Harry S. Truman	907	117	7.78	9538–10431
Dwight D. Eisenhower	484	61	8	10432–10913
John F. Kennedy	214	75	2.84	10914–11127
Lyndon B. Johnson	325	63	5.17	11128–11451
Richard Nixon	346	62	5.55	11452–11797
Gerald R. Ford	169	69	2.45	11798–11966
Jimmy Carter	320	80	4	11967–12286
Ronald Reagan	381	48	8	12287–12667
George Bush	166	42	4	12668–12833
William J. Clinton	364	46	8	12834–13197
George W. Bush	291	36	8	13198–13488
Barack Obama	276	35	8	13489–13764
Donald J. Trump	92	46	2	13765–13856

the Law Revision Counsel at http://uscode.house.gov/tables/usctable4
.htm. Executive orders do not always make it into the *Federal Register*, as
noted above.

In addition to the *Federal Register* and the *Code of Federal Regulations*,
Title 3, you will also find executive orders in the *Weekly Compilation of
Presidential Documents* (now known simply as the *Compilation of Presidential Documents*). Presidential issuances are generally not published in
the *Public Papers of the Presidents*, but they are referenced in an appendix
at the end of each year. Due to publication schedules, other than the White
House website, the first official place to look for EOs is the *Federal Register*
and the *Compilation of Presidential Documents*. The *Code of Federal Regulations*, Title 3, is not fast, being published annually, but it is an excellent
place for a listing of issuances throughout an entire year.

Because of the varying dates of coverage for the above resources, the
best starting point when researching EOs is the American Presidency Project (*site:presidency.ucsb.edu executive orders*) and the National
Archives and Records Administration (NARA) (https://www.archives.gov
/federal-register/executive-orders/). The NARA site is both browsable and
searchable from 1937 to the present. For very recent EOs, go to the White
House website (*site:whitehouse.gov executive orders*). The American Presidency Project has the full text of most executive orders from President
Washington to several months ago. NARA only has full text of EOs back
to 1995.

As far as these unofficial sites go, executive orders tend to show up first
on the White House website, then in the NARA disposition tables, and
finally in the American Presidency Project. A word of warning: the White
House website does not contain the official version of documents, including executive orders. In 2017, *USA Today* noted that the incorrect versions
of EOs had been posted on the White House site (Korte 2017).

The most important aspect of the NARA site is the invaluable disposition tables. It is important to know the current status of an EO and whether
it has been overturned. Typically, when a president of the opposing
party assumes office, they quickly issue EOs that overturn EOs from the
previous administration with which the new administration has policy
disagreements.

The print resource *Codification of Presidential Proclamations and
Executive Orders* is no longer in print, but it is available online via NARA
(*site:archives.gov Codification of Presidential Proclamations and Executive
Orders*).

National Archives and Records Administration. Office of the Federal Reg-
ister. *Codification of Presidential Proclamations and Executive Orders,
April 13, 1945–January 20, 1989.* Washington: Government Printing
Office, 1989. (HT 003781646).

Disposition for Executive Orders from 1937 to the present can be found on the NARA site at: https://www.archives.gov/federal-register/executive-orders. Because executive orders are often overturned, it is important to keep track of their disposition and whether they are currently in force or have been repealed or amended. Although not a definitive legal authority, the *Codification of Presidential Proclamations and Executive Orders* covers April 13, 1945 through January 20, 1989 (Truman administration through the Reagan administration; SuDocs AE 2.113:) and is a useful reference tool. (HT 003781646).

ProQuest claims to have the only complete collection of presidential executive orders and proclamations from 1789 to present (*site: site:-proquest.com Executive Orders and Presidential Proclamations*) (CIS Index 1987) in their add-on module to the ProQuest Congressional database.

Here is a sampling of selected famous executive orders:

1863 January 1. Lincoln Emancipation Proclamation

1933 Roosevelt. Confiscation of Gold EO 6102

1935 Roosevelt. Works Progress Administration EO 7034

1941 Roosevelt. Manhattan Project. EO 8807

    6 FR 3207, July 2, 1941

    Amended by: EO 9389, October 18, 1943

    Superseded by: EO 9913, December 26, 1947

1941 Roosevelt. Japanese Internment EO 9066, Signed: February 19, 1942

    7 FR 1407, February 25, 1942

    See: Transfer Order 40 of the Secretary of Defense dated July 22, 1949 (14 FR 4908); Proc. 4417, February 19, 1976

    Note: Proclamation 2714 of December 31, 1946, formally proclaimed the cessation of WWII hostilities.

1948 Truman. Desegregation of the Military EO 9981

    Signed: July 26, 1948

    13 FR 4313, July 28, 1948

    Revoked by: EO 11051, September 27, 1962

April 8, 1953. Truman. Nationalizing the Steel Industry EO 10340

    Signed: April 8, 1952

    17 FR 3139, April 10, 1952

1963 Johnson. Warren Commission EO 11130

    Signed: November 29, 1963

    28 FR 12789; December 3, 1963

On September 24, 1964, President Johnson sent a letter to each of the commission members discharging the commission.

Presidential Proclamations

Proclamations are most often used for ceremonial matters and usually do not have any legal significance. When they are important, they may be included in the US Code, Table V—Proclamations (https://uscode.house.gov/tables/usctable5.htm). Their publication patterns follow those of executive orders.

Here is a sampling of selected presidential proclamations:

1863 Lincoln. Emancipation Proclamation. Proclamation 95

1914 Wilson. Mother's Day Proclamation 1268

Sept. 8, 1974. Ford Proclamation 4311 Pardoning Nixon

2015. Obama. Leif Erikson Day, 2015, Proclamation 9344

2018. Trump American Red Cross Month, 2018. Proclamation 9700

Other Presidential Issuances

Other presidential issuances include presidential determinations, memoranda, notices, and orders. These generally follow the same publication practices as executive orders and presidential proclamations. Memoranda sometimes appear in the *Federal Register* but most often do not (Cooper 2001).

For an excellent overview of presidential issuances and directives generally, please see "Presidential Directives: Background and Overview" (Relyea 2008).

Sources of Presidential Documents

Presidential issuances are generally published in multiple places. The sources here are generally listed from first source in which the issuance tends to appear to the last.

- White House website. This is often the first place, although unofficial, to find issuances of all types (Google: *site:whitehouse.gov executive orders*).

- *Federal Register.* Often, presidential issues are released (prereleased) in unpublished form at federalregister.gov. The site will state when the official version will be published. The official version will be available via Govinfo.gov.

The Federalregister.gov site also has useful index pages to all issuances back to 1994 (Clinton): https://www.federalregister.gov/presidential-documents.

- *Compilation of Presidential Documents.* Formerly known as the *Weekly Compilation of Presidential Documents* and now the Daily Compilation, so for simplicity Govinfo.gov uses the *Compilation of Presidential Documents.* In practice, however, it still seems like a weekly (or greater) compilation.

- *Code of Federal Regulations*, Title 3. The is the only volume of CFR that doesn't supersede. Each year contains the issuances of that calendar year. Title 3 is published in January of each year and contains the issuances of the previous calendar year.

- *Public Papers of the Presidents.* The text of issuances does not appear in the Public Papers, only a listing with references to the *Federal Register.*

- Individually Published Materials. An example of this is the volume published by the Government Printing Office that compiles proclamations and executive orders of Herbert Hoover (GPO 1974).

The sources of issuances and their relative publication speed are summarized in Table 5.2.

The tool to see how presidential issuances affect the U.S. Code is found in the "tables" volumes of the Code. The easiest way to browse these online is through the U.S. House Office of the Law Revision Counsel. Table IV provides references in the Code to executive orders in the Code (http://uscode.house.gov/tables/usctable4.htm). Table V does the same thing for presidential proclamations (http://uscode.house.gov/tables/usctable5.htm). Table VI covers reorganization plans contained in the Code (http://uscode.house.gov/tables/usctable6.htm).

Another tool that is particularly helpful in locating how presidential issuances affect regulations is the "Parallel Table of Authorities and Rules," found within the separate volume, "CFR Index and Finding Aids" (Figure 5.1). Beginning in 2017, these can be found in Govinfo.gov. Select previous years,

Table 5.2   Sources of presidential issuances and speed of publication

Source	FR	CPD	3 CFR	PPP
Publication Speed	Next govt. day	Up to three weeks later	Annually in January	About five years after
Executive Orders	Full text	Full text	Full text	Indexing only
Proclamations	Full text	Full text	Full text	Indexing only
Determinations	Full text	Full text	Full text	Indexing only

back to 2009, can be found here: https://www.govinfo.gov/help/cfr.

[WEEKLY] COMPILATION OF PRESIDENTIAL DOCUMENTS

President Lyndon Johnson desired to have presidential statements and writings released on a more frequent basis than the *Public Papers of the Presidents*. As a result, beginning in 1965, the *Weekly Compilation of Presidential Documents* was initiated. With the beginning of the Obama administration in January 2009,

Authorities

Executive Orders—Continued	CFR
13626	40 Part 300
13628	31 Part 560
13637	15 Parts 730, 734, 743, 750
	22 Parts 120, 121, 122, 123, 124, 125, 126, 127, 128, 129, 130
	27 Part 447
13638	33 Part 138
13651	19 Part 12
13658	29 Part 10
13660	31 Part 589
13661	31 Part 589
13662	31 Part 589
13664	31 Part 558
13667	31 Part 553
13668	31 Part 576
13672	41 Parts 60-1, 60-2, 60-4, 60-50, 60-20
13706	Part 13
13712	31 Part 554
13808	45 Part 32

Determinations:	
2003-23	15 Parts 742, 746, 747, 750
2007-7	15 Part 746

Directives:	
May 17, 1972	22 Part 9A
	40 Part 11
Dec. 7, 1979	44 Part 351
June 25, 1982	12 Part 403
Mar. 11, 1983	12 Part 403

Memorandums:	
Nov. 10, 1961	5 Part 960
Aug. 21, 1963	47 Part 213
Dec. 30, 1977	40 Part 1515
Feb. 18, 1983	48 Part 2527
July 8, 2003	5 Part 724
May 11, 2010	5 Part 213

Reorganization Plans:	
1946 Plan No. 2	20 Part 25
1946 Plan No. 3	15 Parts 9, 10, 16
	43 Parts 1870, 3590
1950 Plan No. 2	8 Parts 3, 1003
1950 Plan No. 3	25 Parts 150, 250
	36 Parts 63, 64, 68, 71, 72

Reorganization Plans—Continued	CFR
	43 Parts 6, 1780
1950 Plan No. 5	15 Parts 4, 15, 30, 60
1950 Plan No. 6	20 Parts 1, 10, 701, 702, 703, 704, 718, 722, 725, 726, 801, 802
	29 Parts 19, 70, 71, 93, 541, 579, 580
	31 Part 21
1950 Plan No. 19	29 Parts 1, 3, 5, 6, 7, 8, 29, 30
1950 Plan No. 19	20 Parts 25, 61
1950 Plan No. 21	46 Parts 206, 294, 310, 385
1950 Plan No. 26	31 Parts 8, 10, 14
	45 Parts 7, 16, 204
1953 Plan No. 2	7 Parts 2, 11, 1902
1958 Plan No. 1	46 Parts 345, 346, 347
1961 Plan No. 3	14 Parts 384, 385
1961 Plan No. 7	46 Parts 202, 206, 294, 310, 385, 501
1965 Plan No. 2	15 Part 903
1968 Plan No. 2	24 Parts 1, 2
	49 Part 601
1968 Plan No. 3	40 Part 190
1970 Plan No. 2	2 Parts 1, 175
	41 Parts 101-37, 102-33
1970 Plan No. 3	40 Parts 2, 112, 121, 150, 160, 177, 178, 179, 190, 194
1970 Plan No. 4	50 Part 260
1973 Plan No. 1	31 Part 9
	46 Parts 345, 346, 347
1977 Plan No. 2	22 Parts 62, 63, 64, 65, 518
1978 Plan No. 1	29 Parts 1614, 1620, 1621, 1625, 1626, 1627, 1690
1978 Plan No. 2	5 Parts 151, 179, 850
1978 Plan No. 3	44 Parts 1, 2, 6, 8, 9, 15, 18, 59, 60, 61, 62, 63, 64, 65, 66, 67, 68, 70, 71, 72, 73, 75, 78, 79, 80, 150, 151, 201, 207, 208, 209, 295, 300, 302, 304, 312, 321, 323, 327, 329, 330, 331, 350, 351, 354, 360, 361
1978 Plan No. 4	26 Part 1
	29 Parts 2510, 2550, 2570
1979 Plan No. 3	15 Part 2009
1980 Plan No. 1	10 Part 1
1900 Plan No. 5	14 Part 30

Figure 5.1 Parallel Table of Authorities and Rules from *CFR Index and Finding Aids*, 2018, showing C.F.R. parts affected by various presidential issuances

publication was changed from weekly to daily, and the official name was changed to the *Daily Compilation of Presidential Documents*. GPO hosts the official version of the weekly and daily versions on Govinfo.gov, giving them a title that includes both, *Compilation of Presidential Documents*.

There are some differences between the early years of the Weekly Compilation and the Public Papers. In the Weekly Compilation, presidential issuances (executive orders and proclamations) are integrated with the daily happenings of the president. However, the corresponding Public Papers volumes merely list these in an appendix, with reference to the full text in the *Federal Register*. The same goes for announcements of intentions to nominate or other plans. They are listed in abbreviated form in an appendix at the end of the volume. Each issue of the Weekly Compilation has a section at the end of each issue with a list of nominations submitted to the Senate, acts approved by the president, and a Checklist of White House press releases.

PUBLIC PAPERS OF THE PRESIDENTS

In 1957 the *Public Papers of the Presidents* was established as the official published source for the president's public statements and formal issuances. It is published by the Office of the Federal Register (under NARA).

GPO has digitized the entire run of the Public Papers from Herbert Hoover through recent presidents (there is always about a six- to seven-year time lag, in which case you need to consult the *Compilation of Presidential Documents*). The exception (and it is a huge exception) are the papers of President Franklin Delano Roosevelt, whose papers were privately published and are not in the public domain.

Roosevelt, Franklin D. *Public Papers and Addresses of Franklin Delano Roosevelt.* Compiled by Samuel I. Rosenman New York, NY: Russell and Russell, 1969. 13 volumes. Available via HeinOnline.

A work-around for FDR is to use the American Presidency Project site (https://www.presidency.ucsb.edu/), where you will find most of his speeches and other presidential texts. This University of California, Santa Barbara project is the go-to place for texts of historic presidents from Washington onward. The site is nicely organized by category, such as eulogies, news conferences, inaugural addresses, state of the union addresses, weekly addresses, and so forth, and then by date.

On occasion, speeches planned by a president but never given are included. For example, two speeches that were prepared to be delivered ("advance text") by President Kennedy on November 22, 1963 but never were because of his assassination are included in the 1963 volume of the Public Papers.

GPO hosts the official, authenticated version of Public Papers, but full text of the digitized, printed volumes can also be found at the University of Michigan Digital Library (https://quod.lib.umich.edu/p/ppotpus/), the HathiTrust (HT 003932060), and in the Internet Archive (archive.org).

Volumes of the Public Papers prior to 1991 are made available through GPO's digitization efforts and are viewable at the volume-level, rather than individual statements, remarks, part, appendices, and photograph level.

The biggest differences between the Public Papers and the Compilation is that the Public Papers includes official photographs of the president at various events throughout the year and various appendices.

There is an official publication of presidential messages and papers from Washington through the beginning of the McKinley administration:

Richardson, James D. *A Compilation of the Messages and Papers of the Presidents, 1789–1897.* 10 vol. Washington, DC: Executive Office of the President: U.S. G.P.O. (SuDocs: Y 4.P 93/1:3/; also in Serial Set, Serial 3265-1 through 3265-10). HT 100335482, and in the Internet Archive (archive.org).

Richardson, James D. *A Compilation of the Messages and Papers of the Presidents.* New York, NY: Bureau of National Literature, 1917. 20 volumes. (HT 001137867).

SOCIAL MEDIA AND THE PRESIDENCY

Presidential and Federal Records Act Amendments of 2014 (P.L. 113-187, 128 Stat. 2003, 44 U.S.C. Ch. 22) brings the Presidential Records Act up-to-date with references to electronic records (that would include social media content). In *Knight First Amendment Institute at Columbia Univ. v. Trump* (928 F.3d 226, United States Court of Appeals for the Second Circuit, July 9, 2019, Decided) the court held that even the personal Twitter account of President Trump (@realdonaldtrump) is not independent of the presidency, and he cannot block users from that public account. Social media have forever altered the communication between the president and citizens. Barack Obama's YouTube channel (https://www.youtube.com/user/BarackObamadotcom/) was influential in his 2008 presidential campaign. Instagram was also used (https://www.instagram.com/barackobama/). President Trump followed suit with his Instagram (https://www.instagram.com/realdonaldtrump/) and YouTube presence. And then there are the generic White House social media accounts:

- https://www.youtube.com/user/whitehouse/
- https://www.instagram.com/whitehouse/
- https://www.facebook.com/WhiteHouse/
- https://twitter.com/whitehouse with the handle @WhiteHouse

May 18, 2015, was the first tweet from @POTUS, the official Twitter account of the president. The president's tweets are considered presidential records (National Archives 2017). While @POTUS works for the current occupant of the White House, for archiving purposes, the Twitter handle is modified after a presidential transition. President Obama's official tweets are now filed under @POTUS44 in Twitter. After President Trump leaves office, he will be @POTUS45. Stay tuned to the National Archives for further developments in archiving the social media records of the president.

TREATIES AND OTHER INTERNATIONAL AGREEMENTS

The word treaty has different meanings in international law and in U.S. law. Under U.S. law, the Constitution states that a treaty is an agreement made "by and with the Advice and Consent of the Senate" (Constitution, Article II, Section 2, Clause 2). Under international law, it refers to any legally binding agreement between nations. There is likely no government publication that does a better job of tracing the historical background of the treaty process from the beginnings of the country to the present day than "Treaties and Other International Agreements: The Role of the United States Senate" (U.S. Senate Committee on Foreign Relations 2001). This is another example of a congressional committee print that provides (in over 400 pages) extensive topical research.

Treaties can be highly complex. They are generally agreed to by the president and must be ratified by the Senate. This is where Senate Treaty Documents come in. They contain the text of a treaty as it is submitted to the U.S. Senate for ratification by the president.

Treaty Complexities

Nomenclature Differences

Various terms are used to refer to treaties. Sometimes the terms treaty, international agreement, international convention, charter, pact, accord, and do forth are used interchangeably; other times they have significant differences. Under U.S. law, there is a significant difference between the term treaty and the term executive agreement. Article II, Section 2, of the Constitution specifies that treaties are made "by and with the Advice and Consent of the Senate." A treaty is a binding international agreement. But under U.S. law, an executive agreement does not need the consent of the Senate, but it is only binding on domestic law, not internationally. To illustrate this, President Obama put the Paris Agreement through as an executive agreement ("Remarks Announcing the United States Formal Entry into the United Nations Framework Convention on Climate Change Paris Agreement in Hangzhou, China." Compilation of Presidential Documents, September 3, 2016). He did not submit it to the Senate for ratification. On June 1, 2017, President Trump announced that the United States would withdraw from the Paris Agreement. Because the United Nations' rules only allow a country to initiate a withdrawal three years after an agreement goes into force, the earliest date at which such action could take place would be November 4, 2019. Had the Paris Agreement been treated as a treaty under U.S. law rather than an executive agreement, it would have taken the consent of the Senate to withdraw.

Who Is Party?

The first question to ask when attempting to locate treaties is who is party to the treaty? In other words, what country or countries are involved? Is it bilateral (just between two countries) or multilateral (more than two countries)? Is the United States one of the parties or not? The State Department publication, *Treaties in Force*, published annually, contains two sections, one for bilateral treaties and the other for multilateral (*site:state .gov treaties in force*).

What Are the Treaty Dates?

There is much shifting of definitions among countries when it comes to treaties and treaty dates. The first treaty action is generally the signature by the head of state (the president in the case of the United States). The final date is ratification. There are other possible dates as well, such as date of accession. The United Nations Treaty Collection provides a glossary of terms relating to treaty actions that is helpful both for definitions and for clarity about treaty dates (*site:treaties.un.org Glossary*).

What Is the Treaty Status?

One needs to determine if the treaty is still in force. For treaties for which the United States is a party, the *Treaties in Force* document from the State Department is the go-to resource. For multilateral treaties, it is useful to go beyond U.S. publications and into UN document territory. Historically a print publication and now online, *Multilateral Treaties Deposited with the Secretary-General* (*site:treaties.un.org Multilateral Treaties*) presents dates of signature, accession (or succession), and ratification for all treaties organized under the UN Charter. This is a quick and useful way to compare the treaty status of the United States with other nations.

Treaty Text Sources

The earliest treaties of the United States were contained within *United States Statutes at Large*. Treaties continued to be included in the Statutes at Large through 1949. In 1950 treaties were published in *United States Treaties and Other International Agreements* (UST). This set is woefully behind in publication, as no volumes have been published since 1984. To access treaty text after 1984, *Treaties and Other International Acts Series* (TIAS) can be consulted. The following resources are essential in doing treaty research:

United States. Department of State. 1950–1984. *United States Treaties and Other International Agreements*. Washington, DC: Dept. of State; GPO, [vols. 1–35, 1950–1984]. SuDocs S 9.12:; Abbreviated UST. (HT 000888531).

United States. Department of State. 1946– *Treaties and Other International Acts Series*. Washington: GPO. SuDocs S 9.10:; Abbreviated TIAS. Issues from 1981 to present available on State Dept site. https://www.state.gov/tias/. (HT 003915471).

United States. Department of State. –1945. *Treaty Series*. Covers 1795–1945. This is the precursor to TIAS. Abbreviated TS. SuDocs: S 9.5/2:. (HT 001300856).

Wiktor, Christian L. 1976–1994. *Unperfected Treaties of the United States of America, 1776–1976*. Dobbs Ferry, NY: Oceana Publications. 9 vols.

KAV Agreements. Igor I. Kavass made a point to collect treaties before they showed up in the official sources, and, as a result, many treaties in this collection never show up in any other sources. Many federal depository libraries have KAV microfiche, but these are all online through the HeinOnline Treaty Library.

Kavass, Igor I., and Adolf Sprudz. 1982–. *Kavass's Current Treaty Index*. Buffalo, NY: William S. Hein. Companion service to *United States Treaty Index*.

Kavass, Igor I. 2001. *United States Treaty Index, 1776–2000 Consolidation*. Buffalo, NY: W. S. Hein. Indexes the KAV Agreements.

Most of the above publications can be accessed through the HeinOnline U.S. Treaties and Agreements Library. Older treaties are easily access through various treaty compilation volumes, listed below.

Malloy, William M., Denys P Myers, and Garfield Charles. 1910–1938. *Treaties, Conventions, International Acts, Protocols, and Agreements between the United States of America and Other Powers*. Compiled by William M. Malloy from 1910 through 1938, this compilation covers treaties issued from 1776 to 1937. Referred to as "Malloy." SuDocs: S 9.6:. (HT 001755414).

Miller, Daniel Hunter. 1931–1948. *Treaties and Other International Acts of the United States of America*. Washington, DC: GPO. 8 vols. Referred to as "Miller." SuDocs: S 9.5/1:. (HT 011354556).

Bevans, Charles I. 1968–1976. *Treaties and Other International Agreements of the United States of America, 1776–1949*. 13 volume set compiles treaties to which the United States was party from 1776–1949. Usually referred to as "Bevans," the name of the compiler. SuDocs: S 9.12/2 (HJT 001152265).

Kappler, Charles J. 1904–1941. *Indian Affairs: Laws and Treaties*. Stillwater, OK: Oklahoma State University Library. 7 vols. https://dc.library

.okstate.edu/digital/collection/kapplers. Also available in LLMC Digital, HeinOnline. Referred to as "Kappler." Originally 2 vols. in the Serial Set. S. Doc. 57-452, pts. 1 and 2; Serial 4153 and 4254; S. Doc. 58-319, pts. 1 and 2; Serial 4623 and 4624. Volume 2 reprints U.S. treaties with American Indians from 1778 to 1883. (HT 004384258, 000084638).

It is also helpful to note that volume 7 of *U.S. Statutes at Large* (7 Stat.) is itself a compilation of early Indian treaties from 1778 to 1842, and volume 8 (8 Stat.) is a compilation of early foreign treaties from 1778 to 1845.

Since treaties are, by definition, international in nature, it is often necessary to consult resources on foreign or international body websites. Many larger international treaties have their own websites replete with documentation. A drafting history of a treaty is called a *travaux préparatoires*. These documents serve a function similar to the legislative histories of U.S. public laws in that they supplement the interpretation of treaty text when the meaning is ambiguous or obscure (Dag Hammarskjöld Library 2018). Using this term in a web search will help greatly in locating relevant resources.

Several United Nations resources are helpful in determining the status of treaties whether the United States is party to them or not. Starting from the United Nations treaty website (https://treaties.un.org/), it is possible to access the entire United Nations Treaty Series from volume 1 (1947) to recent to get official treaty text in official languages. To see the status of multilateral treaties, go to the Status of Treaties Deposited with the Secretary-General (https://treaties.un.org/Pages/ParticipationStatus.aspx). This provides links to certified copies of treaty text; country participants; and dates of signature, acceptance, succession, and any declarations or reservations.

PRESIDENTIAL LIBRARIES

American presidents from Herbert Hoover onward have active presidential libraries, and some have museums as well. These are under the purview of the National Archives and Records Administration's Office of Presidential Libraries. The NARA website links to each of these libraries: https://www.archives.gov/presidential-libraries. In addition, a web search across all presidential libraries can be found at: https://www.archives.gov/presidential-libraries/search.html. This tool searches across events, press releases, exhibits, and other materials in the various libraries. This search engine does not serve as a replacement for browsing the finding aids maintained by each of the libraries.

EXERCISES

1. What was the exact quote from George W. Bush about the difference between a squirrel and a bomb?

    a) Find this quote in the *Weekly Compilation of Presidential Documents*. Give the exact citation.

    b) Find the same quote in the *Public Papers of the Presidents of the United States*. Give the exact citation.

2. There was an executive order, "Increasing Seat Belt Use in the United States." Give the following information:

    a) E.O. number:

    b) Date:

    c) Citation from *Code of Federal Regulations*: (___ C.F.R. ___) URL:

    d) Citation from *Federal Register*: (___ Fed. Reg. ___) URL:

    e) Citation from *Weekly Compilation of Presidential Documents*: (___ Weekly Comp. Pres. Doc. _____) URL:

    f) Using the archives.gov site, find the disposition of this E.O. Report everything that is stated about the disposition.

3. What was the first executive order issued by George W. Bush after September 11, 2001?

    a) E.O. number:

    b) Date:

    c) Title:

    d) All the sources in which this document text can be found.

4. In the *Code of Federal Regulations*, Title 6 concerns Homeland Security. Using LSA, find the section of the 6 CFR that changed during June 2006.

    a) Give the CFR part affected and the FR page. Copy and paste the heading and summary information only [no need to paste entire text from FR], OR, if using HeinOnline, provide the permanent URL.

    b) Find that section in CFR and copy and paste the first page only, OR, if using HeinOnline, provide the permanent URL.

5. The infamous Japanese internment presidential action was Executive Order 9066 (7 FR 1407, February 19, 1942; 3 CFR 1938–1943 Comp, pp. 1092–93). Using HeinOnline provide the following:

    a) a permanent link to the *Federal Register* citation.

    b) a permanent link to the CFR citation.

    c) a permanent link to the presidential proclamation issued by President Ford rescinding this EO (in the *Federal Register*).

    d) find the disposition of EO 9066 in the *Codification of Presidential Proclamations and Executive Orders*.

6. A student wants help researching the "Brady Bill." Provide the following:

   a) The actual short title of the act.

   b) The enacted bill number.

   c) The public law number.

   d) The citation to Statutes at Large.

   e) The permanent link to this public law in HeinOnline.

   f) The SuDocs numbers of two House reports on this act.

   g) The SuDocs numbers of two hearings.

   h) The SuDocs number of a GAO report about the implementation of the act.

   i) Bibliographic information about a CRS report concerning the act.

7. In 1984, a new SuDocs stem was created for the National Archives and Records Administration (NARA)—the AE stem. Previously, the GS class had been used for these materials. Find the background of why this happened. Be sure to document all resources used in the answer, using SuDocs numbers (if relevant), report numbers (if relevant), and other citations as necessary.

REFERENCES

American Presidency Project. 2019. "Executive Orders." Accessed September 29, 2019. https://www.presidency.ucsb.edu/statistics/data/executive-orders.

CIS Index to Presidential Executive Orders & Proclamations. 1987. Washington, DC: Congressional Information Service. 2 vols. in 21. Also available as an add-on module to ProQuest Congressional.

Cooper, Phillip J. 2001. "The Law: Presidential Memoranda and Executive Orders: Of Patchwork Quilts, Trump Cards, and Shell Games." *Presidential Studies Quarterly* 31, no. 1: 126–141.

Dag Hammarskjöld Library. 2018. "What Are Travaux Préparatoires and How Can I Find Them?" Accessed August 23, 2019. http://ask.un.org/faq/14541.

GPO (Government Printing Office). 1974. *Herbert Hoover: Proclamations and Executive Orders, March 4, 1929 to March 4, 1933.* Washington, DC: Government Printing Office. 2 vols. (HT 001137881, 004731703).

Korte, Gregory. 2017. "White House Posts Wrong Versions of Trump's Orders on Its Website." *USA Today* (online version). February 14. Accessed July 28, 2019. https://www.usatoday.com/story/news/politics/2017/02/14/white-house-posts-wrong-versions-trumps-orders-its-website/97845888/.

Lord, Clifford L., ed. 1944. *Presidential Executive Orders, Numbered 1-8030; 1862–1938.* New York: Archives Publishing Co. 2 volumes. (HT 011421358; also available via Internet Archive).

Lord, Clifford L., ed. 1979. *List and Index of Presidential Executive Orders: Unnumbered Series (1789–1941).* Wilmington, DE: Michael Glazie. 2 pts. Originally published in 1944. Available via HeinOnline.

Mayer, Kenneth R. 1999. "Executive Orders and Presidential Power." *Journal of Politics* 61, no. 2: 445–66.

National Archives. 2017. "Letter from the Archivist of the United States to Senators Claire McCaskill and Tom Harper". March 30. Accessed August 29, 2019. https://www.archives.gov/files/press/press-releases/aotus-to-sens -mccaskill-carper.pdf.

Relyea, Harold C. 2008. "Presidential Directives: Background and Overview." Congressional Research Service, 98-611 GOV. Updated November 26, 2008.

U.S. Senate Committee on Foreign Relations. 2001. "Treaties and Other International Agreements: The Role of the United States Senate." A Study Prepared for the Committee on Foreign Relations, United States Senate, by the Congressional Research Service, Library of Congress. Committee Print. S. Prt. 106-71. January 2001. Accessed August 23, 2019. http://purl .access.gpo.gov/GPO/LPS11657. (SuDocs: Y 4.F 76/2:S.PRT.106-71; HT 011338660).

6

Executive Branch Information Sources

The government organizational chart from the *United States Government Manual* (Figure 6.1) shows the extent of executive branch agencies (including independent and quasigovernmental entities). Since the days of FDR, the size and scope of government has increased enormously, and the more agencies there are, the more the publications proliferate.

How do we measure the extent of publications emanating from the executive branch? One way might be to examine the HathiTrust visualization of the distribution of federal documents in their repository (Figure 6.2).

In Figure 6.2, the Y classification represents congressional publications, particularly hearings and committee prints (Y 4), and publications of congressional commissions (Y 3) as represented in the HathiTrust digital collection. Nearly everything else on the visualization would be executive branch publications (with the exception of the judicial branch publications in the J or JU classifications or other legislative branch publications, such as GA (Government Accountability Office) or GP (Government Publishing Office). Of course, not all documents, especially current ones, are represented in Figure 6.2, but overall, it provides an understanding that executive branch documents are a larger proportion of documents than congressional documents (the Y SuDocs classification).

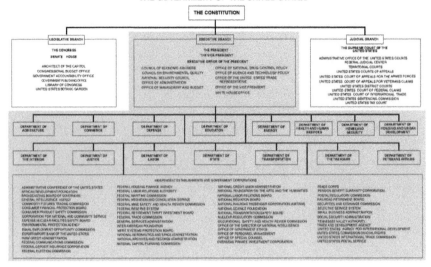

Figure 6.1 Organizational chart of the U.S. government focusing on the executive branch. *Source: U.S. Government Manual*, 2019.

Superintendent of Documents (SuDoc) Call Number Stem

This chart includes a breakdown of assigned SuDoc numbers. The default view is the top 10, but the chart can be manipulated to include all SuDocs or a single stem.

All SuDocs

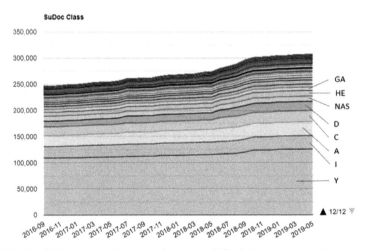

Figure 6.2 HathiTrust visualization of most prolific SuDocs stems. Courtesy of HathiTrust: https://www.hathitrust.org/usdocs_registry/stat_overview.

PROQUEST EXECUTIVE BRANCH DOCUMENTS

There is no reference tool more helpful to historical executive branch publications than the 1909 Checklist (mentioned in chapter 2). We repeat the citation here.

Checklist of United States Public Documents, 1789–1909: Congressional to Close of Sixtieth Congress, Departmental to End of Calendar Year 1909, compiled under the direction of the Superintendent of Documents. 3rd ed., rev. and enl. Washington, DC: GPO, 1911. (GP 3.2:C 41/2). (HT 001168034, 102499857).

For many years the Checklist had been considered a reliable (yet incomplete) account of publications of the executive branch from 1789 onward. In the 1990s, Congressional Information Service issued a microfiche collection with a corresponding index and finding aid that contains nearly all the documents mentioned in the original 1909 Checklist.

Congressional Information Service. *CIS Index to U.S. Executive Branch Documents, 1789–1909: Guide to Documents Listed in Checklist of U.S. Public Documents, 1789–1909, Not Printed in the U.S. Serial Set.* Bethesda, MD: Congressional Information Service, 1990–1997.

But after ProQuest acquired CIS publications with their purchase of LexisNexis government content, this entire series, along with additional documents not in the original series, was made available online for purchase or subscription as an add-on to the ProQuest Congressional database. Keep in mind that there are many documents that were not included in the 1909 Checklist, and these have been fugitive documents for many years. Also, the CIS project was unable to scan everything in the Checklist for the fiche project. However, a very high percentage has now been made available through the ProQuest online platform. Libraries fortunate enough to have access to this digitized collection have a high percentage of what a regional depository library would have in its collection when it comes to historical federal publications.

ANNUAL REPORTS OF EXECUTIVE AGENCIES

One thing executive agencies are known for is producing annual reports. Either because they are required by statute, by Congress, or some other way, annual reports are an excellent source for chronicling events, accomplishments, and failings of executive agencies. Over the years, tens of thousands of these serial publications have been issued.

In the SuDocs classification system, annual reports are usually designated as ".1:." For example, the annual report of the Department of Agriculture will

Table 6.1   Selected examples of federal annual reports with SuDocs classification

Agency	SuDocs Stem for Annual Reports
Agricultural Research Service	A 77.1:
National Technical Information Service	C 51.1:
Department of the Navy	D 201.1:
Energy Information Administration	E 3.1:
National Park Service	I 29.1:
Federal Bureau of Prisons	J 16.1:
Bureau of Labor Statistics	L 2.1:
Copyright Office	LC 3.1:
Council on Environmental Quality	PREX 14.1:
Agency for International Development	S 18.1:
Customs Service	T 17.1:
Federal Transit Administration	TD 7.1:
National Council on Disability	Y 3.D 63/3:1
Upper Colorado River Commission	Y 3.Up 6/4:1

be classed at A 1.1:; Department of Commerce at C 1.1:; Department of Defense at D 1.1:, and so forth. This pattern also holds true not only for the top-most part of cabinet-level agencies but also for subordinate agencies. Table 6.1 provides examples of some of these.

Annual reports tend to give a year in review, including statement of mission, goals, and objectives and performance review, accomplishments, expenditures, and often financial audit information. Perhaps the best way to see which agencies issue annual reports is to consult the *Guide to U.S. Government Publications* ("Andriot"), mentioned in chapter 2.

We will now focus on selected publications, databases, and services of selected executive branch agencies, as well as quasi agencies of the federal government.

EXECUTIVE OFFICE OF THE PRESIDENT

Established in 1939 (Reorganization Act of 1939 (5 U.S.C. 133-133r, 133t note) and E.O. 8248 of September 8, 1939), the Executive Office of the President now oversees many entities, including the Council of Economic Advisors, the National Security Council, the Office of Management and Budget (OMB), the Office of National Drug Control Policy, the Office of

Policy Development, the Office of Science and Technology Policy, and the Office of the United States Trade Representative.

BUDGET OF THE UNITED STATES GOVERNMENT

The massive *Budget of the United States Government* is issued annually by the Office of Management and Budget. It is published by the Government Publishing Office, usually in February or March of each year.

According to the Constitution, budget responsibilities lie with Congress. The House Committee on the Budget is responsible for drafting a budget resolution. By law, this must be enacted by April 15 (Congressional Budget and Impoundment Control Act of 1974, P.L. 93-344, 88 Stat. 297), but, in reality, this deadline has only been met six times from 1975 to present (CRS 2015).

The budget reconciliation process is described in detail, with tables showing several decades of legislative action and how long the reconciliation process took under the modern laws, the Congressional Budget and Impoundment Control Act of 1974, as amended (CRS 2015, 2016).

Budget Calendar

The timetable in Table 6.2 highlights the scheduled dates for significant budget events during a normal budget year.

The two main components of the budget are mandatory (also called entitlement) spending and discretionary spending, as well as paying interest on the national debt. Table 6.3 shows the major categories of budget revenue and spending.

OMB versus CBO

The Office of Management and Budget (OMB) has existed since 1939, with Reorganization Plan No. 1. However, the Congressional Budget Office (CBO) was created by the Congressional Budget and Impoundment Control Act of 1974 (P.L. 93-344, 88 Stat. 297) to provide Congress with an independent analysis and economic forecasts that were nonpartisan. The OMB provides the executive branch perspective on the budget, but the CBO provides its own analysis. It is common for annual estimates of the deficit to differ considerably between the two agencies.

Sources of Budget Documents

Budget documents back to 1923 can be found in the Federal Reserve Bank of St. Louis's Fraser project (https://fraser.stlouisfed.org/title/54/d16182).

Table 6.2   Budget calendar during a "normal" budget year

On or Before	Action to Be Completed
Between the 1st Monday in January and the 1st Monday in February	President transmits the budget.
Six weeks later	Congressional committees report budget estimates to Budget Committees.
April 15	Action to be completed on congressional budget resolution.
May 15	House consideration of annual appropriations bills may begin, even if the budget resolution has not been agreed to.
June 10	House Appropriations Committee to report the last of its annual appropriations bills.
June 15	Action to be completed on "reconciliation bill" by the Congress.
June 30	Action on appropriations to be completed by House.
July 15	President transmits Mid-Session Review of the Budget.
October 1	Fiscal year begins.

Source: Section 300 of the Congressional Budget Act of 1974, as amended (P.L. 93-344, 2 U.S.C. 631).

Table 6.3   Budget income and spending

Revenue (Income)	Spending
Individual Income Taxes	*Mandatory Spending*
Payroll Taxes	Social Security
Corporate Income Taxes	Medicare
Other	Medicaid
	Discretionary Spending
	Defense
	Non-Defense (Transportation, Education, Veteran's Benefits, Health, Housing Assistance, and Other Activities)
	Net Interest

Source: CBO 2019.

This is by far the easiest way to access older budget materials. In addition to the entire reports in PDF, Fraser also has an index in which individual tables with links to the year's tables with the same title are featured.

Budgets from 1996 to current can be found on Govinfo.gov. Older documents can be found in HathiTrust. (HT 002137316, 102222283). Individual selected years of the budget are easily navigable via the Internet Archive (search: *budget of the united states government*).

Navigating the Budget Documents

The federal budget is a multivolume work with great detail and complexity. The main budget document contains the president's goals and priorities in textual format, highlighting programs and priorities. Then, department by department, more in-depth goals are laid out. Summary tables toward the end provide projections 10 years into the future of anticipated receipts and outlays of money and their effects on the deficit. It also contains estimates of the previous year's expenditures compared with the request for the coming fiscal year.

The "Analytical Perspective" volume contains analyses that highlight selected budget areas. Economic assumptions, long-term budget outlook, trends in the federal debt and interest on the debt, trends in employment, household consumption, educational outcomes, health conditions, crime and security, and environment and energy are among the many topics considered in historical perspective in light of the proposed budget. Justification will be provided for any government reorganization, proposed new programs, or elimination of existing programs or agencies. Special topics in the volume include aid to state and local governments, "Strengthening Federal Statistics" (mentioned in greater detail in chapter 9 on statistics), research and development, and topics of current interest such as cybersecurity, drug control, and credit and insurance.

A massive appendix volume contains information designed primarily for use by appropriations committees. It provides great detail, not just for the proposed budget but for actual expenditures for the past fiscal year.

The Historical Tables volume is a wealth of data, often going back to 1789, showing budget receipts, outlays, surpluses, and deficits over time. Additional volumes are published and may vary from year to year.

ECONOMIC REPORT OF THE PRESIDENT

The *Economic Report of the President* is an important publication. It is written annually by the chairman of the Council of Economic Advisors (administratively under the Executive Office of the President). It is transmitted to Congress no later than ten days after the submission of the budget.

This is a major statistical publication, with up to 50 years of time series data on economic topics from gross domestic product, gross value added by sector, personal consumption expenditures, disposition of personal income, sources of personal income, civilian labor force, changes in consumer price indexes, and historical stock prices. It is transmitted to Congress, and thus shows up in the Serial Set as a House document "document edition." It is also issued as a "department edition" and is classed using the SuDocs stem of the president under whom it was issued. The series began in 1947 under President Truman. From 1947 through 1952, midyear reports were also issued. For easy access, these reports have been collected in one place in the American Presidency Project (Google: *site:presidency.ucsb.edu economic report president*). The St. Louis Federal Reserve's FRASER project has all reports digitized back to 1947, with the additional capability of drilling down to individual tables in each of the reports: https://fraser.stlouisfed.org/title /45. The HathiTrust has multiple records, with various years available. (HT 000517807, 007405907, 100942759, 100892746). Official texts going back to 1995 can be found on Govinfo: https://www.govinfo.gov/app/collection/ERP.

Since the *Economic Report of the President* is sent to Congress, it is included in the Serial Set. Thus, there are two places one can find this: the documents edition (under SuDocs stem as noted in Table 6.4 and in the Serial Set. Searching for the titles *Economic Report of the President* or *Midyear Economic Report of the President* in any of the commercial Serial Set products will bring up the document editions of these reports. Table 6.4 will be useful for those accessing print versions in depository libraries. Keep in mind, however, that individual libraries may elect to shelve these materials under only one of these numbers (perhaps the latest one) to make life easier for users.

EXECUTIVE BRANCH INFORMATION RESOURCES

Executive branch agencies and independent agencies have published many important resources over the years. This section is an attempt to call attention to some of them. The listing is format-independent, meaning that I will sometimes refer to print resources, other times to online, and sometimes the resources will be in both formats. In some cases, the government information is offered through commercial vendors. Resources mentioned in other parts of this book will not necessarily be duplicated here. Many agency resources are listed chapters on statistics, census, mapping, intellectual property, or technical and scientific information. Individual titles can be cross-checked using the index at the end of the book.

Table 6.4   SuDocs numbers for locating the *Budget of the United States* and the *Economic Report of the President* in depository libraries

Administration	Budget	Economic Report
Roosevelt, F.D. (1933–1945)	T 51.5:932, 933, 934, 935, 936, 937, 938, 939, 940	
	PR 32.107:[941-946]	
Truman (1947–1953)	PR 33.107	PR 33.10
Eisenhower (1954–1961)	PR 34.107	PR 34.10
Kennedy (1962–1963)	PREX 2.8	PR 35.9
Johnson (1964–1969)	PREX 2.8	PR 36.9
Nixon (1970–1974)	PREX 2.8	PR 37.9
Ford (1975–1977)	PREX 2.8	PR 38.9
Carter (1978–1981)	PREX 2.8	PR 39.9
Reagan (1982–1989)	PREX 2.8	PR 40.9
Bush, H. W. (1990–1993)	PREX 2.8	PR 41.9
Clinton (1994–2001)	PREX 2.8	PR 42.9
Bush, G. W. (2002–2009)	PREX 2.8	PR 43.9
Obama (2010–2017)	PREX 2.8	PR 44.9
Trump (2018–)	PREX 2.8	PREX 1.30

It is impossible to cover all the helpful tools and databases offered by executive branch agencies. This section will highlight selected resources. Also see Appendix F, where additional resources are mentioned.

DEPARTMENT OF AGRICULTURE

The department of agriculture (SuDocs stem: A) has a rich publication history, given that for many years the United States was largely an agriculture-driven economy. In 1880, 43.8 percent of the population lived on farms (Historical Statistics 2006).

Yearbook of Agriculture

An important historical publication documenting the nation's agricultural contributions is the *Yearbook of Agriculture* (1895–1992). Since 1938, each volume also has a distinctive title. The title varies a bit through the years: 1894–1919, *Yearbook of the United States Department of Agriculture* (HT 007417728); 1920–1922, *Yearbook* (HT 007412342); 1923–1925,

Agriculture Yearbook (HT 007395638); 1926–1978, *Yearbook of Agriculture* (HT 007395770); 1979, *United States Department of Agriculture Yearbook* (HT 102263725) (SuDocs A 1.10:). The online versions within the Internet Archive are especially fun to peruse. The individual volumes can be most easily used through the Internet Archive: https://archive.org/details/usda-yearbookofagriculture.

ARS and ERS

Several agencies within the department stand out for their research and publication contributions. The Agricultural Research Service (ARS) (SuDocs stem A 77) is the main scientific research agency within the department of agriculture. Research topics include human nutrition, food safety, animal health, aquaculture, plant diseases, crop production, water availability, watershed management, soil and air, and biorefining. A Google search such as this: *site:ars.usda.gov filetype:pdf* will pull up thousands of PDF files demonstrating the breadth and depth of their research projects.

The mission of the Economic Research Service (ERS) (SuDocs stem A 93) is to anticipate trends and emerging issues in the realms of agriculture, food, and the environment to inform policy-makers and the public. ERS contains a treasure trove of dozens of agriculture-related databases. Topic include farm income and wealth statistics, food price outlook, adoption of genetically engineered crops, crop statistics for all major crops, bioenergy, commodity outlook, hurricane impacts on agriculture, animal products, textile data, and fertilizer use—and I'm just scratching the surface. In the Food Environment Atlas, there is mapping showing the change in numbers of fast-food restaurants (SuDocs: A 93.64/2:; http://purl.access.gpo.gov/GPO/LPS120190).

Over 70 databases are listed on their website, but among them is Ag and Food Statistics: Charting the Essentials; Agricultural Baseline Database; Agricultural Productivity in the U.S.; Cost Estimates of Foodborne Illnesses; County-Level Data Sets [county level population change, poverty rates, education attainment, and unemployment rates/median household income]; Data Visualizations; Farm Income and Wealth Statistics; Food Price Outlook; Major Land Uses; State Fact Sheets; and U.S. Bioenergy Statistics.

Agricola versus PubAg

The National Agriculture Library's online catalog (Agricola) contains two subsets of records. The first contains indexing and abstracting for journal articles, and the other is bibliographic records for books, serials, and other formats typically found in a library.

PubAg (https://pubag.nal.usda.gov/) is the National Agricultural Library's (NAL) search system. It contains selected full-text articles, as well as citations to peer-reviewed content that can be found elsewhere. PubAg has some overlapping coverage with Agricola, but its emphasis is on peer-reviewed journal articles, whereas Agricola emphases more popular magazine articles. Also, the interface is different. Serious searchers should consult both interfaces to have more complete results.

Want to find out the nutrient value of foods that you eat? The *USDA Food Composition Database* (Google: *USDA Food Composition Database*) can be searched by brand name or nutrient.

DEPARTMENT OF COMMERCE

The Department of Commerce (SuDocs stem C) has an amazing array of subagencies including the Bureau of Economic Analysis, International Trade Administration, National Centers for Environmental Information, Census Bureau, and the National Oceanic and Atmospheric Administration.

Bureau of Economic Analysis

According to their website, they produce "some of the world's most closely watched statistics." This small agency has great power with its reporting of the gross domestic product (GDP), personal income and outlays, and U.S. International Trade in Goods and services regular data releases (*site:bea.gov news release archive*). Its partnership with the Federal Reserve Bank of St. Louis's FRED project (Federal Reserve Economic Data) enables smartphone users with the FRED app easy access to current economic data.

Export Administration Regulations (EAR)

The Bureau of Industry and Security's rather obscure name conceals the agency's real purpose: export control, treaty compliance, ensuring U.S. strategic technology leadership, monitoring the U.S. defense industrial base, and supporting U.S. technology leadership in industries essential to national security. The site contains Export Administration Regulations (EAR) (*site:doc.gov ear*; http://purl.access.gpo.gov/GPO/LPS5135; SuDocs: C 63.25/2:; HT 002709969, 000072622, 101745129), statistical analyses of trade with selected countries, and downloadable datasets. The EAR site presents the regulations from 15 CFR 730–774.

International Trade Administration

Businesses exporting products to foreign countries will benefit from publications and data from the International Trade Administration (ITA). From their "Basic Guide to Exporting" to their web portal export.gov, the agency provides assistance to businesses interested in going global. Statistics and infographics are provided that show export impact by U.S. state, by jobs supported, and by industry.

The U.S. Commercial Service is the trade promotion arm of the ITA. Representatives operate in over 100 U.S. cities and over 75 countries to assist businesses. Power Google searching for this agency needs to consider both *site:trade.gov* and *site:export.gov* in search strategies.

National Centers for Environmental Information (NCEI)

The NCEI is part of the National Oceanic and Atmospheric Administration (NOAA) and hosts dozens of databases covering bathymetric data; climate modelling; monthly, seasonal, and annual climate reports; earthquake data; storm data; tsunami data; ocean climates; geomagnetism; world ocean database; paleoclimatology database; land-based station data sets; and interactive radar, just to mention a few (*site:ncei.noaa.gov access*). "Monthly Climatic Data for the World" (*site:noaa.gov monthly climatic data world*); http://purl.access.gpo.gov/GPO/LPS2871; SuDocs: C 55.287/63:) has data back to 1948. "Climate Data Online" (*site:noaa.gov climate data*; SuDocs: C 55.287/64:; http://purl.fdlp.gov/GPO/gpo9262) has searching, mapping, and data access tools to unlock years of climate research. "Local Climatological Data" provides weather station data for the United States (*site:noaa.gov local climatological data*; SuDocs: C 55.286/6-[number for state]).

Long-time users may recall its former name, the National Climatic Data Center. Up until 2009, NCDC data was offered via subscription but was freely available in depository libraries. In 2009, it was opened up to all with no more usage fees.

United States Census Bureau

This book already devotes two chapters to census matters. We discuss in great detail the Decennial Census of Population and Housing and the Economic Census in chapters 10 through 12. However, we need to highlight here some other publications and databases published by the bureau. Census publication can be found in depository libraries with SuDocs stem C 3.

The Census website is most helpful. It not only points to topics featured on its own site, but directs users to the appropriate site with when the bureau is not the primary source of information. For example, when searching for *births and deaths* on the Census web index, results in the message, "The U.S. Census Bureau is not the primary source for data on births and deaths. The primary source is the National Center for Health Statistics (NCHS). NCHS can provide information on number of births, percent unmarried mothers, number of deaths, infant mortality and more." Similar messages are provided for searches on *marriage, obesity, crime,* and *mental health.*

Statistical Abstract of the United States

For many years the *Statistical Abstract of the United States* (SuDocs stem C 3.134:) was considered a "bible" of sorts for U.S. government statistics. A complete archive of these annual publications can be found on the Census website, from 1878 until 2012, when it ceased publication (*site:census.gov statistical abstract*). These volumes are also available from the Internet Archive and HathiTrust (007911858, 004487756). One of the noteworthy features of the publication was inclusion of nongovernmental statistical tables. These sources included the American Medical Association, the American Osteopathic Association, National Education Association, ACT (college testing), National Center for State Courts, Investment Company Institute, National Academy of Social Insurance, National Automobile Dealers Association, Airlines for America, National Ski Areas Association, National Collegiate Athletic Association, and National Sporting Goods Association, to mention just a few.

ProQuest took it upon themselves to continue publishing a fee-based commercial version of the *Statistical Abstract* that included a browsable and searchable archive going back to the 1878 edition.

Other digitized print materials on the Census website include *Historical Statistics of the United States, Colonial Times to 1970* (HT 000707742, 007169391; SuDocs: C 3.134/2:H 62/789-970/) (*site:census.gov Historical Statistics of the United States*). This resource is online and brought up-to-date by Cambridge University Press's fee-based Historical Statistics of the United States: Millennial Edition Online, where tables are downloadable in PDF and Excel formats.

Among the many other bureaus/agencies within the Commerce Department are the Bureau of Economic Analysis, the International Trade Administration, National Institute of Standards and Technology, National Oceanic and Atmospheric Administration, National Technical Information Service, and the U.S. Patent and Trademark Office.

What's with All the Book Colors?

It is very common to use shorthand terminology to refer to government-related publications. Red book, Blue book, Green book, Plum book—all these refer to different publications. Here is a partial list of these resources in the context of government information. Of course, there are many color books that aren't related to governmental contexts. We aren't addressing the blue book for car values, for example. Don't worry, we won't look at your "little black book"!

Red book—*Principles of Federal Appropriations Law* (SuDocs: GA 1.14:F 31; *site:gao.gov "red book"*), also known as the Red book, is the Government Accountability Office's multivolume treatise concerning federal fiscal law. Red Book can also be a reference to New York State's legislative manual.

Blue book—State blue books are generally government manuals issued by state governments or legislatures. These are not to be confused with "Project Blue Book," an investigation into UFO reports between 1947 and 1969 Google: *site:fbi.gov project blue book vault*.

In the closely allied legal community, the "Bluebook" is the official citation style manual. *The Bluebook: A Uniform System of Citation* is the style manual used by attorneys and legal scholars.

Green book—*Background Material and Data on the Programs within the Jurisdiction of the Committee on Ways and Means* (HT 002574525, 100892781; SuDocs: Y 4.W 36:WMCP [Congress-number]; *site:house.gov "green book"*). Published by House Committee on Ways and Means, it lists all the social welfare programs of the United States. It also contains many statistical tables on families, poverty, employment and unemployment, earnings, and budget tables. Typically issued as Committee Print.

But "green book" is also used to refer to two more obscure government titles, the first one being *Standards for Internal Control in the Federal Government.* (HT 011422373; SuDocs: GA 1.13/21:[rept. no.]; *site:gao.gov "green book"*). Published by the Government Accountability Office, this work sets the standards for an effective internal control system for federal agencies.

The second other "green book" is published by the Treasury Department's Bureau of Fiscal Service. *Green Book [year]: A Guide to Federal ACH Payments and Collections.* (HT 003581361; SuDocs: T 63.119:G 82; http://purl.access.gpo.gov/GPO/LPS4942; *site:treasury .gov "green book"*). The Automated Clearing House (ACH) is an electronic funds transfer system that facilitates payments throughout the United States.

Beige book—*Summary of Commentary on Current Economic Conditions by Federal Reserve District* is the official title (*site:federalreserve.gov beige book*). This Federal Reserve System title is published eight times per year, showing information on current economic conditions in each of the twelve districts.

Orange book—*Approved Drug Products with Therapeutic Equivalence Evaluations.* Published by the Food and Drug Administration (HT 000069691, 000681350; SuDocs: HE 20.4715/2; http://purl.fdlp.gov//GPO/gpo986; *site:fda.gov orange book*), it identifies drugs approved by the Food and Drug Administration based on their safety and effectiveness.

Pink book—*Epidemiology and Prevention of Vaccine-Preventable Diseases.* Published by the Centers for Disease Control and Prevention. (HT 102440146; SuDocs: HE 20.7970:; http://purl.access.gpo.gov/GPO/LPS227; *site:cdc.gov pink book*).

Plum book—*United States Government Policy and Supporting Positions.* Published by the Senate Committee on Homeland Security and Governmental Affairs and House Committee on Government Reform alternately after each Presidential election. The Plum book lists over 7,000 federal civil service leadership and support positions in the legislative and executive branches of the federal government. (HT 007415533; SuDocs: Y 4.P 84/10:P 75/; https://purl.access.gpo.gov/GPO/LPS6760). Google: *plum book site:gov.*

Yellow book—*Government Auditing Standards,* again from the Government Accountability Office (GAO), provides background information for conducting financial audits. (HT 011326717, 101690920; SuDocs: GA 1.2:AU 2/14; http://purl.access.gpo.gov/GPO/LPS37283; *site:gao.gov "yellow book"*).

Yellow book may also refer to commercial directories published by Leadership Connect. Although these are not government publications, they assist in navigating complex government bureaucracies. Titles include *Congressional Yellow Book, Federal Yellow Book, Federal Regional Yellow Book, State Yellow Book, Municipal Yellow Book, Judicial Yellow Book, Directory of State Court Clerks and County Courthouses,* and *Federal-State Court Directory.*

DEPARTMENT OF DEFENSE

The Department of Defense (SuDocs stem D) was created after World War II (63 Stat. 597). The original military department was the War Department (SuDocs stem W), and briefly there was the Military Establishment (1947–49) (61 Stat. 495).

As noted in chapter 1, the .gov internet domain accounts for the most U.S. government websites, but second to that is the .mil internet domain for the various branches of the armed forces. Yet not all military or defense-related sites are .mil. The Defense Department itself is defense.gov. Using the site-specific Google searching described in chapter 1, the primary ".mil" websites can be effectively searched by topic or file type.

- Army: https://www.army.mil/
- Navy: https://www.navy.mil/
- Marines: https://www.marines.mil/
- Air Force: https://www.af.mil/
- Coast Guard: https://www.uscg.mil/

Center of Military History

The Center of Military History (SuDocs Stem D 114) has published hundreds of monographs covering military history. Although many of their more recent works are accessible through their website (*site:army.mil military history*), by browsing the *Publications of the U.S. Army Center of Military History* (HT 003117742), you can see titles that you can, in turn, pull up in HathiTrust.

Military Records and Research

Military records are transferred to the National Archives and Records Administration (NARA), which is the ultimate source for historical military and veterans' records. These are paper records only and are not available online. Most commonly requested are the military personnel and/or medical records that are necessary for filing for benefits or entitlements. But historians and genealogists also have an interest in older materials. See the NARA website (archives.gov) for complete instructions for requesting records. NARA has records for military service from the Revolutionary War onward, most of which can be discovered by searching the NARA catalog at https://catalog.archives.gov/. Since many of these pages are open to Google searching, you should also try some creative searching. For example, *site:archives.gov Service Record Cards*; *site:archives.gov Service Record Anthony Gallatin*; or *site:archives.gov regiment casualty list*.

An excellent starting point for research into military and genealogy records at NARA is:

Eales, Anne Bruner, and Robert M. Kvasnicka, eds. 2000. *Guide to Genealogical Research in the National Archives of the United States*. Washington, DC: National Archives and Records Administration. (HT 003834362).

Military registers serve as an important record for commissioned officers of military branches. Larger depository libraries may have some of these holdings in print, as indicated by the SuDocs numbers in the citations below. The large runs are also available through HathiTrust.

U.S. Army Register. War Department 1802–1950 by the War Department, Adjutant General's Office (W 3.11) National Military Establishment, Adjutant General's Office 1947-48 (M 108.8), Department of Defense, Adjutant General Directorate 1949– (D 102.9). Available in HathiTrust (HT 012314227, 010045437, 101744825, 100113493).

Register of the Commission and Warrant Officers of the Navy of the United States, Including Officers of the Marine Corps. United States. Bureau of Naval Personnel. (N 1.10). Later title: *Register of Commissioned and Warrant Officers of the United States Navy and Marine Corps and Reserve officers on Active Duty* (HT 010111371).

Ancestry.com has incorporated numerous government records into its database, including muster rolls (lists of soldiers or sailors and the units or ships to which they were assigned) and draft registration records.

DEPARTMENT OF EDUCATION (SUDOCS STEM ED)

The Department of Education was created in 1979 by P.L. 96-88 (93 Stat. 671), and its documents are classified in the ED SuDocs stem. Before it was a separate department, it was classed as follows (Table 6.5):

Education Resources Information Center (ERIC)

The Education Resources Information Center was created in 1966 and is now administratively under the National Library of Education (founded

Table 6.5   Historical development of education agencies in the United States as seen through SuDocs numbers

SuDocs Stem	Agency Name	Dates
I 16	Education Bureau	1867–1929
I 16	Education Office	1929–1939
FS 5	Education Office	1939–1969
HE 5	Education Office	1970–1972
HE 19.100	Education Office	1972–1979
ED 1	Education Department	1979–

in 1994). The ERIC database is used by academics, educators, researchers, policymakers, and the general public to find peer-reviewed journal articles, book chapters, theses and dissertations, and other published materials in the broad fields of education. It is important to know a bit about the history of the product in order to understand what kinds of materials are being indexed and how to locate them.

The ERIC database contains two kind of materials, ERIC Documents (designated with an ED prefix to the document number (ex. ED295201)) and ERIC Journals (designated with an EJ prefix (e.g., EJ1149893)). In the print era the ERIC documents were indexed in *Resources in Education*, a government publication (ED 1.310). Journal articles were indexed in *Current Index to Journals in Education: CIJE* (ED 1.310/4). Although the indexes were distributed through the depository program, the materials being indexed were generally not government publications themselves—kind of analogous to the situation with the *PubMed* database where the database itself is a government production, but the materials indexed are not.

Originally the database indexing was done by 16 subject-based clearinghouses, most of which were affiliated with colleges or universities. The original dissemination plan (for the ED documents) was a state-of-the-art technology of the time: microfiche. Although microfiche distribution was halted in 2004, many academic libraries still maintain their fiche collections. There are occasions when there may be full text available on ERIC fiche that is not currently available online, which is why some institutions are reluctant to part with their collections. ERIC is now an all-electronic service, and the 16 clearinghouses are no longer necessary. Those wishing to delve further into the early history of the ERIC project should read "50 Years of ERIC," available on their website (https://eric.ed.gov/pdf/ERIC _Retrospective.pdf).

The ERIC database currently indexes over 1,000 journals and contains over 1.6 million items. Over 350,000 of the ED documents are available in full text through the ERIC site. Those that are not include commercially published books, doctoral dissertations, and other materials with copyright restrictions. Many of these materials are "gray literature," such as conference papers, reports, or independently submitted papers. The EJ materials are generally peer-reviewed materials, whereas the ED materials are not.

The government version of the ERIC database is fully functional and integrated with the ERIC thesaurus. The thesaurus is extremely well developed and generally follows international standards for thesaurus development (https://www.niso.org/publications/ansiniso-z3919-2005-r2010). It is both searchable and browsable (https://eric.ed.gov/?ti=all).

Since the database records themselves are the product of a government agency, they are available for commercial vendors to fold into their content offerings. Vendors such as ProQuest, EBSCO, and Ovid are among the many vendors that take the ERIC database content, as well as the thesaurus, and fold it into their own interfaces. They add value to the content by providing full-text links to the EJ content (something the government ERIC database does not do) and, at the same time, points to the ED content that is hosted on the ERIC website.

College Navigator

Although we pay more attention to the National Center for Education Statistics in chapter 9, College Navigator (https://nces.ed.gov/college navigator/) deserves attention here. The database provides excellent background for those shopping for a college or university, whether for an undergraduate degree or higher. Users can browse for programs by major and limit to public, private, two-year, four-year, and so forth. Background information for each institution is given, including tuition, financial aid, enrollment, admission percent admitted and enrolled, retention and graduation rates, athletics, accreditation, and campus crime.

DEPARTMENT OF ENERGY

Another rather new department in terms of government agencies, the Department of Energy's materials are classed in SuDocs stem E. Depository libraries tend to have lots of microfiche from the Energy Department, either as Es from the 1980s or Atomic Energy Commission fiche. Prior to 1997, the DOE disseminated most of its technical reports in microfiche (Whitson and Davis 2001). Now these are largely available through OSTI .gov (see discussion in chapter 14).

Energy Videos

Over 400 educational videos are viewable from the video site (https://www.energy.gov/videos). The searchable and browsable interface covers topics ranging from energy efficiency, energy sources and usage, to science and innovation.

Science.gov

Science.gov is an interagency collaboration between the Departments of Agriculture, Commerce, Defense, Education, Energy, Health and Human Services, Homeland Security, and Transportation; the Environmental

Protection Agency; the National Aeronautics and Space Administration; the National Science Foundation; and the U.S. Government Publishing Office. Since the site is maintained by the Department of Energy, it is mentioned here. It is the U.S. contribution to WorldWideScience.org (https://www.science.gov/about.html).

Records in the database come from about 60 databases of the collaborating agencies. Clicking on a title will launch the bibliographic record from the site of origin (PubMed, NASA Astrophysics Data System, ERIC, PubAg, etc.).

DEPARTMENT OF HEALTH AND HUMAN SERVICES

Now classed as SuDocs stem HE, the health and human services functions were previously class as FS, as shown in Table 6.6.

The current website is https://www.hhs.gov/, and just a few of their many resources are highlighted below.

National Library of Medicine

The National Library of Medicine produces PubMed/Medline and the MeSH controlled vocabulary to go along with it. See chapter 14 for a more complete discussion.

Medicare Coverage Database

The Medicare Coverage Database (*site:cms.gov medicare coverage database*) contains all national and local coverage determinations (in other words, what Medicare will pay for and what it will not pay for).

Table 6.6   Historical development of health and human services agencies in the United States as seen through SuDocs numbers

SuDocs Stem	Agency Name	Dates
FS 1	Health, Education, and Welfare Department, Office of Secretary	1953–1969
HE 1	Health, Education, and Welfare Department, Office of Secretary	1970–1979
HE 1	Health Human Services Department, Office of Secretary	1979–

Grants.gov

Grants.gov (https://www.grants.gov/) is governed by the Office of Management and Budget, but it is managed by the Department of Health and Human Services. It is a centralized location for discovering and applying for federal funding opportunities. Over 1,000 grant programs are promoted through this database. The search interface defaults to all available grants, with facets on the left to limit to funding type, eligibility, major category (agriculture, business, disaster relief, education, environment, health, humanities, etc.), and agency. Free user registration is required, but users can apply directly from the database interface.

DEPARTMENT OF HOMELAND SECURITY

After the events of September 11, 2001, a major reorganization of national security-related agencies resulted in the creation of the Department of Homeland Security. The Homeland Security Act of 2002 (P.L. 107-296, 116 Stat. 2135) created the Department of Homeland Security, bringing under one umbrella agencies that previously had been under several different departments. S. Rpt. 107-175 provides a vivid example of the legislative background and intent leading to the creation of this act. In the "Background and Need for Legislation" section of this report is a confounding chart used by the White House to keep track of all homeland–security–related agencies. Tables 6.7 through 6.13 below show how the histories through the SuDocs numbers of several of the agencies brought under the Homeland Security umbrella.

Table 6.7   U.S. Customs and Border Protection Bureau

SuDocs Stem	Agency Name	Dates
T 17	Customs Division	1870–1927
T 17	Customs Bureau	1927–1973
T 17	Customs Service	1973–2003
HS 4.100	U.S. Customs and Border Protection Bureau	2003–

Table 6.8   Transportation Security Administration (TSA)

SuDocs Stem	Agency Name	Dates
TD 4.800	Federal Aviation Administration	1967–2002
TD 1.200	Transportation Security Administration	2002–2003
HS 4.300	Transportation Security Administration	2003–

Table 6.9   Federal Emergency Management Agency (FEMA)

SuDocs Stem	Agency Name	Dates
D 14	Defense Civil Preparedness Agency	1972–1979
GS 13	Federal Preparedness Agency	1976–1979
HH 12	Federal Disaster Assistance Administration	1973?–1979
FEM 1	Federal Emergency Management Agency	1979–2003
HS 5.100	Federal Emergency Management Agency	2003–

Table 6.10   U.S. Fire Administration

SuDocs Stem	Agency Name	Dates
C 58	National Fire Prevention and Control Administration	1974–1978
C 58	United States Fire Administration	1978–1979
FEM 1.100	United States Fire Administration	1979–2003
HS 5.200	U.S. Fire Administration	2003–

Table 6.11   U.S. Coast Guard

SuDocs Stem	Agency Name	Dates
T 24	Life-Saving Service	1878–1915
T 33	Revenue-Cutter Service	1894–1915
T 47	Coast Guard	1915–1917
N 24	Coast Guard	1917–1919
T 47	Coast Guard	1946–1966
TD 5	Coast Guard	1966–2003
HS 7	U.S. Coast Guard	2003–

Table 6.12   U.S. Citizenship and Immigration Services

SuDocs Stem	Agency Name	Dates
T 21	Immigration Bureau	1891–1903
C 7	Immigration Bureau	1903–1906
C 7	Immigration and Naturalization Bureau	1906–1913
L 3	Immigration Bureau	1913–1933
L 6	Naturalization Bureau	1913–1933
L 15	Immigration and Naturalization Bureau	1933–1940
J 21	Immigration and Naturalization Service	1940–2003
HS 8	U.S. Citizenship and Immigration Services	2003–

Table 6.13   U.S. Secret Service

SuDocs Stem	Agency Name	Dates
T 34	U.S. Secret Service	1865–2003
HS 9	U.S. Secret Service	2003–

FEMA Data Visualizations

The Federal Emergency Management Agency (FEMA) has several data visualization tools that enable easy access to disaster data. The Summary of Disaster Declarations and Grants (*site:fema.gov summary disaster declarations visualization*) features clicking on a state and viewing total numbers (since 1953) of severe storms, floods, tornadoes, snow events, droughts, hurricanes, and so forth. Data can be viewed down to the county level. There are also data visualizations for fire incidents and disaster housing assistance.

National Incident Management System

FEMA also hosts the National Incident Management System (*site:fema .gov National Incident Management System*), a database that is intended to be used by local governments, nongovernmental organizations, and individuals to learn best practices for dealing with natural and human-caused disasters (incidents).

Homeland Security Digital Library

HSDL is sponsored by the Department of Homeland Security's National Preparedness Directorate, FEMA, and the Naval Postgraduate School Center for Homeland Defense and Security in Monterey, California. The database contains not just metadata, but also the full content of most of what it features. When searches are performed, they search not only the metadata (author, title abstracts) but also the full content, meaning that they return very rich search results. The database covers not only typical national security topics; most public policy subjects will turn up very satisfying and relevant results for students.

Content includes selected content from CRS Reports; masters theses from the Naval Postgraduate School; congressional reports, documents, and hearings; journal articles from military and peace-related journals; GAO Reports; presidential documents; treaties; training materials; and many other resource types.

There are several levels of access to the content. The general public has access to about half of it. When going to https://www.hsdl.org/ as a general web user, you may think you are getting all the available results, but you are not. "Organization-wide" accounts are available to military institutions; federal, territorial, tribal, state, or local U.S. government agencies; and public-sector research institutions or university libraries. Depository libraries are included in this group. On July 3, 2019, the "full collection" available to organization-wide accounts, was 182,800 documents, while the "public collection" had 107,100 documents. So, you definitely will want to go to a depository library or a public university library that has signed up for access.

DEPARTMENT OF HOUSING AND URBAN DEVELOPMENT

The Department of Housing and Urban Development oversees housing needs nationwide, ensures fair housing opportunities, and seeks to create strong, sustainable, and inclusive communities (SuDocs Stem: HH).

Huduser.gov is a web portal with research reports and publications on all housing topics, including affordable housing, housing discrimination, homeownership, community and economic development, and fair housing. Publications can be browsed by author, date, title, and year. Data sets on these topics are also available through the portal. The Low-Income Housing Tax Credit Database (https://lihtc.huduser.gov/) can be used to locate affordable housing options and to see any income restrictions, number of bedrooms, amount of HUD subsidies, and other data points.

DEPARTMENT OF THE INTERIOR

There are many interesting agencies under the Department of the Interior (SuDocs Stem: I), including the Bureau of Indian Affairs, Bureau of Land Management, Bureau of Reclamation, and the National Park Service. The agency that stands out as having a massive publication history and fascinating dynamic databases is the United States Geological Survey (USGS).

USGS has many tools covering the diverse topic under its purview. Earthquakes (*site:usgs.gov earthquakes*), water conditions (*site:usgs.gov water conditions*), floods (*site:usgs.gov real time flood*), geomagnetism (*site:usgs.gov real time geomagnetism*), remote sensing (*site:usgs.gov real time remote sensing*), landslides (*site:usgs.gov real time landslides*), volcanoes (*site:usgs.gov real time volcanoes*), droughts (*site:usgs.gov real time droughts*), and wildfires (*site:usgs.gov real time wildfires*) are among the real-time databases available.

USGS Publications Warehouse (*site:usgs.gov publications*) contains indexing to over 160,000 publications authored by USGS scientists for over 100 years. When USGS has rights to digitize the content, the files are viewable and downloadable. In the case of peer-reviewed journal articles, there may be a DOI or other link to online content hosted by the vendor. The interesting innovation with this database is that if the scientific study focuses on a specific geographic area, the GPS latitude/longitude coordinates present users with a map showing the study area.

DEPARTMENT OF JUSTICE

The Drug Enforcement Administration publishes its annual *National Drug Threat Assessment* (SuDocs: J 1.112/2:; http://purl.access.gpo.gov /GPO/LPS78671). Coverage includes transnational criminal organizations; information on gangs and gang terminology; controlled prescription drugs; and lengthy discussion of individual drugs, including heroin, fentanyl, and other synthetic opioids, as well as methamphetamine, cocaine, marijuana (with discussion of legalization in the various states), and new psychoactive substances. The illicit financing of drug operations is also discussed. Statistical data with city-level available data is also presented.

Drug Labs in the United States: National Clandestine Laboratory Register Data (*site:dea.gov national clandestine register*) contains addresses of locations where law enforcement agencies discovered chemicals or related items that indicate the presence of clandestine drug laboratories or dump sites.

The Bureau of Prisons Federal Inmate Locator (*site:bop.gov federal inmate locator*) allows the lookup of federal prisoners by any of several registration numbers. You can also look up by name. If you don't know any names, just look for web pages that list notorious inmates (current or former) of the famous Supermax facility in Florence, Colorado (its formal name is much less memorable: U.S. Penitentiary Florence ADMAX).

DEPARTMENT OF LABOR

Historic publications of the Department of Labor (SuDocs: L) include those of the Bureau of Labor Statistics (1913–; SuDocs: L 2), the Children's Bureau (1913–1946; SuDocs: L 5), and the Women's Bureau (1971–; SuDocs: L 36).

Occupational Outlook Handbook (SuDocs: L 2.3/4:) has been around since 1949 (HT 000046071; http://purl.fdlp.gov/GPO/gpo25035). It is considered an authoritative source for current data and trends for specific occupations. For each job title, there is information on median pay, education requirements, number of jobs, and job outlook, as well as brief summaries of required licenses, certifications, or registrations required.

Monthly Labor Review (HT 010304346) has been published since 1915. It combines statistics with textual analysis of the labor situation. Current issues are available from the Department of Labor website (http://purl .access.gpo.gov/GPO/LPS806).

DEPARTMENT OF STATE

The State Department (SuDocs: S) stands as an exception to the annual reports of other government agencies. Its annual report is the *Foreign Relations of the United States*, issued at least 30 years after the fact.

Archived Content

Another way in which the State Department is a bit different from other cabinet-level agencies is that it maintains its own archive of websites of previous administrations. See Table 6.14.

Official Register of the United States

A long-standing serial publication of interest to genealogists is the *Official Register of the United States*. This is an annual listing of persons occupying administrative and supervisory positions in the legislative, executive, and judicial branches of the federal government. In its own

Table 6.14   Archived State Department website content

Obama Administration	
State Department Website (2009–2017)	https://2009-2017.state.gov/
Foreign Press Center (2009–2017)	https://2009-2017-fpc.state.gov/
Keystone XL Pipeline site (2012)	https://2012-keystonepipeline-xl.state .gov/
U.S. Mission to the United Nations (2009–2017)	https://2009-2017-usun.state.gov/
George W. Bush Administration	
State Department Website (2001–2009)	https://2001-2009.state.gov/
William J. Clinton Administration	
State Department Website (1998–2001)	https://1997-2001.state.gov/

words: "Containing a list of officers and employees in the civil, military and naval service." The publication has been under the purview of four separate government agencies over its long history. Since it originated with the Department of State, it is featured here:

- Department of State 1816–1860 (SuDocs: S 1.11:; HT 009014267, 009014268)

- Department of the Interior 1861–1905 (SuDocs: I 1.25:; HT 011712478)

- Bureau of the Census 1907–1932 (SuDocs: C 3.10:; HT 011712460, 100931495)

- Civil Service Commission 1933–1959 (SuDocs: CS 1.31:; HT 100931495)

A fascinating brief history of the publication can be found in Deeben (2004). A resource like this is a gold mine for those doing genealogical research, as it gives insights into job titles throughout time, in addition to names of government employees.

Foreign Relations of the United States (FRUS)

Without question, this is the most important publication of the State Department. Unlike other executive branch agencies, the State Department does not issue a typical annual report. FRUS was considered to be the closest equivalent (McAllister et al. 2015). In the SuDocs classification system, FRUS occupies the place of the annual report (S 1.1). But be assured, the State Department issues agency financial reports just like other agencies.

FRUS is the official documentary record of U.S. foreign policy. The series began in 1861 with the Lincoln administration and now comprises over 450 volumes. Each volume is filled with valuable primary source materials gathered from presidential libraries, government agencies, National Security Council, Central Intelligence Agency, Agency for International Development, and private papers of individuals.

The Foreign Relations Authorization Act of 1991 (P.L. 102-138, 105 Stat. 647) charges the Advisory Committee on Historical Diplomatic Documentation to the Department of State with overseeing the preparation of the publication of FRUS, as well as monitoring the declassification and release of State Department records. According the 22 U.S.C. § 4351, the FRUS series "shall be a thorough, accurate, and reliable documentary record of major United States foreign policy decisions and significant United States diplomatic activity." Further, "The Secretary of State shall ensure that the FRUS series shall be published not more than 30 years after the events recorded." The 30-year rule is not always followed, as documented by the Advisory Committee on Historical Diplomatic Documentation to the Department of

State (2018). Publication progress can be monitored on the State Department website. Because the URLs change so frequently, it is best to search Google like this: *site:state.gov Status Foreign Relations of the United States.*

The University of Wisconsin-Madison Libraries, in collaboration with the University of Illinois at Chicago Libraries, hosts a freely available FRUS site (Google: *frus site:wisc.edu*). Nearly 400 available volumes can be browsed or searched. Once a volume is retrieved, keyword searches within the retrieved volume can be searched. The scans from this project are of exceedingly high quality. PDFs are also downloadable for each volume, although they have not been subjected to optical character recognition (i.e., they are not OCRed).

HeinOnline has a vendor version of FRUS in its "Foreign Relations of the United States" subsection. It is browsable by presidential administration, and then by volume, and it is searchable across all volumes or across a presidential administration. This is perhaps the easiest-to-use online collection, but it is not free. LLMC Digital also hosts FRUS by subscription.

Each version of FRUS has its own strengths, which is why I mention the various interfaces so that you can see which features work best for you.

State Department Noteworthy Publications

Principal Officers and Chiefs of Mission

The State Department has a long history of publications documenting their principal officers and chiefs of mission. These include the Biographic Register (HT 002137466, 010426377) and Principal Officers of the Department of State and United States Chiefs of Mission, 1778–1990 (HT 102475768). All this information has been folded into a database format, with entries going back to 1778 at: https://history.state.gov/department history/people/principals-chiefs (or *site:state.gov Principal Officers and Chiefs of Mission*). This is an invaluable resource for genealogists.

Country Reports on Terrorism

This is an annual report (SuDocs: S 1.138:) in compliance with 22 U.S.C. § 2656f that requires the State Department to report on countries that engage in terrorism, as defined by the Act (Google: *site:state.gov country reports on terrorism*; http://purl.access.gpo.gov/GPO/LPS68317).

Diplomatic List

This is the official directory of foreign embassies and consular offices in the United States. (HT 000073383, 102186011); SuDocs: S 1.8:; https://purl

.fdlp.gov/GPO/gpo119554 [current]; http://purl.access.gpo.gov/GPO/LPS2407 (archived content); *site:state.gov "diplomatic list"*.

Key Officers of Foreign Service Posts/Key Officers List

This lists ambassadors and other State Department personnel services at embassies and consular offices in foreign countries (HT 000067361); SuDocs: S 1.40/5:; http://purl.access.gpo.gov/GPO/LPS121119 (current); *site:state.gov "key officers list"*.

Report on International Religious Freedom

Covers religious demography for each country, as well as threats to freedom from governments and society (HT 007602157); *site:state.gov Report on International Religious Freedom*; http://purl.access.gpo.gov/GPO /LPS11558; http://purl.access.gpo.gov/GPO/LPS70283.

Trafficking in Persons Report

The TIP Report is a comprehensive resource for anti-trafficking efforts (including sex trafficking, labor trafficking, and human trafficking) (HT 012279576); *site:state.gov Trafficking in Persons*; http://purl.access.gpo.gov /GPO/LPS53214.

U.S. Bilateral Relations Fact Sheets

These fact sheets contain valuable information on U.S. relations with 200 foreign countries. They include the countries' memberships in international organizations and the economic assistance given to those countries (*site:state.gov bilateral relations fact sheets*).

United States Participation in the United Nations

(HT 012261468, 001291912); *site:state.gov United States Participation in the United Nations*.

Voting Practices in the United Nations

(HT 003145605, 000943792); *site:state.gov voting practices in the United Nations*; http://purl.access.gpo.gov/GPO/LPS16005.

International Narcotics Control Strategy Report

(HT 002498595); *site:state.gov International Narcotics Control Strategy Report*; http://purl.access.gpo.gov/GPO/LPS3635.

DEPARTMENT OF TRANSPORTATION (SUDOCS STEM TD)

In the category of audio files is the Federal Aviation Administration's Accident and Incident Data (https://www.faa.gov/data_research/accident _incident/; *site:gov Air traffic control accident incident*). The website includes not only audio files, but also data and PDF reports of the incidents.

Flight Delay Information (*site:faa.gov flight delay*) from the FAA shows a map of the United States, with color-coded status for each of the nation's major commercial airports. This tool can be used to see if there are weather of other delays currently being experienced at airports.

National Traffic and Road Closure Information (*site:dot.gov National Traffic and Road Closure*). For professional drivers and the general public, this resource links to each state's local information for road closures and weather conditions affecting travel.

DEPARTMENT OF THE TREASURY (SUDOCS STEM T)

Not popular but highly used, the Internal Revenue Service provides all tax forms and instructions online (*site:irs.gov tax forms*). The Treasury Department (SuDocs stem T) has many publications relating to the public debt and taxation. Many of these current and historic publications can be found in the FRASER project of the Federal Reserve Bank of St. Louis (https://fraser.stlouisfed.org).

Account of the Receipts and Expenditures of the United States. (HT 001719475, 008608751 SuDoc: T 32.5:; http://purl.fdlp.gov/GPO/gpo35334).

Many historic Treasury Department publication can be found on the St. Louis Fed's Fraser site—https://fraser.stlouisfed.org/author/#33.

DEPARTMENT OF VETERANS AFFAIRS (SUDOCS STEM VA)

It is not common for government agencies (other than the Census Bureau) to preserve and host many historical documents. However, the Department of Veterans Affairs has historic annual reports going back to 1922 (*site:va.gov historical annual reports*) and also reports for predecessor agencies—Bureau of War Risk Insurance, Federal Board of Vocational

Education, National Home for Disables Volunteer Soldiers, and the Public Health Service.

SECURITIES AND EXCHANGE COMMISSION

Public companies in the United States are required to file their reports electronically through the EDGAR system (Electronic Data Gathering, Analysis, and Retrieval). High-priced databases such as Hoovers, Mergent, and ValueLine take the freely available EDGAR data and add value to it by providing their analyses, ratios, and number crunching. This same data is freely available to all who take the time to learn how to do some analysis of their own.

The Securities and Exchange Commission grew out of the stock market crash of 1929. The Securities Act of 1933 (Title I of P.L. 73-22, 48 Stat. 74, Ch. 38), together with the Securities Exchange Act of 1934 (P.L. 73-291, 48 Stat. 881, Ch. 404), created the Securities and Exchange Commission, designed to restore confidence in the capital markets. The Electronic Data Gathering, Analysis, and Retrieval system (EDGAR) was phased in during the 1990s to facilitate online filing of required filings for public companies. The EDGAR database (https://www.sec.gov/edgar/searchedgar/company search.html) searches these filings back to the mid-1990s. Although there are many types of filings available, most researchers and students will be interested in the 10-K filings (annual reports). Many commercial databases take the EDGAR filings, add value to them (such as ratios and comparative analyses), and charge hefty subscription prices. But the raw data is freely available to all.

Here is an example of what EDGAR can do. Suppose you are looking for public companies involved with providing euthanasia services within the field of veterinary medicine. By going to the EDGAR advanced search page, and then selecting full-text search, you can do a search like this: *veterinary AND euthanasia*. You can then discover the public companies that are involved in this field.

ENVIRONMENTAL PROTECTION AGENCY

Technical reports and data sets are numerous on the various EPA websites (SuDocs stem EP). Although the EPA is an independent federal agency and is not a department parallel to agriculture or energy, the administrator of the EPA sits on the president's cabinet. Featured below are just a few of the EPA initiatives.

National Service Center for Environmental Publications (NSCEP)

National Environmental Publications Internet Site (NEPIS) was folded into NSCEP in 2007, just to make things a bit confusing. In fact, when searching the database, you can still see the NEPIS acronym used throughout the search experience.

The NSCEP system is available for searching or browsing at https://www.epa.gov/nscep. Documents can be browsed by publication number or title. Full-text PDFs are available for most documents or, if not, may be available in hard copy from the EPA or from NTIS (likely for a small fee). The size of the database is quickly approaching 100,000 documents.

In some cases, it may be easier to search the NSCEP content using Google like this: *site:nepis.epa.gov "Safe Drinking Water Act Protecting America's Public Health"*. It is nearly impossible to discover this title using the native search engine.

Brownfields

A brownfield, as defined by the EPA, is land that contains the presence or potential presence of a hazardous substance, pollutant, or contaminant. Users can browse or search the site (https://www.epa.gov/brownfields) for brownfield sites near them or anywhere in the United States.

Superfund

Growing out of infamous contaminated sites in the 1970s such as Love Canal (Niagara Falls, NY) and Valley of Drums (Brooks, KY), Congress established the Comprehensive Environmental Response, Compensation, and Liability Act (CERCLA), commonly known as Superfund (P.L. 96-510, 94 Stat. 2767, 42 U.S.C. 9601 note). The EPA Superfund database (https://www.epa.gov/superfund) lets users search for sites by city or site name or browse by state. A map view ("Where you live map") plots each site out using its GPS coordinates.

FEDERAL ELECTION COMMISSION

A stunning feature on the FEC website is the Campaign Finance Data utility (https://www.fec.gov/data/). Campaign monies raised or spent by all presidential candidates back to 1980 are presented in graphic format, making this both an excellent teaching and research resource.

NATIONAL ARCHIVES AND RECORDS ADMINISTRATION (NARA)

The National Archives and Records Administration is the nation's record keeper. Most of the records will not be permanently retained, but about 3 percent of them have permanent historical value. NARA is tasked with managing not only the physical records, but the electronic ones as well.

The primary finding aid is their catalog (https://catalog.archives.gov/). Content includes records of government agencies, political posters, presidential records, maps and charts, and photographs.

Multiple file formats are indexed in the catalog, including images formats, text formats, Microsoft Word and Excel documents, audio visual files (MP4, WMV), sound files (MP3), PDF format, and many others. Some content is viewable online from the catalog. Record groups are generally located in NARA facilities around the country. Also available is the NARA Microfilm Catalog (*site:eservices.archives.gov microfilm catalog*). Many of these microfilm records are available for purchase through NARA. In many cases, local libraries may have already purchased these, so check the OCLC WorldCat database for possibilities.

CENTRAL INTELLIGENCE AGENCY

World Factbook

Originally published from the mid-1970s as the *National Basic Intelligence Factbook* (HT 000550522), the *World Factbook* (HT 000532922; SuDocs: PREX 3.15) began in 1981 and is one of the most well-known of all U.S. federal publications. This famous ready reference work no longer appears in print format—only online (http://purl.fdlp.gov/GPO/gpo66764). The official website provides links to archived versions back to 2000. The *Factbook* is famous for its political and physical maps; gallery of flags of the world; directory of chiefs of state and cabinet members of foreign governments; and its coverage of the economy, demographic profiles, and statistics of around 200 countries of the world.

The Foreign Broadcast Information Service Daily Reports

With the United States engulfed in World War II in Europe and the Far East, it was evident that American leadership, as well as its citizens, needed access to the foreign press in translation. In 1941, the Foreign Broadcast Monitoring Service was established under the auspices of the Federal

Communications Commission. It was soon transferred to the War Department and, in 1947, found its permanent home in the Central Intelligence Agency (Roop 1969).

Originally focusing on broadcast news, over the years, it added print news sources from in-country news entities. Many depository libraries received FBIS reports in paper and fiche (PREX 7.10), and there was a significant lag time between the time of the broadcast and availability in libraries. Finding aids were generally lacking, so these valuable resources were underutilized for most of their lifetime.

Tangible distribution of FBIS materials ceased after 1996, and the entire database was offered through the Department of Commerce's NTIS program via vendors such as Dialog and later ProQuest. When Readex came out with a digital version of the tangible Daily Reports around 2010, new life was breathed into this series. Readex coverage is available from 1941 to 1996 in various modules. It is important to include the FBIS report numbers in citations of older FBIS materials. This immediately signals knowledgeable researchers to the source of the citation, making it easily findable.

FBIS Daily Report indexing only (not full text) can be found in a separate Newsbank database, Foreign Broadcast Information Service Electronic Index covering 1975–1996. For older materials, users can search event indexes or the *New York Times* index, which provides excellent worldwide event coverage. Then go the FBIS materials within several days of the event occurrence.

Researching names using the various FBIS research tools is challenging. Many names in Arabic, Chinese, Russian, and other languages are rendered in various ways, meaning that researchers should search by multiple name variants. For example, the commonly accepted form for the Libyan leader's name is Muammar Gaddafi, yet the most common form in FBIS is Mu'ammar al-Qadhdhafi, or simply Al-Qadhdhafi. Chinese names are sometimes rendered using the pinyin style preferred by the Chinese Communist Party and is more generally accepted by most scholars today; for example, Deng Xiaoping for the Chinese leader. But entries will still be found for the older, but less linguistically preferred Wade-Giles system, which would render the former Chinese leader's name as Teng Hsiao-Ping. Mikhail Gorbachev's name also shows up under Gorbachov and Gorbachyov.

Importance of the Daily Reports for academic research can be found in an article by Solso, "The KAL 007 Tragedy: The Use of FBIS in Cross Cultural Research" (1986).

While the Readex FBIS Daily Reports full-text database covers from 1941 to 1996, after print was no longer distributed, electronic FBIS documents were vended through NTIS. World News Connection was the database that carried these electronic documents from 1995 through 2013. World News Connection and the FBIS project ceased to exist after December 31, 2013, but it is still a valuable news service for non-American perspectives for its time period. The database is still available from East View Information Services.

Joint Publications Research Service Reports

Joint Publication Research Service Reports (JPRS) is a sister publication series to the FBIS series (PREX 7.13). Covering 1957–1975, these translated reports cover a wide range of topics in science and the social sciences. Abstracts from Russian and East European scientific and engineering journals; surveys of agriculture in North Korea, China, and Eastern Europe; and summaries of the foreign press are only a few of the topics covered. Report types include biographies, conference proceedings, statistical compilations, technical reports, and many other materials. To have access to primary source materials on such a broad variety of topic from the Cold War era in English translation is an extremely valuable resource.

Readex has released a sister database to their FBIS database, Joint Publications Research Service (JPRS) Reports with full text of nearly all extant reports.

EXERCISES

1. Using your Google site-specific search skills, find speeches made by HUD officials going back to the 1990s.

2. Find a current organizational chart for the Department of the Interior. Now find one from 1980. Give the sources and the URLs.

3. Find the annual report for the Federal Bureau of Prisons from 1974. Give the source and the URL.

4. How many company-operated stores did Starbucks have as of September 30, 2018? Give the total for the United States: _____ and total for world _____. [Hint: Starbucks is a public company].

5. Create a list of all institutions of higher education that offer advanced degrees in "Library and Information Science" in the United States. How many institutions are on your list? How many of these institutions are in your state?

REFERENCES

Advisory Committee on Historical Diplomatic Documentation to the Department of State. 2018. "2017 Report of the Advisory Committee on Historical

Diplomatic Documentation." August 13. Accessed July 17, 2019. https://fas
.org/sgp/advisory/state/hac2017.html.

Congressional Budget Office. 2019. "The Federal Budget in 2017: An Infographic."
Accessed August 12, 2019. https://www.cbo.gov/publication/53624.

CRS (Congressional Research Service). 2015. "Congressional Budget Resolutions:
Historical Information." RL30297. Updated November 16, 2015. Accessed
August 14, 2019. https://crsreports.congress.gov/product/pdf/RL/RL30297.

CRS (Congressional Research Service). 2016. "The Budget Reconciliation Process:
Timing of Legislative Action." RL30458. Updated February 23, 2016.
Accessed December 12, 2019. https://crsreports.congress.gov/product/pdf
/RL/RL30458.

Deeben, John P. 2004. "The Official Register of the United States, 1816–1959."
Genealogy Notes 36, no. 4. Accessed December 12, 2019. https://www
.archives.gov/publications/prologue/2004/winter/genealogy-official
-register.html.

Historical Statistics of the United States. 2006. Millennial Edition Online, edited
by Susan B. Carter, Scott Sigmund Gartner, Michael R. Haines, Alan L.
Olmstead, Richard Sutch, and Gavin Wright. Cambridge University Press.
TABLE Da14–27 Farms—number, population, land, and value of property:
1850–1997 [Census years].

McAllister, William B., Joshua Botts, Peter Cozzens, and Aaron W. Marrs. 2015.
*Toward "Thorough, Accurate, and Reliable": A History of the "Foreign Rela-
tions of the United States."* Washington, DC: U.S. Department of State,
Office of the Historian, Bureau of Public Affairs. Accessed August 16, 2019.
https://static.history.state.gov/frus-history/ebooks/frus-history.pdf.

Roop, Joseph E. 1969. *Foreign Broadcast Information Service History; Part I: 1941–
1947.* Washington, DC: Central Intelligence Agency. Accessed December
12, 2019. http://purl.access.gpo.gov/GPO/LPS116843.

Solso, Robert L. 1986. "The KAL 007 Tragedy: The Use of FBIS in Cross Cultural
Research." *Government Publications Review* 13, no. 2: 203–208.

Whitson, Thurman L., and Lynn Davis. 2001. "Best Practices in Electronic
Government: Comprehensive Electronic Information Dissemination for
Science and Technology." *Government Information Quarterly* 18, no. 2:
79–91.

7

The Regulatory Process

THE REGULATORY PROCESS

Regulations, or administrative law, cannot come into existence without underlying statutory authority (Figure 7.1). In this chapter, we will look at how regulations are promulgated, how to find full text, and how to relate them to their underlying statutes. We will also examine the various methods for finding official text for both current and superseded regulations.

The Office of Information and Regulatory Affairs of the Office of Management and Budget published extensive background information on the rule-making process. Most helpful is their "Reg Map," available at https://www.reginfo.gov/public/reginfo/Regmap/regmap.pdf, covering the finer details of the complex regulatory processes.

Regulations can come into being in any number of ways. The usual way is for Congress to grant rule-making authority to a federal agency to implement regulations. There is a process for creating regulations—the rule-making process—and, once made, these regulations have the full force and effect of law. The question comes to mind then, if members of Congress are "lawmakers," why are they delegating their authority to agencies? The primary answer is that the agencies are the experts in the field, and they are dealing in the details that members of Congress have no time or expertise to focus on. Congress retains its general legislative authority, but members spend their time on the big picture rather than delving into details. The 1946 Administrative

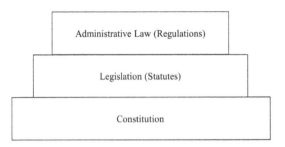

Figure 7.1   Regulations in relation to statutes and the Constitution

Procedure Act (APA) (P.L. 79–404, 60 Stat. 237, ch. 324, 5 U.S.C. ch. 5, § 500 et seq.) institutes a number of procedural controls on agencies to ensure that the public can participate and provide comments (CRS 2019).

In some cases, Congress may not want to delegate rule-making authority. After all, agency personnel are not directly accountable to the electorate, as members of Congress are. Unless an agency's authorizing statute states otherwise, the rule-making process, as outlined in the Administrative Procedure Act, is to be followed (CRS 2019).

Figure 7.2 illustrates the rule-making process in a clear manner.

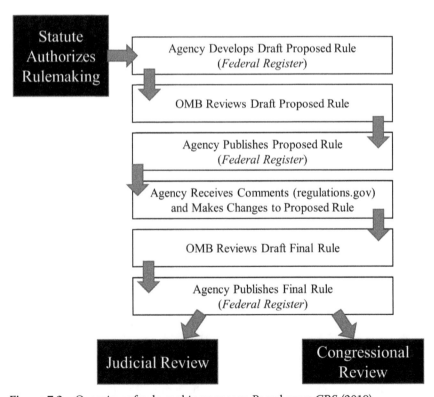

Figure 7.2   Overview of rule-making process. Based upon CRS (2019).

Note that the *Federal Register*, discussed in greater detail below, is the essential information pathway in the rule-making process. A bit of background is necessary to understand the role of the Office of Management and Budget, under the Executive Office of the President, in this process. EO 12291, issued by President Reagan, established a centralized review of most agencies' rules through the Office of Information and Regulatory Affairs (OIRA) within the Office of Management and Budget (OMB). In 1993, President Clinton replaced Reagan's executive order with EO 12866. The centralized process remained intact, but agencies were required to conduct a cost-benefit analysis. In January 2017, President Trump issued EO 13771 which initiated a "one-in, two-out" requirement. Agencies were required to offset the costs of new rules by eliminating at least two previously issued rules of equivalent costs. Undoubtedly subsequent executive orders will further amend these procedures, but, for now, OBM review is required at two points in the process. Notice that public comment today is solicited using the website regulations.gov.

Congressional oversight and judicial review of the regulatory process were also envisioned within the APA. Congress has ultimate statutory control over any agency action. They can use the Congressional Review Act (CRA) (P.L. 104-121, Subtitle E; 110 Stat. 847), part of the Contract with America Advancement Act of 1996, to overturn rules through enactment of a joint resolution of disapproval. Through the end of 2018, President Trump signed 16 disapproval resolutions, putting an end to various rules issued at the end of the Obama administration (CRS 2018). Up until the Trump administration, the CRA had only been used once to overturn a rule early in the administration of George W. Bush (P.L. 107-5, 115 Stat. 7) (Carey et al. 2016). One easy way to view these is to search Congress.gov like this: *"congress disapproves" rule* (with limit to 115th Congress and limit to status of legislation → became law).

Congress has other forms of oversight of rule making available to it, such as holding hearings or gathering information on an agency's activities regarding rule making. If Congress does not approve of an agency's direction, it can also invoke its appropriations authority, thus cutting funding to the agency.

Judicial review through the courts is another check on rule making. A court may vacate an agency rule if it determines that it violates the Constitution, exceeds statutory authority, or if it is deemed arbitrary or capricious.

THE UNIFIED AGENDA

The full name is "The Unified Agenda of Federal Regulatory and Deregulatory Actions," but it is generally known simply as the "Unified Agenda."

Executive Order 12866 (58 FR 51735) and the Regulatory Flexibility Act (5 U.S.C. 602) require agencies to publish semiannual regulatory agendas describing actions they are planning or have already completed. This is required of executive branch agencies only not legislative branch agencies. Published each spring and fall by the Office of Information and Regulatory Affairs of the Office of Management and Budget, under the Executive Office of the President, the document is a semiannual compilation of agency plans for regulations that are under development. In addition to general regulation plans, agencies must delineate the effects their regulations will have on small businesses and other small entities. The "Unified Agenda" can be found on the reginfo.gov site, although much of the information is also published in the *Federal Register*. It is important to note that reginfo.gov contains regulatory information that does not appear in the *Federal Register*. Govinfo.gov also contains the "Unified Agenda," but it is not the easiest place to access current information. It points to the relevant parts of the *Federal Register* and pulls those parts together for easy access. Its primary value is for past agenda information, going back as far as 1994.

FEDERAL REGISTER

Although federal regulations existed before the administration of Franklin D. Roosevelt, it wasn't until the Federal Register Act of 1935 (P.L. 74-220, 49 Stat. 500, 44 U.S.C. §1501) and the first issue of the *Federal Register* in 1936 that there was a systematic process for publishing federal regulations. The *Federal Register* (abbreviated FR) serves effectively as the official journal of the executive branch of the government. The FR is the place where notices of proposed rules were to be first published and made available for public comment. When the rules are finalized, they are published in the *Code of Federal Regulations* (abbreviated CFR). The CFR is organized into 50 titles, resembling the original 50 titles of U.S. Code, although those parallels broke down very quickly.

The *Federal Register* contains regulations, but it also contains more than that. A typical FR issue contains the following sections:

- **Contents**. This is not really the same as a table of contents in other publications. It is more of an index, since it presents things by agency. The "Contents" section has subheadings for government agencies and their rules, notices, and proposed rules. If that day's issue is multipart, this will be noted in a section labelled "Separate Parts in this Issue."
- **CFR Parts Affected in This Issue.** Notes changes to the *Code of Federal Regulations* by CFR title, and the FR page. This is just an index to changes in the issue at hand; the "Reader Aids" section at the end of

each FR issue has a cumulated list of CFR parts affected for the entire month.

- **Presidential Documents**. Includes executive orders, presidential proclamations, determinations, memoranda, and other issuances.

- **Rules and Regulations**. Includes policy statements and interpretations of rules. This is the final stage of the rule-making process, before final publication in CFR. This section gives dates when a rule is effective, very often the date of the FR publication or shortly thereafter.

- **Proposed Rules.** Includes petitions for rule-making and other advance proposals. Instructions for making public comment are provided. Some of these are formal notices of proposed rule-making (NPRM) notices. Others are simply "proposed rules." Under this section, the "Unified Agenda" is published semiannually, usually under the heading "Semiannual Regulatory Agenda."

- **Notices**. Includes scheduled hearings and meetings open to the public, grant applications, administrative orders, and other announcements of government actions.

- **Reader Aids**. In addition to explaining how to subscribe to FR, where to find it on the web, and how to get email notifications, it contains CFR parts affected not just in "this issue" but for the entire month. It also contains a breakdown of pages of FR for the month to date.

In addition to the sections listed above, P.L. 94-409 (90 Stat. 1241), the Government in the Sunshine Act, requires that meetings open to the public be listed in the *Federal Register*. These will be clearly marked as a "Sunshine Act Meeting." If there are any corrections to be noted from previous issues, they will also be noted in the contents.

When you think about it, there are really two ways you might want to view the *Federal Register*'s table of contents: by agency first, and then by notice type or by notice type, and then by agency. The print version accommodates the first way, and Federalregister.gov accommodates the second.

If a daily edition is too large, it will be split into separate parts. For example, the issue for November 16, 2018 is 513 PDF pages long. As a result, it is divided into parts. These parts are not of equal lengths. The first part is 138 pages long, but part ix is only two pages long, a title page and one page of content. In all, there are 29 parts to this particular FR issue.

For those wanting further assistance, the National Archives has a helpful tutorial available (*site:archives.gov federal register tutorial*).

The Regulatory Study Center at George Washington University keeps track of total pages within the *Federal Register* year-by-year, number of final rules each year, economically significant rules each year, and many other interesting research points (https://regulatorystudies.columbian

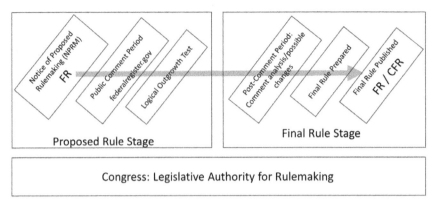

Figure 7.3 Overview of rule-making process. Adapted from https://www .regulations.gov/docs/FactSheet_Regulatory_Timeline.pdf.

.gwu.edu/reg-stats). From this, we can see that a typical year in the life of the *Federal Register* will yield around 70,000 to 80,000 pages, with 2016 setting a record at 95,894 pages.

Figure 7.3 presents a graphic overview of the rule-making process.

Overview of Online Interfaces

Because there are so many new and creative interfaces to access and comment on the rule-making process, the following overview of online databases is provided.

Reginfo.gov

Reginfo.gov is the Office of Information and Regulatory Affairs of the Office of Management and Budget's portal to information on the regulatory process. The site is one of the most helpful primers for an introduction to the regulatory process, including the "Unified Agenda." Reginfo .gov is the easiest place to see all the "Unified Agenda" versions all in one place. A pulldown menu provides easy access to the current "Unified Agenda" plans for each agency. Summary statistics in graphical form and navigation links to agency data show the regulatory process from a top-level perspective.

The three sections of the site are the "Unified Agenda," "Regulatory Review," and "Information Collection Review." A colorful graphical interface shows how many activities are under review within each section. Clicking on a section of the chart will retrieve actions within that category.

Federalregister.gov

Federalregister.gov is published by NARA. It conveniently breaks down the current issue into the three main categories of the FR: notices, proposed rules, and rules. If all you want is the current day's FR in PDF format, it has a link for that as well, pointing to the authenticated version from Govinfo.gov.

Federalregister.gov provides links to web-enabled HTML versions of the FR text, or, if you prefer, to the official PDF page that is more official looking, authenticated, and easily printed. It also provides citations all along the way for legal and sourcing purposes. Older documents can be searched by FR citation. It interlinks with Regulations.gov (for public comment) and Govinfo.gov (for the official GPO pages).

Regulations.gov

The Environmental Protection Agency's eRulemaking Program Management Office, under an interagency agreement, manages the Regulations .gov public-facing portal, where the public can submit comments on proposed rules, as well as the Federal Docket Management System (FDMS) back end for government agencies. Public comments range from a single sentence or paragraph to complex analyses with thousands of pages.

Govinfo.gov

This is the official authenticated version of the *Federal Register* in PDF format, including the "Unified Agenda." Hosted by the Government Publishing Office, the interface goes all the way back to the first issue of FR on March 14, 1936. The older scanned issues take a long time to load—sometimes several minutes. It may be faster to consult the *Federal Register* using a database like HeinOnline instead.

Having all these sites is meant to be helpful, but to the information professional, it can seem very confusing. Figure 7.4 is meant to help alleviate this confusion.

Regulatory Histories

For those interested in detailed histories of regulations, the subscription databases ProQuest Regulatory Insight will provide that information. It traces the notices, proposed rules, and public comments before a rule becomes final. Then it also traces actions after a final rule is published, such as subsequent changes to the regulations and legislation that amends or revokes the regulations. Unlike legislative histories, regulatory histories are never finished and can always be amended.

Figure 7.4   Relationship of regulatory sites to each other

Users can start with a public law and find all the regulations issued in the implementation of that law through the agencies. On the other hand, citations to the *Federal Register* within the *Code of Federal Regulations* can also be the starting point. Regulatory Insight also traces the histories of Executive Orders.

CODE OF FEDERAL REGULATIONS

Arrangement and Publication

As noted above, the current *Code of Federal Regulations* (CFR) is organized into 50 titles. Unfortunately, they do not all parallel the topics in the United States Code. Notice in Appendix E that in approximately half of the cases, there is a topical correspondence between USC and CFR. Other cases are wildly off.

CFR has an interesting publishing schedule. It is not published at one time, as the U.S. Code is (every six years with annual supplements). Rather, it is published on a quarterly basis throughout the year.

- Titles 1–16 are updated as of January 1
- Titles 17–27 are updated as of April 1
- Titles 28–41 are updated as of July 1
- Titles 42–50 are updated as of October 1

Another thing to consider is the relative size of individual CFR titles. Though there are 50 titles, the full set consists of approximately 200 physical volumes. Some are a single volume (Title 8 Aliens and Nationality [2019]) while others have multiple volumes (Title 26 Internal Revenue has 47 physical volumes [2019]).

GPO's Govinfo.gov contains the official, authenticated version of CFR, but that doesn't mean it is the most user-friendly way to access it. Govinfo.gov allows users to browse the regulations (1996 to present), as well as to search them. It also allows users to go directly to a CFR citation. The CFR on Govinfo.gov is current with the published print editions, but it is not updated daily as is eCFR. HeinOnline, available in law libraries and larger academic libraries, provides access via subscription to the entire run of CFR.

Title 3: The President

Other titles of CFR supersede on an annual basis. Title 3 is an exception. For libraries that keep print CFR titles, this title containing presidential issuances should be kept permanently. It contains a record of executive orders, proclamations, and other issuances. An index at the beginning of each annual Title 3 volume shows which annual compilation contains each numbered proclamation and executive order. Also contained in Title 3 are regulations issued by the Executive Office of the President.

Parallel Table of Authorities and Rules (PTOA)

One tool that you need to be familiar with is the Parallel Table of Authorities and Rules. This is contained in the index volume (the last volume) of the annual CFR. In Govinfo.gov, it usually comes after Title 50 and is in the volume with the CFR Index and Finding Aids.

The table has four sections:

• US Code
• US Statutes at Large
• Public Laws
• Presidential Documents (Proclamations, Executive Orders, and Reorganization Plans)

In the left-hand column will be the U.S. Code, statutes, public laws, or presidential document citation, and in the right-hand column will be the current CFR sections that relate to these authorities.

Online Access

Govinfo.gov is the official and authenticated version of CFR, but as of this writing, it only goes back to 1996. Current access (with daily changes incorporated into CFR) is available via ecfr.gov.

Some nongovernmental sources also provide access to CFR. These include Govregs.com and Cornell's Legal Information Institute (https://www.law.cornell.edu/cfr/). HeinOnline is perhaps the easiest way in an academic library setting to access older annual editions and compilations. Although back issues of CFR are available via HathiTrust (HT 008701565, 006222388, 003911273), these volumes are too difficult to navigate, and this access method is not recommended.

CORRELATING FR AND CRF

List of CFR Sections Affected

Since the CFR codification is published annually in four quarterly installments, how are users supposed to know what the current state of regulations is at any given time? The answer for years has been a publication called *List of CFR Sections Affected* (abbreviated LSA). LSA serves as a crosswalk between the daily *Federal Register* and the annual *Code of Federal Regulations*.

To see what the current regulations in force are, researchers must perform the following process:

1. Consult the current CFR volume for the latest annual regulations
2. Consult the latest cumulation of the LSA (if applicable)
3. Consult the latest monthly LSA
4. Examine each daily FR issue on the topic

For example, suppose you were interested in tracking updates to 8 CFR, the volume on "Aliens and Nationality." You would first consult the most-recently available volume of 8 CFR. This is one of the volumes published January 1 of each year, so you would need to somehow find out what has changed between the date of the CFR you are now looking at and all subsequent FR issues. You don't need to look at each and every FR issue, thanks to LSA. LSA is published monthly and cumulated quarterly. You would only need to consult the most recent LSA cumulation, and then each subsequent month since the publication of 8 CFR to see what changes had been made. LSA gives the page number to FR where relevant changes can be found. But since LSA is published monthly, you would still need to check the most-recently available issue of FR. Each issue has a section titled "CFR Parts Affected in this Issue," but at the end of each issue, in the

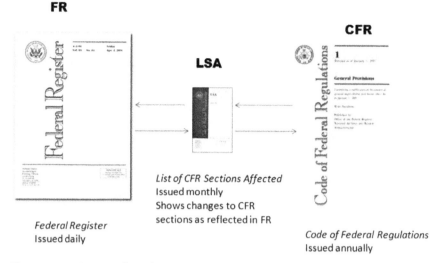

Figure 7.5   Crosswalking between FR and CFR

"Readers Aids" section, is a cumulative index to "CFR Parts Affected during [Whichever Month]." Figure 7.5 illustrates the process.

Kind of complicated, isn't it? But don't quit quite yet. Read the next section.

e-CFR

Now that you know how to use LSA to coordinate FR to CFR, I'll tell you that all of that isn't necessary, thanks to e-CFR! Though branded as "e-CFR," the URL is actually eCFR.gov—a bit confusing. This is a daily updating of CFR, folding in all daily changes that have affected it from the *Federal Register*. Although not the "official" version of the regulations (as the content on Govinfo.gov is), it surely can be trusted as the current state of regulations. You will notice on the main website that a currency date is posted, "e-CFR data is current as of [date]." This is the first of the stunning features of this GPO-administered site. Future plans are to make the regulations in this site official, although it is difficult to say when that will be. Here is a quote from the site:

> The e-CFR will be maintained as an unofficial editorial compilation until all remaining technical and performance issues are satisfactorily resolved. When this is accomplished, the OFR/GPO partnership will propose to the ACFR that the e-CFR become an official edition of the CFR and a permanent record of the United States Government. (https://www.ecfr.gov /—FAQs)

The second stunning feature is that e-CFR has the ability to show what regulations were in force on a particular day, going back to January 1, 2015. This is an amazing feature that simply wasn't possible several years ago. Just as you could do a "rollback" of the U.S. Code via the uscode.house.gov website, you can do a similar thing with e-CFR. The House OLRC site allows users to see the state of the U.S. Code back to 1994. But the e-CFR site allows you to view daily integration of FR regulations in the CFR back to 2015—not as far back, but it does allow daily integration. You can't beat that!

It's obvious how attorneys would like this feature, since they need to see what regulations were in force at different periods of time. But social scientists should consider making use of this feature as well.

OTHER ADMINISTRATIVE LAW RESOURCES

In addition to what has been covered so far regarding regulations issued by the executive branch, covered by Administrative Procedure Act, and subject to review by the Office of Management and Budget, there are other regulations, those of independent regulatory agencies (also called independent regulatory commissions, or IRCs), that do not serve at the pleasure of the president and whose rules are not reviewed by the OMB (McKinney 2018). According to 44 U.S.C. § 3502,

> the term "independent regulatory agency" means the Board of Governors of the Federal Reserve System, the Commodity Futures Trading Commission, the Consumer Product Safety Commission, the Federal Communications Commission, the Federal Deposit Insurance Corporation, the Federal Energy Regulatory Commission, the Federal Housing Finance Agency, the Federal Maritime Commission, the Federal Trade Commission, the Interstate Commerce Commission, the Mine Enforcement Safety and Health Review Commission, the National Labor Relations Board, the Nuclear Regulatory Commission, the Occupational Safety and Health Review Commission, the Postal Regulatory Commission, the Securities and Exchange Commission, the Bureau of Consumer Financial Protection, the Office of Financial Research, Office of the Comptroller of the Currency, and any other similar agency designated by statute as a Federal independent regulatory agency or commission.

These IRCs can issue rules that do not show up in the *Federal Register* (CRS 2012). The first independent regulatory agency was the Interstate Commerce Commission, established in 1887. The ICC was abolished in 1995, with the Surface Transportation Board taking over its functions.

Regulations issued by IRCs can usually be found on their websites. Just do a Google search, and you will find current case information, reports, dockets, and enforcement actions.

ADMINISTRATIVE LAW RESOURCES

Certain executive branch agencies have authority to direct, supervise, and implement certain legislative acts or statutes. Administrative law is that which governs the work of government agencies. Many agencies have enforcement authority and may publish decisions, cases, or other actions in response to noncompliance.

Also, depository libraries have many of these decisions in print or microfiche format. For example, the FCC Record is available in many larger depository libraries in print. Agencies that no longer exist, such as the Interstate Commerce Commission (1897–1995) published several series of cases in their *Interstate Commerce Commission Reports.* These are also available in HathiTrust.

Here is a sampling of administrative law decisions. Many of these are older series but are generally all available via two subscription services (LLMC Digital and HeinOnline) and freely available via HathiTrust. In addition, selected volumes may be available through the UNT Digital Library (https://digital.library.unt.edu/), agency websites, and other sources that a Google search would uncover.

Agriculture Decisions. 1942—. (HT 000523748, 100946972).

Atomic Energy Commission Reports. 1956–1975. 8 vols. (HT 001530705).

Civil Aeronautics Board Reports. 1938–1984 105 vols. (HT 002138250, 010117895, 010069860).

Decisions of Commissioner of Patents and U.S. Courts in Patent and Trademark and Copyright Cases. 1869–1968. (HT 003585000, 012158844).

Decisions of the Federal Maritime Commission, 1919–1985. (HT 007912365, 006125227).

Environmental Administrative Decisions. 1972–. (HT 003110237).

Federal Communications Commission Reports, Series 1 (1934–1965) and Series 2 (1965-86) (Series 1: HT 007407818, 010014317; Series 2: HT 001531692).

Federal Energy Regulatory Commission Reports. (FERC), 1977–. (HT 002998905).

Federal Mine Safety and Health Review Commission Decisions, 1979–. (HT 011325905).

Federal Trade Commission Decisions, 1915–. (HT 005577048, 001531691).

Interstate Commerce Commission Reports. First Series 1887–1984; Second Series 1984–1994. (HT 003916145).

Interstate Commerce Commission Reports. Motor Carrier Cases. 1936–1986. (HT 007912215, 003916144).

Interstate Commerce Commission Reports. Valuation Reports, 1918–1964. (HT 003919131).

Interior Dept., *Board of Contract Appeals Decisions,* 1970–1983.

Interior Dept., *Board of Indian Appeals Decisions,* 1970–1995.

Interior Dept., *Board of Land Appeals Decisions/Orders,* 1970–1987.

Interior Dept., *Board of Mine Operations Appeals Decisions,* 1970–1978.

Interior Dept., *Indian Claims Commission Decisions,* 1948–1978.

Interior Dept., *Indian Decisions,* 1972–.

Interior Dept., *Interior Department Decisions.* 1881–1994. (HT 000505680, 007929238, 000505683).

Interior Dept., *Decisions of the Department of the Interior in Appealed Pension and Bounty-land Claims.* 1887–1930. (HT 008697589).

Justice Dept., Admin. Dec., Employer Sanctions, 1988–. *Administrative Decisions under Employer Sanctions, Unfair Immigration-related Employment Practices, and Civil Penalty Document Fraud Laws.* (HT 003255999).

Justice Dept., Admin. Dec., Immigration/Naturalization Laws, 1940–. *Administrative Decisions under Immigration & Nationality Laws.* (HT 001719567).

Justice Dept., Attorney General Opinions, 1790–1982 *Official Opinions of the Attorneys General of the United States.* (HT 011325978, 010418561).

Justice Dept., *Federal Antitrust Decisions,* 1890–1931. (HT 100227280, 008921275).

Justice Dept., Office of Legal Counsel Opinions, 1977– *Opinions of the Office of Legal Counsel of the United States Department of Justice.* (HT 000679607).

Labor Dept., Federal Labor-Management Relations, 1970–1978. *Decisions and Reports on Rulings of the Assistant Secretary of Labor for Labor-Management Relations.* (HT 000052854).

Labor Dept., Federal Labor Relations Authority, 1979–. *Administrative Law Judge Decisions Report.* (HT 102113716, 006176541).

Labor Dept., Federal Labor Relations Council, 1970–1978. *Decisions and Interpretations of the Federal Labor Relations Council.* (HT 007150268).

Labor Dept., Federal Merit Systems Protection Board, 1979–1983. *Decisions of the United States Merit Systems Protection Board.* (HT 002973863, 010317862).

Labor Dept., National Labor Relations Board, 1935–. *Decisions and Orders of the National Labor Relations Board.* (HT 002140855).

Labor Dept., Occupational Safety/Health Review Commission, 1952–1968. *OSAHRC Reports: Decisions of the Occupational Safety and Health Review Commission.* (HT 001719311, 011325907).

Labor Dept., Office of Administrative Law Judges, 1987–1993. *Decisions of the Office of Administrative Law Judges and Office of Administrative Appeals.* (HT 011412302).

Nuclear Regulatory Commission Opinions, 1975–. *Nuclear Regulatory Commission Issuances.* (HT 003919030, 012448062, 102223114).

Opinions and Decisions of the Federal Power Commission, 1931–1977. (HT 007929236).

Post Office, Solicitor's Opinions. *Official Opinions of the Solicitor of the Post Office Department.* (HT 010424008, 100187889).

Securities & Exch. Commission, 1934– *Decisions and Reports.* (HT 100948099, 011329639).

Surface Transportation Board Reports, 7v., 1996–2004. *Surface Transportation Board Reports.* (HT 003440961).

Transportation Safety Board, 1967–. *National Transportation Safety Board Decisions.* (HT 012448063, 102609627, 003919633).

Treasury Dept., Comptroller, 1st, 1880–1894. *Decisions of the Comptroller of the Treasury.* (HT 007908779, 008959853).

Treasury Dept., Customs Bulletin, 1967– *Customs Bulletin.* (HT 012448068, 000888066).

Treasury Dept., IRS, Cum. Bull., Tax Rul., 1919–1921. *Cumulative Bulletin ... Income Tax Rulings.* (HT 005824036).

Treasury Dept., IRS, Cumulative Bulletin, 1922– *Internal Revenue Cumulative Bulletin.* (HT 003925119, 100892898).

Treasury Dept., Treasury Bulletin, 1939–. *Treasury Bulletin.* (HT 000517883, 007132016).

Treasury Dept., Treasury Decisions., 1868–1966. (HT 010424084).

Veterans Affairs Dept., Dec. Administrator Veteran Affairs, 1931–1955. *Decisions of the Administrator of Veterans' Affairs.* (HT 010068909).

EXERCISES

1. Can pigs fly? In other words, are there any circumstances under the law in which a pig can travel in the passenger cabin of a commercial aircraft? Be sure to support you answer with primary sources.

2. Are there any current proposed rules on the topic of raisins in the *Federal Register* that are available for public comment? What tool did you use to find this answer?

3. According to the July 2019 issue of LSA, changes were made to 11 CFR 101.1. Print out this section of CFR from July 2019, as well as how CFR looked at this section on May 1, 2019.

4. The U.S. Fish and Wildlife Services maintains listings of threatened and endangered animals (https://www.fws.gov/endangered/). They also have a list of species proposed for listing. How would you go about keeping up with the status of these listings? Which of the many resources presented in this chapter are most helpful in tracking these listings?

REFERENCES

Carey, Maeve P, Alissa M. Dolan, and Christopher M. Davis. 2016. "The Congressional Review Act: Frequently Asked Questions." Congressional Research Service Report, R43992, November 16, 2016. Accessed December 12, 2019. https://crsreports.congress.gov/product/pdf/R/R43992.

CRS (Congressional Research Service). 2012. "Independent Regulatory Agencies, Cost-Benefit Analysis, and Presidential Review of Regulations." November 16, 2012. R42821. Accessed December 12, 2019. https://crsreports.congress.gov/product/pdf/R/R42821.

CRS (Congressional Research Service). 2018. "The Congressional Review Act (CRA)." In Focus, IF10023. Updated December 18, 2018. Accessed December 12, 2019. https://crsreports.congress.gov/product/pdf/IF/IF10023.

CRS (Congressional Research Service). 2019. "An Overview of Federal Regulations and the Rulemaking Process." In Focus, IF10003. Updated January 3, 2019. Accessed December 12, 2019. https://crsreports.congress.gov/product/pdf/IF/IF10003.

McKinney, Richard J. 2018. "Federal Administrative Law: An Overview." Revised July 9, 2018. Accessed December 12, 2019. https://www.llsdc.org/assets/sourcebook/fed-admin-law.pdf.

8

Judicial Branch Information Sources

A quick perusal of Govinfo.gov, combined with searches within GPO's chief cataloging tool, catalog.gpo.gov, shows that the judicial branch seems to be getting the short shrift. The structure of the federal judiciary, combined with their history of commercial publication, are two major reasons for this.

We have three equal branches of government in this country, but in terms of available publications, the judicial branch doesn't feel equal. Having covered the extensive, almost out-of-control publications of the executive branch and the slightly more controlled publications of the legislative branch, we now come to the judicial branch, where the tonnage of documents seems much lighter. There are several reasons for this. One is that the purpose of courts is to render judicial decisions, not to create ephemeral reports, scientific studies, or other issuances that the other two branches are so famous for producing. Another reason is that private publishers carry much of the weight for the judicial branch.

COMMERCIALIZATION OF LEGAL RESOURCES

As noted in chapter 1, early government publications from all three branches of government were published by commercial publishers. *100 GPO Years* documents the early years of commercial printers in the years before the establishment of the Government Printing Office in 1861. Until 1861, "public printing" was controlled by private printers (Barnum 2011).

Legal information has taken much more of a commercial bent than other kinds of federal government information. Legal information is an industry, and a very lucrative one. The two dominant players today are Lexis (owned by RELX) and Westlaw (owned by Thomson Reuters). The issue is that they take freely available public information, add value to it in the form of headnotes, controlled vocabularies, and timeliness, and place their ownership on it. These services are necessary to the research process, one in which finding "all and only" relevant case history is essential to finding materials. While most of the legal cases can be found on court websites or even in Google Scholar, the topical linkages provided by the controlled vocabularies of these two publishers, together with their citation tools, render searching without them a huge investment of time. While cases might be findable in the public domain, it cannot easily be determined if they are "good law"—that is, if they have been overturned or have been affected positively or negatively by subsequent court actions.

This is not the sourcebook for exhaustive legal research. Many tomes have been authored by and for law librarians that cover these topics in amazing breadth and depth. What I hope to cover here is a thumbnail sketch of the resources and skills needed to answer the most commonly asked legal questions by public library users and students in academic libraries.

THE JUDICIARY

The Federal Judicial Center (https://www.fjc.gov/), chaired by the chief justice of the United States, is the judiciary's research and education agency. Here you will find historical information on all federal judges, courts, the judicial branch, courthouses, famous federal trials, and many other fascinating topics. As states have been added to the Union, the federal judicial circuits have evolved as well. This site has an interesting visualization showing the federal circuit court districts over time (https://bit.ly/2XziI7H).

In the federal court system, there are 94 district courts that are organized into 12 circuits, or regions (Figure 8.1). The purpose of this book is not to explain all the complexities of court rules and procedures but, rather, to assist in locating the documents and sources you need.

Links to all federal courts are kept up-to-date on the U.S. Courts' website (*site:uscourts.gov court website links*). There is also a federal court finder tool (https://www.uscourts.gov/federal-court-finder/search) that is easy to search. Just put in a place name or a zip code, and the result set lists federal district courts, bankruptcy counts, probation offices, and federal defenders in that area.

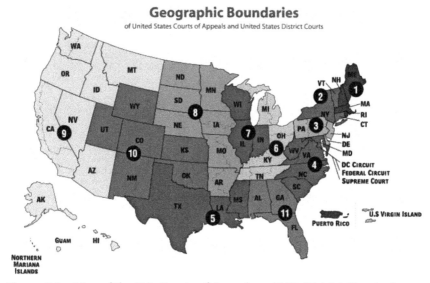

Figure 8.1   Map of the U.S. Courts of Appeals and U.S. District Courts. *Source:* https://www.uscourts.gov/about-federal-courts/federal-courts-public/court -website-links.

West's National Reporter System has become a standard for U.S. case law. The National Reporter System consists of a series of reporters (books that contain reports of decisions by courts) that have become the standard source for court decisions.

Federal district court cases are published in the *Federal Supplement.* These are trial level courts, and only a subset of cases is reported. Citation format examples: 952 F. Supp. 1119; 263 F. Supp. 2d 1219. Federal district court cases, heard in the 13 circuit courts of appeal, are found in the *Federal Reporter.* Citation format examples: 703 F.2d 1233; 572 F.3d 962). Under the West system, Supreme Court cases are found in the *Supreme Court Reporter.* Citation format example: 116 S. Ct. 1620. Keep in mind that the West reporters are necessary for cases below the Supreme Court, since the commercial publisher, West, has a monopoly on these publications. But in the case of Supreme Court cases, you can rely on the official *United States Reports* set published by the GPO. The West set adds value, however, by including their key number system.

Other federal West reporters include the *Bankruptcy Reporter, Federal Rules Decisions, Military Justice Reporter,* and *Federal Claims Reporter.*

There are seven West regional reporters, and the map doesn't at all correspond to the U.S. Courts of Appeals map. Table 8.1 shows the state coverage for each of the seven reporters.

Table 8.1   West's Regional Reporter state coverage

Title	Abbreviation	Case Coverage
Atlantic Reporter	A. A.2d A.3d	CT, DE, MD, ME, NH, NJ, PA, RI, VT, and DC
North Eastern Reporter	N.E. N.E. 2d	IL, IN, MA, NY, OH
North Western Reporter	N.W. N.W. 2d	IA, MI, MN, ND, NE, SD, WI
Pacific Reporter	P. P.2d P.3d	AK, AZ, CA, CO, HI, ID, KS, MT, NV, NM, OK, OR, UT, WA, WY
South Eastern Reporter	S.E. S.E. 2d	GA, NC, SC, VA, WV
Southern Reporter	So. So. 2d	AL, FL, LA, MS
South Western Reporter	S.W. S.W. 2d S.W. 3d	AR, KY, MO, TN, TX

SEARCHING FOR CASES

It is necessary to have a basic understanding of legal publishing practices in order to successfully search for cases. We will limit our discussion here to cases on the federal level, although the principles generally apply to state cases as well.

Published Opinions

Case law that is published can be used as precedent for other cases. Published cases are collected in print books, called reporters. This is important to point out, since many readers will not have access to legal databases such as Nexis Uni or Westlaw Campus Research and will want to consult the print reporters instead. Judges can decide if cases have precedential value or not. For more on unpublished cases, please see Gerken (2004).

These opinions are generally published through West's National Reporter System. As we mentioned earlier in chapter 1, early government publishing in the United States was controlled by private interests. That tradition has held on in the case of most published legal cases. It is important to note the major series of cases so that your next visit to a law library will not be as mysterious.

West's federal cases have the following formats:

Supreme Court Reporter—102 S. Ct. 1388

Federal Reporter (U.S. Circuit Courts of Appeal)—34 F.3d 1048

Federal Supplement (U.S. District Courts)—204 F. Supp. 2d 1309

West's division of the legal world greatly differs from the federal district courts. Here is the state coverage through the West National Reporter System.

Atlantic Reporter—CT, DC, DE, MD, ME, NH, NJ, PA, RI, VT

South Eastern Reporter—GA, NC, SC, VA, WV

Southern Reporter—AL, FL, LA, MS

North Eastern Reporter—IL, IN, MA, NY, OH

South Western Reporter—AR, KY, MO, TN, TX

North Western Reporter—IA, MI, MN, ND, NE, SD, WI

Pacific Reporter—AK, AZ, CA, CO, HI, ID, KS, MT, NV, NM, OK, OR, UT, WA, WY

For coverage of West's National Reporter System, please consult the publisher's website by searching Google like this: *site:westlaw.com regional reporters map.*

SUPREME COURT OPINIONS

We will start with the Supreme Court of the United States for several reasons. These are among the most requested decisions, the court is closely watched for landmark decisions, and they are most often cited by those interested in public policy and lobbying efforts. Also, unlike most other court decisions, these are freely available.

Slip Opinions

In the print days, when Supreme Court opinions were first released, they were on slips of paper (or a pamphlet of many pages). Thus, they were called "slip opinions." Since they were not yet bound into the permanent volumes, they had no page numbering. In the digital world, the same situation occurs with digital slip opinions. Notice that in Figure 8.2, there is no pagination given for the case. This follows the common patterns across government of an initial document being released independently, and then later being bound into a permanent book form. In the digital age,

Cite as: 587 U. S. ___ (2019)   1

Opinion of the Court

NOTICE: This opinion is subject to formal revision before publication in the preliminary print of the United States Reports. Readers are requested to notify the Reporter of Decisions, Supreme Court of the United States, Washington, D. C. 20543, of any typographical or other formal errors, in order that corrections may be made before the preliminary print goes to press.

SUPREME COURT OF THE UNITED STATES

No. 17–778

JAMAR ALONZO QUARLES, PETITIONER v.
UNITED STATES

ON WRIT OF CERTIORARI TO THE UNITED STATES COURT OF
APPEALS FOR THE SIXTH CIRCUIT

[June 10, 2019]

JUSTICE KAVANAUGH delivered the opinion of the Court.

Section 924(e) of Title 18, also known as the Armed Career Criminal Act, mandates a minimum 15-year prison sentence for a felon who unlawfully possesses a firearm and has three prior convictions for a "serious drug offense" or "violent felony." Section 924(e) defines "violent felony" to include "burglary." Under this Court's 1990 decision in

Figure 8.2   A digital slip opinion displaying no pagination

slip opinions first show up in the U.S. Supreme Court website (https://www.supremecourt.gov/).

United States Reports

Final, official opinions are published in the print (and online) title *United States Reports* (abbreviated simply as U.S.). Pay heed to the caution on the Supreme Court website that only the bound version of their opinions is official:

Only the printed bound volumes of the *United States Reports* contain the final, official opinions of the Supreme Court of the United States. In case of discrepancies between a bound volume and the materials included here—or any other version of the same materials, whether print or electronic, official or unofficial—the printed bound volume controls. (https://www.supremecourt.gov/opinions/boundvolumes.aspx)

The early bound volumes of *U.S. Reports* were known by the names of the reporters and may bear a citation with the reporter's name (thus they are called the "nominative reporters"). Thus, 5 U.S. would be the same as 1 Cranch. Thus, the citation *Marbury v. Madison*, 5 U.S. (1 Cranch) 137 (1803). The early Supreme Court reporters and coordinated with *U.S. Reports* volumes in Table 8.2.

After volume 90 of *U.S. Reports*, the names of reporters are not generally used in citations to opinions.

Supreme Court opinions are the only ones distributed through the FDLP. They can be found in print in depository libraries under the SuDocs number JU 6.8:. HeinOnline's Supreme Court Library, available at colleges and universities with law schools, has an easily accessible online collection of the entire set, back to volume 1. The Library of Congress digital collections contain digital versions of every case going back to volume 1 of *U.S. Reports.* Although the collection is searchable, it is not browsable. Perhaps the easiest way to see all cases within a particular volume of the Supreme Court set is

Table 8.2   **Early Supreme Court reporters coordinated with volumes of**
U.S. Reports

Reporter	*U.S. Reports* Vol.	Reporter Vol.
Alexander J. Dallas (1790–1800)	1 U.S.–4 U.S.	1 Dall.–4 Dall.
William Cranch (1801–1815)	5 U.S.–13 U.S.	1 Cranch–9 Cranch
Henry Wheaton (1816–1827)	14 U.S.–25 U.S.	1 Wheat.–12 Wheat.
Richard Peters (1828–1842)	26 U.S.–41 U.S.	1 Pet.–16 Pet.
Benjamin Chew Howard (1843–1860)	42 U.S.–65 U.S.	1 How.–24 How.
Jeremiah Sullivan Black (1861–1862)	66 U.S.–67 U.S.	1 Black–2 Black
John William Wallace (1863–1874)	68 U.S.–90 U.S.	1 Wall.–23 Wall.

to search Google like this: *site:loc.gov 435 u.s.* Govinfo.gov lists *U.S. Reports* in its index, but it merely links out to the Library of Congress content.

The Oyez Project

Every Supreme Court session begins with the Marshal saying "Oyez, oyez, oyez." According to dictionaries, the term goes back to the fifteenth century and is an imperative form of the verb "to hear." The website oyez .org, sponsored by Cornell University's Legal Information Institute (LII), Justia, and Chicago-Kent College of Law, not only provides links to case syllabi, opinions, and dissenting opinions, it also features audio files of oral arguments and opinion announcements, when available. This certainly makes court decisions more compelling, interesting, and dramatic. Biographies of Supreme Court justices, current and historic, are also available.

C-SPAN Videos

C-SPAN has a video library covering the Supreme Court (https://www.c -span.org/supremeCourt/). C-SPAN programming covering landmark cases, and the workings of the Supreme Court can generally be found here, as well as selected oral arguments going back to the 1990s.

WESTLAW AND LEXIS

As you may have noticed in the GPO tool Govinfo.gov (if you are reading this book in consecutive order), there are relatively few resources for the judicial branch. This is largely because the legal information industry has been taken over by two commercial publishers, Westlaw and Lexis (Arewa 2006).

48 F.Supp.2d 1212 (1999)

SONY COMPUTER ENTERTAINMENT INC., et al., Plaintiffs,

v.

CONNECTIX CORPORATION, Defendant.

No. C-99-0390-CAL.

United States District Court, N.D. California.

April 20, 1999.

1213   *1213 Joel Linzner, Townsend & Townsend & Crew LLP, San Francisco, CA, Riley R. Russell, Sony Computer Entertainment America, Inc., Foster City, CA, for plaintiffs.

William Sloan Coats, Howrey & Simon, Menlo Park, CA, Bonnie E. Fought, Connectix Corporation, San Mateo, CA, for defendant.

ORDER ON MOTION FOR PRELIMINARY INJUNCTION

LEGGE, District Judge.

1214   Now before the court is plaintiff's motion for a preliminary injunction. On January *1214 27, 1999 plaintiff Sony filed its complaint alleging copyright infringement and other causes of action against defendant Connectix Corporation. Since that date, Sony made two applications for temporary restraining orders against Connectix' product, the Virtual Game System ("VGS"). This court granted the second application for a temporary restraining order, for the reasons stated on the record in open court on March 11, 1999. After expedited discovery by the parties, the present motion was filed. Sony has also amended its complaint, but this motion for a preliminary injunction is evaluated in the context of plaintiff's original complaint.

Figure 8.3   Example of a publicly available court opinion. *Source:* Google Scholar.

These two publishers do an amazing job of adding value to court opinions, but they also make it more difficult for those without adequate financial resources to gain access to these materials. Figure 8.3 shows the publicly available court opinion from the U.S. District Court for the Northern District of California.

Figure 8.4 shows the Nexis Uni version of the same opinion.

Notice how much value is added to the official opinion: controlled vocabulary, hyperlinking to subsequent history, judge information, citations in the U.S. Code, and the ability to export citation information. Notice as well that the Nexis Uni version displays a stop sign, warning researchers that this case has a subsequent negative history, meaning that this case is not the final word on this area of law.

It is always better to use the Westlaw (or Westlaw Campus) or Lexis (or Nexis Uni) version, if you are fortunate enough to have access. That way you can get the value-added content and also see if the case you are viewing has had subsequent positive or negative treatment in the courts.

PACER

PACER is controversial. Begun in the 1980s before GPO's successful GPO Access initiative that emphasized free public access in electronic format, PACER was allowed by Congress to charge fees for everything except Supreme Court filings. The access costs have risen over the years, and today, it is very expensive to access materials. It shouldn't be that way (Schultze 2017). It was originally intended that the database charge money to recover costs, not to compete with expensive databases from the private sector for which one can be the priciest. Recent legislation has been introduced to change this, but it has not passed yet.

Figure 8.4 Nexis Uni version of *Sony Computer Entertainment, Inc. v. Connectix Corp.* Reprinted from Nexis Uni with permission. Copyright 2019 LexisNexis. All rights reserved.

The PACER website (https://www.pacer.gov/) states that "Public Access to Court Electronic Records (PACER) is an electronic public access service that allows users to obtain case and docket information online from federal appellate, district, and bankruptcy courts." Their definition of public access services certainly differs from that of GPO. True, there have been pilot projects over the years between PACER and GPO's FDLP to attempt to make the database more accessible, but, in the end, users are still stuck with paying fees for their own government information.

The value of PACER is that it contains more than opinions of federal appellate, district, and bankruptcy courts; docket sheets contain lists of background documents related to the cases. These materials are valuable to researchers trying to understand all the information underlying a court's ultimate decision.

Some of these materials may be freely available through individual court websites, although not systematically across all federal courts as PACER is. For example, many court sites contain audio files of oral arguments.

In the case of the Supreme Court, briefs, or materials submitted to the court in advocacy for a particular side in a case, are available in many law libraries and in larger academic libraries.

Gale's *Making of Modern Law: U.S. Supreme Court Records and Briefs, 1832–1978,* provides easy access to scans of briefs filed. ProQuest's Supreme Court Insight is a comprehensive collection of all Supreme Court documents from 1975 to recent years.

SECONDARY SOURCES BEFORE PRIMARY SOURCES

In general, it is advisable to seek out secondary legal sources before trying to delve into primary sources (unless you really want to get confused and lost). Secondary sources, such as legal encyclopedias (*American Jurisprudence* [AmJur] and *Corpus Juris Secundum* [CJS]), law review articles (found in HeinOnline and Google Scholar), and legal guidebooks (such as the *West Nutshell Series*) are excellent ways to quickly acquire sufficient background information, specific citations to statutes and regulations, and references to legal cases, not only by plaintiff/defendant but by legal citation. This makes finding primary sources much faster. Otherwise, you will be adrift in the unsorted haystack of almost relevant, but not exactly correct, primary sources.

Google can be a great tool in legal research, as long as you use it with care. Wikipedia is often prominently featured in Google result sets, and the legal citations there are usually accurate. You just need to verify that this is the case. I have found errors in Wikipedia and sometimes have spent several hours trying to untangle the citation mess. But at least Google searches can (usually) get you on the right track.

For example, if you were looking for the landmark Supreme Court case involving sexual orientation from Colorado, you might search Google like this: *sexual orientation colorado supreme court.* This would lead you to the Wikipedia page that mentions *Romer v. Evans,* 517 U.S. 620 (1996), and there you have your citation. The same strategy usually works well for statutes and compilations.

WHERE TO GET CASES

If you have access to Nexis Uni or Westlaw Campus Research, these will serve you well. Not only do they provide access to precedent-setting case law but they also show the disposition of the cases (that is, whether they are "good law" or not). You need to know if a case was later overturned on appeal or if it still stands today. Searching free sources will not necessarily give you that essential information.

You can search Google Scholar for case law. You may have noticed the "Case law" radio button on the Scholar main search page. Google allows you to select courts from lists of federal and state jurisdictions. For example, you may want to set Scholar to search for your state courts, as well as the federal district court that covers your state and the relevant federal circuit court of appeals. Google Scholar results often (although not always) give you the official West citation, which is essential in properly citing the case and also useful in locating the case in Nexis Uni, Westlaw Campus Research, or other commercial databases. The Google Scholar version of opinions may lack parallel citation references, prior history, headnotes (value-added controlled vocabulary), and references to legislative and regulatory codes, but it will have the basic opinion as originally published on the court website.

There is also a "How Cited" feature that works very much like Google Scholar's citations. However, it lacks the nuances of the Lexis Shepard's Citation Service features or Westlaw's KeyCite. These two commercial services clearly point out if a point in a case is "good law" or not and if it should be used as precedent with caution. The Google "how cited" feature merely gives citations without clearly giving the status of the case.

Many depository libraries and law libraries allow public access to databases like Nexis Uni and Westlaw Campus Research, and some even allow limited access to the full Westlaw and Lexis for checking the status of cases. It never hurts to search for a depository library or law library near you to inquire about access. Table 8.3 summarizes sources of court cases from commercial sources, as well as those that are freely available.

Table 8.3   Sources of federal court cases from commercial and freely available sources

Supreme Court	
Commercial Sources	Freely Available
West's Supreme Court Reporter and *United States Supreme Court Reports, Lawyers' Edition*; Online via Nexis Uni and Westlaw Campus Research	• United States Reports (SuDocs:); Online via https://www.supremecourt.gov/ from 1988 to present • Via Govinfo at https://www.govinfo.gov/app/collection/uscourts/ for selected cases since April 2005 • *United States Reports* in HathiTrust (HT 000063625, 009782035) • *United States Reports*, Selected volumes in Internet Archive • Google Scholar

(*continued*)

Table 8.3 (continued)

Circuit Courts of Appeal

Commercial Sources	Freely Available

Print: *Federal Reporter,* as well as in the regional reporters: *Atlantic Reporter, North Eastern Reporter, North Western Reporter, Pacific Reporter, South Eastern Reporter, Southern Reporter, South Western Reporter, California Reporter, New York Supplement*; Online via Nexis Uni and Westlaw Campus Research	• Older cases (pre-1923) in HathiTrust:
	  • *Federal Reporter* (HT 100663455)
	  • *Atlantic Reporter* (HT 007855027, 007822946)
	  • *North Eastern Reporter* (HT 100663277, 006665169)
	  • *North Western Reporter* (HT 006665167)
	  • *Pacific Reporter* (HT 100334005, 100671815, 010085292)
	  • *South Eastern Reporter* (HT 006665168)
	  • *South Western Reporter* (HT 010116986, 100333420)
	  • *California Reporter* (HT 100836372)
	  • *New York Supplement* (HT 100682352, 006665360)
	• Via Govinfo at https://www.govinfo.gov/app/collection/uscourts/ for selected cases for past 20 years or so
	• Google Scholar

District Courts

Commercial Sources	Freely Available
Print: *Federal Supplement*; Online via Nexis Uni and Westlaw Campus Research	• Older cases (pre-1923) in HathiTrust: • *Federal Supplement* (HT 009922654) • Via Govinfo at https://www.govinfo.gov/app/collection/uscourts/ for selected cases for past 20 years or so • Google Scholar

Bankruptcy Courts

Commercial Sources	Freely Available
Print: *Bankruptcy Reporter*; Online via Nexis Uni and Westlaw Campus Research	• Via Govinfo at https://www.govinfo.gov/app/collection/uscourts/ for selected cases for past 20 years or so • Google Scholar

Tax Court

Commercial Sources	Freely Available
Online via Nexis Uni and Westlaw Campus Research; HeinOnline	• HathiTrust from 1942 onward (HT 004510567, 100946969, 002637456) • *Reports of the United States Tax Court* (SuDocs: JU 11.7/A 2:) • Google Scholar

ISSUANCES: PRELIMINARY VERSUS FINAL

As you likely noticed when reading this book, many important publications are first issued in a preliminary form, and later in a final version. This may not be as apparent in the online world, but it was very apparent in the pre-web days. This practice occurs in all three branches of government. Table 8.4 shows the print title of both the preliminary and final versions of selected key publications.

Table 8.4   Preliminary print publications and final publications across three branches of government

Legislative Branch		
Category	**Preliminary Title**	**Final Title**
Debate and Proceedings	*Congressional Record* Daily Edition	*Congressional Record* Permanent (Bound) Edition
Congressional Reports	Slip Reports	Bound in the *U.S. Congressional Serial Set*
Public and Private Laws	"Slip Laws"	*United States Statutes at Large*
Executive Branch		
Category	**Preliminary Title**	**Final Title**
Final Rules	*Federal Register*	*Code of Federal Regulations*
Treaties	"Slip Treaties" *Treaties and Other International Acts Series* (TIAS)	*United States Treaties and Other International Agreements* (UST)
Presidential Speeches and Issuances	*Weekly Compilation of Presidential Documents*	*Public Papers of the Presidents*
Judicial Branch		
Category	**Preliminary Title**	**Final Title**
Supreme Court Opinions	Slip Opinions	*United States Reports*

The same thing occurs in the online world, but the distinctions are not as apparent. Even with online dissemination, the gap time between preliminary version and final version has not necessarily shortened. The time gap may be a year to a year-and-a-half, as in the case of rules in the *Federal Register* being published in the *Code of Federal Regulations*, or to longer than 30 years, as is the case with slip treaties.

COMMERCIAL ONLINE SERVICES

Most people have heard of Westlaw and Lexis. These commercial databases are pricey and are the services used by attorneys. They are also offered to law school students free of charge while they are enrolled, in hopes of getting them addicted to the respective services. More recently, Bloomberg Law has become a popular option as well.

Many colleges and university libraries subscribe to the academic analogs of Westlaw and Lexis, Westlaw Campus Research and Nexis Uni, respectively. The same legal cases are accessible through these databases, it's just that many of the legal practice aids are not included in the interfaces. Either of these databases are excellent ways to search for cases on legal topics and to discover if cases are "good law"—that is, if they can still be relied upon or if they have been overturned by a higher court. This is not very easy to do when searching freely available cases, such as are found in Google Scholar.

EXERCISES

1. The case *Romer v. Evans* went to the Supreme Court. Give the citation from *United States Reports* and provide a summary of the holding in this case.

2. If the Supreme Court comes out with a decision today, where should you look to find the official opinion? Where will it eventually be published?

3. You see a citation that reads 131 L. Ed. 2d 985. Provide the parallel citations from *United States Reports* and *Supreme Court Reporter*. Also give the name of this case.

4. Look up any legal case using Google Scholar. Now look up that same case in Nexis Uni or Westlaw Campus Research. What do the commercial databases tell you about your case that was not available in Google Scholar?

REFERENCES

Arewa, Olufunmilayo B. 2006. "Open Access in a Closed Universe: Lexis, Westlaw, Law Schools, and the Legal Information Market." *Lewis and Clark Law Review* 10, no. 4: 797–839.

Barnum, George. 2011. "Public Documents Our Specialty"—GPO's Public Documents Library 1895–1971 Part 1: A Library for GPO. Updated March 18, 2013. Accessed December 12, 2019. https://www.fdlp.gov/all-newsletters/featured-articles/1084-public-documents-library.

Gerken, Joseph L. 2004. "A Librarian's Guide to Unpublished Judicial Opinions." *Law Library Journal* 96, no. 3: 475–502.

Schultze, Stephen J. 2017. "The Price of Ignorance: The Constitutional Cost of Fees for Access to Electronic Public Court Records." *Georgetown Law Journal* 106, no. 4: 1197–1228.

9

Statistical Sources
(Not Including Census)

The federal government has always been interested in gathering and publishing statistics. After all, the census is instantiated in the Constitution. The earliest volumes of the *American State Papers* and the Serial Set are replete with statistical tables. The problem is not a lack of statistics but a fear among the public, and even among librarians, of statistics—especially government-issued statistics. In this chapter, we are not concerned about things such as probability, p-values, mean, median, average, chi-square curves, cluster samples, random samples, or scary-looking equations. We won't be discussing using SAS, SPSS, R, or other statistical software packages. There are already many books about that. What we are concerned with here is knowing what is available from government sources and how to find them.

First, we will consider a general framework for approaching the search process for government statistics, and then we will look at specific databases. The following chapters will focus especially on census statistics, since that is such a specialized application of statistics.

BASIC STATISTICAL STARTING STRATEGIES

Before we examine a selected collection of federal statistical databases, we need to discuss general statistical search strategies. Many people, librarians included, experience a sense of fear and trembling when confronted with a request for government statistics. Statistics themselves bring about a fear factor, and the category of government statistics only compounds that fear. There are several reasons we can suggest for these fears. First, we are accustomed to searching for textual information. We put words in a search box, and inevitably we get relevant results. Numerical information is quite different. While you can search for words, terms, subjects, names of people, how do you effectively search for numbers? You don't know what the answer will be, so you are unable to frame a question. You often cannot even guess what the categories are, what the x and y axes on a chart would look like, or what the data availability is. In addition, when using a search engine like Google, you are dissatisfied with the results because you simply don't know how to search.

One reason might be that we don't get good results when attempting direct-style searches. A direct-style search is when you simply put the question into a search engine. Actually, a Google search does a much better job now at getting results than it did a decade ago. As an example, take a question I recently received. The user wants "hospital patient discharge rates and average length of stay at the county level." Putting those exact words into Google comes pretty close to getting excellent results. That would be an example of a direct-style search.

An indirect search, on the other hand, takes a step back and considers what kind of resource would likely contain the statistics or data that are being sought. It is likely that a database related to health care, hospital administration, or patient outcomes would be the likely source. So instead of searching as in the paragraph above, you could search like this: *hospital discharge statistics database.* Or perhaps like this: *patient length of stay database.*

Another common reason is that, while they get close to the desired answer, they don't get down to exactly to what they, or their library patron, wants. For example, they may not have the correct geography. The geography they find is commonly too general, maybe down to the state level, but they need statistics down to the place, zip code, or census block level. Another reason some find statistics intimidating is that they don't go through the thought process of considering what agency or group would be interested enough in the type of statistics you're after to collect them. After collecting the data, how might they make that information available? Might they put it on the web for free, or are they more likely to lock in into a fee-based database?

There are some steps that you can take to make these questions less intimidating.

Strategy 1: Use Google Web for Direct and Indirect Search Strategies

That's right, Google Web. I purposely call it Google Web to distinguish it from Google Scholar and Google Books. Searching Google takes a bit of skill for statistical information. That's because you cannot usually search directly for the statistics, since the information is often contained in a database that is opaque to Google's indexing. First try searching directly. You just might find what you are looking for. If that doesn't work well, then try an indirect search strategy. For example, let's say you are looking for the number of housing units in the 80210 zip code that are renter-occupied versus the number that are owner-occupied. Typing that question into Google will help a little bit. Many times, Google will provide direct statistics, with links to source information. In most cases, you will need an authoritative series of statistics. In these cases, you need to perform indirect Google searches. We might search Google for the renter-occupied question like this: *housing statistics.* Google suggests the U.S. Census Bureau, pointing to a helpful guide page with links to available datasets.

Let's try this with another question. Say you are looking for the trade balance with Japan. You really want a U.S. government perspective on this. In this situation, you could search Google like this: *site:gov trade balance with japan.* Some of the results may directly answer the question at hand, but, more importantly, you need to make a list of government entities that have an interest in this topic. Here is a list of potential government agencies related to this question:

- U.S. Census Bureau: census.gov
- United States Trade Representative: ustr.gov
- Bureau of Economic Analysis: bea.gov [under the Commerce Dept.]
- United States International Trade Commission: usitc.gov [independent agency]
- CRS Reports: crsreports.congress.gov
- International Trade Administration: trade.gov [under the Commerce Dept.]
- White House: whitehouse.gov
- U.S. Department of Agriculture: usda.gov
- U.S. Senate: senate.gov

- National Oceanic and Atmospheric Administration: noaa.gov [under the Commerce Dept.]
- Central Intelligence Agency: cia.gov
- Bureau of Transportation Statistics: bts.gov [under the Transportation Dept.]
- State Department: state.gov
- National Science Foundation: nsf.gov [independent agency]
- Government Accountability Office: gao.gov [independent agency under Congress]
- International Trade Administration's Export.gov: export.gov

The list goes on. As you can see, it would not be in our best interest to stop with the first result offered up by Google. But our work is just beginning. Now we need to take each of the domains we have uncovered and continue to drill down into the sites to look for more perspectives on our statistical question. Like this:

site:census.gov trade balance with japan

site:ustr.gov trade balance with japan

site:bea.gov trade balance with japan

site:usitc.gov trade balance with japan

site:crsreports.gov trade balance with japan

site:trade.gov trade balance with japan—and so forth.

TIPS FOR SEARCHING GOOGLE FOR STATISTICS

1. Try to find the statistics by asking your statistical question in the Google search box. I call this the "go for the gold" approach. You just might get lucky and turn up the statistics right away.

2. Try an indirect search strategy. Search Google for terms like *statistics maritime interdictions*; or a similar search: *data crimes at sea international*. Use your synonym skills to change up the terms you search by.

3. Try using Google advanced search techniques, like domain-specific searching. Try searching like this: *site:un.org maritime statistics crime*; or again: *international data maritime interdictions site:org*.

4. Use Google's "filetype" command to find statistics kept in database formats like Excel. Excel uses file extensions ".xls" or ".xlsx". You can from a search like this with Google: *pet ownership statistics filetype:xls*. Since newer Excel files have the .xlsx extension, you can rerun the search with that alternation: *pet ownership statistics filetype:xlsx*. Your results will likely be different.

Let's try an even less direct strategy. Let's look for government databases on the topic. Previously, we were seeking government agencies that addressed a specific topic, but now we just want to look generally for databases that could be searched. The idea here is that often, database content is not exposed to Google. As a result, some of this content might not have been revealed with more specific searching. A search on same topic as above might look like this:

site:gov foreign trade database

What did this search uncover?

1. The Census Bureau as *USA Trade Online* (https://usatrade.census.gov/). Somewhat annoyingly, users must register first. That's because the Commerce Department used to sell access to this database. Now we still need to go through the annoying process of selecting a password following strict rules:

     Both user password and maintenance password should be minimum 12 characters. At least one uppercase, one lowercase, one numeric, and one special character. No spaces.

     Special characters: !,@,#,$,%,^,&,and ' are allowed.

     When the Commerce Department will join the rest of free government information in the twenty-first century is unknown.

2. The U.S. International Trade Commission has a database, dataweb .usitc.gov that provides merchandise trade and tariff data.

3. The International Trade Administration has several searchable databases including Trade Policy Information System and Exporter Database. To find all of these, search Google: *site:trade.gov trade statistics databases.*

4. Export.gov has their TradeStats Express database with two sections titled Global Patterns of U.S. Merchandise Trade and Product Profiles of U.S. Merchandise Trade with a Selected Market.

There are other databases as well, but this illustrated how a less direct search can produce excellent results on a topic.

Let's summarize. I showed how to use Google three different ways to find government statistics:

•   Direct searching: "Go for the gold." Just type in your statistical question and see if it works. It often does.

•   Domain searching for the topic. Two steps here: first discover which government entities care about the topic with a *site:gov* search. Then repeat the search using the specific government subdomain to drill down more deeply agency by agency.

•   Database searching. Deliberately do not search for your question. Instead search broadly for government entities that might have databases related to the content of interest.

Strategy 2: ProQuest Statistical Insight

If Statistical Insight is available to you, it can be quite useful. Ask yourself the question "who cares"—that is, what organization or government cares enough to publish the kind of statistics you are looking for. Statistical Insight will likely be able to help answer that question with names of U.S. government agencies, state government agencies, international organizations, and foreign governments that care enough about the topic to issues statistical publications. The following description of Statistical Insight's historical background explains what it contains and what its value is. (This is an example of why it is important to know the physical analog versions of a database.) Before the database was with ProQuest, it was owned by Lexis-Nexis, who bought it from Congressional Information Service (CIS). CIS issued this reference tool as three print indexes. The first was *American Statistics Index*, or ASI, which covered U.S. statistics. This index featured statistics issued in government publications and provided a valuable index to depository collections back when everything was in print. International and foreign statistics were the focus of *Index to International Statistics*, or IIS. This index covered two categories: statistics emanating from international bodies such as the United Nations, its organs, and other international bodies; and foreign governments, such as the governments of Germany, Japan, and so forth. Their third statistical index, *Statistical Reference Index*, or SRI, covered statistics from sources that fell outside the scope of ASI and IIS. The SRI portion was the most complex, as it covered six categories of statistical-issuing entities. Thinking of them in terms of their pneumonic associations may be a useful way to help remember all six (Table 9.1).

When all else fails, this resource provides a helpful pathway. I don't often use *Statistical Insight* to find actual statistics; rather, I use it to get a frame of reference, to inform me of "who cares" about the statistics I am looking for (that is, who publishes the statistics). Then I search for the statistics from the website of the issuing agency, since the *Statistical Insight* tables are likely too old for what I am looking for.

Table 9.1 Six categories within CIS's *Statistical Reference Index*

Abbreviation	*Statistical Reference Index* Category
A	Associations
B	Business
C	Commercial Publishers
R	Research Institutes
S	State Agencies
U	Universities

We can try this strategy with our question about finding statistics on the trade balance with Japan. Placing *trade balance japan* in the Statistical Insight search box retrieves results from these categories:

- International organizations
- Federal agencies
- Commercial publishers
- Associations
- Research organizations
- State agencies
- Business organizations
- Universities

Notice how the result categories align with the previous discussion about the print CIS publications. For the purposes of the question at hand, we will focus on the federal agencies category.

The agency breakdown is much like the result sets we were getting from our Google searches. The emphasis here, however, is on specific published tables from agency publications. The numbers are to number of tables, not numbers of web pages. Statistical Insight presents the results in descending order of the number of tables available:

- International Trade Administration (973)
- Department of State (762)
- Foreign Agricultural Service (490)
- U.S. International Trade Commission (463)
- Bureau of Economic Analysis (Department of Commerce) (401)
- Economic Research Service (USDA) (363)
- Bureau of Census (288)
- Federal Reserve Board of Governors (263)
- Energy Information Administration (201)
- Bureau of Labor Statistics (181)

I have to confess, I don't actually use Statistical Insight for the actual tables. I use it to get ideas of what agencies care about the topic, what publications (or databases) contain the data, and how I can find more recent information on the web.

The first question we need to ask in any statistical question is: Who cares? What entity cares enough about this data to publish it? And that's where Statistical Insight comes in.

Strategy 3: ProQuest Statistical Abstract of the United States

For years, reference librarians kept the Census Bureau's *Statistical Abstract of the United States* close at hand. If it wasn't in what was called a "Ready Reference Collection," it was kept inside a drawer so that it would never be checked out and would always be at hand for the inevitable statistical questions that came to those who gave informational directions. It was with great shock when it was announced in March 2011 that it would cease publication after the 2012 edition because of budget constraints and an emphasis on digital dissemination of Census Bureau statistics (U.S. Census Bureau 2012).

ProQuest has taken over publication of a resource that was published from 1878 through 2012 by the U.S. Census Bureau and was the "bible" for U.S. statistics. In a partnership with Bernan Press, through their Rowman and Littlefield imprint, a print version is available for libraries that still want to feature it.

ProQuest has conveniently folded in all the previous years into the interface, providing cross-searching capability for all years. The ProQuest fee-based version follows the same principles of organization and citation as previous editions. Every table cites to the original table and how users can find more detailed information on the topic. If you don't have access to the ProQuest Statistical Abstract, then you could consult the historic versions of Stat Abs, all of which are online through the Census Bureau (*site:census.gov statistical abstract of the united states*), and you will see the Census website featuring online versions back to 1878. The strategy involves looking at older volumes of Stat Abs is to see where the data came from. Every table in Stat Abs gives attribution to the source. More recent annual volumes have URLs in them. The URLs may have changed since publication, but at least you will know the name of the issuing agency. This will give us a clue as to where to look for current data. If you need older statistics from the *Statistical Abstract*, a much better source than the annual version is the *Historical Statistics of the United States* (see below).

One of the greatest features of the old Stat Abs, and one that still exists in the ProQuest continuing version, is the inclusion of nongovernmental sources of statistics. For example, the table for summary characteristics of hospitals includes data provided by the American Hospital Association. The Investment Company Institute provides statistics on individual retirement accounts (IRAs). Data on credit card holders is provided by the *Nilson Report*, a respected newsletter of the industry. When ProQuest took over publication of Stat Abs, I wondered if these nongovernmental associations and commercial entities would be willing to give their statistics to ProQuest, since it is a for-profit company. For the time being, it appears that these data sets are making their way into the publication.

Strategy 4: Going beyond U.S. National Sources

We discuss the official statistical program of the United States below. The main function of this book is to feature U.S. federal resources, but it is often helpful to go beyond U.S. statistical sources and venture into foreign and international sources.

International Agencies

On the international side of things, the United Nations Statistics Division has a helpful site that lists statistical programs of the UN as well as other autonomous organizations (https://unstats.un.org/home/international _agencies/), or search Google: *site:un.org statistical international agency partners*. You can also just Google: *united nations programmes agencies* to find more about the many agencies that exist that may offer international statistics. The common "go to" UN agencies that have statistics are the Food and Agriculture Organization (FAO), International Labour Organization (ILO), International Telecommunication Union (ITU), United Nations Educational, Scientific and Cultural Organization (UNESCO), and the World Health Organization (WHO).

The UN isn't the only international organization with statistics. You might also want to consider organizations such as the African Development Bank, Asian Development Bank, Caribbean Community (CARICOM), European Development Bank, Eurostat (European Union), International Energy Agency (IEA), International Monetary Fund (IMF), Inter-American Development Bank, Organisation for Economic Cooperation and Development (OECD), Organization of the Petroleum Exporting Countries (OPEC), the World Bank, and the World Trade Organization (WTO).

Since there are over 3,000 international bodies, often referred to as international organizations (IGOs), you should search the freely available IGO search feature from the Union of International Organizations (http://www.uia.org/igosearch).

Foreign National Sources

The U.S. Census Bureau comes to our aid when trying to locate foreign national statistics (*site:census.gov international statistical agencies*). Academic libraries often have comprehensive listings of foreign statistical agencies (*foreign statistical agencies list site:edu*). Although it is usually a better use of time to get individual country information from one of the UN agencies (because foreign data differs so much from country to country), there are times when in-country statistics on the provincial, prefectural (or whatever a country calls its subdivisions) level.

Table 9.2   Top level domains from selected countries

Afghanistan	.af
Argentina	.ar
Brazil	.br
China (People's Republic of)	.cn
Japan	.jp
Netherlands	.nl
Saudi Arabia	.sa
South Africa	.za
Spain	.es
Thailand	.th
United Kingdom	.uk

It is often beneficial to search foreign government statistical information using the top-level internet domain assigned to the country, and then attempting to discover the statistical entity within the country. To find a list of top-level domains for each country, search Google like this: *TLD*. That's it! Generally, the Wikipedia page for "List of Internet Top-Level Domains" is first or second on the list, but there are other lists as well. I like the Wikipedia list because it also has country flags, a nice graphical touch. Table 9.2 shows TLDs from a sampling of countries.

Let's try finding foreign statistical agencies from several countries.

Let's try Afghanistan. Using the Wikipedia list, we discover that the TLD is *af*. Next, searching Google like this: *site:af government*, we see that the country uses *gov.af* for government sites. Now we can search *site:gov.af statistics*. We immediately discover that they have a Central Statistics Organization (cso.gov.af) and a Statistical Yearbook.

Now we will try Japan. From the Wikipedia page for TLDs, we see that the top-level domain for Japan is *jp*. Searching Google again for *site:jp government* yields results that show us that go.jp is the secondary domain for the government of Japan. Just a note here—don't make assumptions about what the government domain for a country is (or even that there is one). Now we can do the final search: *site:go.jp statistics*. We discover the Statistics Bureau home page, a guide to statistics, and the *Statistical Handbook of Japan*.

Please see Appendix C for a list of government domains for countries of the world.

Strategy 5: Do a Literature Search

If you are totally lost, try searching the scholarly literature in the field to see how other researchers approach the topic and what statistical sources

> ### What Is the Difference between International Statistics and Foreign Statistics?
>
> Good question, and often a source of great confusion.
>
> International Statistics. By "international" we mean more than one country, multinational, global, or worldwide. The United Nations is a major publisher of international statistics. But don't forget about the many subsidiary entities of the UN (https://unstats.un.org/home/international_agencies/).
>
> Foreign Statistics. Foreign statistics are issued by individual countries. Please see the section on foreign government publications to see how to search within the internet top-level domains for each country of the world. Most countries have a statistical bureau or agency with publicly available data. Because foreign data differs so much from country to country, it is usually a better use of time to get individual country information from one of the UN agencies. But there are times, for example, when searching for subnational statistics (that is, statistics on the provincial, prefectural, or whatever a country calls its subdivisions) level, that in-country statistics will help the most.

they use. You can do this using general aggregator databases, such as EBSCO's Academic Search, ProQuest Central, or Gale's Academic One-File. Another approach is discipline-specific databases (see the relevant chapters within this book). Finally, you can use Google Scholar to find scholarly articles that may cite the statistical series you are looking for. Scholars writing in academic journal literature often cite the resources they used in doing their research. By tracking down the sources they used, you can either find the same statistics they used, or use this information as a basis to acquire more current statistics.

PUTTING THE TOOLS TO WORK

Example Search: Let's say that we want to find statistics on fisheries. We want all available statistics, from government statistics to commercial statistics.

Going to ProQuest Statistical Insight, I type *fisheries* into the search box. This will give me the categories that harken back to the origins of this tool, because I get results from international organizations (IIS), federal agencies (ASI), and five of the six categories from SRI (see Table 9.3). Further drilling down gives me the actual documents (if your institution subscribes to this content). I can then search for more current statistics, or use the tables within Statistical Insight, if they meet my needs,

Table 9.3   Selected examples from _Statistical Insight_ of agencies mentioned in SRI having statistics related to the search: _fisheries_

Statistical Insight Facet	Entity with Fishery Statistics
Commercial Publishers	ProQuest (Commercial Publishers)
	Bernan Associates
	Commodity Research Bureau
State Agencies	Hawaii Dept. of Business, Economic Development, and Tourism
	Alaska Dept. of Labor and Workforce Development
	Florida Dept. of Agriculture and Consumer Services
Associations	Council of Better Business Bureaus
	National Association of State Budget Officers
	Foreign Policy Association
	Regional Airline Association
Research Organizations	Center for American Progress
Universities	University of Florida: Bureau of Economic and Business Research

From my fisheries search in Statistical Insight, I see the following federal entities that issue statistics on this topic:

U.S. Federal Agencies

- All federal agencies (11,026)
- National Marine Fisheries Service (1,873)
- National Marine Fisheries Service (Department of Commerce) (1,397)
- Department of State (1,131)
- Foreign Agricultural Service (USDA) (1,126)
- International Trade Administration (688)
- Bureau of Census (316)
- Fish and Wildlife Service (295)
- Office of Management and Budget (254)
- U.S. International Trade Commission (240)
- Department of Agriculture (191)

Now for International Organizations:

International Organizations

- All international organizations (10,062)
- International Bank for Reconstruction and Development (United Nations: World Bank Group) (1,898)

- European Union (803)
- Asian Development Bank (664)
- Thailand National Statistics Office (Thailand) (505)
- Statistics Bureau of Japan, Ministry of Internal Affairs and Communications (Japan) (329)
- All China Marketing Research (China, People's Republic) (304)
- Food and Agriculture Organization (United Nations) (282)
- Organisation for Economic Cooperation and Development (276)
- Economic Commission for Latin America and the Caribbean (United Nations) (224)
- International Monetary Fund (United Nations) (208)

One difference should be noted from the print CIS resources. With the *Index to International Statistics*, the coverage included international organization and foreign government entities together in the series. However, the ProQuest product has chosen to present things differently (maybe that's a good thing). The foreign government tables are not listed in the "Source" section of the result facets but rather in the "Countries and Regions" facets. This makes for a clearer presentation of results, but users will need to know to navigate to a different facet. On the topic of fisheries, we would expect countries like Norway and Japan to have major statistics series on the topic, and indeed they do.

Statistical Insight also has listings for data from commercial publishers, state agencies, associations, research organizations, and universities (as denoted in Table 9.3).

Whereas Statistical Insight gives us more of the viewpoint of traditional publications, especially those issued serially over time, we might also try using Google to locate fishery statistics (as in strategy 1 above). First, we need to locate the entities (organizations, governments, associations) that would likely issue such statistics. To do that, we can start by searching Google like this: *fisheries statistics*. Looking over these initial search results we see that the interested statistical-issuing organization include the United Nations Food and Agriculture Organization (fao.org), U.S. National Oceanic and Atmospheric Administration (noaa.gov), the European Commission (europa.eu), and the Organisation for Economic Co-operation and Development (oecd.org). There are likely other entities as well.

We would want to structure domain-specific Google searches like this:

site:fao.org fisheries statistics

site:noaa.gov fisheries statistics

site:europa.eu fisheries statistics

site:oecd.org fisheries statistics

We should also look up country-specific information, first by finding the top-level domains (TLDs) for relevant countries, finding government sub-domains, and then doing site-specific searching. Using the Wikipedia page for TLDs (https://en.wikipedia.org/wiki/List_of_Internet_top-level_domains), we note that the domains of several relevant countries for which fishing is important: Philippines (*.ph*), Norway (*.no*), and Japan (*.jp*) to get us started. Searching Google for *site:ph government* we discover that *gov.ph* is the government domain; for Norway it appears to be *dep.no;,* and Japan is *go.jp*. There is no uniformity of second-level government domains across countries. It takes a bit of persistence to discover these. We are now prepared to set up searches like this:

site:gov.ph fisheries statistics

site:dep.no fisheries statistics

site:go.jp fisheries statistics

For more insights about searching freely available statistics using Google, I recommend my book about Google searching, *Harnessing the Power of Google: What Every Researcher Should Know* (Brown 2017).

DIVING INTO STATISTICAL DATABASES

We don't have the luxury within the confines of this text of introducing you to every sophisticated statistical database on the market, in addition to the free resources out there. Rather than doing that, let's recall the principles of how to approach learning new databases and their features.

- Determine the database scope. If you don't know the scope, you don't know how to dive in. What data is included? How was the data collected? What are the dates of coverage?
- What is this database all about? Is it about people, companies, countries, cities?
- Who collects the data? What are their methods?
- What are the geographies?
- What are the dates?
- How is the data collected?

With these background considerations in mind, let's dive in to several databases.

Example Search 1: Let's try to find the difference in the cost of living in Denver and San Francisco. We might start by using Google: *cost of living database*. We see some nongovernmental databases, but to get authoritative data, let's restrict results to the .gov domain: *cost of living database site:gov.* We see the result for Consumer Price Index from the Bureau of Labor Statistics, and we go there. After poking around in the various CPI databases, we find what we want in the Average Price Data section.

Example Search 2: We want to find which cities in Colorado have the highest violent crime rates. There are many possible ways we could search for a good database, but we start by searching Google like this: *violent crime database site:gov.* We find the Uniform Crime Reporting Statistics Database from the FBI here: https://www.ucrdatatool.gov/. Looking at the choices in the left margin, it seems that the best selection for this question is "local law enforcement agencies (city and county)—multiple agencies, one variable." We then select all agencies in Colorado and select our one variable, violent crime rate, and quickly retrieve a table with crime rates for 57 Colorado agencies from 1985 to present.

Example Search 3: The FEMA website, at least as of June 2019, is very challenging to navigate. Even though it is supposed to have statistics, being a nonprincipal statistical agency (see below), nothing in the navigation tools suggests that. You want to find hurricane disaster relief statistics. To find these, search Google like this: *site:fema.gov hurricane disaster relief statistics.* This will get you much closer to finding results than browsing the FEMA website.

These examples show how you can search for data without having any idea ahead of time what agency will have the data you need. Of course, it isn't always so easy. There are times when you will need to send an email to a listserve or ask a statistics librarian about the best data source.

HISTORICAL STATISTICAL RESEARCH

Several tools are useful when researching historical government statistics. Before rushing off to the older volumes of the *Statistical Abstract of the United States* (available on the Census Bureau website, HathiTrust, and the Internet Archive), consider consulting the *Historical Statistics of the United States* (Google: *site:census.gov historical statistics of the united states*; HT 007169391, 000707742). Published by the Bureau of the Census, this resource normalizes statistics over long stretches of time. Topics include wealth and income; population characteristics and migration; vital statistics, health, and nutrition; labor force, wages, and working conditions; agriculture; land, forestry, and fisheries; minerals and power; construction and housing; manufactures; transportation; price indexes; balance of payments and foreign trade; banking and finance; and government. A commercial version of this book is available as an online database vended by Cambridge University Press. Many university libraries subscribe to this resource. It updates the statistical tables that ended in the print version in the 1970s and makes tables available for downloading in PDF or Excel formats.

Another resource worth consulting is *The Statistical Work of the National Government* (Schmeckebier 1925). Coverage includes Census publications and also all other statistical publications issued as serials, monographs, within the *American State Papers*, and in the U.S. *Congressional Serial Set*. This is an extremely valuable resource for navigating complex statistical series such as wholesale prices scattered in various numbers of the *Bulletin* of the Bureau of Labor, or the places where statistics on telephones show up. This work is available in full view via HathiTrust.

In addition to all that, the Serial Set itself contains many statistical releases in annual reports, congressional reports, and other miscellaneous tables. Both the ProQuest Serial Set and the Readex Serial Set allow for searching of tables, many of which are statistical tables. In ProQuest, look for the field "Table Title (Serial Set Only). In Readex, use the option to "Limit to Tables."

No source is better for historical economic, banking, and financial statistics than the FRASER project from the Federal Reserve Bank of St. Louis (Google: *fraser fed*). You will also want to use their companion databases FRED and ALFRED. FRED allows for downloading, graphing, and tracking of many time series from 87 sources. ALFRED stands for Archival FRED, intended to access legacy data. Economists can greatly benefit from these important statistical tools applied to historical data.

EXECUTIVE BRANCH STATISTICAL AGENCIES

In past years FedStats could be relied on as a valuable resource for discovering federal statistical information. The FedStats website was established in 1997, in the early days of the web. However, the site unceremoniously disappeared from the internet sometime around February 2018 (Sunlight Foundation 2018).

One of the most useful features of FedStats was the way they featured the statistical programs of the nations, both the principal programs and the others. Of course, we could do what we do whenever we discover "disappeared" government sites: that is: go to the Wayback Machine. For many years, FedStats was hosted on fedstats.gov (https://web.archive.org/web /2015*/fedstats.gov). Since 2015, it has been at fedstats.sites.usa.gov (https://

web.archive.org/web/2018*/http://fedstats.sites.usa.gov/). The best substitute for FedStats is an official publication, *Statistical Programs of the United States Government.*

Each year the Office of Management and Budget publishes *Statistical Programs of the United States Government* (HT 002882166; SuDocs: PREX 2.10/3:; https://purl.fdlp.gov/GPO/gpo112260 [current]; https://purl.access .gpo.gov/GPO/LPS3897 [archived]). This details the Federal Statistical System and its structure. An abbreviated version of this appears each year in the *Analytical Perspectives* volume of the *Budget of the United States Government*, focusing on budgets for these programs.

There are thirteen Principal Statistical Agencies (PSAs) (Table 9.4) and about 100 non-PSA statistical agencies associated with the executive branch. They generate statistics on such topics as the economy, workforce, energy, agriculture, foreign trade, education, housing, crime, transportation, and health.

The OMB's *Statistical Programs of the United States* provides authoritative background information for the over 100 other executive branch agencies that maintain statistics. This resource essentially does what FedStats did, it's just not as well-known as a statistical resource. We will follow their

Table 9.4   The thirteen Principal Statistical Agencies (PSAs) of the federal government

Principal Statistical Agency	URL
Bureau of the Census	https://www.census.gov/
Bureau of Economic Analysis (BEA)	https://www.bea.gov/
Bureau of Justice Statistics (BJS)	https://www.bjs.gov/
Bureau of Labor Statistics (BLS)	https://www.bls.gov/
Bureau of Transportation Statistics (BTS)	https://www.bts.gov/
Economic Research Service (ERS)	https://www.ers.usda.gov/
Energy Information Administration (EIA)	https://www.eia.gov/
National Agricultural Statistics Service (NASS)	https://www.nass.usda.gov/
National Center for Education Statistics	https://nces.ed.gov/
National Center for Health Statistics	https://www.cdc.gov/nchs/
National Center for Science and Engineering Statistics (NCSES), NSF	https://www.nsf.gov/statistics/
Office of Research, Statistics and Policy Analysis, SSA	https://www.ssa.gov/policy/
Statistics of Income Division, IRS	https://www.irs.gov/statistics

Source: Strengthening Federal Statistics, 2019.

breakdown by executive branch. Names of agencies are given, together with their acronyms. It wouldn't be a government agency without an acronym, would it?

Although URLs are given to agencies below, keep in mind that the web can be volatile—websites can change without notice at any time. In addition, government reorganizations occur often. Use a Google search to try to straighten out bad URLs. Consult the OMB's annual *Statistical Programs of the United States* to see if there have been any changes to these programs.

Although the tables below emphasize statistical agencies within departments, we will also draw attention to selected databases and their features.

Department of Agriculture

The two principal statistical agencies Economic Research Service (ERS) and National Agricultural Statistics Service (NASS) were mentioned in the previous section. Seven other agencies also maintain statistical programs on topics such as current demographic statistics, soils, forest, fish, wildlife, public wetlands, agriculture, and labor statistics. Table 9.5 shows both PSA and non-PSA agency statistical agencies under the USDA.

Another agriculture-related statistical resource deserves mention—The National Agricultural Statistics Service (NASS) https://www.nass.usda .gov/ (SuDocs A 92). NASS publisher *Agricultural Statistics* (an annual

Table 9.5   Statistical agencies under the Department of Agriculture

Principal Statistical Agencies	URL
Economic Research Service (ERS)	https://www.ers.usda.gov/
National Agricultural Statistics Service (NASS)	https://www.nass.usda.gov/
Non-PSA Agencies	**URL**
Agricultural Research Service (ARS)	https://www.ars.usda.gov/
Food and Nutrition Service (FNS)	https://www.fns.usda.gov/
Foreign Agricultural Service (FAS)	https://www.fas.usda.gov/
Forest Service (FS)	https://www.fs.fed.us/
Natural Resources Conservation Service (NRCS)	https://www.nrcs.usda.gov/wps/portal/nrcs/site/national/home/
Risk Management Agency (RMA)	https://www.rma.usda.gov/
World Agricultural Outlook Board (WAOB)	https://www.usda.gov/oce/commodity/

publication, available online in PDF format) as well as the Census of Agriculture, currently taken every five years on the years ending in "2" and "7."

When we think "census," our thoughts immediately go to the Census Bureau's Decennial Census of Population and Housing and to the Economic Census. Among the many other censuses is the Census of Agriculture, not under the purview of the Census Bureau but under the Department of Agriculture. The website is a treasure trove of historical census publications, going back to the 1840 agricultural census.

Department of Commerce

The two principal statistical agencies under the Department of Commerce are the Bureau of Economic Analysis and the Census Bureau. One cannot help but notice the diversity of programs and statistical offerings under the administrative purview of this department: demographic information (population and housing) economic and business information (Census Bureau, Bureau of Economic Analysis, Economics and Statistics Administration, International Trade Administration), and science and engineering (covering satellite data, fisheries, etc.).

Prior to 2018, the Economics and Statistics Administration (http://www .esa.doc.gov/) had been listed as one of the Department of Commerce's non-PSA agencies. However, according to the 2018 "Statistical Programs of the United States" report, the ESA ceased operations. As of June 2019, the site www.esa.doc.gov was not working. For previous iterations of the site, use the Internet Archive's Wayback Machine (https://web.archive.org/web /*/http://www.esa.doc.gov/). The site has also been intermittently archived by the End of Term Web Archive (http://eotarchive.cdlib.org/).

Table 9.6 shows both PSA and non-PSA agency statistical agencies under the Commerce Department.

Table 9.6   Statistical agencies under the Department of Commerce

Principal Statistical Agencies	URL
Bureau of the Census	https://www.census.gov/
Bureau of Economic Analysis (BEA)	https://www.bea.gov/
Non-PSA Agencies	**URL**
International Trade Administration	https://www.trade.gov/
National Environmental Satellite, Data, and Information Services (NESDIS)	https://www.nesdis.noaa.gov/
National Marine Fisheries Service (NMFS)	https://www.fisheries.noaa.gov/

Table 9.7   Statistical agencies under the Department of Defense

Non-PSA Agencies	URL
Army Corps of Engineers (ACE)	https://www.usace.army.mil/
Office of People Analytics (OPA)	https://opa.defense.gov/

Department of Defense

There are no principal statistical agencies within the Defense Department. Table 9.7 shows the two non-PSA agency statistical agencies under the Department of Defense.

The department has their own data site: https://data.defense.gov/. This serves as a subset of data submitted to data.gov. Data sets available include defense budget estimates, U.S. active-duty military casualty deaths, FOIA requests, and administrative decisions from military hearings and appeals boards.

Numerous statistical databases can be uncovered from all the service branches by putting to use your Google Search skills, like this:

- *site:army.mil statistics*
- *site:navy.mil statistics*
- *site:marines.mil statistics*
- *site:af.mil statistics*
- *site:uscg.mil statistics*

Department of Education

The Department of Education has one principal statistical agency, the National Center for Education Statistics, as well as eight other agencies that maintain education and health statistics. Table 9.8 shows both the PSA and non-PSA statistical agencies under the Department of Education.

Several statistical databases from the Education Department deserve attention.

NCES Datalab (https://nces.ed.gov/datalab/index.aspx) allows exploration of education data from kindergarten to postsecondary and adult education. Data sets for enrollment and attendance, education history, employment after graduation, faculty and staff profiles and compensation, finances and financial aid, parent and family data, school and institutional characteristics, school districts, special education, and student characteristics are among the many categories that can be explored with this system.

Table 9.8   **Statistical agencies under the Department of Education**

Principal Statistical Agency	URL
National Center for Education Statistics	https://nces.ed.gov/

Non-PSA Agency	URL
Institute of Education Sciences, excluding NCES (IES)	https://ies.ed.gov/
Office of Career, Technical, and Adult Education (OCTAE)	https://www2.ed.gov/about /offices/list/ovae/
Office for Civil Rights (OCR)	https://www2.ed.gov/about /offices/list/ocr/
Office of Elementary and Secondary Education (OESE)	https://www2.ed.gov/about /offices/list/oese/
Office of Innovation and Improvement (OII)	https://innovation.ed.gov/
Office of Planning, Evaluation, and Policy Development (OPEPD)	https://www2.ed.gov/about /offices/list/opepd/
Office of Postsecondary Education (OPE)	https://www2.ed.gov/about /offices/list/ope/
Office of Special Education and Rehabilitative Services (OSERS)	https://www2.ed.gov/about /offices/list/osers/

International Data Explorer (https://nces.ed.gov/surveys/international /ide/) compares education in the United States with that of other countries using an interactive interface for topics such as reading literacy, math and science literacy, financial literacy, and assessment of adult competencies.

NCES has search tools allowing searches of all public schools (https:// nces.ed.gov/ccd/schoolsearch/), the public school districts to which they belong (https://nces.ed.gov/ccd/districtsearch/), and private schools (https:// nces.ed.gov/surveys/pss/privateschoolsearch/).

NCES's Common Core of Data program (https://nces.ed.gov/ccd/) contains data files on the United States' public schools. The mapping tool (https://nces.ed.gov/ccd/schoolmap/) allows mapping of schools or school districts.

The Database of Postsecondary Institutions and Programs (https://ope .ed.gov/dapip/) searches accreditation agencies and the institutions they have accredited. The downloadable data set includes accreditation actions taken against institutions.

The well-known print publication, *Condition of Education*, has coverage back to 1989 from the NCES website (*site:nces.ed.gov condition of education*) and back to its beginnings in 1975 via HathiTrust (HT 003912476).

Table 9.9   Statistical agencies under the Department of Energy

Principal Statistical Agency	URL
Energy Information Administration (EIA)	https://www.eia.gov/
Non-PSA Agency	**URL**
Office of Environment, Health, Safety, and Security (OEHSS)	https://www.energy.gov/ehss /environment-health-safety-security

Department of Energy

The Energy Information Administration is the principal statistical agency of the Department of Energy, which also has one non-PSA agency. The DOE provides statistics on energy, minerals, and health statistics. Table 9.9 shows the statistical agencies under the DOE.

The Energy Information Administration has a visually attractive Statistics Data Browser: https://www.iea.org/statistics/ that features interactive data for energy-related topics.

Department of Health and Human Services

The principal statistical agency of HHS is the National Center for Health Statistics, mentioned above. There are 12 additional agencies that provide statistical programs. One of these is the Centers for Disease Control and Prevention (CDC), which has nine centers, and the National Institutes of Health (NIH), with its 13 institutes, offices, and centers, each offering statistics. Table 9.10 shows non-PSA agency statistical agencies under the HHS.

Department of Homeland Security

The Department of Homeland Security (DHS) has three agencies that provide statistics. Topics include safety, crime and justice, and current demographic and economic statistics. Table 9.11 shows non-PSA agency statistical agencies under the Department of Homeland Security.

An often-consulted reference resource, originally published by the Department of Justice, and now by Homeland Security, is the *Yearbook of Immigration Statistics*. It was originally published as *Statistical Yearbook of the Immigration and Naturalization Service*.

Yearbook of Immigration Statistics [2002—present] (*site:gov Yearbook of Immigration Statistics*; HT 004909197; SuDocs: HS 8.15:[year]; http:// purl.access.gpo.gov/GPO/LPS5957).

Table 9.10   Statistical agencies under the Department of Health and Human Services

Principal Statistical Agency	URL
National Center for Health Statistics	

Non-PSA Agency	URL
Administration for Children and Families (ACF)	https://www.acf.hhs.gov/
Administration for Community Living (ACL)	https://acl.gov/
Agency for Healthcare Research and Quality (AHRQ)	https://www.ahrq.gov/

Centers for Disease Control and Prevention (CDC):

Center for Global Health	https://www.cdc.gov/globalhealth/
National Center on Birth Defects and Developmental Disabilities (NCBDDD)	https://www.cdc.gov/ncbddd/
National Center for Chronic Disease Prevention and Health Promotion (NCCDPHP)	https://www.cdc.gov/chronicdisease/
National Center for Emerging Zoonotic and Infectious Diseases (NCEZID)	https://www.cdc.gov/ncezid/
National Center for Environmental Health (NCEH)	https://www.cdc.gov/nceh/
National Center for HIV/AIDS, Viral Hepatitis, Sexually Transmitted Disease and Tuberculosis Prevention (NCHHSTP)	https://www.cdc.gov/nchhstp/
National Center for Immunization and Respiratory Diseases (NCIRD)	https://www.cdc.gov/ncird/
National Institute for Occupational Safety and Health (NIOSH)	https://www.cdc.gov/niosh/
Office of Public Health Scientific Services (PHSS)	https://www.cdc.gov/ddphss/
Centers for Medicare and Medical Services (CMS)	https://www.cms.gov/
Food and Drug Administration (FDA)	https://www.fda.gov/
Health Resources and Services Administration (HRSA)	https://www.hrsa.gov/
Indian Health Service (IHS)	https://www.ihs.gov/dps/

(continued)

Table 9.10   (Continued)

Non-PSA Agency	URL
National Institutes of Health (NIH):	
National Cancer Institute (NCI)	https://www.cancer.gov/
National Center for Complementary and Integrative Health (NCCIH)	https://nccih.nih.gov/
National Heart, Lung, and Blood Institute (NHLBI)	https://www.nhlbi.nih.gov/
National Human Genome Research Institute (NHGRI)	https://www.genome.gov/
National Institute on Aging (NIA)	https://www.nia.nih.gov/
National Institute on Alcohol Abuse and Alcoholism (NIAAA)	https://www.niaaa.nih.gov/
National Institute of Allergy and Infectious Diseases (NIAID)	https://www.niaid.nih.gov/
National Institute of Biomedical Imaging and Bioengineering (NIBIB)	https://www.nibib.nih.gov/
National Institute of Child Health and Human Development (NICHD)	https://www.nichd.nih.gov/
National Institute of Deafness and Other Communication Disorders (NIDCD)	https://www.nidcd.nih.gov/
National Institute of Diabetes and Digestive and Kidney Diseases (NIDDK)	https://www.niddk.nih.gov/
National Institute on Drug Abuse (NIDA)	https://www.drugabuse.gov/
National Institute of Mental Health (NIMH)	https://www.nimh.nih.gov/
Office of the Director (NIH/OD)	https://www.nih.gov/institutes-nih/nih-office-director
Office of the Assistant Secretary for Planning and Evaluation (ASPE)	https://aspe.hhs.gov/
Office of Population Affairs (OPA)	https://www.hhs.gov/opa/
Substance Abuse and Mental Health Services Administration (SAMHSA)	https://www.samhsa.gov/

Table 9.11   Statistical agencies under the Department of Homeland Security

Non-PSA Agency	URL
Customs and Border Protection (CBP)	https://www.cbp.gov/
Federal Emergency Management Agency (FEMA)	https://www.fema.gov/
Office of Immigration Statistics (OIS)	https://www.dhs.gov/immigration-statistics

Statistical Yearbook of the Immigration and Naturalization Service [1978–2001] (HT 002973860; SuDocs: J 21.2:St 2; J 21.2/10:[year];).

Department of Housing and Urban Development

HUD has three agencies providing statistical programs (Table 9.12).

Department of the Interior

Five agencies under the Interior Department maintain statistical programs, covering energy and minerals, soil, fish, wildlife, and public lands (Table 9.13).

Department of Justice

The Bureau of Justice Statistics is the PSA for the DOJ, but there are four other agencies that also maintain statistical programs (Table 9.14).

Of special interest here is the Uniform Crime Reporting Program (https://www.fbi.gov/services/cjis/ucr). Publications of the Department of Justice (SuDocs stem: J) include *Crime in the United States*, with the previous title *Uniform Crime Reports for the United States* (HT 007406857;

Table 9.12   Statistical agencies under the Department of Housing and Urban Development

Non-PSA Agency	URL
Office of Housing	https://www.hud.gov/program_offices/housing
Office of Policy Development and Research (PD&R)	https://www.huduser.gov/portal/
Office of Public and Indian Housing (PIH)	https://www.hud.gov/program_offices/public_indian_housing

Table 9.13   Statistical agencies under the Department of the Interior

Non-PSA Agency	URL
Bureau of Ocean Energy Management (BOEM)	https://www.boem.gov/
Bureau of Reclamation (USBR)	https://www.usbr.gov/
Fish and Wildlife Service (FWS)	https://www.fws.gov/
Geological Survey (USGS)	https://www.usgs.gov/
Office of Natural Resources Revenue (ONRR)	https://www.onrr.gov/

Table 9.14   Statistical agencies under the Department of Justice

Principal Statistical Agency	URL
Bureau of Justice Statistics	https://www.bjs.gov/
Non-PSA Agency	**URL**
Bureau of Prisons (BOP)	https://www.bop.gov/
Drug Enforcement Administration (DEA)	https://www.dea.gov/
Federal Bureau of Investigation (FBI)	https://www.fbi.gov/
Office of Juvenile Justice and Delinquency Prevention (OJJDP)	https://www.ojjdp.gov/

http://purl.access.gpo.gov/GPO/LPS9179), data from the National Incident-Based Reporting System, *Law Enforcement Officers Killed and Assaulted* (LEOKA) (HT 003248547, 003248500), and *Hate Crime Statistics* (HT 002782512, 102495590; http://purl.access.gpo.gov/GPO/LPS9179). Each of these series has historical data going back several decades.

Department of Labor

The Bureau of Labor Statistics is the Labor Department's Principal Statistical Agency. Four other agencies also provide statistics (Table 9.15).

Bureau of Labor Statistics Databases has an index of available databases, tables, and calculators at https://www.bls.gov/data/. Among the more well-known publications of the Department is the *Consumer Price Index.*

Consumer Price Index. Title varies: *Retail Costs of Food . . . Release* (HT 009178700). *Consumers' Price Index and Retail Prices of Food* [1945–1952] (HT *Consumer Price Index* (HT 007424267). Later title: *CPI Detailed Report* (HT 000500950).

Department of State

The Department of State has only one statistical agency (Table 9.16).

Department of Transportation

The Bureau of Transportation Statistics is the principal statistical agency of the DOT. There are seven other programs under the department (Table 9.17). Topics include all forms of transportation and related topics, including automobiles, trucking, highways, railroads, pipelines, transit, and shipping.

Table 9.15   Statistical agencies under the Department of Labor

Principal Statistical Agency	URL
Bureau of Labor Statistics	https://www.bls.gov/

Non-PSA Agency	URL
Chief Evaluation Office (CEO)	https://www.dol.gov/asp/evaluation/
Employment and Training Administration (ETA)	https://www.doleta.gov/
Occupational Safety and Health Administration (OSHA)	https://www.osha.gov/
Wage and Hour Division (WHD)	https://www.osha.gov/

Table 9.16   Statistical agencies under the Department of State

Non-PSA Agency	URL
Office of the U.S. Global AIDS Coordinator (OGAC)	https://www.state.gov/s/gac/ [Note: although this site is listed in Statistical Program, the URL is not working Sept. 20, 2019].

Table 9.17   Statistical agencies under the Department of Transportation

Principal Statistical Agency	URL
Bureau of Transportation Statistics	https://www.bts.gov/

Non-PSA Agency	URL
Federal Aviation Administration (FAA)	https://www.faa.gov/
Federal Highway Administration (FHWA)	https://www.fhwa.dot.gov/
Federal Motor Carrier Safety Administration (FMCSA)	https://www.fmcsa.dot.gov/
Federal Railroad Administration (FRA)	https://railroads.dot.gov/
Federal Transit Administration (FTA)	https://www.transit.dot.gov/
National Highway Traffic Safety Administration (NHTSA)	https://www.nhtsa.gov/
Pipeline and Hazardous Materials Safety Administration (PHMSA)	https://www.phmsa.dot.gov/

Department of the Treasury

The sole statistical agency under Treasury is their PSA (Table 9.18).

The U.S. Department of the Treasury, Bureau of the Fiscal Service created USASpending.gov. The site is the official source for spending data for the U.S. government. Spending can be viewed by high-level categories,

Table 9.18   Statistical agency under the Department of the Treasury

Principal Statistical Agency	URL
Statistics of Income (SOI)	https://www.irs.gov/statistics

agency, or object class (that is, spending grouped by types of items and services). Results are presented graphically in a heat map format. Clicking on an area of the map produces a visualization with greater granularity.

Treasury Bulletin contains a mix of narrative and statistical data covering financial commitments of the federal government, international statistics, and federal financial operations. (*site:treasury.gov treasury bulletin*; HT 000517883, 007132016).

Department of Veterans Affairs

The VA has three agencies that maintain statistical programs (Table 9.19).

Social Security Administration (SSA)

The Social Security Administration is an independent agency and not under any of the departments, yet it has one PSA and one non-PSA agency (Table 9.20).

Other Agencies That Maintain Statistical Programs

Table 9.21 shows the remaining statistical agencies presented in *Statistical Programs of the United States.*

LEGISLATIVE BRANCH STATISTICAL SITES

The legislative branch has almost no statistical presence on the web. The official Senate website does have a link to "Statistics and Lists" (*site: site:senate.gov statistics and lists*), but it is mostly lists that occupy the links. The House maintains official federal election statistics from elections from 1920 to present: *Statistics of the Presidential and Congressional Election of* . . . . (SuDocs: Y1.2:El 2/[year]; Y 1.2/10:[year]).

Congressional Research Service reports (crsreports.congress.gov) can be a source of government statistics for all three branches of government. Although not necessarily systematic in nature, CRS reports often report out current and historical statistics on varied topics.

Table 9.19   Statistical agencies under the Department of Veterans Affairs

Non-PSA Agency	URL
National Center for Veterans Analysis and Statistics (NCVAS)	https://www.va.gov/vetdata/
Veterans' Benefits Administration (VBA)	https://benefits.va.gov/benefits/
Veterans' Health Administration (VHA)	https://www.va.gov/health/

Table 9.20   Statistical agencies under the Social Security Administration

Principal Statistical Agency	URL
Office of Research, Demonstration, and Employment Support (ORDES)	https://www.ssa.gov/disabilityresearch/
Non-PSA Agency	**URL**
Office of Retirement Policy (ORP)—now merged with the Office of Research, Statistics and Policy Analysis, SSA	https://www.ssa.gov/policy/

Table 9.21   Statistical agencies under miscellaneous statistical agencies

Non-PSA Agency	URL
Consumer Product Safety Commission (CPSC)	https://www.cpsc.gov/
Corporation for National and Community Service (CNCS)	https://www.nationalservice.gov/
Environmental Protection Agency (EPA)	https://www.epa.gov/
National Aeronautics and Space Administration (NASA)	https://www.nasa.gov/
National Science Foundation, excluding NCSES (NSF)	https://www.nsf.gov/
U.S. Agency for Global Media, formerly known as the Broadcasting Board of Governors (BBG)	https://www.bbg.gov/
U.S. Agency for International Development (USAID)	https://www.usaid.gov/

The Government Accountability Office (GAO) site (gao.gov) does not have a statistics database, but many of their reports include valuable statistical tables and charts.

The Congressional Budget Office (CBO) produces cost estimate statistics for legislation. These estimates can be accessed from the CBO website (cbo.gov) or from within a bill in Congress.gov.

JUDICIAL BRANCH STATISTICAL SITES

U.S. Courts Website

The U.S. Courts website contains statistical reports (https://www.us courts.gov/statistics-reports). Another way to find statistics that may work better for certain topics is to search Google (*site:uscourts.gov statistics*).

The Federal Judicial Center, working with the Administrative Office of the U.S. Courts, provides public access to its Integrated Data Base (IDB): https://www.fjc.gov/research/idb. Here you can find statistics on civil, criminal, appellate, and bankruptcy cases. Data sets can be downloaded or searched interactively. The interactive search allows for limiting by circuit, district, nature of suit (for civil cases), nature of offense (for criminal cases), disposition of case, origin, and jurisdiction. This is a most impressive database.

TRACFED

TRACFED (tracfed.syr.edu) is a unique subscription tool worth mentioning here. Housed at Syracuse University, TRACFED is comprised of statistics generated from continual FOIA requests made of the federal judiciary. The site is divided into six basic navigation sections:

- Criminal Enforcement. Prosecutions, convictions, and sentencing statistics.
- Civil Enforcement. Cases by district, office, nature of suit, and jurisdiction.
- Administrative Enforcement. Available for Internal Revenue Service, Immigration, and Social Security.
- People and Staffing. Reports on judges, prosecutors, administrators, and staffing.
- Federal Funds. On state, district, or county level.
- Community Context. Many areas; for example, wages and salaries.

One of the most useful features is to find prosecutions or convictions by charge from the U.S. Code. Although TRACFED is subscription-based, there is a free site called TRAC (trac.syr.edu). This is a free public site that provides access to published reports about federal enforcement issues.

FEDERAL COMMITTEE ON STATISTICAL METHODOLOGY

We should also mention the Federal Committee on Statistical Methodology. Housed on the Department of Education's NCES website (https://nces.ed.gov/FCSM/), the committee is an interagency effort dedicated to improving the quality of federal statistics. Reports can be found on the site covering modernization of federal statistics, transparency in reporting, statistical methodology, and other topics including integrated data, big data, and statistical standards.

PRINT TOOLS, STATISTICAL AND CENSUS

Andriot, John L. 1998. *Guide to U.S. Government Statistics.* 3rd ed. McLean, VA: Documents Index.

Cook, Kevin L. 1986. *Dubester's U.S. Census Bibliography with SuDocs Class Numbers and Indexes.* Westport, CT: Libraries Unlimited.

Historical Statistics of the United States, Colonial Times to 1970. 1975. Washington, DC: U.S. Dept. of Commerce, Bureau of the Census. (HT 000707742, 007169391; SuDocs: C 3.134/2:H 62/789-970/; *site:census .gov Historical Statistics of the United States*), http://www.census.gov /prod/www/abs/statab.html.

Measuring America: The Decennial Censuses from 1790 to 2000. Washington, DC: U.S. Dept. of Commerce, Economics and Statistics Administration, U.S. Census Bureau: For sale by the Supt. of Docs., U.S. G.P.O., 2002. (HT 007423519; SuDocs: C 3.2:M 46/2). http://www.census.gov /prod/2002pubs/pol02marv.pdf.

United States. Bureau of the Census. *Bureau of the Census catalog of publications, 1790–1972.* 1974. Washington, DC: U.S. Dept. of Commerce, Social and Economic Statistics Administration, Bureau of the Census. (HT 000732965; SuDocs: C 56.222/2-2:970-972).

EXERCISES

1. You want to compare the number of passengers flying out of Chicago's O'Hare Airport with the number of passengers flying out of Chicago's Midway Airport for the most recent available year. You want to find the ranking of these two airports compared with other airports in terms of passenger traffic. You also want to do a time study of the past 10 years of data. [Hint: There are two federal agencies that collect this data, but they do not have the data presented in the same manner, and their numbers are slightly different].

2. What federal agencies have statistics on opioid use?

3. You want to do some research on credit card complaints.

   a. Try to solve this with statistics from federal agencies.

   b. Try to get specific complaints from federal agencies.

   c. Try to download a large data set about this topic.

4. What resource would you use to find how much milk cost in 1950? How much did it cost?

REFERENCES

Brown, Christopher C. 2017. *Harnessing the Power of Google: What Every Researcher Should Know.* Santa Barbara, CA: Libraries Unlimited.

Budget of the U.S. Government, Fiscal Year 2020. 2019. "Strengthening Federal Statistics." In *A Budget for a Better America: Analytical Perspectives.* Washington, DC: GPO, pp. 249–254. Accessed September 29, 2019. https://www.govinfo.gov/content/pkg/BUDGET-2020-PER/pdf/BUDGET-2020-PER.pdf.

Schmeckebier, Laurence F. 1925. *The Statistical Work of the National Government.* Baltimore, MD: Johns Hopkins Press. (HT 001306622).

Sunlight Foundation. 2018. "Removal of the FedStats Website and Reduction in Access to Statistical Methods Reports, Including Sexual Orientation and Gender Identity Resources, on the Federal Committee on Statistical Methodology Website." Accessed July 31, 2019. http://sunlightfoundation.com/wp-content/uploads/2018/03/AAR-1-FedStats-FCSM-Report-180301.pdf.

U.S. Census Bureau. 2012. "Census Bureau's Statistical Abstract Honored for 133 Years as Premier Reference Book." Accessed July 31, 2019. https://www.census.gov/newsroom/releases/archives/miscellaneous/cb12-245.html.

10

Census Basics and Background

The census is a specialized kind of statistics. It is a frequent request in libraries of all types including academic, public, and special. There are many layers of complexity to census research. The Census Bureau has made things easy in terms of the basic population and economy statistics that most people desire. But when it comes to finding data for specific census geographies, doing longitudinal studies of population trends, or examining microdata for specific correlations, a much deeper background is necessary.

A census is an actual count (at least as much as humanly possible). Actual counts are quite expensive, which is why they are only done every ten years. Thanks to the science of statistical sampling, the Census Bureau has been able to finely tune its methodology over time. Whatever sampling is done between decennial censuses can be righted by the time the next decennial census comes around.

THE CENSUS AND REAPPORTIONMENT

The need for a census (enumeration) was established in our founding document, the U.S. Constitution, although the controlling law for the census is Title 13 of the U.S. Code. The enumeration was crucial to equitably determine representation of each state in the House of Representatives. It was originally stated that "the Number of Representatives shall not exceed one for every thirty Thousand" and that "each State shall have at Least one Representative" (U.S. Constitution, Art. 1, Sect. 2).

Further, the census was to be administered every ten years so that adjustments could be made to the number of representatives among the states. After the 2010 census, the average apportionment population was 710,767. Compare that with the apportionment size after Census 2000 of 646,952 per congressional district (Table 10.1).

After each decennial census, there are winners and losers: some states gain congressional districts, while others must lose them. As a result of census counts in 2000 and 2010, 12 seats were shifted in each of these counts (Burnett 2011). Notice the shifts in congressional redistricting from 1940 to 2010 among the states, all a direct result of the decennial census (Figure 10.1).

The results of decennial censuses are used for much more than reapportionment, as important as that is. They are used by historians, economists, and other social scientists to track changes in living arrangements, income distribution, employment (or lack thereof), economic well-being, languages spoken at home, and migration patterns, to mention just a few topics. Businesses, both large and small, use census data to predict trends—where to place shopping malls, what communities are experiencing upward mobility, and how to plan mass-mailing campaigns. Governments use census data for city planning, zoning restrictions, traffic flows, and land-use patterns.

HISTORY OF THE DECENNIAL CENSUS

The first census in the United States was the 1790 census. Things were done very differently back then. There were six basic questions: (1) name of the head of the household, (2) number of free white males of 16 years and upward, (3) number of free white males under 16 years, (4) number of free white females, (5) number of all other free persons, and (6) number of slaves. The census was taken in all of the original 13 states, plus the districts of Kentucky, Maine, and Vermont, and the Southwest Territory (Tennessee). As still happens after the census in modern times, the final counts were received with skepticism. Both George Washington and Thomas Jefferson thought that the 3.9 million inhabitants counted in the census was too low (U.S. Census Bureau 2009).

The Census website contains histories of each decennial census from 1790 onward, including the authorizing legislation, enumeration procedures, technological advancements, questions asked, and examples of the forms used to collect the information. Herman Hollerith's famous electronic tabulating machine was used to process Census punch cards.

Times have certainly changed. From the Census website, you can discover that one of the questions on the 1830 census was, "The number of

Table 10.1   Population base for apportionment and the number of
Representatives apportioned, 1790–2010. Based on U.S. Census Bureau
(1993) and updated recent statistics.

Census Year	Population Base[1]	Number of Representatives[2]	Ratio of Apportionment Population to Representative
2010......................	309,183,463	435	710,767
2000......................	281,424,177	435	646,952
1990......................	249,022,783	435	572,466[3]
1980......................	225,867,174	435	519,235
1970......................	204,053,025	435	469,088[4]
1960......................	178,559,217	435	410,481
1950......................	149,895,183	435	344,587
1940......................	131,006,184	435	301,164
1930......................	122,093,455	435	280,675
1920[5]......................	...	435	...
1910......................	91,603,772	435	210,583
1900......................	74,562,608	386	193,167
1890......................	61,908,906	356	173,901
1880......................	49,371,340	325	151,912
1870......................	38,115,641	292	130,533
1860......................	29,550,038	241	122,614
1850......................	21,766,691	234	93,020
1840......................	15,908,376	223	71,338
1830......................	11,930,987	240	49,712
1820......................	8,972,396	213	42,124
1810......................	6,584,231	181	36,377
1800......................	4,879,820	141	34,609
1790......................	3,615,823	105	34,436
Constitution	...	65	30,000[6]

[1]Excludes the population of District of Columbia; the population of the
territories; prior to 1940, the number of American Indians not taxed; and, prior
to 1870, two-fifths of the slave population. In 1990 and 1970, includes selected
segments of Americans abroad.
[2]This figure is the actual number of representatives apportioned at the beginning
of each decade.
[3]Ratio of resident population to representative in 1990 is 570,352.
[4]Ratio of resident population to representative in 1970 is 465,468.
[5]No apportionment was made on the basis of the 1920 census.
[6]The minimum ratio of population to representative, as stated in Article 1,
Section 2 of the United States Constitution.

UNITED STATES	435	435	0
California	23	53	+30
Florida	6	27	+21
Texas	21	36	+15
Arizona	2	9	+7
Georgia	10	14	+4
Washington	6	10	+4
Colorado	4	7	+3
Nevada	1	4	+3
Hawaii	*	2	+2
Maryland	6	8	+2
Utah	2	4	+2
Virginia	9	11	+2
Alaska	*	1	+1
New Mexico	2	3	+1
North Carolina	12	13	+1
Oregon	4	5	+1
South Carolina	6	7	+1
Delaware	1	1	0
Idaho	2	2	0
New Hampshire	2	2	0
Rhode Island	2	2	0
Vermont	1	1	0
Wyoming	1	1	0
Connecticut	6	5	-1
Maine	3	2	-1
Minnesota	9	8	-1
Montana	2	1	-1
Nebraska	4	3	-1
North Dakota	2	1	-1
South Dakota	2	1	-1
Tennessee	10	9	-1
Alabama	9	7	-2
Indiana	11	9	-2
Kansas	6	4	-2
Louisiana	8	6	-2
New Jersey	14	12	-2
Wisconsin	10	8	-2
Arkansas	7	4	-3
Kentucky	9	6	-3
Michigan	17	14	-3
Mississippi	7	4	-3
Oklahoma	8	5	-3
West Virginia	6	3	-3
Iowa	8	4	-4
Massachusetts	14	9	-5
Missouri	13	8	-5
Ohio	23	16	-7
Illinois	26	18	-8
Pennsylvania	33	18	-15
New York	45	27	-18

* Not a state in 1940.

Figure 10.1 Reapportionment as a result of the decennial census over several decades. *Source:* U.S. Census Bureau (2010a).

White persons and the number of 'slaves and colored persons' who were deaf and dumb." In the 1860 census, one question included "Was the person deaf and dumb, blind, idiotic, pauper, or convict?" From the 1890 questionnaire, for the question of race, enumerators were instructed to write "'White,' 'Black,' 'Mulatto,' 'Quadroon,' 'Octoroon,' 'Chinese,' 'Japanese,' or 'Indian.'" In most years, there were considerable changes to the decennial questionnaires, making longitudinal research somewhat challenging.

Every census questionnaire is different. The Census Bureau's website is a treasure trove of historic census documents, questionnaires, maps, and tutorials. Table 10.2 shows selected development over time.

STATISTICS VERSUS RECORDS

Let's clear up one thing at the outset. Many people get confused between census statistics and census records (sometimes also referred to as census schedules, enumerations, enrollments, or rolls). Census statistics are the aggregated numbers from the various decennial censuses. These include general population counts, as well as specific demographic characteristics

Table 10.2   **Selected historical developments in decennial census history**

Census Year	Selected Historical Developments
1790	Marshals in judicial districts were enumerators, submitting schedules without uniformity. Questions: head of family; number of persons: free white males 16+; free white males under 16; free white females; other free persons; slaves.
1800	Until 1840, marshals reported to the secretary of state. Name of head of family; free white males and females by ages: under 10, 10–15, 16–25, 26–44, 45 and over; number of other free persons (except Indians not taxed), and number of slaves.
1810	Basic questions identical to 1,800 questions. First questions about manufacturing.
1820	Added question about free white males, 16–18. Asked number of free colored persons and slaves, by sex and by age. Asked if engaged in agriculture, commerce, or manufacturing and the number of foreigners not naturalized. More details about population.
1830	Age categories expanded: white males and females: under 5, 5–10, 10–15, 15–20, 20–30, 30–40, 40–50, 50–60, 60–70, 70–80, 80–90, 90–100, 100+. Slaves and colored persons, by sex, by age: under 10, 10–24, 24–36, 36–55, 55–100, 100+. Also asked about blind and white foreigners not naturalized. Uniform printed schedules began.
1840	Asked the number of persons in each family employed in mining; agriculture; commerce; manufacture and trade; navigation of the ocean; navigation of canals, lakes, and rivers; and learned professional engineers. Name and age of pensioners for Revolutionary or military service. Number of colleges or universities, primary schools, and grammar schools, and numbers of students associated with each. Number of white persons under 20 who could not read and write. Asked about white blind, insane, and idiots and colored persons who were deaf, dumb, blind, insane, and idiots. Questions added for school attendance, illiteracy, and occupation. Household, not individual, was the unit of enumeration.
1850	One schedule for free and another one for slaves. District subdivisions provided by marshals. Additional social statistics (taxes, crime, wages, value of estates, morality, etc.).

(continued)

Table 10.2   (continued)

Census Year	Selected Historical Developments
1860	Two questionnaires again. Slave questionnaire same as 1850. Free one added questions about profession, occupation, or trade; value of real estate and personal estate; place of birth; marital status; school attendance; literacy; and whether person was deaf and dumb, blind, idiotic, pauper, or convict.
1870	Question for color: Enumerators could mark "W" for white, "B" for black, "M" for mulatto, "C" for Chinese [a category that included all east Asians], or "I" for American Indian. Questions about parents' foreign birth. Greater detail about marriage; school attendance; literacy; and whether deaf and dumb, blind, insane, or idiotic. Males asked if citizens aged 21+. Rudimentary tabulating machine used in 1872.
1880	Questions about past year unemployment and marital status, including whether divorced. Questions about sickness and disability. Enumerators forbidden to disclose census info. Greater detail for many questions. Census office established in Interior Dept. Specially appointed supervisors and enumerators replaced marshals.
1890	First year the census distinguished between those of East Asian descent: white, black, mulatto, Quadroon, Octoroon, Chinese, Japanese, or Indian. Great detail in questions. More questions about family home and mortgages. Supplemental surveys for farms, mortgages, indebtedness of corporations and individuals. Punch cards and electric tabulating machines used to process data.
1900	Asked about ability to speak English. Separate Indian population schedule.
1910	Last-minute addition of "mother tongue" question.
1920	Slightly shorter than 1910. No separate schedule for American Indians.
1930	Basically the same as 1910 and 1920. Racial classification changes: "W" for white, "Neg" for black, "Mex" for Mexican, "In" for American Indian, "Ch" for Chinese, "Jp" for Japanese, "Fil" for Filipino, "Hin" for Hindu, and "Kor" for Korean. All other races were to be written out in full. No more mulatto classification.
1940	Considered the first contemporary census, employing sampling and other advanced statistical techniques. First census to include a census of housing.

Table 10.2   (continued)

Census Year	Selected Historical Developments
1950	Fewer questions (20); 5 percent asked sample questions. Used an electronic computer in 1951 to tabulate data.
1960	Place of work and means of transportation to work added. Filling in small circles on schedules aided in computer processing. U.S. mail used extensively for general (100 percent) questions. Enumerators visited sample population households.
1970	Separate questionnaire (booklet) for each household, to be completed by the respondent.
1980	Housing costs asked. Spanish origin asked of 100 percent. Sample rate at 50 percent for places under 2,500 population, but 17 percent elsewhere.
1990	"Short form" questionnaire contained the 100 percent inquiries asked of each household member. "Long form" included the short-form questions, plus additional questions on population, housing, social and economic questions asked of a sample of households.
2000	Short and long form continued. Long form asked 29 questions in addition to the 8 short-form questions.
2010	First time since 1940 that short-form/long-form pattern not used. A single questionnaire was distributed to all households with 10 questions. The American Community Survey took the place of the former long form questionnaires.

Sources: GPO (1979); U.S. Census Bureau (2002); and U.S. Census Bureau (2019).

in the aggregate. Obviously, the Census Bureau has statistics on each household and each individual from the recent census counts and surveys, but these are not reported individually or by individual household, to protect personal privacy. We cover that a bit later under public use metadata samples. These census records contain the information recorded by the census enumerators (things were done differently in the early years—no computers and no mailing of census forms!).

By law, these records are kept confidential for 72 years (P.L. 95-416, 92 Stat. 915, Oct. 5, 1978). The "72-Year Rule" is clearly explained on the Census website (just use a search engine to search for *census 72-year rule*). Records for later census records can only be obtained by the person named in the record, or their heir, after submitting form BC-600 (Google it!). In April 2012, the 1940 census records became available, to the delight of the genealogical community. You will see headlines again in April 2022, when the 1950 census records are made public.

The Census Bureau does not have these records. They are housed at the National Archives and Records Administration (NARA) (see https://www .archives.gov/research/census). Microform reels are available for purchase from NARA, and many public and academic libraries have these census records for their local areas. In reality, the easiest way to get to these records is through one of the online services, either Ancestry.com or Familysearch.org. Ancestry.com is now a publicly traded company and is available for personal subscriptions. Many libraries, both public and academic, subscribe to a library edition of Ancestry.com. Familysearch.org is a service of the Church of Jesus Christ of Latter-Day Saints.

Now for some bad news: most of the 1890 census records were destroyed in a fire in January 1921. The Census Bureau has suggestions for accessing 1890 records that still exist (*site:census.gov Availability of 1890 Census*).

We've already covered some of the basic principles of the Census of Population and Housing, so let's discuss some additional basic concepts.

SAMPLING

The most important thing to bear in mind when thinking about a census and a survey is the methodology. A census is an attempt at a complete enumeration, whereas a sample is an extrapolation from a partial result. Taking a complete count is obviously much more expensive, which is why sampling is very attractive. With sampling, there is always a margin of error. The Census Bureau has been performing sampling for a long time, having used it in the 1940 decennial census (U.S. Census Bureau 2010b). Sampling is common in the business world; in fact, it is really the only method. Businesses cannot afford to do censuses of all people to discover how they feel about their tennis shoes. The census sampling is sort of analogous to political polling. Before a national election, pollsters feverishly take sample surveys to try to predict the outcome of an election, but the ultimate truth is found in the election results. In the same way, ACS samplings are done in the years between decennial censuses. The accuracy of ACS samplings will be borne out (or not) by the next decennial census.

PERSONALLY IDENTIFIABLE INFORMATION (PII)

Federal law restricts the Census Bureau from releasing information identifying individuals. The Census Bureau is required by 13 U.S.C. § 9 to maintain confidentiality when collecting survey data.

The data exposed in the census tables does not divulge any personally identifiable information. Another way to say this is that you cannot drill down to detail levels that would expose personal information. Detail goes down to the census tract level, as long as there are 100 or more people in the tract. If not, then the data are only available down to the county level for purposes of anonymity. If a geography is too small, then the information will be suppressed. The degree of data suppression differs depending on the survey. These suppression rules are detailed in *American Community Survey: Data Suppression* (U.S. Census Bureau 2016).

Let's use a ridiculous case to see why data suppression is necessary. Suppose you live in a small town (or "place," to use census terminology) that has just 25 dwelling units. Nobody is very well-off in this community, except for one multimillion-dollar mansion on the edge of town. You have always wondered how much income this family makes, so you go to the most recent American Community Survey data to find out the answer, thinking you can find out the income of this household. But the threshold rules prevent this information from being revealed. You will have to wait for the 72-year rule to kick in!

CENSUS GEOGRAPHIES

You will not get very far when researching census statistics if you only have vague assumptions about census geographies. Some geographies are straightforward (such as state or county), but other definitions are nuanced and need some explanation (like place or census tracts).

Although it was published in 1994, the *Geographic Areas Reference Manual* (*site:census.gov Geographic Areas Reference Manual*) is a good work for background on the way the Census Bureau looks at geographic subdivisions. There are two kinds of geographic entities: (1) legal and administrative entities and (2) statistical entities. Selected geographic entities include:

Nation. Legal entity.

Regions. Statistical entity.

Divisions. Statistical entity.

States. Legal entity.

Counties. Legal entity.

Place. Legal entity.

Census Tracts. Statistical entity. Optimally contain 4,000 people, but range from 1,200 to 8,000 people.

Block Groups. Statistical entity. A combination of census blocks that is a subdivision of a census tract or block numbering area.

Blocks. Statistical entity. The smallest geographic area for which statistics are gathered.

Urban Areas. Statistical entity. There are two types of urban areas: (1) urbanized areas of 50,000 or more people and (2) urban clusters of 2,500 to 50,000 people. All other areas are considered "rural areas." Note: The definition of urban areas may change for the 2020 census.

Zip Code Tabulation Areas (ZCTAs). These are "calculated" geographies, approximate zip code distributions. They do not nest cleanly within other geographic entities.

Metropolitan Statistical Areas. One or more counties that contain a city of 50,000 or more inhabitants, or contain a Census Bureau-defined urbanized area and have a total population of at least 100,000 (75,000 in New England).

Counties or County Equivalents. There are counties in 48 states (Louisiana has parishes, and Alaska has cities, boroughs, municipalities, and census areas). Puerto Rico has *municipios*. American Samoa has islands and districts. The Northern Marianas have municipalities. The Virgin Islands have islands. The District of Columbia and Guam are each treated as county equivalents.

County Subdivisions. This gets rather complicated. The 50 states make use of Minor Civil Divisions (MCDs) and Census County Divisions (CCDs) differently.

Census County Divisions (CCDs). Statistical entities.

Figure 10.2 is the way the Census Bureau illustrates the hierarchy of Census geographies.

American Indian, Alaska Native, and Native Hawaiian Areas are more complex. This requires a customized graphical representation (Figure 10.3).

Figure 10.4 clearly shows the easiest way to think about the census geographies from the county level down to the block level.

2010 CENSUS NATIONAL GEOGRAPHIC TALLIES

It is helpful to know what we are dealing with when we discuss geographic entities. How many census tracts are there? How many counties? How many places? Table 10.3 provides the official tallies from the 2010 decennial census. The tallies here are for the 50 states and the District of Columbia. They do not include Puerto Rico and the Island Areas.

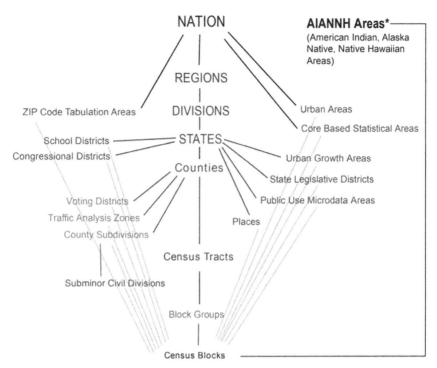

Figure 10.2 Standard hierarchy of Census geographic entities. From https://www2.census.gov/geo/pdfs/reference/geodiagram.pdf.

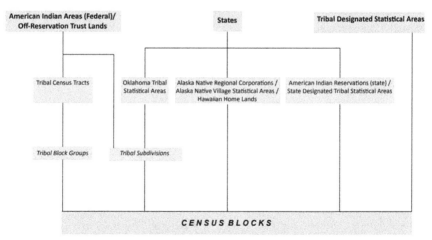

Figure 10.3 Hierarchy of American Indian, Alaska Native, and Native Hawaiian Areas. From https://www2.census.gov/geo/pdfs/reference/geodiagram.pdf.

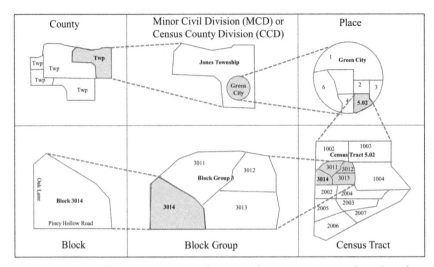

Figure 10.4 Smaller census geographies in relation to one another. Based on https://www.census.gov/content/dam/Census/data/developers/geoareaconcepts.pdf.

Table 10.3   Geographic tallies from the 2010 decennial census

Geographic Entities	United States
American Indian/Alaska Native/Native Hawaiian Areas	695
Alaska Native Regional Corporations	12
Tribal Subdivisions	492
Tribal Tracts	480
Tribal Block Groups	914
Block Groups	217,740
Census Blocks	11,078,297
Census Tracts	73,057
Counties and Equivalents	3,143
County Subdivisions	35,703
Consolidated Cities	7
Places	29,261
Incorporated Places	19,540
Census Designated Places	9,721
Metropolitan and Micropolitan Statistical Areas and Related Statistical Areas	
Metropolitan Statistical Areas	366
Micropolitan Statistical Areas	576
Metropolitan Divisions	29

Table 10.3   (continued)

Geographic Entities	United States
Combined Statistical Areas	125
Metropolitan New England City and Town Areas (NECTAs)	21
Micropolitan New England City and Town Areas (NECTAs)	22
New England City and Town Area (NECTA) Divisions	9
Combined New England City and Town Areas (CNETCAs)	10
Congressional Districts	436*
State Legislative Districts	
Upper	1,967
Lower	4,745
Voting Districts	177,808
School Districts	13,709
Elementary	2,304
Secondary	514
Unified	10,891
ZIP Code Tabulation Areas (ZCTAs)	32,989
Regions	4
Divisions	9
States and Equivalents	51

*There are 435 congressional districts and 1 delegate at large (District of Columbia).

Source: https://www.census.gov/geographies/reference-files/time-series/geo/tallies.html.

ADJUSTED GEOGRAPHIC BOUNDARIES

Because census geographic boundaries are always shifting, it is useful to be able to map newer data on to older census boundaries. For this reason, you will sometimes see in the Social Explorer database (see more in chapter 11) data sets such as "Census 1970 on 2010 Geographies," "Census 1980 on 2010 Geographies," and so forth.

An effective way to search the many available Census files on this topic is to search Google: *site:census.gov geographic boundaries by year.* There you will find updates on boundaries for legal and statistical areas.

STATE DATA CENTERS

Each of the 50 states, Puerto Rico, and island areas have data centers that partner with the Census Bureau. The purpose of these data centers is to promote Census Bureau products and to assist users, businesses, and governments in accessing and understanding the data. The bureau lists all the state data centers with contact information (*site:census.gov state data center member network*).

DATA VISUALIZATIONS

Hundreds of data visualizations are available from the Census site (https://www.census.gov/library/visualizations.html) featuring data back to the mid-2000s.

SPECIAL CENSUS REPORTS

Not only does the Census Bureau gather and disseminate statistical data from their survey and census projects, they also produce many interesting specialized reports and customized database tabulations. An example of one such tabulation is the Post-Secondary Employment Outcomes (PSEO). Released in August 2019, the PSEO provide earnings and employment outcomes for college and university graduates by degree level, degree major, and post-secondary institution. Only the Census Bureau would be capable of performing this analysis, since they are using state-of-the art confidentiality mechanisms to match university transcript data with a national database of jobs. Use Google to locate the data: *site:census.gov pseo*.

The most well-known of the special reports is the Current Population Survey. Beginning in the 1940s, the Bureau focused on timely topics of general interest that show the economic situation of families, individuals, and the economy of the nation. Among the reports are the following, each of which is available in full text from the Census website:

- Family and Individual Money Income in the United States: 1945 and 1944
- Income of Families and Persons in the United States: 1948
- Mobility of the Population for the U.S.: April 1950–April 1951
- Components of Population Change: 1950–1960
- Voter Participation in the National Election: November 1964
- Socioeconomic Trends in Poverty Areas: 1960–1968
- College Plans of High Schools Seniors: October 1973
- Families Maintained by Female Householders: 1970–1979
- Computer Use in the United States: 1984
- Trends in Relative Income: 1964–1989

- Statistical Brief: Our Scholastic Society: 1994
- The Older Foreign-Born Population in the United States: 2000
- Fertility of American Women: June 2004
- Custodial Mothers and Fathers and Their Child Support: 2011
- Educational Attainment in the United States: 2015
- Characteristics of Voters in the Presidential Election of 2016

This is just a sampling of the special reports that are available from the Census Bureau and demonstrates the national-level research they can produce with their unique access to such massive amounts of data. For a complete checklist of Census reports over time, consult Cook (1996).

The Current Population Survey collects data that is not included in the decennial census or the American Community Survey. For example, data about voting and voter registration is broken down by race or Hispanic characteristics, age, and sex. Data goes back several decades. Other publications in the series include health insurance coverage, the supplemental poverty measure, postsecondary education enrollment, geographic mobility, households with grandparents, fertility of women, child support, computer and internet use, effect of taxes on income and poverty, the older foreign-born population, and reasons for moving.

The easiest way to access the CPS is to search like this: *site:census.gov current population survey.*

EXERCISES

1. Play a little prediction game. Go to the Census website and see what the current population count is for your state, as well as the number from the previous decennial census. Then look for population estimates for the most recently available year. Now, make your own population projection to the next decennial census year (2020 or 2030). Does the difference in numbers argue for gaining or losing congressional seats? You might also see if the projection data is available on your state demographer's website. It likely is.

2. Using data.census.gov, find business and economic information for the community where you live.

3. Find the data center for your state on your state's website. After examining the resources available, summarize how resources available from the state data center augment what is available from the Census Bureau. Does your state data center have data that is more recent than that available from the Census Bureau?

REFERENCES

Burnett, Kristin D. 2011. "Congressional Apportionment." 2010 Census Briefs. Accessed July 23, 2019. https://www.census.gov/prod/cen2010/briefs/c2010br-08.pdf.

Cook, Kevin L. 1996. *Dubester's U.S. Census Bibliography with SuDocs Class Numbers and Indexes.* Westport, CT: Libraries Unlimited.

GPO (Government Printing Office). 1979. *Twenty Censuses: Population and Housing Questions, 1790–1980.* Washington, DC: GPO. (SuDocs: C 3.2:C 33/33; HT 000094175). Accessed December 12, 2019. https://www.census.gov/history/pdf/20censuses.pdf.

U.S. Census Bureau. 1993. "Apportionment of the U.S. House of Representatives." In *Census of Population and Housing. Population and Housing Counts.* Series 1990 CPH-2-1. Issued October 1993. Accessed September 29, 2019. https://www.census.gov/prod/3/98pubs/CPH-2-US.PDF.

U.S. Census Bureau. 2002. *Measuring America: The Decennial Censuses from 1790 to 2000.* Washington, DC: U.S. Census Bureau. (HT 007423519; SuDocs: C 3.2:M 46/2). Accessed December 12, 2019. http://purl.access.gpo.gov/GPO/LPS50135.

U.S. Census Bureau. 2009. "1790 Overview." Last updated May 30, 2019. Accessed July 21, 2019. https://www.census.gov/history/www/through_the_decades/overview/1790.html.

U.S. Census Bureau. 2010a. "2010 Apportionment Results." Accessed September 29, 2019. https://www.census.gov/population/apportionment/data/2010_apportionment_results.html.

U.S. Census Bureau. 2010b. "Developing Sampling Techniques." Accessed July 23, 2019. https://www.census.gov/history/www/innovations/data_collection/developing_sampling_techniques.html.

US Census Bureau. 2016. "American Community Survey: Data Suppression." September 27, 2016. Accessed July 23, 2019. https://www2.census.gov/programs-surveys/acs/tech_docs/data_suppression/ACSO_Data_Suppression.pdf.

U.S. Census Bureau. 2019. "Index of Questions." Accessed January 14, 2020. https://www.census.gov/history/www/through_the_decades/index_of_questions/.

11

Census Data for People and Housing

Data.census.gov is a deep and complex database. It is the official Census portal for accessing census data. One of the reasons it is complex is that it is a single interface used to access dissimilar types of data. For example, population and housing statistics have completely different fields and data relationships than those in the business and economic census data. It is important at the outset to have a clear understanding of the content that is accessible via Data.census.gov.

UNDERSTANDING DATA STRUCTURES

To really grasp Data.census.gov, it is essential to understand the relationship of the data sets and tables to the programs contained within the portal. This is essential since, for example, the data types between the Decennial Census of Population and Housing differ greatly from those of the Economic Census. Not only are the geographies different in some cases, but the Economic Census uses NAICS industry codes, a classification system that is not applicable to individuals and households. Figure 11.1 attempts to show the various census terms and how they relate to each other.

Programs

Programs can be divided into three areas, demographic programs (people and housing), economic programs (business and industry), and governments.

Data Sets

Data sets are specific censuses or surveys within programs. Take the American Community Survey as an example. Within that, we have the 2017 ACS five-year estimates, 2017 ACS one-year, 2017 one-year supplemental estimates, 2016 five-year estimates, 2016 one-year estimates, and so forth. These are each data sets within the ACS program. The same holds true for each of the demographic, economic, and governments programs. Table 11.1 shows the relationship of data sets to programs.

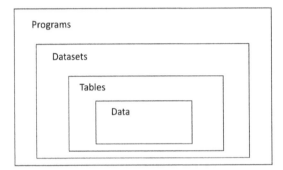

Figure 11.1   Relationship of key Census concepts

Table 11.1   Organization of programs in American FactFinder, assumed to be replicated in Data.census.gov (Census Bureau 2016b)

Program Type	Data Set
Demographic Programs	Decennial Census
	American Community Survey
	American Housing Survey
	Equal Employment Opportunity (EEO) Survey
	Population Estimates Survey
Economic Programs	Economic Census
	Annual Survey of Manufactures
	Business Patterns
	Commodity Flow Survey
	Nonemployer Statistics
	Survey of Business Owners
Governments Programs	Census of Governments
	Annual Survey of Public Pensions
	Annual Survey of State Government Finances
	Annual Survey of State Government Tax Collections

Tables

Tables show individual statistics in rows and columns. They each have a title and an identification number. For example:

POPULATION 60 YEARS AND OVER IN THE UNITED STATES
  TableID: S0102

MEANS OF TRANSPORTATION TO WORK BY SELECTED CHARAC-
  TERISTICS FOR WORKPLACE GEOGRAPHY TableID: S0804

ZIP Code Business Statistics: Zip Code Business Patterns by Employment
  Size Class: 2016 TableID: CB1600ZBP.

Data

Data are facts about people, places, businesses, and so forth that are collected via censuses, surveys, and through administrative records (such as birth certificates). These data collections can be referred to as statistics (U.S. Census Bureau 2016a).

By understanding the way that the Census Bureau thinks about data, which are within tables, which are within datasets, which are within programs, we can successfully navigate the advanced search features of the search tools, whether in print, CD-ROM, American FactFinder, or Data .census.gov.

DECENNIAL CENSUS VERSUS AMERICAN
COMMUNITY SURVEY

The Decennial Census of Population and Housing is taken every 10 years on the "zero" years. This is obviously not often enough for anyone in this era of daily polling, business intelligence, and statistical inquisitiveness. To deal with this problem, starting in 2003, the Census Bureau initiated the American Community Survey. Often called a "rolling sample survey," the ACS samples subsections of the population, and then extrapolates the numbers on to census geographies.

The decennial census counts one point in time (April 1 of the census year), whereas the ACS is a sample survey that takes place over several years, with estimates applied to the various geographies. The earlier ACS through 2012 provide data down to the census-tract level, and later surveys go down to the block group level.

The annual data from the ACS results in three different annual datasets: one-year estimates, three-year estimates, and five-year estimates, although the three-year estimates were discontinued after 2013. To understand when to use which data, see Table 11.2.

Table 11.2 Details of American Community Survey estimates

1-year estimates	1-year supplemental estimates	3-year estimates*	5-year estimates
12 months of collected data. *Example:* 2017 ACS 1-year estimates *Date collected between:* January 1, 2017 and December 31, 2017	12 months of collected data *Example:* 2017 ACS 1-year supplemental estimates *Date collected between:* January 1, 2017 and December 31, 2017	36 months of collected data *Example:* 2011–2013 ACS 3-year estimates *Date collected between:* January 1, 2011 and December 31, 2013	60 months of collected data *Example:* 2013–2017 ACS 5-year estimates *Date collected between:* January 1, 2013 and December 31, 2017
Data for areas with populations of 65,000+	Data for areas with populations of 20,000+	Data for areas with populations of 20,000+	Data for all areas
Smallest sample size	Smallest sample size	Larger sample size than 1-year	Largest sample size
Less reliable than 3-year or 5-year	Less reliable than 5-year	More reliable than 1-year; less reliable than 5-year	Most reliable
Most current data	Most current data	Less current than 1-year estimates; more current than 5-year	Least current
Annually released: 2005–present	Annually released: 2014–present	Annually released: 2007–2013	Annually released: 2009–present
Best used when	**Best used when**	**Best used when**	**Best used when**
Currency is more important than precision. Analyzing large populations.	Currency is more important than precision. Analyzing smaller populations. Examining smaller geographies because the standard 1-year estimates are not available.	More precise than 1-year, spans fewer years than 5-year. Analyzing smaller populations. Examining smaller geographies because the standard 1-year estimates are not available.	Precision is more important than currency. Analyzing very small populations. Examining tracts and other smaller geographies because 1-year estimates are not available.

*ACS 3-year estimates have been discontinued. The estimates already in Data.census.gov will remain available to users, but no new estimates are being produced after 2013 (U.S. Census Bureau 2018b).

The ACS has over 1,400 detailed tables. There are two views of many of these tables, the B tables, with the most complete breakdown, and the C tables, which is a collapsed version. For example, detailed race is Table B02003. This table has 71 columns, but the corresponding C, or collapsed table, has only 19 columns. Depending on the research needs, it is often easier to use the collapsed table.

Decennial censuses from 1940 through 2000 had two different versions of questionnaires, a short-form and a long-form. The short-form was sent to a majority of households and asked basic questions, with a long-form asking additional questions. The history of the questionnaires and all the questions asked can be found at the Census Bureau's index of questions page (*site:census.gov index of questions*). The 2010 census is a "short-form only" census, since it integrates ACS data to take the place of what was previously supplied in the long form. The plan going forward is for the ACS to complement the decennial census, eliminating the need for a long form.

RACE AND ETHNICITY

The Census Bureau's definitions of race, ethnicity, Hispanic, Latino, and so forth, come from an Office of Management and Budget directive, originally issued in 1977 and revised in 1997. (Statistical Policy Directive No. 15, Race and Ethnic Standards for Federal Statistics and Administrative Reporting, revised Oct. 30, 1997 [62 FR 58782]). (Access hint: just put *62 FR 58782* into Google, and you should immediately pull up the official text of FR from Govinfo.gov!) In fact, all government agencies must adhere to this standard. To see just how many government agencies discuss these standards, try this Google search: *site:gov Race and Ethnic Standards for Federal Statistics and Administrative Reporting.* Based on the OMB standards, these are the race classifications used by the Census Bureau:

White—A person having origins in any of the original peoples of Europe, the Middle East, or North Africa.

Black or African American—A person having origins in any of the black racial groups of Africa.

American Indian or Alaska Native—A person having origins in any of the original peoples of North and South America (including Central America) and who maintains tribal affiliation or community attachment.

Asian—A person having origins in any of the original peoples of the Far East, Southeast Asia, or the Indian subcontinent, including, for example, Cambodia, China, India, Japan, Korea, Malaysia, Pakistan, the Philippine Islands, Thailand, and Vietnam.

Native Hawaiian or Other Pacific Islander—A person having origins in any of the original peoples of Hawaii, Guam, Samoa, or other Pacific Islands (U.S. Census Bureau 2014b).

Many federal programs require race data for making policy decisions, particularly in civil rights matters. States use race data to meet legislative redistricting principles. Examining possible racial disparities in employment opportunities and health risks are other uses for the data.

Self-Identification

You are who you say you are—according to the Census Bureau. An individual's response to race questions on census forms or surveys is based on self-identification. Nobody will come around from the Census Bureau to make corrections or offer interpretations. Survey respondents may report multiple races.

Hispanic Origin

One census concept that runs contrary to the beliefs of some is that of Hispanic origin. Ethnicity, not race, determines whether a person is of Hispanic origin or not.

From the Census website:

> Hispanic origin can be viewed as the heritage, nationality, lineage, or country of birth of the person or the person's parents or ancestors before arriving in the United States. People who identify as Hispanic, Latino, or Spanish may be any race. (U.S. Census Bureau 2014a)

Hispanics may report as any race. Ethnicity in census questionnaires and the resultant tables will be broken out in two categories: Hispanic or Latino, or Not Hispanic or Latino.

PUBLIC USE METADATA SAMPLES (PUMS)

Census data, whether found in the decennial census print materials or through Data.census.gov, is aggregated data. That is, it is overall data about the selected geography and in no way gives any indication of what any person or household is like. Aggregate data and data suppression mask individual responses by mashing them together and giving the characteristics of a group of people. The individual census responses for individuals and households will eventually become available after the 72-year waiting period.

But there is great value in being able to see how individuals and households each answered the census questions. This is where public use metadata samples (PUMS) come in. PUMS are a sample set of anonymized data. Since the ACS itself is a sample, we could say that PUMS is a sampling of the sample.

Recent PUMS data is available through the Census website at data .census.gov. Several years of older data is available via the Census FTP site. Data is available is CSV or SAS format. (CSV is a text format that opens up seamlessly in Microsoft Excel. SAS is a common statistical format ready for statistical analysis.)

PUMAs, the PUMS Geography

Because the PUMS data contain sampling of individual responses to census surveys, it is not possible to use the same geographies as the decennial census or the American Community Survey use. For this reason, Public Use Microdata Areas (PUMAs) are used instead. PUMAs:

* Nest within states or equivalent entities

* Contain at least 100,000 people

* Cover the entirety of the United States, Puerto Rico, Guam, and the U.S. Virgin Islands

* Are built on census tracts and counties

* Should be geographically contiguous (U.S. Census Bureau 2018a)

The Census Bureau website has all PUMA reference maps available for download. This is essential, since almost nobody is familiar with these divisions. Google: *site:census.gov pumas reference maps.*

iPUMS Data from the Minnesota Population Center

Downloading data directly from the Census Bureau involves downloading the entire data set for the desired PUMAs, but then making selections of fields within the statistical analysis tool. The Minnesota Population Center of the University of Minnesota has provided a tool that makes working with PUMS data much easier. The iPUMS project deals with more than just U.S. census materials, although that is the focus of this section. They also provide enhanced access to microdata from the Census Bureau's Current Population Survey, boundary files from the National Historical Geographic Information System, environmental data, historical time use survey data, health surveys, historical survey data on the science and engineering workforce, global health survey data, and the world's largest collection of census microdata covering nearly 100 countries.

The focus here will be on iPUMS USA, microdata from the 1850 census onward, incorporating American Community Survey data for recent years. The project can be found at https://usa.ipums.org/. However, I usually access the project by simply searching *iPums Minnesota* in Google. Through their site, there is sufficient help to guide the novice user through the process. Before doing anything, however, users must register for access—but registration is free. This is necessary because it takes time to process data extractions and make them available to users through individual accounts. Numerous geographic files are available. GIS boundary files, all the various PUMAs over time are available with easy-to-view maps.

The basic steps for creating a data extract are these:

- Select your samples. These might be ACS one-year, three-year (for the years that the three-year samples existed), or five-year samples or any of the available decennial census samples from 1850 to the most recently available one. The sample selection page clearly spells out the percent size of the sample, with links to more specific documentation.

- Select your variables. Variables can be for households or for individuals. Each variable is presented in table format, showing which surveys contain data for that variable. Although it takes some time to get used to the selection process, I find that as I walk users through the steps, they quickly understand the process.

- Submit your request. Long, more complex data extracts take longer. When the file is complete, users receive an email notifying them that the file is ready to download.

RETIRED CENSUS DATA TOOLS

Earlier Data Tools

In preparation for the 1990 decennial census release, the Census Bureau released software developed in-house called GO and EXTRACT to access the data. The 1990 census was released in print and also on CD-ROMs. Many depository libraries still have these CD-ROMs, but the software cannot run on current software systems (Figure 11.2).

Thankfully, access to data is much simpler today!

In 1999 the Bureau launched American FactFinder, the original version (which I'll refer to as AFF1). It was wildly popular with users of all types: academics, small businesses, grant writers, and government users. By 2011, a new look and feel was rolled out, American FactFinder 2 (AFF2). The new version was suited to serve up decennial census and American Community Survey data and also included the economic census and many of the surveys (Annual Survey of Entrepreneurs, Annual Survey of Manufactures, Annual Survey of Public Pensions, Annual Survey of School Finance Systems, State and Local Government Finances, Business Expenses Survey, County and Zip Code Business Patterns, Census of Governments, Commodity Flow Survey, Equal Employment Opportunity Tabulations, Enterprise Statistics, Government Employment and Payroll, Nonemployer Statistics, Population Estimates, State Government Finances, State Government Tax Collections, and the Survey of Business Owners).

Several Data Base Software Options Let You Do More

What's great about the simple *GO* retrieval software is that it's a snap to use! Perhaps the best news is that it comes right on the CD-ROM. The *GO* software will meet the needs of most users.

   "But I need some freedom to move," you say. You've got it! Our CD-ROM's allow you to use many different software packages.

Census Bureau's *EXTRACT* for Specialized Tabulations

   We have developed another software package for IBM PC-compatible microcomputers—known as *EXTRACT*—for use with the economic census data on disc.

   EXTRACT was designed to help users load subsets of the large files stored on CD-ROM's into spreadsheets, graphics packages, and other commercial software. Our simple *GO* software (described on page 13) allows users to find one record at a time—say, for one census tract or county. *EXTRACT* allows you to select multiple areas—say, all block groups within a place or all counties with 50 or more Hispanic residents.

   EXTRACT works with all dBASE-compatible Census Bureau discs, including STF 1, but you must first obtain auxiliary files to work with the discs.

   You can download the *EXTRACT* software and documentation free from the Census Bureau's Electronic Bulletin Board (call 301-763-1580 for information) or from the CD-ROM software clearinghouse maintained by the Center for Electronic Data Analysis at the University of Tennessee (615-974-5311).

Applications Software Sources

Census Bureau Electronic
   Bulletin Board
U.S. Bureau of the Census
Data User Services Division
Washington, DC 20233
Information: 301-763-1580

Center for Electronic
   Data Analysis
University of Tennessee
316 Stokley Management Center
Department of Marketing,
   Logistics, and Transportation
Knoxville, TN 37996
Information: 615-974-5311

Figure 11.2   GO and EXTRACT software used by the Census Bureau for the 1990 Census. *Source:* Census Bureau, 1992.

Yet, not all data sets were contained in AFF2. For example, the 1990 Census data, which had previously been included in AFF1, was not migrated over to AFF2, much to the consternation of the government information community. While it is unrealistic to expect the Census Bureau to continue to migrate all past data into new interfaces, users need to develop new strategies to get to older data. It should be noted that the Census Bureau does make the 1990 census data, and many other surveys as well, available via file transfer protocol (FTP) (ftp://ftp2.census.gov/).

American FactFinder—Going Away

In 2019, the bureau announced that they were replacing American Fact-finder with Data.census.gov. As of June 2019, no new content was being added to AFF, and by the following June, AFF would be completely gone. The replacement is Data.census.gov. Although there are many slick, new features with the new interface, not all the features in the old AFF will be possible, at least not at first.

Disappearing Censuses

It is always disappointing to the government information community when resources disappear. In one sense, we can understand; government agencies never were tasked with the mission of archives or libraries. It takes a lot of resources to support the hosting of previously published, out-of-date material. It is one thing to host a lot of old PDF documents (which the Census Bureau does to an amazing degree). It is on another level to support old data files that have a different data structure and to back-integrate them into a current system. This is likely the reason that the 1990 census files never make it into AFF2. We have yet to see how many census files will make their way into Data.census.gov.

PRINT CENSUS RESOURCES

The statistics from each of the censuses are available in print format in many depository libraries. Generally, the larger academic depository libraries will have these available, depending on their collection strengths. Individual libraries may elect to shelve these volumes in a single area, while others may shelve them in the SuDocs stem, according to the agency under which they were issued. Originally, the Census Bureau was organized under the Interior Department. Keep in mind that the SuDocs system had not been invented until the late 1800s/early 1900s, so these SuDocs stems are an attempt at retrospectively imputing numbers for the sake of demonstrating the provenance of the materials. Table 11.3 shows the SuDocs classification for libraries that chose to follow that and also gives search tips for retrieving the online versions of these works in both HathiTrust and the Internet Archive.

The Census Bureau does much more than count people every ten years. After the enumerations, many reports are generated from the data. Keeping track of historical reports would be nearly impossible without *Dubester's U.S. Census Bibliography* (Cook 1996).

DATA.CENSUS.GOV

As I write this chapter, it is a particularly awkward time for Census tools. Data.census.gov streamlines many of the tools that previously existed for separate functions into a single tool. Separate tools, such as Tigerweb, County Business Patterns, Easy Stats, DataFerrett, Census Business Builder, and American FactFinder will all be folded into a single interface, saving support and development time of programmers.

American FactFinder will be up and running until June 2020, and then it will be completely gone. If I took screen captures of AFF, they would be irrelevant by the time this book is published. Data.census.gov does not yet have all the data loaded into it, nor does it have all the features it will eventually have. The point I want to communicate is that it really doesn't

Table 11.3   Guide for locating historical census publication in depository libraries and in the HathiTrust or Internet Archive

Census	SuDocs classification for locating print	Suggested initial search terms for HathiTrust (catalog search) and Internet Archive
1st Census, 1790	I 2	census office 1st census 1790
2nd Census, 1800	I 3	census office 2nd census 1800
3rd Census, 1810	I 4	census office 3rd census 1810
4th Census, 1820	I 5	census office 4th census 1820
5th Census, 1830	I 6	census office 5th census 1830
6th Census, 1840	I 7	census office 6th census 1840
7th Census, 1850	I 8	census office 7th census 1850
8th Census, 1860	I 9	census office 8th census 1860
9th Census, 1870	I 10	census office 9th census 1870
10th Census, 1880	I 11	census office 10th census 1880
11th Census, 1890	I 12	census office 11th census 1890
12th Census, 1900	I 13	census office 12th census 1900
13th Census, 1910	C 3.14–C 3.17	thirteenth census 1910
14th Census, 1920	C 3.28	fourteenth census 1920
15th Census, 1930	C 3.37	fifteenth census 1930
16th Census, 1940	C 3.940	sixteenth census 1940
17th Census, 1950	C 3.950	"bureau of the census" 1950 decennial
18th Census, 1960	C 3.223	"bureau of the census" 1960 decennial
19th Census, 1970	C 3.223	"bureau of the census" 1970 decennial
20th Census, 1980	C 3.223	"bureau of the census" 1980 decennial
21st Census, 1990	C 3.223	"bureau of the census" 1990 decennial

matter what tools the Census Bureau makes available to access the data, as long as users have a clear understanding of the way the surveys are carried out and the way the data structures are organized and reasonable expectations of what the data looks like, then any tool can be mastered.

It is not possible to provide a complete manual of all the functions of Data.census.gov in this context. Knowing the thoroughness of the Census

Bureau, by the time Data.census.gov is in full release, there will be plenty of training videos, help files, and tutorials.

Single Search Bar

The easiest way for basic searching is to use what the Census Bureau calls the "single search bar," the search box at the top of the Data.census .gov initial page. There are some tricks to getting the best results efficiently. With few words, type your topic and then your geography. Here are some examples of effective searches. As you type, wait for the suggestions from the interface to make more exact selections. If you start typing *Asians in Chicago*, the system will suggest *Asians in Chicago city, Illinois*. This aligns your search with census nomenclature for geographic places. Try these types of searches in the single search bar:

Education in Denver, CO

Unemployment in Ithaca, NY

Health insurance in Seattle, WA

Grandparents in Paducah, KY

Japanese language in Downey, CA

Results are presented in several clusters. In the main section of the search results, you will see tables and maps. The same selections are presented as selections in the top navigation panel. The interface features the top three tables and the top three maps, with a button to view all tables relevant to the search. Upon entering a map, it is easy to change the geography. For example, if you are viewing a city, you can switch to census tracts or zip code tabulation area.

Another excellent feature is the ability to retrieve exact table numbers. For example, if you know that the table in the ACS for educational attainment is S1501, you can just type that into the simple search bar, followed by a geography.

The bottom of the Data.census.gov entry page features topical buttons that launch general subject searches on population, economic matters, education, business, emergency preparedness, employment, families and living arrangements, health, housing, income and poverty, international trade, and the public sector. These topics pull relevant tables from multiple sources including the American Community Survey, the decennial census, the economic census, and various annual surveys.

The far-right section of the results page features a summary of the selected geography. Depending on the geography, it features a profile of the geography and several related searches.

Advanced Search

While the simple search bar might meet the needs of most users, I always recommend that users with specific data needs use the advanced search function. One important reason to use advanced search is that not all geographic types are available via the simple search bar. There are so many surveys over time, with varying fields and idiosyncrasies, and the advanced search gives the user great control over which data sets are searched. There is no substitute for knowledge of the differences between the decennial census, the American Community Survey and their one-year and five-year samplings, and other surveys.

Advanced search will be somewhat familiar to users of AFF2, with the breakdown of topics and geographies. As was the case with American FactFinder, different surveys are presented together in a single interface, which can be a source of confusion to the novice user. Differences between data for individuals and households will have a vastly different shape from data for businesses and industry, which is why we spent time initially covering the many survey types the Census Bureau offers.

As with AFF2, tables that are not available for a certain selection are grayed out. This is important to keep in mind. If you really want data about a certain census tract (a very granular geography selection), then it is helpful to do your geography select first, followed by a topic. Otherwise frustration will set in as you see too many tables unavailable.

Best practice: Data.census.gov works best if you don't try to mix simple searches with advanced searches.

For example, try finding the number of people from El Salvador in San Bernardino County, California. The difficulty here is knowing which topic this will be found under. Information might be found in tables on ancestry, citizenship, foreign born, migration, or place of birth. To make things easier, just put a search term in the "topic or table name" field. In this case, just put "Salvador." Then you will find tables beginning with "Place of Birth for the Foreign-Born Population." This saves you the time of trying to figure out how the Census Bureau classifies this.

Table Types

Data Profiles

These contain the most frequently requested social, economic, housing, and demographic data. Tables include Selected Social Characteristics (DP02), Selected Economic Characteristics (DP03), Selected Housing Characteristics (DP04), and ACS Demographic and Housing Estimates (DP05). To see data for smaller populations, see the supplemental tables below.

There are four categories of data profiles. Understanding these will help when:

- Social Characteristics—includes Education, Marital Status, Relationships, Fertility, Grandparents
- Economic Characteristics—includes Income, Employment, Occupation, Commuting to Work
- Housing Characteristics—includes Occupancy and Structure, Housing Value and Costs, Utilities
- Demographic Characteristics—includes Sex and Age, Race, Hispanic Origin, Housing Units

The easiest way to generate data profiles is to search Google like this: *site:census.gov data tables.*

Narrative Profiles

Narrative profiles are short economic reports derived from data from the ACS five-year estimates. They are available for a variety of geographies: nation, state, county, place, census tract, zip code tabulation area, metropolitan/micropolitan statistical area, and American Indian area/Alaska Native area/Hawaiian Home Land. The easiest way to generate a narrative profile is *site:census.gov narrative profiles.*

Subject Profiles

There are several dozen subject profiles. Age and Sex (S0101), Characteristics of People by Language Spoken at Home (S1603), Characteristics of People with a Marital Event in the Last 12 Months (S1251), Children Characteristics (S0901), Commuting Characteristics by Sex (S0801), Earnings in the Past 12 Months (S2001), Field of Bachelor Degree for First Major (S1502), Health Insurance Coverage Status (S2701), School Enrollment (S1401), Selected Characteristics of the Native and Foreign-Born Populations (S0501), and Types of Computers and Internet Subscriptions (S2802) are just a few of the interesting profiles. The subject profiles default to the national geography, but the geography can be changed to state, if that is desired. An easy way to get subject profiles from Data.census.gov is to first examine all existing subject tables (*site:census.gov subject tables*). Then simply take the table number and put it in the main search bar in Data .census.gov. Then adjust the geography as necessary.

Ranking Tables

Ranking tables typically show a title number for the United States, followed by ranking by state from highest to lowest. This is a quick and easy way to fulfill a commonly requested task. Topic examples include Percentage of People Who Are Foreign Born (R0501), Percentage of People 5 Years and over Who Speak English Less Than "Very Well" (R1603), Median Household Income (R1901), Median Family Income (R1902), Percentage of Households with Retirement Income (R1903), Percentage of Housing Units That Are Mobile Homes ((R2501), Percentage of Grandparents Responsible for Their Grandchildren (R1001), and Average Household Size (R1105).

Supplemental Tables

These tables provide ACS with one-year estimates for geographies with a population from 20,000 to 64,999 people. Geography can be selected by state, county, place, or metropolitan/micropolitan area.

Dealing with Geographies

In Data.census.gov, you can select geographies by putting the geography in the search box, by preselecting the geography under advanced search, by doing a geography limit using the filtering system after results are displayed, or by using the maps feature. When viewing a map, you can include more geographies of the surrounding areas using the rectangle selection tool in the lower right corner of the map.

Context-Sensitive Table Elimination

Like the old American FactFinder, Data.census.gov takes away tables that do not meet the selection criteria you have selected. This is a good feature, but if you don't understand what is going on, it becomes very unhelpful. When you enter Data.census.gov, all tables are available to you. Depending on how you perform your selections, the system subtracts tables that do not meet the criteria you selected.

Suppose you are looking for census tract data. Not all data is available down to the tract level. To escape the disappointment of coming up with a nice research topic, only to find that the data is not granular down to the census tracts, do your geography select before going your topic.

If your most important criterion is geography, then start with a geography select. If you don't care about the degree of granularity or which census program your data comes from, then start with a topic.

Confusion often comes about because Data.census.gov is the container for both population and housing data, as well as economic census data. This creates confusion on several levels. Geographies from both survey types are represented in the geography selections. If you happen to select, for example, NAICS industry code 236210, industrial building construction, and then try to do a geography select for place, you will notice that place (geography 160) is grayed-out. It is not selectable. Instead, you will see that economic place (geography E 60 is selectable). Similar care should be taken when which survey is used matters to you. In some cases, you need data from ACS five-year surveys, but in other cases one-year data works best.

THIRD-PARTY STATISTICAL TOOLS

Social Explorer

Social Explorer, distributed by Oxford University Press, is one of most valuable demographic tools on the market. It gets regular data feeds from the Census Bureau for population and housing data (no economic data at this time). This includes the decennial censuses and also all the American Community Survey data. They have also folded in all the legacy data from the first census onward. The interface will be familiar to those how have been around the documents community for a while—it follows the design and interface of the original American FactFinder (AFF1).

Other data sets folded into Social Explorer include U.S. Census population estimates; Business Patterns (County and Zip Code); two sources of U.S. Religion data (one from the Religions Congregations and Membership Study and the other from InfoGroup—both nongovernmental); U.S. Crime data from the Uniform Crime Report and the FBI; U.S. Health data from County Health Rankings and Roadmaps, a nongovernmental organization; U.S. Census data from the Centers for Disease Control and Prevention and the Centers for Medicare and Medicaid Services; and the Canadian census, the United Kingdom census, European statistics from Eurostat, and the World Development Indicators from the World Bank.

There are two ways to approach the database. The tables selection allows users to see data by making selections for desired geographies, topics, and other criteria, as appropriate for the database. Data can then be viewed or downloaded into Excel, CSV, SAS, SPSS, or Stata, popular file formats for statistical analysis.

The really stunning feature is the mapping tools. Maps can be created for selected data (not all tables are available for mapping) and prepared as presentations. Users can create their individual logins so that searches and presentations can be saved. A time comparison map can be created, with the ability to swipe from one map to another. For example, the population of New York City in 1980 can be compared with that of 2010, and swiping across the page will show population growth pockets.

One question I often get is for mapping showing income growth surrounding the Coors Field baseball stadium in Denver from 1990 (just before construction) to present day. I show students how to create a slide show of maps: one map from 1990, another from 2000, another from 2010, and another from the most recent year available. We then save each map as a separate slide, export the maps to PowerPoint, and the student now has a presentation with maps that can be used in class.

PolicyMap

PolicyMap is a different concept from Social Explorer. Launched in 2008, it was originally founded by the Reinvestment Fund, but is a separate entity. Social Explorer allowed users to explore one data set at a time, but PolicyMap allows users to create various layers of data. By incorporating government data from various governmental sources (Census Bureau, USDA, FCC, FEMA, FBI, US DOT, and Health Resources and Services Administration [HRSA], to mention just a few), as well as incorporating selected commercial and nonprofit data sets (ESRI, the Reinvestment Fund, the Institute of Museum and Library Services [IMLS], the National Center for Charitable Statistics [NCCS] at the Urban Institute, etc.), much additional value can be added to basic census data.

A question I have received on several occasions is related to "food deserts." The first time I received this question was over email. I had not heard of food deserts before, and I started thinking about all kinds of sweet things I shouldn't eat. With PolicyMap, you can create a base map with poverty levels for a city area, and then on top of that you can plot points for "Limited Supermarket Access (LSA) Areas." This creates an effective presentation and shows how Census data can be integrated with other data sources.

SimplyAnalytics

SimplyAnalytics, formerly known as SimplyMaps, is more similar to PolicyMap than to Social Explorer. It uses current data rather than reaching back to older data sets. It also involves creating layers. It has many of the same data sets as PolicyMap but also many different ones, making it a complementary subscription for libraries that can afford it. It has some business statistics folded in, which the other two databases do not seem to have. It is possible to map businesses by NAICS code onto a topical map, an excellent tool for small businesses trying to write business plans.

Consumer expenditure statistics are easily mapped into the map, showing money spent on food away from home, very granular data on apparel expenditure (for example, money spent on women's active sportswear); vehicle purchases; average health care expenditure; and amount spent on sports events, plays and concerts, and movies.

Table 11.4   Comparison of features and coverage of three commercial tools incorporating census data

Commercial Product	Features	Coverage
Social Explorer	Historic and current data. Tables and maps.	Decennial censuses back to 1790, ACS, selected other datasets.
PolicyMap	Data from Census Bureau, other governmental and other sources. Primarily maps, but tables possible. Layers can be added.	Current data.
Simply Analytics	Primarily maps, but tables possible. Layers can be added.	Current data with selected historical as well.

SimplyAnalytics will take longer to get used to, but the final results may be more gratifying than PolicyMap. Both tools take a bit of time to get used to.

Table 11.4 provides a brief summary of features and coverage of these three commercial products.

EXERCISES

1. Which congressional district has the highest population? Which one has the lowest? How many single-family units are there in Denver, Colorado? How many homes use solar energy in [geography]?

2. You read an article stating that certain cities attract out-of-staters (Google: *cities attract out-of-staters*). How can we find out the data behind this claim?

3. You have just bought a beachfront rental property in Myrtle Beach, South Carolina, and are not sure what to charge in rent. Using the most recent American Community Survey, which cash rent range has the higher number of renter-occupied units?

4. You work in an economic development office that monitors the job market in the Bronx, Brooklyn, and Manhattan boroughs of New York. Using the ACS one-year estimates, which borough has the higher number of females with a bachelor's degree or higher living below the poverty level in the last 12 months? Map your results.

5. Using the American Community Survey five-year estimates for Boston, Massachusetts, what is the number of the population 65 years and over with no health insurance?

REFERENCES

Cook, Kevin L. 1996. *Dubester's U.S. Census Bibliography with SuDocs Class Numbers and Indexes.* Westport, CT: Libraries Unlimited.

U.S. Census Bureau. 1992. *Census, CD-ROM, and You! New Horizons for Microcomputer Users of Census Bureau Data.* HT 007415430.

U.S. Census Bureau. 2014a. "Hispanic Origin." Accessed July 23, 2019. https://www.census.gov/topics/population/hispanic-origin.html.

U.S. Census Bureau. 2014b. "Race." Updated January 23, 2018. Accessed September 29, 2019. https://www.census.gov/topics/population/race/about.html.

U.S. Census Bureau. 2016a. "Migration/Geographic Mobility." Accessed September 29, 2019. https://www.census.gov/topics/population/migration/data.html.

U.S. Census Bureau. 2016b. "Programs, Datasets and Tables in American FactFinder." Accessed July 23, 2019. https://factfinder.census.gov/help/en/programs_datasets_tables.htm.

U.S. Census Bureau. 2018a. "Public Use Microdata Areas (PUMAs)." Accessed July 19, 2019. https://www.census.gov/programs-surveys/geography/guidance/geo-areas/pumas.html.

U.S. Census Bureau. 2018b. "When to Use 1-year, 3-year, or 5-year Estimates." Accessed September 29, 2019. https://www.census.gov/programs-surveys/acs/guidance/estimates.html.

12

Economic Census and Related Business Data

We'll now shift from discussing the decennial census, mandated by the Constitution, to the economic census, created by statutes. From the beginning of the country, there has been an interest in the nation's economic activities. The first census of manufactures was in 1810. To the third census, an additional order was given to the marshals (enumerators of the day) to take "an account of the several manufacturing establishments and manufactures within their several districts, territories and divisions" (2 Stat. ch. 38, sec. 2; May 1, 1810). This practice of asking economy-related questions continued until 1905, when the manufacturing census was taken out of the decennial census and spun off as its own separate census. This was also the first census taken by mail. In 1930, the first census of business was taken covering not just manufacturing, but also wholesale and retail trade (U.S. Census Bureau 2009a). A more complete history of the economic census can be found on the Census Bureau website (*site:census.gov history economic census*).

The economic census in not optional but is required by law (13 U.S.C. § 131). Since 1977, the economic census has been taken every five years on the years ending in "2" and the years ending in "7."

There are separately issued censuses that touch on other aspects of the economy, the census of agriculture and the census of governments. The census of agriculture was administered by the Census Bureau though the 1992 census. In 1995, those responsibilities were transferred to the National Agricultural Statistics Service under the USDA. The census of governments is still administered by the Census Bureau and can be accessed via their tools.

Economy-wide statistics are available from several Census-hosted sources. A guide to these sources can be found on the bureau's website (*site:census.gov economy wide statistics*). It is interesting to note that there are a few exceptions to the "economy-wide" part of this, as these NAICS codes are excluded from the economic census: NAICS 111-112, agricultural production; NAICS 482, rail transportation; NAICS 491, postal service; and NAICS 814, private households. Coverage of NAICS 525, funds, trusts, and other financial vehicles, varies from program to program. In general, governmental activities, such as public schools, are excluded, although certain governmental activities are consistently included, such as hospitals (U.S. Census Bureau 2009b).

ECONOMIC CENSUS GEOGRAPHIES

The economic census uses different geographies than the census of population and housing at some points. For example, instead of the notion of "place," the economic census uses "economic place." Economic places include incorporated places of 2,500 or more people; county subdivisions of 10,000 or more people in 12 designated states; and census designated places in Hawaii. Any residual area within a state is delineated into economic places so as not to cross the boundaries of any consolidated city, county subdivision in 12 designated states, metropolitan area in New England, or county. More details can be found on the economic census geographic on the Census website (*site:census.gov economic census geographies*).

Economic data are available by state, metropolitan area, country, and economic place levels, with the national level data added at the end. Geographic Area Series reports contain statistics for about 21,000 geographic areas.

SIC: STANDARD INDUSTRIAL CLASSIFICATION SYSTEM

The Standard Industrial Classification System (SIC) was developed in 1937 to organize industries for statistical reporting purposes, among other uses. SIC is a four-digit system, although over the years, many business and private statistical entities have added additional digits to accommodate new industries or subcategories.

The SIC Manual gives a clear presentation of the logic of the system. The manual was last updated in 1987 (HT 102418926) but is still available in an online format from the Occupational Safety and Health Administration (OSHA) website: https://www.osha.gov/pls/imis/sic_manual.html.

Below, in Table 12.1, are the ten divisions and the major groups (numbering 01–99, with some gaps). As you examine this list, notice how much emphasis there is on heavy industries, and how little emphasis there is on services or modern technologies.

Table 12.1   Standard Industrial Classification major groups

SIC Divisions	SIC Major Groups
Division A: Agriculture, Forestry, and Fishing	Major Group 01: Agricultural Production Crops Major Group 02: Agriculture Production Livestock and Animal Specialties Major Group 07: Agricultural Services Major Group 08: Forestry Major Group 09: Fishing, Hunting, and Trapping
Division B: Mining	Major Group 10: Metal Mining Major Group 12: Coal Mining Major Group 13: Oil and Gas Extraction Major Group 14: Mining and Quarrying of Nonmetallic Minerals, Except Fuels
Division C: Construction	Major Group 15: Building Construction General Contractors and Operative Builders Major Group 16: Heavy Construction Other Than Building Construction Contractors Major Group 17: Construction Special Trade Contractors
Division D: Manufacturing	Major Group 20: Food and Kindred Products Major Group 21: Tobacco Products Major Group 22: Textile Mill Products Major Group 23: Apparel and Other Finished Products Made from Fabrics and Similar Materials Major Group 24: Lumber and Wood Products, Except Furniture Major Group 25: Furniture and Fixtures Major Group 26: Paper and Allied Products Major Group 27: Printing, Publishing, and Allied Industries Major Group 28: Chemicals and Allied Products Major Group 29: Petroleum Refining and Related Industries

Table 12.1   (continued)

SIC Divisions	SIC Major Groups
	Major Group 30: Rubber and Miscellaneous Plastics Products
	Major Group 31: Leather and Leather Products
	Major Group 32: Stone, Clay, Glass, and Concrete Products
	Major Group 33: Primary Metal Industries
	Major Group 34: Fabricated Metal Products, Except Machinery and Transportation Equipment
	Major Group 35: Industrial and Commercial Machinery and Computer Equipment
	Major Group 36: Electronic and Other Electrical Equipment and Components, Except Computer Equipment
	Major Group 37: Transportation Equipment
	Major Group 38: Measuring, Analyzing, and Controlling Instruments; Photographic, Medical and Optical Goods; Watches and Clocks
	Major Group 39: Miscellaneous Manufacturing Industries
E. Division E: Transportation, Communications, Electric, Gas, and Sanitary Services	Major Group 40: Railroad Transportation
	Major Group 41: Local and Suburban Transit and Interurban Highway Passenger Transportation
	Major Group 42: Motor Freight Transportation and Warehousing
	Major Group 43: United States Postal Service
	Major Group 44: Water Transportation
	Major Group 45: Transportation by Air
	Major Group 46: Pipelines, Except Natural Gas
	Major Group 47: Transportation Services
	Major Group 48: Communications
	Major Group 49: Electric, Gas, and Sanitary Services
Division F: Wholesale Trade	Major Group 50: Wholesale Trade—Durable Goods
	Major Group 51: Wholesale Trade—Non-Durable Goods
Division G: Retail Trade	Major Group 52: Building Materials, Hardware, Garden Supply, and Mobile Home Dealers
	Major Group 53: General Merchandise Stores
	Major Group 54: Food Stores
	Major Group 55: Automotive Dealers and Gasoline Service Stations
	Major Group 56: Apparel and Accessory Stores
	Major Group 57: Home Furniture, Furnishings, and Equipment Stores
	Major Group 58: Eating and Drinking Places
	Major Group 59: Miscellaneous Retail

(*continued*)

Table 12.1   (continued)

SIC Divisions	SIC Major Groups
Division H: Finance, Insurance, and Real Estate	Major Group 60: Depository Institutions Major Group 61: Non-Depository Credit Institutions Major Group 62: Security and Commodity Brokers, Dealers, Exchanges, and Services Major Group 63: Insurance Carriers Major Group 64: Insurance Agents, Brokers, and Service Major Group 65: Real Estate Major Group 67: Holding and Other Investment Offices
Division I: Services	Major Group 70: Hotels, Rooming Houses, Camps, and Other Lodging Places Major Group 72: Personal Services Major Group 73: Business Services Major Group 75: Automotive Repair, Services, and Parking Major Group 76: Miscellaneous Repair Services Major Group 78: Motion Pictures Major Group 79: Amusement and Recreation Services Major Group 80: Health Services Major Group 81: Legal Services Major Group 82: Educational Services Major Group 83: Social Services Major Group 84: Museums, Art Galleries, and Botanical and Zoological Gardens Major Group 86: Membership Organizations Major Group 87: Engineering, Accounting, Research, Management, and Related Services Major Group 88: Private Households Major Group 89: Miscellaneous Services
Division J: Public Administration	Major Group 91: Executive, Legislative, and General Government, Except Finance Major Group 92: Justice, Public Order, and Safety Major Group 93: Public Finance, Taxation, and Monetary Policy Major Group 94: Administration of Human Resource Programs Major Group 95: Administration of Environmental Quality and Housing Programs Major Group 96: Administration of Economic Programs Major Group 97: National Security and International Affairs Major Group 99: Nonclassifiable Establishments

Source: https://www.osha.gov/pls/imis/sic_manual.html.

One problem with the SIC Manual was that, even though it had been updated many times over the years, it was increasingly difficult to accommodate new industries in a way that made sense. When they didn't know what to do with an industry, it seems as though they stuck it in the 99s somewhere. As an example of this, here is the breakdown of SIC 5999: "Miscellaneous Retail Stores, Not Classified Elsewhere:

> Architectural supplies—retail, Art dealers—retail, Artificial flowers—retail, Artists' supply and material stores—retail, Auction rooms (general merchandise)—retail, Autograph and philatelist supply stores—retail, Awning shops—retail, Baby carriages—retail, Banner shops—retail, Binoculars—retail, Cake decorating supplies—retail, Candle shops—retail, Coin shops—retail, except mail-order, Cosmetics stores—retail, Electric razor shops—retail, Fireworks—retail, Flag shops—retail, Gem stones, rough—retail, Gravestones, finished—retail, Hearing aids—retail, Hot tub—retail, Ice dealers—retail, Monuments, finished to custom order—retail, Orthopedic and artificial limb stores—retail, Pet food stores—retail, Pet shops—retail, Picture frames, ready-made—retail, Police supply stores—retail, Religious goods stores (other than books)—retail, Rock and stone specimens—retail, Rubber stamp stores—retail, Sales barns—retail, Stamps, philatelist—retail: except mail-order, Stones, crystalline: rough—retail, Swimming pools, home: not installed—retail, Telephone stores—retail, Telescopes—retail, Tent shops—retail, Tombstones—retail, Trophy shops—retail, Typewriter stores—retail, Whirlpool baths—retail

What use is it to have art dealers—retail in with the same category as tombstones—retail? Or pet food stores—retail in with hearing aids-retail? Clearly some reorganization was necessary.

NAICS: THE CLASSIFICATION SYSTEM

The North American Industry Classification System was officially launched in 1997 (notice the pattern of the original release of the SIC Manual in 1937 and periodic updates to the manual in the "7" years). The release was a long-overdue reworking of the way business statistics are organized.

One reason for retooling the classification manual was changes in industries. Think about the entire megashift for the country (and the whole world for that matter) moving from an industrialized society to a service-based society. Think about the changes that would be needed to accommodate the world of an online economy, spurred on by the adoption of the World Wide Web from 1993 and onward. A second motivation for reworking the classification manual was the North American Free Trade Agreement (NAFTA) (KAV 3417)—the major trade treaty between the United

States, Canada, and Mexico that went into effect on January 1, 1994. The NAICS project was a cooperative effort between the United States, Canada, and Mexico.

NAICS is divided into 20 industrial sectors with 1,170 industries, of which nearly 360 are new. Reflecting the move toward a more service-based economy, 565 of these industries are service-based (Inc. 2010). Although SIC was (and still is) hosted on the OSHA website, NAICS is hosted by the Census Bureau (Google: *naics census*). There you will find all the classification systems, updated every five years, beginning with 1997. NAICS is a five-digit system. That's right—officially it is the five digits that are agreed upon between the three countries of the United States, Canada, and Mexico. A sixth digit is used to provide country-specific detail (U.S. Census Bureau 2018). It is a hierarchical arrangement, with the digits having meaning as illustrated with NAICS code 511140:

51 = Information sector

511 = Publishing Industries (except internet) (subsector)

5111 = Newspaper, Periodical, Book, and Directory Publishers (industry group)

51114 = Directory and Mailing List Publishers (NAICS industry)

511140 = Directory and Mailing List Publishers (National industry)—this "0" is the sixth digit added by the United States for country-specific detail (although it doesn't seem to have been used for that purpose yet).

Obviously, your next question will be, "How do we translate SIC codes to NAICS codes, and vice versa?" This "cross-walking" is done with the concordances, found on the NAICS website. The earliest concordances provide cross-walks from 1987 SIC to 1997 NAICS as well as to 2002 NAICS. At each additional five-year interval concordances can be found to step from previous iterations of NAICS to the then-current edition. So many of the "99s" from SIC have been classified into meaningful numbers under NAICS (Table 12.2).

Notice how these industries that were previously classed under a miscellaneous grouping have been assigned meaningful NAICS industry codes. This means that, for these industries, meaningful data will be available.

So many new industries now represented in the current NAICS classification were not even envisioned in 1987, the last year of the SIC Manual update. Take, for example, NAICS code 519130 Internet Publishing and Broadcasting and Web Search Portals:

> This industry comprises establishments primarily engaged in (1) publishing and/or broadcasting content on the Internet exclusively or (2) operating web sites that use a search engine to generate and maintain extensive

Table 12.2 Example of the 1987 SIC to 1997 NAICS concordance

SIC (1987)		NAICS (1997)
7699	Repair Shops and Related Services Not Elsewhere Classified	
7699	• Boiler Cleaning	23511 Plumbing, Heating, and Air-Conditioning Contractors (pt)
7699	• Custom Picture Framing	442299 All Other Home Furnishings Stores (pt)
7699	• Locksmith Shops	561622 Locksmiths
7699	• Cesspool and Septic Tank Cleaning	562991 Septic Tank and Related Services (pt)
7699	• Furnace Ducts, Chimney, and Gutter Cleaning Services	56179 Other Services to Buildings and Dwellings (pt)
7699	• Sewer Cleaning and Rodding	562998 All Other Miscellaneous Waste Management Services (pt)
7699	• Ship Scaling	48839 Other Supporting Activities for Water Transportation (pt)
7699	• Other Non-Automotive Transportation Equipment and Industrial Machinery and Equipment	81131 Commercial and Industrial Machinery and Equipment (except Automotive and Electronic) Repair and Maintenance (pt)
7699	• Retailing New Bicycles from a Storefront and Repairing Bicycles	45111 Sporting Goods Stores (pt)
7699	• Farriers	11521 Support Activities for Animal Production (pt)
7699	• Camera Repair	811211 Consumer Electronics Repair and Maintenance (pt)

(continued)

Table 12.2 (continued)

SIC (1987)		NAICS (1997)
7699	• Typewriter Repair	811212	Computer and Office Machine Repair and Maintenance (pt)
7699	• Dental Instrument Repair, Laboratory Instrument Repair, Medical Equipment and Other Electronic and Precision Equipment Repair, Except Typewriters	811219	Other Electronic and Precision Equipment Repair and Maintenance (pt)
7699	• Lawnmower Repair Shops, Sharpening and Repairing Knives, Saws and Tools	811411	Home and Garden Equipment Repair and Maintenance
7699	• Taxidermists, and Antique Repair and Maintenance, Except Antique Car Restoration	71151	Independent Artists, Writers, and Performers
7699	• Gas Appliance Repair Service, Sewing Machine Repair, Stove Repair Shops, and Other Non-Electrical Appliances	811412	Appliance Repair and Maintenance (pt)
7699	• Leather Goods Repair Shops, Luggage Repair Shops, Pocketbook Repair Shops	81143	Footwear and Leather Goods Repair (pt)
7699	• Except Industrial, Electronic, Home and Garden, Appliance, Locksmith, and Leather Goods	81149	Other Personal and Household Goods Repair and Maintenance (pt)

databases of Internet addresses and content in an easily searchable format (and known as web search portals). The publishing and broadcasting establishments in this industry do not provide traditional (non-Internet) versions of the content that they publish or broadcast. They provide textual, audio, and/or video content of general or specific interest on the Internet exclusively. Establishments known as web search portals often provide additional Internet services, such as email, connections to other websites, auctions, news, and other limited content, and serve as a home base for Internet users. (NAICS code 519130 in NAICS Manual 2017)

Illustrative Examples:

- Internet book publishers
- Internet sports sites
- Internet entertainment sites
- Internet video broadcast sites
- Internet news publishers
- Internet periodical publishers
- Internet radio stations
- Internet search portals
- Web search portals
- Internet search websites
- Internet social networking sites (North American Industry Classification System 2017)

There was no web economy in 1987 when the SIC Manual was updated for the last time. These industries would have wound up in some kind of "99" classification under SIC. In fact, the subscription database ReferenceUSA, in assigning NAICS codes to business, also attempts to assign outdated SIC codes. For businesses with a 519130 NAICS code, they often use SIC codes 7389 Business Services Not Elsewhere Classified or 7373 Computer Integrated Systems Design, neither of which captures the essence of these businesses. It's difficult to keep trying to force new industries into an old and outmoded classification system.

NAICS SECTORS

Compare Table 12.3 with the SIC Major Sectors (Table 12.1). The entire list of NAICS Major Groups (down through group number 99) is too long to include in the table, but if you are interested, you can consult the current NAICS manual (*site:census.gov naics manual filetype:pdf*).

Notice that the 10 SIC divisions are replaced by 20 NAICS sectors.

THE SIC ZOMBIE

So, SIC is dead, right? It died in 1997, as NAICS was being launched, right? Well, sort of, but not exactly. The Standard Industrial Classification

Table 12.3   NAICS sectors and description (from 2017 Manual)

NAICS Sector	NAICS Description
11	Agriculture, Forestry, Fishing, and Hunting
21	Mining, Quarrying, and Oil and Gas Extraction
22	Utilities
23	Construction
31–33	Manufacturing
42	Wholesale Trade
44–45	Retail Trade
48–49	Transportation and Warehousing
51	Information
52	Finance and Insurance
53	Real Estate and Rental and Leasing
54	Professional, Scientific, and Technical Services
55	Management of Companies and Enterprises
56	Administrative and Support and Waste Management and Remediation Services
61	Educational Services
62	Health Care and Social Assistance
71	Arts, Entertainment, and Recreation
72	Accommodation and Food Services
81	Other Services (except Public Administration)
92	Public Administration

system just doesn't seem to want to die. Many commercial publishers still insist on employing it. Is it because they have added their own additional codes beyond the official four-digits, and they don't want to lose that added value? Is it because users are so accustomed to SIC that publishers don't want to disappoint them? We don't exactly know. But this "undead" system can be seen in these commercial offerings:

- First Research database (Mergent) Searchable by SIC or NAICS
- Many Dun & Bradstreet products
- ReferenceUSA

I'm sure there are others as well. But it is not only commercial publishers who continue to push an outdated classification system. Certain agencies of the U.S. government still use this superseded system. The Securities and Exchange Commission EDGAR database for searching for filing from public companies, has a search form option for SIC codes but not for NAICS. Because the SEC's EDGAR system still uses SIC, many accounting firms do the same. SIC codes are apparently still used by the importing and exporting government communities, as mentioned on the export.gov and cbp.gov sites.

ECONOMIC CENSUS DATA ONLINE

American FactFinder had contained economic census data from 2002 onward. Economic census data is now available via Data.census.gov, but, at this point, it is not clear how much of the older economic census data will be available. Just like the population and housing census and the ACS, when filters are selected via facets or via the advanced search functions, tables that don't qualify are knocked out of the result set. Thus, it is crucial to select geographies that have meaning in the context of the economic census. For example, you need to select "economic place" rather than "place." Failure to do so would rule out all economic census tables.

BUSINESS PATTERNS

One of the most useful economic surveys is Business Patterns. More often referred to as County Business Patterns (HT search *Country Business Patterns [State]*) or Zip Code Business Patterns (because that was their print title version), in Data.census.gov, they are accessed simply under "Business Patterns."

OLDER ECONOMIC CENSUS PUBLICATIONS ONLINE

Business is one of those research areas where there are a lot of fee-based resources (licensed databases, value-added stock statistics, market research reports) and yet much freely available content. In many cases, the free content is compliments of your taxpayer dollars at work—information provided through U.S. federal government agencies. From the business filings required of public companies through the EDGAR program to the dozens of statistics releases from government agencies (see chapter 9), the federal government makes data and research available to the public citizen, as well as to information providers that are able to take this content, add value to it, and sell it back to us. Large businesses may be able to afford the commercial offerings, but this is rarely the case with small businesses. Universities often have contracts with these commercial publishers that prohibit access for those not enrolled in university coursework. With this information so tightly locked down, we need strategies to access the freely available business information provided by the U.S. government's many business-related agencies. Let's survey selected agencies and the business information that is available from them.

To understand the organizational chart and the superordinate and subordinate relationships properly, one should consult the current *United States Government Manual*.

We have already looked at business and economy-related statistics available through the Census Bureau's Data.census.gov in this chapter, but there are many other statistical publications produced by the Census Bureau. One way to get to this information is by using the "Browse by Topic" feature on the Census website. "Business and Economy" is relevant to the topic at hand. Here you will find links to the many economic programs operated by the bureau, including County Business Patterns, Enterprise Statistics, Monthly and Annual Retail Trade, Monthly and Annual Wholesale Trade, Nonemployer Statistics, and Statistics of US Businesses (SUSB). SUSB is an annual serial providing national and subnational data by enterprise size and industry. These series serve as a standard reference resource for small business.

The Census Economic Indicators (*site:census.gov economic indicators*) is an easy way to get current and historic data. Series available include U.S. International Trade in Goods and Services, Manufactures' Shipments, Monthly Wholesale Trade, Construction Spending, New Residential Sales, New Residential Construction, Homeownership Rate, Rental Vacancy Rate, and many others. To dig deeply into Census publications, a Google power search is recommended. Examples: *site:census.gov tourism Colorado*; *site:census.gov black-owned businesses*; *site:census.gov family farms*.

The Census Bureau has scanned all economic census publications from 1967 onward and deposited them in the Internet Archive (archive.org). These publication series include:

• Census of Mineral Industries
• Census of Manufactures
• Census of Retail Trade
• Census of Wholesale Trade
• Census of Service Industries
• Census of Transportation
• Census of Construction Industries

Here are some example searches that can be used as patterns to retrieve the desired publications using the Internet Archive text archive (archive .org):

1987 census of retail trade Wisconsin

1982 census of manufactures New Mexico

1987 census of wholesale trade Maine

1972 census of construction industries

Here are examples of searches that can be run in HathiTrust (catalog search, not full-text search at hathitrust.org). Notice that it is best not to search with an economic census date:

census of service industries

census of retail trade

census of wholesale trade

census of manufactures

census of service industries

census of construction industries

CENSUS BUSINESS BUILDER

A powerful (and free) tool available from the Census Bureau is Census Business Builder. Designed to help small businesses with understanding the business landscape of an area or to assist regional planners as they look across all economic sectors, the tool incorporates ESRI data in partnership with free economic statistics. Users can map data for consumer spending habits over other mapped variables, such as population, building permits, selected demographic characteristics, and selected socioeconomic characteristics like foreign born, educational attainment, average household size, and homeownership rate.

The maps may be a bit awkward to work with, but the reports convey a lot more information for the selected geography in relation to the business sector. Not all business types are represented, but those that are include construction, food services, health care, personal services, professional and business services, and retail trade.

There are two versions of the Census Business Builder. The Small Business Edition allows users to select from one of the available economic sectors (https://cbb.census.gov/sbe/). The Regional Analyst Edition (https://cbb.census.gov/rae/) provides views of all economic sectors or selected sectors. It's a powerful tool for those who are unable to afford the third-party mapping tools described above.

EXERCISES

1. Using tools from the Census website, find which counties in your state have the most retail jewelry stores.

2. Compare and contrast the classification of skiing facilities under the SIC system with the classification under the NAICS system. Which system provides the best statistics?

3. You are helping someone open a beauty salon (NAICS code 812112) in your hometown. Find the number of beauty salons already located there. Has the number of salons been increasing or decreasing in recent years?

REFERENCES

Inc. 2010. "North American Industry Classification System (NAICS)." Accessed July 22, 2019. https://www.inc.com/encyclopedia/north-american-industry-classification-system-naics.html.

North American Industry Classification System, United States. 2017. Executive Office of the President, Office of Management and Budget. Accessed January 1, 2020. http://purl.access.gpo.gov/GPO/LPS26109.

U.S. Census Bureau. 2009a. "Economic Census." Updated May 30, 2019. Accessed July 22, 2019. https://www.census.gov/history/www/programs/economic/economic_census.html.

U.S. Census Bureau. 2009b. "Economy-Wide Statistics." Updated May 21, 2018. Accessed July 25, 2019. https://www.census.gov/econ/economywide.html.

U.S. Census Bureau. 2018. "North American Industry Classification System: Frequently Asked Questions (FAQs)." Updated September 4, 2018. Accessed July 22, 2019. https://www.census.gov/eos/www/naics/faqs/faqs.html.

13

Mapping and Geographic Information Systems

The U.S. government has had a long interest in maps. There are more than 50,000 maps in the Serial Set, and both Readex and ProQuest have dedicated map search interfaces for accessing them. Government-issued maps make up a major percentage of the online David Rumsey Historical Map Collection (https://www.davidrumsey.com/). General George Washington understood the importance of mapping when planning his military strategies: "A good geographer to Survey the Roads and take Sketches of the Country where the Army is to Act would be extremely useful" (Washington 1933, 443).

Through the years, depository libraries have been receiving maps and making them available to historians, geographers, demographers, government workers, and the general public. Regional depository libraries and other large depositories still maintain map collections, with map cases that occupy a significant amount of square footage in their libraries. Others may have opted to put their map collections in offsite storage, making them requestable through their library catalogs.

Georeferencing software has opened up a whole new world for understanding government information. Small businesses want to see metropolitan economic trends displayed on easily understood maps. Community grant writers need to communicate community needs visually, rather than through dry data in tables. Demographers want to make data visualizations to show growing and shrinking industry sectors across states. What was only available to those with expensive software, massive computer servers, and years of training and expertise is now becoming more within reach of the layperson.

Many government agencies provide the tools that are necessary to accomplish the tasks mentioned above. But increasingly, several commercial entities are taking freely available government information and folding it into their value-added subscription database products. These products, although not freely available, are often free to use if you have a large academic library near you (and if they happen to subscribe).

SELECTED MAP-PUBLISHING AGENCIES

Although there are numerous federal agencies that publish maps, several agencies are most commonly accessed.

- Department of Agriculture (SuDocs: A). Forests, grasslands, and recreational maps.
- National Oceanic and Atmospheric Administration (NOAA) (SuDocs C 55.) Nautical charts.
- Defense Mapping Agency (now defunct) (SuDocs: D 5.354:). Maps of the entire world in various scales.
- U.S. Geological Survey (SuDocs: I.19:). Topographic and geological maps.
- Central Intelligence Agency (SuDocs: PREX 3.10/4). Physical and political maps of the world.

Other agencies that produce maps include Federal Emergency Management Agency (FEMA) with flood maps; Federal Aviation Administration (FAA) with their aeronautical charts and VFR maps; the Census Bureau and census maps of places, congressional districts, and other geographies; U.S. Fish and Wildlife Service; Environmental Protection Agency and their LandView maps; and the National Park Service and national parks maps.

Larger university library systems often have map libraries and map librarians who know their collections intimately. These people are essential in getting the maps you need since, in many cases, many of the map holdings of these libraries have not been cataloged. A phone call or email to a map librarian will help you focus your questions and determine which library may have the map resources you need.

TYPES OF MAPS

Maps range from the simple political or physical maps to the highly specialized bathymetric, aerial, and climate maps. Table 13.1 lists several map types, the agencies that publish them, and where to find them on the web.

Insights into military use of land maps can be gleaned from reading "Map Reading and Land Navigation" from the *Army Field Manual* (FM 21-26) (https://fas.org/irp/doddir/army/fm3-25-26.pdf).

Table 13.1   Selected federal government map types online

Map Type	Agency	Where to Find
Aerial Imagery	NOAA and USDA	*site:noaa.gov aerial imagery*
		site:usda.gov aerial imagery
Aeronautical Charts	FAA	*site:faa.gov vfr charts*
Bathymetric Maps (underwater equivalent of topo maps)	NOAA	*site:noaa.gov bathymetric maps*
BLM Maps	BLM	*site:blm.gov maps*
Census Maps	Census Bureau	*site:census.gov maps*
Country Maps	CIA and Perry Castaneda	*site:cia.gov maps*
Flood Maps	FEMA	*site:fema.gov flood maps*
Geologic Maps	USGS	*site:usgs.gov geologic maps*
Land Ownership Maps	BLM and others Land tenure—Colorado—Maps.	*site:blm.gov land tenure maps*
Military Maps	Defense Logistics Agency and others	*site:mil military maps*
Nautical Charts	NOAA	*site:noaa.gov nautical charts*
Topographic Maps	USGS	*site:usgs.gov topographic maps*
Weather and Climate Maps	NOAA	*site:climate.gov maps*

TOPOGRAPHIC MAPS FROM USGS

Since topographic maps are among the most requested map types, we need to take some time to explain what they are and how to use them. Topographic maps detail the topography (detailed physical features—both natural and man-made) of an area. These land maps are produced by the U.S. Geological Survey. Maps covering the topography of the ocean floor are called bathymetric maps. These are produced by NOAA.

USGS has been distributing topographic maps since 1895, but that is largely no longer the case. The best way to find this site is to search Google: *site:usgs.gov us topo maps*. The site explains the difference between traditional USGS topographic maps and the newer U.S. topo maps. The newer maps are completely digitally produced from GIS databases, with no field inspection or data collection. They are computer generated on a three-year publication cycle. They are geocoded and will work with basic no-cost GIS software. Downloads are available for free.

When you read a map, you first need to understand the map's scale. The first number is always "1." After the colon is a second number. This is the ground distance. If the map scale is 1:24,000, then that means that one inch on the map is equal to 24,000 inches in the real world. This is the most commonly used scale in US topo maps. You might sometimes see a 1:25,000 scale. These would be maps based on the metric system, where one centimeter equals 0.25 kilometers. Because of Alaska's immense size, some topo maps are at a scale of 1:63,360. Why 63,360? Because that's how may inches are in a mile. The larger the second number is, the smaller the scale of the map.

Many topographic maps are at a scale of 1:24,000. Maps at this scale cover 7.5 minutes of latitude and 7.5 minutes of longitude. These are commonly referred to as 7.5 minutes quadrangle maps (USGS 2002). Table 13.2 sheds light on common USGS maps and their scales.

The USGS's National Geologic Map Database (https://ngmdb.usgs.gov/) contains the historical USGS topographic maps. The project, completed in 2011, combines high-resolution historical and current maps—more than 178,000 maps. These maps show changes over time to development, buildings, infrastructure, and waterways. They are often used by engineers, scientists, historians, environmentalists, and genealogists in researching particular areas of the country.

Locating maps with USUG's TopoView utility is extremely easy. They can be searched by name of topo map (if you happen to know that), or you can simply click on the map of the United States and select the year of the map you want. The application allows you to select a scale, and then you will see the quad lines. Clicking within a quad will show you the quad name. This is essentially the same function as the old-fashioned map index.

Table 13.2   Common USGS maps with their scales

Series	Scale	1 inch = approx.	1 cm. =	Std. quad size (lat. by lon.)	Quad area (sq. mi.)
7.5 minute	1:24,000	2,000 ft. (exact)	240 meters	7.5 x 7.5 minute	49 to 70
7.5 minute	1:25,000	2,083 ft.	250 meters	7.5 x 7.5 minute	49 to 70
Alaska maps	1:63,360	1 mile (exact)	633.6 meters	15 x 20 to 36 minute	207 to 281
County maps	1:50,000	4,166 ft.	500 meters	County area	Varies
County maps	1:100,000	1.6 miles	1 kilometer	County area	Varies
1 degree by 2 or 3 degrees	1:250,000	4 miles	2.5 kilometers	1° by 2° or 3°	4,580 to 8,669
State maps	1:500,000	8 miles	5 kilometers	State area	Varies
State maps	1:1,000,000	16 miles	10 kilometers	State area	Varies
U.S. sectional maps	1:2,000,000	32 miles	20 kilometers	State groups	Varies

Source: USGS 2002.

Maps can be downloaded with both the National Map (nationalmap .gov) and TopoView (*site:usgs.gov topoview*). Formats available for download include high-resolution JPEG, KMZ format (for use with Google Maps), and two georeferenced file formats, GeoTIFF and GeoPDF. There are numerous tutorials and help files available on the USGS website with more detail on how to download topo maps and what can be done with them.

To read topographic maps, you need to know the meaning of the colored lines and symbols shown on the maps. The USGS publication "Topographic Map Symbols" (*site:usgs.gov Topographic Map Symbols*) will guide you in this.

DEGREES: MINUTES: SECONDS VERSUS DECIMAL

Think for a minute about the changes the digital age has brought to the world of maps. Modern technology has brought about a clashing of standards. In the print realm, maps were described in terms of degrees, minutes, and seconds, and catalogers used that information in their physical descriptions of maps. The catalogers' approach is to describe the area of coverage in terms of latitude and longitude: what the north, south, east,

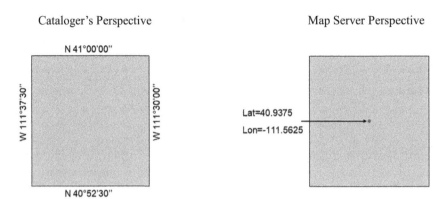

Figure 13.1   Contrast of perspectives in describing maps

and west boundaries are for the map. This information is carried in two MARC fields, the 034 and the 255 fields.

But when linking to an online map, the reference point is not the bounding lat/lon, but the center point of the intended map, and then how far out to go from the center to derive the same size map. Figure 13.1 illustrates the differences in these perspectives. The cataloger describes the bounding areas, N, S, E, and W in degrees, minutes, and seconds, whereas the map server points to the center of the map in decimal referencing of latitude and longitude.

CENSUS TIGER/LINE FILES

Since 1989, the Census Bureau has produced TIGER/Line files. Originally created for the 1990 decennial census, the ease with which we navigate with our smartphones today can be traced back to this census innovation (U.S. Census Bureau 2014). TIGER stands for Topologically Integrated Geographic Encoding and Referencing, which is the name of the system that supports census mapping needs. This is an early technology showing geographic features such as roads, railroads, rivers, lakes, and legal boundaries. The database contains names of features, including latitude and longitude, physical addresses such as numbers on streets, and geographic relationships to other features. It should be noted that these TIGER files need to be loaded into mapping or geographic information system (GIS) software. You cannot just simply view them within your web browser.

Recently the Census Bureau has created TIGER/Line files in the more popular shapefile (.shp) format. These can be found by doing a Google search: *site:census.gov tiger shapefiles*. Shapefiles are a file format (with extension .shp) originally created by ESRI that contain map features with georeferenced features. Places, boundaries, and state lines are among the many features that can be included in these files, which can then be integrated with mapping software to create additional layers of information. This book cannot provide support for all these features. But as you would expect, the Census website provides much basic documentation.

Shapefiles could also be downloaded from the old American Factfinder 2 for any geography. It is anticipated that Data.census.gov will also have this capability, but, as of this writing, this capability has not yet been programmed into the system. I am told that it is coming soon.

NATIONAL GEODETIC SURVEY

Under NOAA, the National Geodetic Survey (https://www.ngs.noaa.gov/) provides the framework for all global positioning activities of the United States. The National Geodetic Survey Data Explorer (Google it for URL!) is a complicated and fascinating dynamic map for finding GPS coordinates and other features. Most of the tools are intended for surveyors and other professionals. But lay users will appreciate remote sensing emergency response imagery from selected historic hurricanes, tropical storms, tornadoes, and flooding events.

NAUTICAL MAPS FROM NOAA

NOAA's Office of Coast Survey has a database of electronic nautical charts for marine navigation. Electronic navigation charts are accessible via the ENC Viewer (*site:noaa.gov electronic navigational charts*). The database covers U.S. coastal waters and the Great Lakes. These maps are also available in PDF format.

PERRY CASTEÑEDA MAP COLLECTION

The Perry Casteñeda Map Collection comes from the University of Texas at Austin. About 70,000 public domain maps are included in this digitized online collection. Most of these maps are government publications. Although they are not georeferenced, they hold much value for teaching and inclusion in publications. Maps are arranged geographically, topically, and by map type. This is the go-to resource for general reference work involving political, geographic, and historical maps for the entire world.

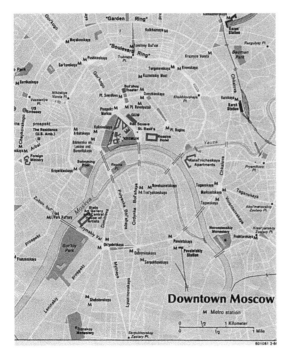

Figure 13.2   CIA map of downtown Moscow

CIA MAPS

Maps can and have been used for political purposes. For example, maps of the former Soviet Union published by their government were falsified for over 50 years by order of the secret police. Maps published by the U.S. Central Intelligence Agency were more accurate. Figure 13.2 shows an excerpt of a CIA map of downtown Moscow, which is more accurate than Soviet-issued maps of the time (Keller 1988).

Using not published maps but land navigation techniques taught by the U.S. military, the CIA misidentified the headquarters of the Yugoslav Federal Directorate for Supply and Procurement (FDSP) in Belgrade, and, as it turned out, the NATO Allied Forces actually bombed the Chinese Embassy (Tenet 1999). Maps that we use will (hopefully) not have such dire life-and-death consequences, but they are nevertheless important to understanding political, social, and economic activities and aspirations. Current CIA maps in PDF or JPG formats can be found on the CIA website (*site:cia.gov maps* OR *site:cia.gov maps* downloads).

MAPS FROM NTIS

Maps and publications released through the Library of Congress from 1971 and through the National Technical Information Service (NTIS) since 1980 may be purchased from NTIS through their National Technical Reports Library (NTRL) (*site:ntis.gov National Technical Reports Library*).

GEOPLATFORM.GOV

Think of GeoPlatform.gov as a data repository for mapping data. Developed by the member agencies of the Federal Geographic Data Committee (FGDC), the tool hosts thousands of datasets from various agencies.

MAPS WITHIN FRASER

FRASER, mentioned earlier in the context of historical economic statistics, contains selected maps from the Statistical Abstract of the United States and other places that illustrate the economic history of the United States (*site:stlouisfed.org maps in fraser*).

SERIAL SET MAPS

Readex Serial Set maps contain georeferencing in their TIFF files. These can be used in creative ways to overlay historic maps over current versions. The Serial Set's many Washington, D.C. maps present a treasure-trove of information, including instances of diseases and fatalities by block, location of schools, location of sewer and water lines, public transportation, and much more. These maps are mostly presented on the same scale and projection, but no coordinates are given. By adding accurate latitude and longitude references, these maps can be compared with other maps, both historical and current, using today's GIS technology. For example, this feature could be used to overlay L'Enfant's original plan form the District of Columbia on top of the current land use (Readex 2005).

COMMERCIAL MAPPING TOOLS

Several commercial mapping tools have become popular for use in academic libraries. These tools typically take free available data from the Census Bureau, add selected commercially available data from sources such as ESRI into the mix, and combine them into a mapping tool of their own. These tools provide valuable resources for students of public policy or business analytics. The Census Bureau recently launched its Census Business Builder, which partners with ESRI and provides consumer data merged with Census data to the general public.

Social Explorer can create maps from all the decennial censuses back to the first in 1790. It can also map American Community Survey and other nongovernmental data sets into a series of maps to show changes over time. PolicyMap and SimplyAnalytics can overlay nongovernmental data sets over census data, providing interesting arguments for policy purposes. For example, data showing limited grocery store availability (food deserts) can be overlaid on poverty data from the Census Bureau.

USGS MAPPING TOOLS

Other publications of the USGS deserve highlighting. The National Atlas of the United States was a prior program of the USGS that was ended in 2014. One of the features of the National Atlas was small-scale maps (meaning that they showed large areas). These maps are still available through the National Map Small-Scale Collection (*site:usgs.gov National Map Small-Scale Collection*). Maps available for viewing and downloading for the entire country or for individual states include climate maps (cooling and heating, humidity, precipitation, temperature), federal lands and Indian reservations, presidential elections, reference and outline maps, and satellite views.

The National Geologic Map Databases (https://ngmdb.usgs.gov/) serves up current and historic topographic maps in various downloadable file formats. Current topo maps can be easily downloaded from https://bit.ly /1YxhdNC (shortened URL necessary here because it is an extremely long URL).

The Historical Topographic Map Collection (HTMC) (*site:usgs.gov Historical Topographic Map Collection*) is a digital repository to USGS 1:250,000 scale and larger (i.e., more detailed) printed maps from 1884 to 2006.

An index to a physical map is a gazetteer. But when you need an index to a digital map, the Geographic Names Information System performs the task. GNIS Features Search, available by searching Google: *geonames gnis feature search*. Very obscure geographic landmarks are included in this database, even with their popular names. It's really quite impressive. Want to get a list of Colorado's 14ers? (for those of you outside of Colorado, those are mountains at least 14,000 feet above sea level). The Geographic Names Information System will do that for you (Figure 13.3).

SHAPEFILES AND GEOREFERENCING

The National Map allows users to download shapefiles for many geographies, including cities and towns, coastline areas, metropolitan statistical areas, urban areas, transportation features (airports, ferry routes, parkways and scenic rivers, ports, railroad and bus terminal stations, railroad, and highways and roads), and water features (dams, streams, and other bodies of water). The Census Bureau is a major destination for acquiring shapefiles of all census geographies.

WHERE CAN I FIND THESE MAPS?

Often, all you need is a reference map. Just a simple map you can print out for teaching or for a publication. This can be a tedious task, since many sites explain their methodologies, their shapefiles, and how to use georeferencing, when all you want is a simple map. Table 13.3 is a brief guide to getting quick reference maps from federal sources.

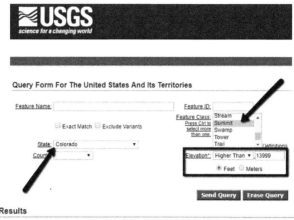

Figure 13.3   USGS's Geographic Names Information System, showing the query set-up and the result set

Table 13.3   Selected reference maps from U.S. federal sources

Map Topic	URL or Search Strategy
Biomass Maps	https://www.nrel.gov/gis/biomass.html
Climate Maps	https://nationalmap.gov/small_scale/printable/climatemap.html
Coastal Barrier Maps	https://www.fws.gov/cbra/maps/
Congressional District Maps	*site:census.gov congressional district maps*
County Maps	https://nationalmap.gov/small_scale/printable/reference.html
County Maps	*site:census.gov bas reference maps*
Crop Production	https://ipad.fas.usda.gov/rssiws/al/global_cropprod.aspx

(continued)

Table 13.3   (continued)

Map Topic	URL or Search Strategy
Federal Lands and Indian Reservations	https://nationalmap.gov/small_scale/printable/fedlands.html
Federal Lands: BLM Administrative Map	https://www.blm.gov/maps/frequently-requested
Flood Maps	https://msc.fema.gov/
Geothermal Maps	https://www.nrel.gov/gis/geothermal.html
Hydrogen Maps	https://www.nrel.gov/gis/hydrogen.html
Marine Maps	https://www.nrel.gov/gis/maps-marine.html
Places, Incorporated	*site:census.gov bas reference maps*
Presidential Election Maps	https://nationalmap.gov/small_scale/printable/elections.html (1789-2012)
Recreation Map, Interactive	https://www.blm.gov/visit
Recreation Maps	https://www.blm.gov/maps/georeferenced-PDFs
Rivers and Lakes of States	https://nationalmap.gov/small_scale/printable/reference.html
School District Reference Maps	*site:census.gov Census School District Reference Maps*
Solar Maps	https://www.nrel.gov/gis/solar.html
State Legislative District Reference Maps	*site:census.gov State Legislative District Reference Maps*
State Legislative District Reference Maps	*site:census.gov state legislative district Reference Maps*
States	https://nationalmap.gov/small_scale/printable/reference.html
States and Capitals	https://nationalmap.gov/small_scale/printable/reference.html
Territorial Acquisitions of the United States	*site:nationalmap.gov territorial acquisitions*
Time Zones	https://nationalmap.gov/small_scale/printable/timezones.html
Topographic Maps, Current	https://bit.ly/1YxhdNC
Topographic Maps, Historic	https://ngmdb.usgs.gov/topoview/
Wind Maps	https://www.nrel.gov/gis/wind.html

RESOURCES

Moffat, Riley Moore. 1985. *Map Index to Topographic Quadrangles of the United States, 1882–1940.* Occasional Paper/Western Association of Map Libraries, no. 10. Santa Cruz, CA: Western Association of Map Libraries. This valuable resource has state-by-state listings of quad names, dates of publication, scale, and southeast coordinates, together with state maps for easy visualization of quads.

Western Association of Map Libraries. 2015. Map Librarian's Toolbox. Available at: http://www.waml.org/maptools.htm. One of the most helpful resource pages for understanding and accessing maps, including U.S. government maps.

EXERCISES

1. Find the topo map for where you live. What is the name of the quad? What years are available for topo maps for this location? What are the scales of these maps?
2. Find a current map of the congressional district where you live.
3. Use the GNIS database to find geographic landmarks near your home.

REFERENCES

Keller, Bill. 1988. "Soviet Aide Admits Maps Were Faked for 50 Years." *New York Times.* September 3, 1988. Accessed January 1, 2020. https://www.nytimes.com/1988/09/03/world/soviet-aide-admits-maps-were-faked-for-50-years.html

Readex. 2005. "Serial Set Maps Frequently Asked Questions." Accessed July 19, 2019. https://www.readex.com/serial-set-maps-frequently-asked-questions.

Tenet, George. 1999. "DCI Statement on the Belgrade Chinese Embassy Bombing." Testimony given to the House Permanent Select Committee on Intelligence. July 22, 1999. Accessed September 29, 2019. https://www.cia.gov/news-information/speeches-testimony/1999/dci_speech_072299.html. Also available as a hearing transcript in ProQuest Congressional. Not published by GPO.

U.S. Census Bureau. 2014. "Census Bureau Celebrates 25th Anniversary of Technology That Propelled GIS, Digital and Online Mapping into the 21st Century." November 19, 2014. Accessed September 29, 2019. https://www.census.gov/newsroom/press-releases/2014/cb14-208.html.

USGS (United States Geological Survey). 2002. "Map Scales." USGS Fact Sheet 015-02. February 2002. Accessed August 8, 2019. https://pubs.usgs.gov/fs/2002/0015/report.pdf.

Washington, George. 1933. *The Writings of George Washington from the Original Manuscript Sources, 1745–1799.* Washington, DC: GPO, vol. 8, p. 443. (SuDocs: Y 3.W 27/2:13/; HT 000366819).

14

Federal STEM Information

STEM—science, technology, engineering, and mathematics—is a hot topic today, and many government agencies are replete with it. Add a second M for medicine to make the acronym STEMM if you like, but the federal government is a major information disseminator in each of these letters. Want proof? Just go to the online Government Manual (https://www .usgovernmentmanual.gov/) and type *technology* or *science* into the search box. You could also try *biology* OR *biological, medicine* OR *medical, environment* OR *environmental*, and similar branches of science or engineering. As you would expect, these many agencies generate seemingly endless technical reports and datasets.

Although many government agencies release scientific information and technical reports, most of this content does not fall under the purview of the FDLP. Some of these entities are under the Commerce Department, most notably, the National Technical Information Service (NTIS), which has statutory authority to charge a minimal fee for technical reports that are not classified. Most of these reports were never distributed to depository libraries. Other entities under the Commerce Department that have, in the past, charged fees include the National Oceanic and Atmospheric Administration (NOAA) and its National Climate Data Center, and USATrade.

TECHNICAL REPORTS

Technical reports present many challenges. Not only are most of them not distributed via the FDLP depository channels but they are also often difficult to classify with SuDocs stems. Many are produced with federal grant money on behalf of multiple federal agencies. Early technical reports were published in microformats or electronic formats that are no longer supported or can only be viewed on specialized machinery. As such, they are perfect candidates for digitization projects.

Technical reports often fall in the category of "gray literature" (often spelled "grey literature")—that is, publications that are not controlled or indexed by commercial publishers. Federal technical reports are further complicated by the fact that sometimes report series were distributed by GPO and sent to depository libraries, only later to be turned over to NTIS for their indexing in their publication *Government Reports Announcements* (title varies), and the online version, the NTIS database (Thompson 2001).

Numerous government agencies publish technical reports. We will highlight several of them here, while omitting many others. To find more technical report databases from the federal government, try a Google search like this: *site:gov technical reports database*.

National Technical Information Service (NTIS) and Its National Technical Reports Library (NTRL)

NTIS was created after World War II to serve as the U.S. government's repository for scientific and technical research and information. It houses over three million publications and survives on a cost-recovery basis by selling documents to interested parties at nominal prices.

Over the years, there have been many discussions about spinning off NTIS as a completely private entity, establishing it as a government corporation, or creating a public or private special-purpose organization (CRS 1987). Yet it remains under the Department of Commerce. Its revenues are generated completely from direct sales of its products and services.

The NTIS Bibliographic Database contains over three million records and is the primary access point for research sponsored by the United States and selected foreign governments. It is available commercially through several database vendors, including ProQuest, EBSCO, Engineering Information (EI), Dialog (ProQuest), Ovid, and STN International/Chemical Abstract Service. Larger academic institutions may also subscribe to enhanced access to technical reports via NTIS's National Technical Reports Library (NTRL).

NTIS is allowed by law to charge money for the technical reports so that it is financially self-sustaining (15 U.S.C. 1153). This runs contrary to the general mission of the Federal Depository Library Program, but at least the prices are relatively reasonable.

The database has come under scrutiny recently because it seems to be adding more older reports to its database while the demand is for newer reports. Also, about 74 percent of items added between 1990 and 2011 were available for free in other places, such as the issuing agency website, usa.gov, or another source findable with a web search (GAO 2012).

As of this writing, users can access the National Technical Reports Library through two URLs: https://classic.ntis.gov/ or https://ntrl.ntis.gov/. The database contains more than three million records and uses a robust descriptor system to classify materials. NTRL consists largely of technical reports but also has conference proceedings, journal articles, and theses. Even if full text is not available in the NTRL database, it may be findable by doing a general web search; a Google Scholar search; or, in the case of dissertations, by searching the ProQuest Dissertations and Theses database. Search tips, including the NTIS subject categories, can be found in the *NTIS Search Guide* at https://classic.ntis.gov/assets/pdf/dbguid .pdf.

OSTI.gov

The Department of Energy's OSTI.gov is an index-based discovery tool that retrieves citations and selected full text. This interface has replaced previously familiar tools such as SciTech Connect, DOE Information Bridge, the E-Print Network, EnergyFiles, and Energy Citations Database. Not only is metadata searchable, but generally full text of technical reports can be searched as well. Much of the indexing contained in the older print indexes, such as *Energy Research Abstracts*, *ERDA Energy Research Abstracts*, *Energy Abstracts for Policy Analysis*, and *Nuclear Science Abstracts* is searchable in OSTI.gov. If you are searching for a known item, such as a technical report title, it is best to place the title in quotes. The search engine does not do a good job of placing relevant items at the top of the results set. Sometimes reports indexed in OSTI .gov are not available in full text within OSTI.gov but are available through NTIS.

Science.gov is an older tool that follows a federated search model. Unlike OSTI.gov, it does not have a central index of metadata but, rather, does a broadcast out to search engines from 15 federal agencies. Users will often experience link failures because of this, and full text of documents is not searched; only metadata is searched.

EPA Documents and the NEPIS Database

The Environmental Protection Agency, whose administrator sits on the president's cabinet, produces an astounding number of technical reports. Through the National Service Center for Environmental Publications (NSCEP), the National Environmental Publications Information System (NEPIS) provides bibliographic information and often full text of environmental reports. The database can be browsed or searched through https://nepis.epa.gov/ or https://www.epa.gov/nscep. Users will notice that the NEPIS database has extremely long URLs that actually persist over time. These URLs are typically 12 lines long when pasted into Microsoft Word with a 12-point font. The secret is to derive a short, durable URL. You will see an information icon on the report page. Clicking that link will give you document properties, including a short URL.

NASA Technical Reports Server (NTRS)

From the National Aeronautics and Space Administration comes the NASA Technical Reports Server (NTRS) (https://ntrs.nasa.gov/), which provides access to citations, full text documents, images, and videos on the broad topics of aerospace from the three collections that have been merged into this single interface: (1) citations and reports from the National Advisory Committee for Aeronautics (NACA, with SuDocs stem Y 3.N 21/5), which existed from 1915 to 1958; (2) citations and documents either produced by or sponsored by the National Aeronautics and Space Administration (1958 to present, with SuDocs stem NAS 1); and (3) the National Image Exchange (NIX) Collection, with links to images and videos.

In 2013, the NTRS was taken down over vague concerns about public access to certain NASA content (FDLP 2013). But in 2016, NASA and the NTRS became GPO partners, ensuring permanent public access to the content (FDLP 2016).

Defense Technical Information Center (DTIC)

The stated purpose of DTIC is "to aggregate and fuse science and technology data to rapidly, accurately and reliably deliver the knowledge needed to develop the next generation of technologies to support our warfighters and help assure national security" (DTIC 2019). Document types include technical reports and papers, journal articles, conference papers, security classification guides, unified research and engineering data, international agreements data, and Department of Defense grant awards. Some records have only citations, and others contain full text. The impressive thing about this database is that it searches deeply into the full text of materials, unlike many library discovery tools today. Since DTIC is exposed to Google, it is also possible to search like this: *site:dtic.mil "atomic bomb"*. Some DTIC documents also find their way into the NTIS database. A subset of DTIC technical reports can be found in the Homeland Security Digital Library.

A searchable or downloadable thesaurus with broader terms, narrower terms, and related terms helps with controlled vocabulary searches (https://discover.dtic.mil/thesaurus/). Full text of OCRed documents is searchable via the database for items that have full text available, making this a very powerful search engine. If you don't like navigating the DTIC website, technical reports are also findable with a Google search (*site:dtic .mil [your keywords]*). A subset of DTIC reports are searchable in the Homeland Security Digital Library database.

The database URL has changed several times over the years. Currently it is https://discover.dtic.mil/. Keep in mind, as has been emphasized throughout this book, that you may need to do a web search to discover the new URL (*site:dtic.mil dtic*). Civilian users will discover the publicly available collections. There are access-controlled (secret or classified) materials for those with security clearances, but those cannot be used in research papers anyway.

Technical Report Archive and Image Library (TRAIL)

TRAIL is a collaborative project originally started by the University of Arizona and the Greater Western Library Alliance (GWLA), in collaboration with the Center for Research Library's Global Resources Network, which now hosts the TRAIL website (http://www.technicalreports.org /trail/search/). The early history and mission of the project can be found in Nesdill et al. (2016).

In the early years of the project, the emphasis was on digitizing pre-1976 technical reports. As time went on, the mission expanded beyond the limitation of early reports. It now includes more recent ones as well. TRAIL digitized content is kept in the University of North Texas Digital Library and the HathiTrust. As of May 2019, UNT Digital Library had 25,246 visible items, and 429 hidden, and HathiTrust had 26,844 full view items, with 373 hidden items.

MEDICAL INFORMATION

The Department of Health and Human Services has 11 agencies under its purview, many of which are involved with medical information.

Prominent in the government information realm are the Centers for Disease Control and Prevention and the National Institutes of Health (and especially the NIH's National Library of Medicine).

Centers for Disease Control and Prevention (CDC)

There are many agencies that publish medical information, and most of them are under the Centers for Disease Control and Prevention (CDC). The CDC website is difficult to navigate, at least in terms of finding publications or other meaningful information within their many centers, institutes, and offices. One way to cut across this situation is to search Google like this: *site:cdc.gov filetype:pdf [disease or condition]*. This limits the results to documents hosted on the CDC website that are in PDF format and contain your topic term.

National Institutes of Health (NIH)

There is a searchable NIH Publications List (*site:nih.gov nih publications list*) which emphasized consumer-oriented pamphlets and publications in English and Spanish. A strategy similar to the Google searching recommended for the CDC above can be done for discovering hidden information on the NIH sites with their 27 institutes and centers: (*site:nih .gov filetype:pdf [disease or condition]*). It is also instructive to browse through these institutes and centers, each with its own government-issued abbreviation: (*site:nih.gov list of NIH institutes Centers*).

National Library of Medicine

The National Library of Medicine is so difficult to find from the NIH main web page that you wouldn't think it is so important—but it is. Founded in 1836, it is the world's largest biomedical library, situated on the campus of the National Institutes of Health in Bethesda, Maryland. The NLM's Medline project is another example, along with the Department of Education's ERIC project, of a government agency creating a premier thesaurus-controlled bibliographic database that indexes nongovernment publications.

PubMed, Medline, and PubMed Central

A little bit of background is necessary here. Since 1960, monthly print indexes, called *Index Medicus*, were published by the National Library of

Medicine, covering journals in all areas of medicine. These would be cumulated annually into *Cumulated Index Medicus*, again a print publication. These cumulations superseded the monthly indexes but still took up a significant amount of shelf space. The online database version, which first appeared as Medline (which stands for Medical Literature Analysis and Retrieval System) has Medical Subject Headings (MeSH) carefully applied to each record by indexing professionals with medical backgrounds.

The entirety of Medline is now incorporated into the broader umbrella known as PubMed and runs under the Entrez browser interface. This is the same interface that hosts the Human Genome Project, the famous DNA mapping project. In all, 39 literature and molecular databases are searchable under this interface (National Library of Medicine 2006). It is important to note that PubMed contains more than the *Cumulated Index Medicus*/Medline content. Because the field of medicine is changing so quickly, researchers and doctors can't wait for indexers to apply Medical Subject Headings to entries before they enter the database. Figure 14.1 shows the relationships between the products as they exist today. A subset of Medline records, PMC, or PubMed Central, are freely available records with accompanying full text. There is a separate search pulldown selection from within the Entrez interface that will retrieve PMC free full text. This is most useful for people who don't have access to college or university subscriptions to premium journal content.

Also contained in PubMed are "ahead of print" records that have not yet been fully indexed and have not yet had MeSH headings applied. It is important for medical professionals to be aware of this information ahead of time. There is also a subset of pre-1966 records that have not been indexed for other reasons. These include articles from medical journals that may not be related to medical fields, such as pieces about plate tectonics or astrophysics. The thesaurus to PubMed is the Medical Subject Headings, also accessed via the Entrez interface.

Another NLM project, Medline Plus, is a web portal for health information geared to

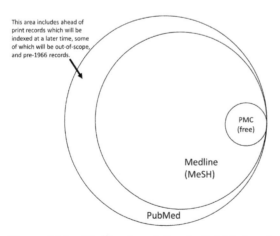

This area includes ahead of print records which will be indexed at a later time, some of which will be out-of-scope, and pre-1966 records.

PMC (free)

Medline (MeSH)

PubMed

Figure 14.1   Medline in relation to PubMed and PubMed Central

patients and the general public. It is not directly related to finding journal articles as are Medline and PubMed.

PubMed has its own controlled vocabulary—the Medical Subject Headings, or MeSH. Access to a controlled vocabulary is essential for medical professions, since their search task is to find "all and only" relevant articles on a topic and not just articles that may happen to mention a word.

Let me be clear on one thing: the articles indexed in PubMed, PubMed Central, and Medline are not government information (well, some of them may be). The finding aids themselves are government productions. That's why you will be asked to pay for access to many of the journal articles (unless you belong to an institution that subscribes). Use PubMed Central if you only want content that is freely available.

STANDARDS

Standards.gov

Branded as Standards.gov, the site flips over to https://www.nist.gov /standardsgov. As you can see from the URL, this is under the purview of the National Institute of Standards and Technology (under the Department of Commerce). NIST publications can be searched from https://www .nist.gov/publications. The database does not contain many standards, but peer-reviewed articles, conference papers, and NIST publications generally related to standards and technology.

Military Standards

Often referred to as "MIL Standards," these are often requested by military contractors and occasionally by veterans or others interested in military history. The ASSIST database is available from the https://assist .dla.mil/ site. It requires free registration to access. "All users must register to obtain a user account and password in order to access ASSIST-Online. Registration data is used by the DODSSP to establish the correct type of account and to manage and audit customer activity. Accounts are available free of charge to all users who need access to standardization document information" (DTIC 2012). Then, after applying, you will receive this message: "In the next few days, an administrator will review your application and contact you via email to inform you of your account status."

Although the primary search form requires registration, a "Quick Search" is available here: https://quicksearch.dla.mil/qsSearch.aspx. Standards go back to the 1930s.

DATA

Researchers want raw data for various reasons. They want to import the data into statistical or scientific software to run their own observations. Students taking business analytics classes often want raw data to learn how to deal with big data and multiple variables.

The data.gov website was launched in May 2009. The scope is not just as a federal government data repository, but also includes state, local, and tribal data sets. The initiative was part of the Obama Administration's Open Government Initiative and was announced in the *Federal Register* at 74 Fed. Reg. 29211.

As of June 2019, the repository had over 252,000 data sets, with 140,000 of them containing geospatial data. Going to the data.gov metrics page (https://www.data.gov/metrics), you can see counts for the number of data sets from various entities, such as federal government, city governments, state governments, and other organizations. On the federal level, the largest contributors to date are the Department of the Interior, Department of Commerce, and NASA. One useful way to approach data.gov is to browse by organization. Using this URL, https://catalog.data.gov/organization, you can browse all organizations together, federal, state, and local.

Even though federal, state, and local data sets are all living together within data.gov, facets on the side make it easy to limit results to only federal data sets. One of the stunning features of searching data.gov is the ability to limit searches to geographic regions. Figure 14.2 shows search results limited to the Denver metropolitan area.

A search for credit card complaints in data.gov yields a result titled Consumer Complaint Database from the Consumer Financial Protection Bureau (Figure 14.3). This large file (over 700 MB) can be downloaded in various formats: CSV, RDF, JSON, or XML.

The data.gov interface is not the only way to get to federally generated data. Some agencies have their own data portals. In many cases, these data sets have also been contributed to data.gov, but one should not assume that this is always the case. Not only is there the likelihood that you will discover different data sets, but the browsing experience is usually different, sometimes making it easier to discover the desired data sets. Using this Google site-specific search, you can see agencies that have data sets following the URL pattern data.xxx.gov: *site:data.*.gov.* The asterisk here serves as a wildcard for the Google domain search. Table 14.1 shows agencies that maintain their own data catalogs.

PRINT TOOLS FOR NTIS TECHNICAL REPORTS

What follows is the serial chain for the cataloging of the print titles that represent the early years of what is now the NTIS database.

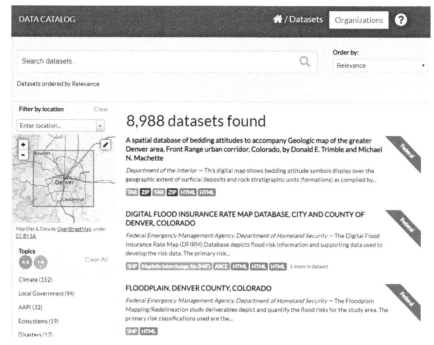

Figure 14.2 Data.gov search limited to geospatial coordinates

	A	B	C	D	E	F	G	H	I	J	K	L	M
1	Date received	Product	Sub-product	Issue	Sub-issue	Consumer complaint	Company	Company	State	ZIP code	Tags	Consumer	Submitt
2	6/18/2019	Debt collection	Other debt	Threatened to contact someo	Talked to a third-party about yc		Company	LJ Ross Associates	OH	436XX			Web
3	6/18/2019	Debt collection	Other debt	Attempts to collect debt not c	Debt was paid			Diversified Consulta	TN	385XX			Web
4	6/18/2019	Payday loan, title loan, or	Personal line o	Getting a line of credit				NAVY FEDERAL CREC	NY	112XX	Servicemember		Web
5	6/18/2019	Payday loan, title loan, or	Payday loan	Problem with the payoff process at the end of the loan				CURO Intermediate	TX	760XX			Web
6	6/18/2019	Credit reporting, credit re	Credit reportin	Incorrect information on your	Information belongs to someone else			ONEMAIN FINANCIA	OH	436XX			Web
7	6/18/2019	Credit reporting, credit re	Credit reportin	Incorrect information on your	Information belongs to someone else			NAVY FEDERAL CREC	OH	436XX			Web
8	6/18/2019	Credit reporting, credit re	Credit reportin	Incorrect information on your	Old information reappears or never goes			Ad Astra Recovery S	CA	903XX			Web
9	6/18/2019	Credit card or prepaid carc	General-purpo	Incorrect information on your	Information belongs to someone else			NAVY FEDERAL CREC	GA	300XX	Servicemember		Web
10	6/18/2019	Mortgage	Conventional h	Trouble during payment process				BAYVIEW LOAN SER	FL	334XX	Older American		Web
11	6/18/2019	Credit reporting, credit re	Credit reportin	Improper use of your report	Credit inquiries on your report that you d			ALLY FINANCIAL INC	SC	29464			Web
12	6/18/2019	Credit reporting, credit re	Credit reportin	Incorrect information on your	Old information reappears or never goes			ALLY FINANCIAL INC	TX	760XX			Web
13	6/18/2019	Credit reporting, credit re	Credit reportin	Incorrect information on your	Account information incorrect			NCC Business Servic	GA	30655			Web
14	6/18/2019	Debt collection	Medical debt	Attempts to collect debt not c	Debt is not yours			Community Health I	MO	63845		Consent w	Web
15	6/17/2019	Credit reporting, credit re	Credit reportin	Incorrect information on your	Old information reappears or never goes			EQUIFAX, INC.	CA	904XX	Older American		Web
16	6/17/2019	Debt collection	Other debt	Attempts to collect debt not c	Debt is not yours		Company	Convergent Resourc	CA	904XX			Web

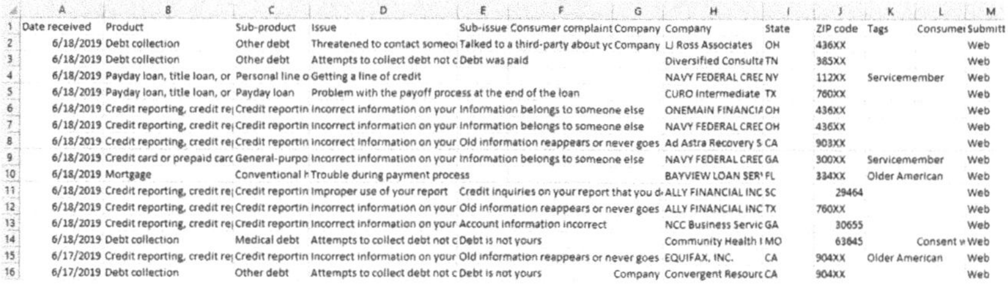

Figure 14.3 Example of a data set, Consumer Complaint Database, available from data.gov

Bibliography of Scientific and Industrial Reports. Washington, DC: Office of Technical Services, U.S. Dept. of Commerce. January 11, 1946–June 1949. (C 35.7: and C 41.21:). (OCLC 1777858). (HT 009487225).

Bibliography of Technical Reports. Washington, DC: Dept. of Commerce. July 1949–September 1954. (C 41.21:). (OCLC 1777859). (HT 009487227).

U.S. Government Research Reports. Washington, DC: U.S. Dept. of Commerce, Office of Technical Services. October 1954–December 1964. (C 41.21:). (OCLC 4354743). (HT 009487229).

Table 14.1   Federal agencies maintaining their own data catalogs

Data Catalog URL Stem	Agency
data.boem.gov	Bureau of Ocean Energy Management (Interior)
data.bsee.gov	Bureau of Safety and Environmental Enforcement (Interior)
data.cdc.gov	Centers for Disease Control and Prevention (Health and Human Services)
data.census.gov	Census Bureau. This is the replacement for American FactFinder (Commerce)
data.cms.gov	Centers for Medicare and Medicaid Services (Health and Human Services)
data.commerce.gov	Commerce Department
data.defense.gov	Defense Department
data.doi.gov	Interior Department
data.faa.gov	Federal Aviation Administration (Transportation)
data.fdic.gov	Federal Deposit Insurance Corporation (Independent)
data.globalchange.gov	U.S. Global Change Research Program (13 Government Agencies)
data.healthcare.gov	Managed by Centers for Disease Control and Prevention (Health and Human Services)
data.hrsa.gov	Health Resources and Services Administration (Health and Human Services)
data.hud.gov	Housing and Urban Development
data.medicaid.gov	Centers for Disease Control and Prevention (Health and Human Services)
data.medicare.gov	Centers for Disease Control and Prevention (Health and Human Services)
data.nasa.gov	National Aeronautics and Space Administration (Independent)
data.nationalservice.gov	Corporation for National and Community Service (Independent)
data.nist.gov	National Institute of Standards and Technology (Commerce)
data.noaa.gov	National Oceanic and Atmospheric Administration (Commerce)
data.nrel.gov	National Renewable Energy Laboratory (Energy)
data.usgs.gov	United States Geological Survey (Interior)

U.S. Government Research and Development Reports. Washington, DC: U.S. GPO, Division of Public Documents, 1965–1971. (C 41.21: and C 51.9/3). (OCLC 1768747). (HT 005134756, 007406672).

Government Reports Announcements. Springfield, VA: National Technical Information Service. March 27, 1971–March 21, 1975. SuDocs: C 51.9/3). (OCLC 2240136). (HT 000541200).

Government Reports Index. Washington, DC: U.S. Dept. of Commerce, National Technical Information Service. April 10, 1971–March 21, 1975. (SuDocs: C 51.9). (OCLC 1751359). (HT 000051438).

Government Reports Announcements and Index. Springfield, VA: U.S. Dept. of Commerce, National Technical Information Service. 1975–1996. (C 51.9/3:). (OCLC 2242215). (HT 000640222).

EXERCISES

1. Find an object at home, school, or work that has a patent number on it somewhere. Not everything has patent numbers, so focus on older items. Look up the number in the patents database from the Patent and Trademark Office. Now look up the same patent using Google Patents.

2. Find the HathiTrust records for either *Energy Research Abstracts, ERDA Energy Research Abstracts,* or *Nuclear Science Abstracts.* The object with this exercise is to judge how much content from either of these indexes is included in the OSTI.gov database (citations only). Did you find any reports that were included in the print index but were not in OSTI.gov?

3. Using tools mentioned in this chapter, find technical reports for magnetic resonance imaging and tumors. Next, find peer-reviewed articles for the same topic only using tools in this chapter.

REFERENCES

CRS (Congressional Research Service). 1987. *Privatization of the National Technical Information Service.* February 25, 1987. Washington, DC: Congressional Research Service.

DTIC (Defense Technical Information Center). 2012. "ASSIST—Register for an Account." Accessed January 1, 2020. https://assist.dla.mil/online/registration/pre_registration.cfm.

DTIC (Defense Technical Information Center). 2019. "DTIC's Mission." Accessed January 1, 2020. https://discover.dtic.mil/mission-statement/.

FDLP (Federal Depository Library Program). 2013. "NASA Technical Reports Server Being Reviewed by NASA." May 23, 2013. Accessed August 9, 2019. https://www.fdlp.gov/news-and-events/1608-nasa-technical-reports-server-being-reviewed-by-nasa.

FDLP (Federal Depository Library Program). 2016. "NASA Scientific and Technical Information Program Technical Reports." August 24, 2016. Accessed August 9, 2019. https://www.fdlp.gov/all-newsletters/partnership-show case/2668-partnership-showcase-nasa-scientific-and-technical-infor mation-program-technical-reports.

GAO (Government Accountability Office). 2012. "Information Management: National Technical Information Service's Dissemination of Technical Reports Needs Congressional Action." November 2012. Accessed August 15, 2019. GAO-13-99. https://www.gao.gov/assets/660/650210.pdf.

National Library of Medicine. 2006. "Entrez Help." Updated May 31, 2016. Accessed September 29, 2019. https://www.ncbi.nlm.nih.gov/sites/books /NBK3836/.

Nesdill, Daureen, Laura Sare, Alice Trussell, and Marilyn Von Seggern. 2016. "Ten Years of TRAIL." *Documents to the People (DttP)* 44, no. 2: 14–18.

Thompson, Larry A. 2001. "Grey Literature in Engineering." *Science and Technology Libraries* 19, no. 3–4): 57–73. DOI: 10.1300/J122v19n03_05.

15

Intellectual Property, Secrets, and Declassified Information

"Information wants to be free," you have heard it said—especially government information. But there are limits to freedom. Inventors want their inventions to be protected—kept secret for a limited time—to allow them to make money. Nobody wants to take the time to write a song, book, or screenplay only to have someone else claim that it as his or her creation.

Governments also want certain information protected. As a measure of national security, the United States doesn't want its missile codes published on the internet. Certain kinds of information are deemed classified—not forever, but for a meaningful period of time.

This chapter deals with information that is secret, unpublished, classified or declassified, and how and when we can expect to access such information.

INTELLECTUAL PROPERTY

Intellectual property is a major area of legal studies, often referred to as "IP." IP consists of three parts, as briefly summarized in Table 15.1.

Table 15.1   Summary of the three parts of intellectual property

IP Category	Brief Summary
Patents	Utility, design, or plant patents that exclude others from making, using, or selling the invention.
Trademarks	Word, phrase, design, symbol that identifies and distinguishes the goods of one party from those of others.
Copyright	Protects original works of authorship. Includes books, journals, music, movies, sound recordings, software, photographs, and other works of original authorship.

Patents

Patents are part of intellectual property, with the other two parts being trademarks and copyrights. The U.S. Patent and Trademark Office (USPTO) is organizationally under the Department of Commerce, but the United States Copyright Office is under the Library of Congress.

Patents are mentioned in the Constitution right along with copyrights. The Congress shall have power "to promote the progress of science and useful arts, by securing for limited times to authors and inventors the exclusive right to their respective writings and discoveries" (Constitution, Article 1, Section 8, Clause 8). There is tension between protecting the rights of innovators with the wider public interest. The protections associated with patents do not occur automatically; inventors must apply with the U.S. Patent and Trademark Office, according to the Patent Law Codification and Revision Act (P.L. 82-593, 66 Stat. 792; 1952) (CRS 2017).

Patents are an exciting and challenging combination of two different skill sets: an engineer (or in the case of plant patents, a botanist) and an attorney. Sometimes patent filings are the opposite of what we try to do in the field of library science. Librarians attempt to create catalog records and index records that fully capture the "aboutness" of the items they are indexing. But with many patents, the titles are anything but clear. It's as if they don't want to be discovered.

Patents are valuable. Think about how pharmaceutical companies make their billions. They endeavor to keep their patents alive for as long as possible. As soon as a drug becomes generic, revenue drops off.

Patents are useful for many purposes, not just the obvious, original one. Inventors, whether individuals or research teams working for large corporations, desire to protect their intellectual property. Beyond the protection of inventions, patents have other uses to those of us who are neither engineers, inventors, nor intellectual property attorneys.

- They show the history of inventions.

- Genealogists find them useful in researching family histories.

- The technical drawings, especially the older ones, can make interesting displayable artwork.

Library users ask for assistance with patents more often than they do for trademarks or copyrights, and that is the focus of this section. What makes patents confusing is their obfuscated titles, difficult-to-access older patents, and obscure classification system. Patents must be indexed with one of the most complex classification schedules known, and this indexing must be accurate. Patents are not generally found by title but by using their precise classification system. Table 15.2 shows some examples of this.

Table 15.2   Examples of popular names of items versus the patent titles

Popular Name	Title of Patent	US Patent Number	Date Patented
Telephone	Improvement in Telegraphy	174,465	Mar. 7, 1876
Razor	Razor	775,134	Nov. 15, 1904
Television	Television System	1,773,980	Aug. 26, 1930
Slinky	Toy and Process of Use	2,415,012	Jan. 28, 1947
Frisbee	Flying Toy	D183,626	Sept. 30, 1958
Twister (game)	Apparatus for playing a game wherein the players constitute the game pieces	3,454,279	July 8, 1969
Drone	Omni-directional, vertical-lift, helicopter drone	3,053,480	Sept. 11, 1962
Global Positioning System	Navigation System Using Satellites and Passive Ranging Techniques	3,789,409	Jan. 29, 1974
Google (one of several early patents)	Information Extraction from a Database	6,678,681	Mar. 9, 2000 (filed); Jan. 13, 2004 (granted)
Facebook (initial patent)	Dynamically Generating a Privacy Summary	8,225,376	July 25, 2006 (filed); July 12, 2012 (granted)
iPhone	Electronic Device	D672,769	Dec. 18, 2012

Types of Patents

There are three primary types of patents in the United States: utility patents, design patents, and plant patents.

Utility Patents. This is the most common type of patent, accounting for about 90 percent of patents in recent years. These involve a process, a machine, a manufacture, a composition of matter, or an improvement of an existing idea. They generally permit their owners to exclude others from making, using, or selling the invention for a period of up to 20 years from the date of patent application filing.

Design Patents. These patents are issued for new, original, and ornamental design for something manufactured. Whereas a utility patent protects the way an article is used and works, a design patent protects the way an article looks. If an invention is distinctive in both its utility and appearance, then both kinds of patents may be obtained (U.S. Patent and Trademark Office 2018). Design patents begin with a "D."

Plant Patents. Patents for plants? Let's get the information straight from the primary source, 35 U.S.C. 161: "Whoever invents or discovers and asexually reproduces any distinct and new variety of plant, including cultivated sports, mutants, hybrids, and newly found seedlings, other than a tuber propagated plant or a plant found in an uncultivated state, may obtain a patent therefor, subject to the conditions and requirements of this title."

Plant patent numbers typically begin with "PP" followed by a five-digit number. These can sometimes be found on plant identification markers in your local nursery. The other day, I purchased a "Red Elf Coreopsis," commonly known as a tickseed plant. The patent number was PP27918. I was easily able to retrieve the patent (Figure 15.1).

One of my favorite trees, the Shiloh Splash Birch, was patented in 2006 as PP16362. Searching that number reveals all the claims, as well as more information about growth rates, leaf patterns, and pest resistance than can be found anywhere else.

Anatomy of a Patent

The front or summary page of a patent contains the title, abstract, and drawings that, together, provide a summary of the technology. The title is very often obscure and rarely reflects a trademarked name. The title usually reflects something in the claims section. Inventors are listed, along with the city in which they live. Under U.S. law, the patent rights are owned by the inventor in most cases. In other cases the inventor assigns the rights

US00PP27918P2

(12) **United States Plant Patent**   (10) **Patent No.:**   **US PP27,918 P2**

Probst   (45) **Date of Patent:**   **Apr. 18, 2017**

(54) **COREOPSIS PLANT NAMED 'RED ELF'**

(50) Latin Name: **Coreopsis hybrid**
Varietal Denomination: **Red Elf**

(71) Applicant: **Darrell R. Probst**, Hubbardston, MA
(US)

(72) Inventor: **Darrell R. Probst**, Hubbardston, MA
(US)

(*) Notice: Subject to any disclaimer, the term of this
patent is extended or adjusted under 35
U.S.C. 154(b) by 97 days.

(21) Appl. No.: **14/545,032**

(22) Filed: **Mar. 18, 2015**

(51) **Int. Cl.**
A01H 5/02   (2006.01)
(52) **U.S. Cl.**
USPC **Plt./417**
(58) **Field of Classification Search**
USPC Plt./417
See application file for complete search history.

(56) **References Cited**

PUBLICATIONS

American Nurseryman 2015 Dec. 2014, retrieved on Aug. 4, 2016,
retrieved from the Internet at <http://www.amerinursery.com/con-
tent/AN/pdf/2015__AN_NewPlants.pdf> pp. 4 and 36.*
Emerald Coast Grower Starter Plants 2014-2015 catalog pp. 1-3,
8-9 and 26-27.*
Pioneer Gardens, Inc. 2014-2015 Program and Availability,
retrieved on Aug. 18, 2016, retrieved from the Internet at <https://
nebula.wsimg.com/
a8e14aaf5f2c1ab73574f0980ec0bb03?AccessKeyId=D4DC3ED
90C9EAD58C2B4&disposition=0&alloworigin=1> Aug. 27, 2014,
pp. 1-20.*

* cited by examiner

Primary Examiner — June Hwu
(74) *Attorney, Agent, or Firm* — Penny J. Aguirre

(57)   **ABSTRACT**

A new cultivar of hybrid *Coreopsis* named 'Red Elf' that is
characterized by its compact plant habit, its nearly sterile
florets result in a floriferous and long bloom season that does
not require deadheading with bloom commencing in late-
June and lasting until frost in Connecticut, its large inflo-
rescences with ray florets that are deep velvety red in color,
its cold hardiness at least to U.S.D.A. Zone 5a, and its
resistance to powdery mildew and leaf spot.

2 Drawing Sheets

Figure 15.1   Example of a plant patent summary page

to his or her employer, so the inventor area may not tell you who was personally involved with the invention.

A section called "prior art" is a list of references used by the examiner in
the research process. These references are included to demonstrate the
validity of your invention. The abstract is a brief summary of the invention
in broad terms. It must be 150 words or fewer.

Nearly all U.S. patents have drawings. These help the reader understand
the invention. Drawings for older patents can be quite artful and are often
suitable for framing. The specification section includes the detailed
description. This is the main technical disclosure part of the patent.

Claims and Prior Art

Arguably, the most important section of a patent is the claims section.
Although we are instantly drawn to the images in patents, the most important part of a patent is the claims—what makes this patent unique and distin-
guishes it from other patents? How is the patent different from similar ones?

Classification

Searching by a classification system is necessary because of the irregularities of keyword searching. U.S. patents are now into their third century. But terminology changes over time. Not only that, but words can have different meanings in different industries. A helpful classification timeline showing the historical evolution of classification can be found at https://www.uspto.gov/sites/default/files/documents/Timeline.pdf.

The U.S. Patent Classification System (USPC) was the original U.S. classification system. The Cooperative Patent Classification (CPC), codeveloped with European Patent Office and updated for newer technologies, replaced it in 2013. Below are two examples of the hierarchical CPC classification system.

A46B 9/04 Toothbrush Bristles Arrangement

A Section

A46 Class

A46B Subclass

A46B 9/00 Maingroup

A46B 9/04 Subgroup

G02C 7/04 Contact Lenses

G Section

G02 Class

G02C Subclass

G02C 7/00 Maingroup

G02C 7/04 Subgroup

A classification search avoids the pitfalls of keyword searching. For example, the word "nail" may refer to fasteners, horseshoe nails, or artificial nails in manicuring or pedicuring. But classifications avoid those ambiguities.

Suggested patent search strategy:

1. Brainstorm terms that describe what you want to search for.
2. Go to USPTO main page and type *CPC scheme [term]*. This enables the search tool to focus only on the CPC schedule and not on the entire website. If you need further search suggestions, use World Intellectual Property Organization's IPC Catchword index. CPC classification is an extension of IPC classification. This resource has recently changed its web address, so it is best to do a Google search: *site:wipo.int catchword*. This should lead you to a PDF version of the catchwords, as well

as an interactive version. This is a brainstorming tool that shows common language terms in relation to the classification system.

3. From the CPC schedule, find the classification definition that most closely fits what you are looking for. Use the cross-references to assist in making more specific searches. You can also use the main USPTO search box to find definitions. For example: *CPC definition [term]*.

4. Search the PatTF database by CPC. The following substeps are important:

    • Enter the CPC classification without spaces.

    • From the Field1 pulldown menu, select Current CPC Classification. *Do not* select Current CPC Class, as that will only search more recent patents.

    • Select years: 1790 to present [entire database].

    • Review the front-page information of all retrieved patents, identifying possibly relevant ones.

    • Review patents in more detail by looking carefully at images, claims, and cited references.

5. Search the AppFT database by CPC. These are patent applications back to 2001. Even if a patent was not ultimately granted, it may be considered prior art.

    • Enter the CPC classification without spaces.

    • From the Field1 pulldown menu, select Current CPC Classification. *Do not* select Current CPC Class

    • Select years: 2001present

    • Review the front page of the patent applications

6. Broaden your search by searching for older U.S. patents using the USPC classification. Also, consider searching for foreign patents using the European Patent Office's worldwide patent search tool, Espacenet (https://worldwide.espacenet.com/), using the same CPC classification number.

The UPSTO website contain a plenty of documentation in print and online tutorials as well.

For help with older patents, the Subject-Matter Index is recommended.

Subject-Matter Index of Patents for Inventions Issued by the United States Patent Office from 1790 to 1873, Inclusive. 1874. Washington, DC: U.S.GPO. 3 volumes. Reprinted in 1976 by Arno Press. (HT 001511246).

Google Patents

Google Patents has opened up a new world of research, not only for patent researchers, but for genealogists. Previously it was extremely difficult to locate patents by assignee for early years. But when Google took the TIF images provided by the Patent Office and applied their optical character recognition technology to them, new pathways opened up.

I'll illustrate this with my own great grandfather. I have always been told that Fred Wegner, of Fairport, New York, was an inventor. He was an engineer who worked for a canning company. But even though I worked in a depository library, there was no easy way to find out what his patents were.

My library did have the *Official Gazette* going back several decades, but the trouble with trying to search it is that since this is a monthly publication, it is a very tedious task to search each issue.

When Google Patents came out, I was able to quickly locate his many patents (Figure 15.2).

Now that I knew the patent numbers and dates of my grandfather's patents, I could search for them in the *Official Gazette*. The *Official Gazette of the United States Patent Office*, 1872–1971 (HT 000498155, 012225984, SuDocs: C 21.5:) exists in many larger depository libraries, but it occupies a massive amount of shelf space. Since the entire run of the *Official Gazette* is searchable and viewable in HathiTrust, I was able to locate my grandfather's patent for a "conveying and feeding mechanism" by "patentees" and by "list of inventions" (see Figures 15.3 and 15.4).

I could have searched the *Annual Report of the Commissioner of Patents for the Year . . .* (HT 002138126). The Wegner entry shows up for 1913 in

Figure 15.2   Using Google Patents to find patents before 1976

the alphabetical list of patentees, as well as in the alphabetical list of inventions. This is much less tedious than searching every month of the Gazette.

Now that I know the patent numbers, I can pull up the patent images from the USPTO database (Figure 15.5).

> ˮeeiaus, Cuuries, �𝘛renton, ᴎ. ᴊ., assignor to ʟ. ᴡolfᶠ
> Manufacturing Company, Chicago, Ill.   Urinal.   No.
> 1,070,643 ; Aug. 19 ; Gaz. vol. 193 ; p. 605.
> Wegner, Fred, Fairport, N. Y.   Conveying and feeding
> mechanism.   No. 1,069,362 ; Aug. 5 ; Gaz. vol. 193 ;
> p. 96.
> Weigel, Albert P., assignor to Kokomo Nail and Brad
> Company, Kokomo, Ind.   Food mechanism for a-ill

Figure 15.3   Wegner entry in patentee index. *Source: Official Gazette of the United States Patent Office*, vol. 193 (August 1913), p. xxxix.

> Conveying and discharging apparatus.   W. G. Wilson.   No.
> 1,069,507 ; Aug. 5 ; Gaz. vol. 193 ; p. 146.
> Conveying and feeding mechanism.   F. Wegner.   No.
> 1,069,362 ; Aug. 5 ; Gaz. vol. 193 ; p. 96.
> Cooker.   P. M. Conkey.   No. 1,070,586 ; Aug. 19 ; Gaz. vol.
> 193 ; p. 587.

Figure 15.4   Wegner entry in list of inventions. *Source: Official Gazette of the United States Patent Office*, vol. 193 (August 1913), p. lx.

Free Patent Search Tools

Several freely available resources from nongovernmental sources exist that are useful in the quest for patents.

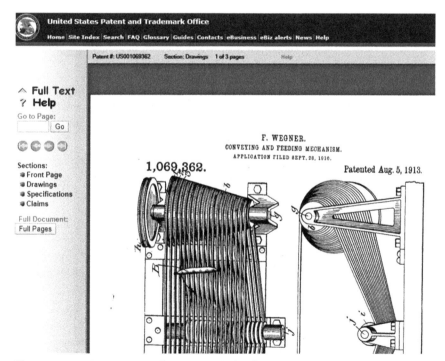

Figure 15.5   Patent image from USPTO database

- Pat2PDF Patent generator. https://www.pat2pdf.org/.This is useful for patents when all you have is a patent number, and you want a quick, multipage PDF.

- Patent Retriever. http://www.patentretriever.com/. Patent generator. Put in a patent number and retrieve a multipage PDF.

- Patent Fetcher. https://free.patentfetcher.com/Patent-Fetcher-Form .php. Another patent PDF generator.

- WIPO Patentscope. https://patentscope.wipo.int/. A search engine that searches across international and national patent collections.

- Free Patents Online. http://www.freepatentsonline.com/. Includes foreign as well as U.S. patents.

Patent and Trademark Resource Centers

Patent and Trademark Resource Centers (PTRCs) are located throughout the country to provide specialized assistance with USPTO databases and resources. Historically, these centers were called Patent and Trademark Depository Libraries, since the patents were actually distributed in a variety of tangible formats, including print, microformats, and CD-ROMs. In addition, they have all the finding aids necessary to research historic patents and selected foreign patents. They do not provide legal advice, but they can point users to the right forms for filing trademarks and patents, demonstrate how to search their databases, and offer assistance on historical research or tracking current research. The easiest way to find these centers is to search Google: *site:uspto.gov ptrc map*. These centers are a mixture of public libraries, academic libraries, state libraries, and one special library.

Trademarks

As with patents, the U.S. Patent and Trademark Office has many helpful booklets, videos, forms, and FAQs to assist with background knowledge, filing, and the trademark registration process. But in terms of government information access, what we really want to do is search the trademark database (Google: *trademark database*). It is currently called TESS, Trademark Electronic Search System. If you like classification systems, then you will love TESS. Otherwise, you might be frustrated. Design marks, the technical term for pictures that are trademarked, are classified with a complex system contained in the online Design Search Code Manual (Google: *Design Search Code Manual site:uspto.gov*).

As an example of the power of this search capability, suppose I wanted to find all marks that had both rainbows and unicorns. I use the code manual to lookup rainbows: 01 Celestial bodies, natural phenomena, geographical maps → 01.15 Natural phenomena → 01.15.01 Rainbows. Then for unicorns: 04 Supernatural beings, mythological or legendary beings, fantastical beings or unidentifiable beings → 04.05 Mythological or legendary animals → 04.05.04 Unicorns.

Now I can combine these codes in the TESS database (be sure to use the Boolean AND operator, since the system defaults to an OR operator). Your search form will look like this:

Search term: 01.15.01 Field: Design Code

Operator: AND

Search term: 04.05.04 Field: Design Code

One of the results is in Figure 15.6.

Figure 15.6   One result of trademark search for rainbows and unicorns together in a trademark

I don't know what to say about a unicorn vomiting a rainbow and stars. But if you do the same search in the trademark database, you will find even more offensive marks.

For older trademarks, it's not OMG, but TMOG that you need to remember. The *Trademark Official Gazette* (Google: *site:uspto.gov trademark official gazette*). It is fully searchable from 2004 to present, as well as downloadable in PDF format. It is also available in the HathiTrust (HT 000498157, 012405264). Older trademarks are contained in the Official Gazette of the United States Patent Office, 1872–1971 (HT 000498155, 012225984).

Copyright

Copyright has its own title in the U.S. Code—Title 17. Copyright law was completely revised in 1976 with the passage of the Copyright Act of 1976 (P.L. No. 94-553, 90 Stat. 2541). The law has been amended since 1976 to incorporate the Semiconductor Chip Protection Act of 1984 (SCPA); the Vessel Hull Design Protection Act (VHDPA); and the Digital Millennium Copyright Act (DMCA) (P.L. No. 105-304, 112 Stat. 2860, 2905). Of course, there have been many amendments to copyright law since then. As a reminder to what was covered in chapter 3, the easiest way to see the current U.S. Code is to access the House Office of Law Revision Counsel version of the code (https://uscode.house.gov/), or simply Google: *house us code.*

One significant different between copyright and the other two kinds of intellectual property is that copyright holders do not need to apply with the government to obtain a copyright. But if a case goes to court (that is, if there is an intent to sue in a federal court), U.S. copyright holders must first register the copyright with the U.S. Copyright Office (CRS 2018).

Unlike patents and trademarks, which have their own office under the Commerce Department (uspto.gov), copyrights are administratively under the Library of Congress (https://www.copyright.gov/). The website is easy to navigate and provides educational resources about copyright, schedule of fees, discussion of mandatory deposit, and frequently asked questions. Links are provided to existing laws, regulations, and rule-making proposals (both open and closed). Forms are provided for those interested in registering copyright for their works. Copyright circulars provide up-to-date and authoritative information for a general audience.

A searchable database of copyright records searches registered copyrights from 1978 to present. When an entity is copyrighted, the data is contributed to the database. If you are familiar with the Library of Congress catalog (the book catalog), this is the same interface, just adapted to copyrights. Here is an example of a record from the database (Figure 15.7).

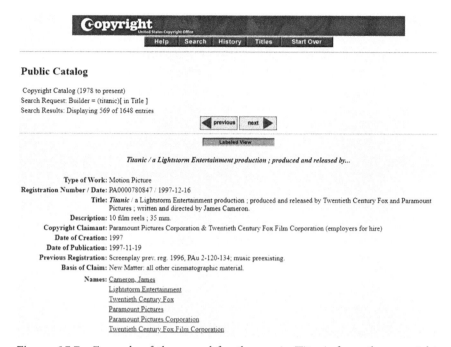

Figure 15.7 Example of the record for the movie *Titanic* from the copyright catalog

Notice that the fields are similar to a library's online catalog, but different fields are prominent. Fields for type of work, registration number, date of creation, date of publication, and rights and permissions are among the fields that differ from library catalog records.

The U.S. Copyright Office Fair Use Index is intended to help lawyers and non-lawyers understand recent decisions on copyright. It does not include the decisions themselves but is an index to the outcomes of cases—whether it was determined that a particular case was fair use or not. Courts included are the Supreme Court, circuit courts of appeal, and federal district courts. Although it does not index all cases on fair use, it provides a helpful summary of the decision of the court.

Those interested in historical copyright research will want to consult the *Catalog of Copyright Entries.*

Catalog of Copyright Entries. Library of Congress. Copyright Office. Other title: *Catalogue of Title Entries of Books and Other Articles entered in the Office of the Register of Copyrights, Library of Congress, at Washington, D.C.* Issued by the Treasury Department from 1891 to June 1906. (SuDocs: LC 3.6/; LC 3.6/5:).

Description: no. 1–782, July 1/11, 1891–June 28, 1906; New ser., v. 1–41, July 5, 1906–1946; 3d ser., v. 1–31, January/June 1947–July/Dec. 1977; 4th ser., v. 1–15, January/June 1978–July/December 1992. Ceased with Fourth series, v. 5, no. 4 (October–December 1992).

New series: pt. 1. Books, pamphlets, leaflets, contributions to newspapers or periodicals, etc., lectures, sermons, addresses for oral delivery, dramatic compositions, and maps, annual indexes, renewals—pt. 2. Periodicals. Periodicals and newspapers, Vols. 1–41, 1906–1946 (quarterly, with annual index)—pt. 3. Musical compositions (Winchell BH 37). Vols. 1–41, 1906–1946 (published compositions, unpublished compositions, renewals, annual index)—pt. 4. Works of art, reproductions of works of art, drawings or plastic works of a scientific or technical character, photographs, prints and pictorial illustrations, motion pictures.; Third series: pt. 1. Books and pamphlets, renewal registrations—pt. 2. Periodicals, renewal registrations—Pts. 3–4. Dramas and works prepared for oral delivery (includes sermons, addresses, lectures, etc.), renewal registrations—pt. 5. Music, published and unpublished, renewal registrations—pt. 6. Maps and atlases, published and unpublished—pt. 7–11A. Works of art, reproductions of works of art, drawings or plastic works of a scientific or technical character, photographs, prints and pictorial illustrations, motion pictures—pt. 11B. Commercial prints and labels—pt. 12–13. Motion films and filmstrips, renewal registrations.; Fourth series: pt. 1. Nondramatic literary works—pt. 2. Serials and periodicals—pt. 3. Performing arts—pt. 4. Motion pictures and filmstrips—pt. 5. Visual arts—pt. 6. Maps—pt. 7. Sound recordings—pt. 8. Renewals.

(HT 006952951; other records also available in HT, *search: Catalog of Copyright Entries*). Although this complex work is largely represented in the HathiTrust, it is most easily access via the Internet Archive. Use this URL: https://archive.org/details/copyrightrecords.

The Library of Congress also published records of motion pictures and filmstrips under the title *Motion Pictures [years]* that cover 1894–1969 (HT 002137632). The Library of Congress scanned all these volumes and contributed them to the Internet Archive. The URLs for each of these files are most easily access by consulting this file: https://www.copyright.gov/circs/circ23.pdf.

Another published finding aid is *Dramatic Compositions Copyrighted in the United States, 1870–1916* (HT 001171577). These two volumes have been scanned by the Library of Congress and contributed to the Internet Archive, as referenced in the circular in the paragraph above.

SECRET, DECLASSIFIED, AND UNPUBLISHED GOVERNMENT INFORMATION

In chapter 1, we discussed the early commitment in the new country to freely disseminate information so that citizens were informed and know what their government was doing. But now we turn to the underside of the freely available world: the world of secrets, nondisclosure, and confidentiality.

Secret Documents and Declassification

The U.S. government has secrets. This is set up in the levels of security clearance available to government employees. There are three levels of sensitivity of information. In ascending order, they are:

- Confidential: disclosure would cause damage to national security
- Secret: disclosure would cause serious damage to national security
- Top Secret: disclosure would cause exceptionally grave damage to national security (CRS 2016).

The National Archives and Records Administration has an office of Controlled Unclassified Information (created by EO 13556 November 4, 2010, "Controlled Unclassified Information"). This created an entirely new way of marking up documents. NARA maintains an extensive list of CUI categories grouped by government organization (Google: *site:archives.gov cui categories*).

Declassified Document Sources

National Security Agency (NSA) Declassified Documents

The National Security Agency (NSA) maintains a public page of declassified documents after review under EO 13526 (*site:nsa.gov Declassification and Transparency*). Among the available declassified document topics:

- C130 Shootdown September 2, 1958
- Cuban Missile Crisis 1960s
- European Axis Signal Intelligence in World War II
- Gulf of Tonkin—November 30, 2005, and May 30, 2006
- John F. Kennedy Assassination
- Korean War

- U.S.S. Liberty Incident, June 8, 1967
- U.S.S. Pueblo Incident, January 28, 1968
- Vietnam Paris Peace Talks 1972–1973
- Vietnam Prisoner of War/Missing in Action (POW/MIA) Documents

Central Intelligence Agency Electronic Reading Room

The CIA has a searchable Electronic Reading Room (https://www.cia
.gov/library/readingroom/). This database is an outgrowth of EO 13526,
December 29, 2009, "Classified National Security Information." The problem is that usually you don't know what to search by. But doing a null
search (that is, just hitting the search button with nothing in the search
box) presents you with browsable categories to limit by date, by keyword,
by NIC function, by NIC geography, and by collection. At present there are
over 70 collections represented, with some collections containing tens of
thousands of scanned images. Among the collections are the following
(with current number of documents in parentheses):

- An Underwater Ice Station Zebra: Recovering a Secret Spy Satellite
  Capsule from 16,400 feet Below the Pacific Ocean (37)
- Argentina Declassification Project—The "Dirty War" (1976–1983) (815)
- Atomic Spies: Ethel and Julius Rosenberg (102)
- Baptism by Fire: CIA Analysis of the Korean War Overview (1355)
- CIA Analysis of the Soviet Navy (82)
- Declassified Documents Related to 9/11 Attacks (6)
- From Typist to Trailblazer: The Evolving View of Women in the CIA's
  Workforce (117)
- Human Rights in Latin America (624)
- Intelligence Warning of the 1957 Launch of Sputnik (59)
- Nazi War Crimes Disclosure Act (56252)
- President Carter and the Role of Intelligence in the Camp David
  Accords (258)
- President Nixon and the Role of Intelligence in the 1973 Arab-Israeli
  War (419)
- President's Daily Brief 1961–1969 (2484)
- Reagan Collection (206)
- Tet Declassified (680)
- UFOs: Fact or Fiction? (243)

FBI Vault

In early June 2019, the FBI released files kept secret since 1976 concerning the legendary Bigfoot, a.k.a. Sasquatch (https://vault.fbi.gov/bigfoot /bigfoot-part-01-of-01/view). Releases of files like these make sensational headlines and give conspiracy theorists more to talk about. Other declassified releases in the FBI Vault include organized crime personalities such as Al Capone, John Gotti, Jimmy Hoffa, and Bugsy Siegel; antiwar files on Abbie Hoffman; FBI Chief J. Edgar Hoover; civil rights personalities including Rodney King, Malcolm X, Martin Luther King, Jr., Cesar Chavez, and Medgar Evers; TWA flight 800; Aristotle Onassis; organizations such as Greenpeace, League of Women Voters, Nation of Islam, National Organization for Women, and the National Rifle Association; popular culture icons such as Frank Sinatra, Muhammad Ali, journalist Mike Wallace, Steve Jobs, Rock Hudson, Ernest Hemingway, and the Beatles; and other unexplained phenomena such as animal mutilation, UFOs, Roswell, and extrasensory perception. The FBI Vault can be browsed at https://vault.fbi.gov/.

National Security Archive

The National Security Archive (https://nsarchive.gwu.edu/), housed at George Washington University, was founded by journalists and scholars to monitor the increasing use of government secrecy. Their major project is the Digital National Security Archive, a curated collection of over 750,000 pages of declassified government records. The records are available through ProQuest's Digital National Security Archive database. Collections within the database include Afghanistan; Argentina, 1975–1980; Berlin Crisis; Chile and the United States; China, 1960–1998; China and U.S. Intelligence, 1945–2010; CIA Covert Operations, from Carter to Obama, 1977–2010; Cuban Missile Crisis; Electronic Surveillance; El Salvador 1977–1994; Guatemala and the United States; Iran-Contra Affair; Iraqgate; Japan and the United States; Kissinger Conversations; Korea, 1969–2010; Mexico-United States Counternarcotics Policy, 1969–2013; Military Uses of Space; Nuclear History; Nuclear Nonproliferation; Peru: Human Rights, Drugs, and Democracy, 1980–2000; Presidential Directives; South Africa; Soviet-U.S. Relations, 1985–1991; Targeting Iraq, 1997–2004; Terrorism and U.S. Policy, 1968–2002; U.S. Espionage and Intelligence; Vietnam War, 1954–1975; and Weapons of Mass Destruction.

U.S. Declassified Documents Online

U.S. Declassified Documents Online, formerly known as the Declassified Documents Reference System, is a Gale database. Many libraries may still have the multivolume print index with corresponding microfiche containing images of the documents. Included in the digital edition are presidential papers that were previously classified, intelligence studies, policy papers, diplomatic correspondence, and domestic surveillance and military reports. Declassified materials from Departments of State, Defense, the CIA, and the FBI are included. Coverage spans the twentieth and the beginning of the twenty-first centuries.

Unpublished Hearings

One major class of unpublished documents is certain congressional hearings. There is no law that they be published; they are published at the discretion of each committee or subcommittee of Congress. Congressional Information Service (now ProQuest) has identified numerous unpublished House and Senate hearings from 1972 through 1992. These are available as an add-on module to the ProQuest Congressional database.

THE FREEDOM OF INFORMATION ACT AND THE PRIVACY ACT

Freedom of Information Act Background

Public Law 89-487 (80 Stat. 250, July 4, 1966, 5 U.S.C. 552) requires executive agencies make available to the public their methods of operation, public procedures, rules, policies, and precedents, and to make available other "matters of official record." FOIA was necessary to amend the Administrative Procedure Act, which was originally intended to lean in favor of making information more publicly available but, in fact, was used to withhold information (this from H. Rept. 89-1497, showing an example of a congressional report being used for legislative intent).

Making FOIA Requests

The Freedom of Information Act opens up government activity to public scrutiny. The Act allows any person to gain access to nonexempt federal records from executive branch agencies. Most federal agencies clearly state their FOIA policies and procedures. FOIA.gov is the federal government's central website for the topic. The site has a link that allows searching by agency name. This leads to agency-specific information.

Each executive branch agency is required to submit annual electronic FOIA reports according to the Electronic FOIA Amendments of 1996

(P.L. 104-231, 110 Stat. 3048). Reports must specify the number of requests received and processed, the types of requests received, the number of requests not fulfilled and the reasons for the decision, number of appeals of decisions, fees collected, and number of staff and staff hours devoted to the requests. Rather than providing a list of each government agency's FOIA instructions and annual reports, it is best just to search Google like this: *site:cia.gov foia*, *site:usda.gov foia*, or *site:energy.gov foia*. But remember, FOIA is only applicable to executive branch agencies.

Many state governments have FOIA-like laws, with some states extending open records requests beyond their executive branches to the legislative or judicial branches. An excellent resource for state information is the National Conference of State Legislatures (ncsl.org).

FOIA Uses

Syracuse University's TracFed database (available by subscription) makes systematic use of FOIA requests to populate their database that tracks enforcement statistics for federal criminal, civil, and administrative legal actions, as they are handled by federal prosecutors and the courts. As an example of the usefulness of this database, let's take criminal enforcement for immigration matters. We can drill down for prosecutions or convictions for either monthly statistics or fiscal year annual statistics. Under that, we can browse by agency (from the 35 agencies with criminal enforcement divisions), federal district (94 districts), program (broad areas including civil rights, environment, immigration, narcotics/drugs, terrorism, and organized crime), detailed program (a more granular version of "program"), or lead charge (section of United States Code for which charges are made). The results are often available in a time-series graph showing differences in enforcement and prosecution over various presidential administrations. This is a most creative and useful application of FOIA information.

Privacy Act

Closely related to the Freedom of Information Act is the Privacy Act. The two Acts sit next to each other in the United States Code (5 U.S.C 552 for FOIA, and 5 U.S.C. 552a for the Privacy Act). The Privacy Act was passed in 1974 (P.L. 93-579, 88 Stat. 1896, 5 U.S.C. 552a), and its purpose is to restrict the disclosure of personally identifiable records. In order to understand what databases are maintained by agencies, a publication called *Privacy Act Issuances* is necessary. Online access to this biennial publication is available on Govinfo.gov (https://www.govinfo.gov/app

/collection/pai). Here you will find descriptions of records maintained about individuals by federal agencies and their record-keeping policies, as well as procedures for requesting the information. Requests are generally limited to "first party" requesters, that is, by the person who would be named in the records.

System of Records Notice (SORNs)

The Privacy Act requires all federal agencies to provide formal notices to the public for all systems (i.e., databases) they use to collect and keep personally identifiable information (PII). They are formally called system of records notices, or SORNs, which makes an easy search hook. These are required to be published in the *Federal Register*. But a more efficient way to see what databases contain this information by agency is to use your Google search skills. For example:

- *site:ed.gov sorns*
- *site:va.gov sorns*
- *site:doc.gov sorns*

You get the idea. The hardest part of FOIA is knowing who keeps what so that you can intelligently request the information.

EXERCISES

1. Find an object around the house that has a patent number on it. When you find something with a number, look up the number in the PatFT database. Then use Google Patents to look up the same number.

2. Use the TESS trademark database to lookup trademarks held by your college, university, or other place you are associated with. Did you discover anything interesting or surprising?

3. Are you worried about what information government agencies have about you? Devise a strategy to find out which agencies might have personal information about you.

REFERENCES

CRS (Congressional Research Service). 2016. "Security Clearance Process: Answers to Frequently Asked Questions." Updated October 7, 2016. R43216. Accessed December 13, 2019. https://crsreports.congress.gov /product/pdf/R/R43216.

CRS (Congressional Research Service). 2017. "Patent Law: A Primer and Overview of Emerging Issues." Updated September 17, 2017. R44962. Accessed December 13, 2019. https://crsreports.congress.gov/product/pdf/R/R44962.

CRS (Congressional Research Service). 2018. "Intellectual Property Law: A Brief Introduction." In Focus. September 19, 2018. IF10986. Accessed December 13, 2019. https://crsreports.congress.gov/product/pdf/IF/IF10986.

U.S. Patent and Trademark Office. 2018. *Manual of Patent Examining Procedure.* 9th ed. March 2014. Latest Revision January 2018 [R-08.2017]. Accessed September 29, 2019. https://www.uspto.gov/web/offices/pac/mpep/ OR this: https://mpep.uspto.gov/.

16

State and Local Government Information

Skills we have learned about locating, finding, and using federal government information are largely transferrable to the state and local levels. Legislation results in slip laws that are codified into state statutes. Regulations are promulgated by state agencies and announced through a daily publication, and later codified into a permanent set of regulations. Agencies produce consumer publications, forms, and serial publications. Most states publish some kind of state manual, often called a "blue book." The website Ballotpedia maintains a page of state blue books (https://ballotpedia.org/State_Blue_Books).

STATE GOVERNMENT WEBSITES

You are likely familiar with the structure of state government resources from the state where you now reside. But often questions arise about states with which we are not as familiar. For this reason, we need to revisit our discussion of using Google to do domain-specific searching. In the early internet days, the designers thought they would be helpful and assigned each of the states its own internet domain: state.al.us for Alabama, state.ak .us for Alaska, and so forth. In these early days of the web, most states posted most of their content on these servers. Over time, however, many administrators realized that users had a difficult time remembering the state's URL pattern—this is the early days when people assumed that everything had to be a "dot com" address. States began to deviate from the initial assigned pattern and purchased their own domains. For example, Florida purchased "myflorida.com."

After 2003, with the opening up of the .gov domain to non-federal government entities (see discussion in chapter 1), most states opted to purchase their own .gov domains, for example, alabama.gov, colorado.gov, mass.gov, texas.gov, and so forth. These sites became the "front servers" for state government information. All users needed to remember was the state name (or abbreviation), followed by .gov. However, much content still remained on the original state.xx.us servers, which I generally refer to as the "back servers."

When attempting to do site-specific searching for state publications, it is important to note the different servers a state uses to host its data. Many states still have a significant amount of materials on their back servers, while a few states have migrated nearly all their content to the front server. This is easy to check, now that you know how to do power Google searching. In the case of California (as of July 25, 2019), here is how the front server/back server situation looks:

site:state.ca.us = 538 results

site:ca.gov = about 5,420,000 results

But many states still have a majority of content on their back servers:

site:state.co.us = about 441,000 results

site:colorado.gov = about 281,000 results

Texas was about evenly split at the time of testing.

site:state.tx.us = about 993,000 results

site:texas.gov = about 994,000 results

site:tx.gov = about 904 results

As a reminder, the reason why this kind of domain-specific searching is necessary is that Google does what it wants with relevance ranking and doesn't bother to tell us what it is doing. Most commercial vendors of library databases will at least tell you which fields are being searched and have at least something to say about how it ranks results. Not Google. Chances are good that the resource you need is buried below the limit where Google will not let you go. Google never lets you access past the 1,000th result in a Google search and usually only down to several hundred results. This means that we need a way to force Google to search the way we want to search.

Another more recent trend is to host state content on multiple domains. Alabama not only uses alabama.gov and state.al.us, they also use alea.gov, alacourt.gov, and alsde.edu (notice the use of a .edu domain for government) to host official state content. Arizona uses azleg.gov, azcourts.gov, azsos.gov, and azed.gov in addition to their front and back servers. This is a trend to keep an eye on.

Another reason to be interested in tracking older state internet domains is for searching for fugitive documents using the Wayback Machine. Even though California no longer actively uses state.ca.us, many older documents can be discovered from the older domain using the Internet Archive's tool. Pennsylvania.gov is completely retired, but documents can be found under that domain in the Wayback Machine.

To help with this, Table 16.1 gives state-by-state information on front server and back server addresses. This table will change. States actively move things around. State administrators change; strategic plans change. So always keep testing away to see what your state is up to.

URL PATTERNS BELOW STATE LEVEL

Local governments, meaning counties, cities, and other places such as villages, share a similar URL situation to that of states. Counties were originally assigned a URL structure under the .us domain. A county such as Arapahoe County, Colorado, was assigned co.arapahoe.co.us. The first "co" here refers to "county," whereas the second "co" refers to Colorado. This can be seen clearly in the case of Walworth County, Wisconsin: co .walworth.wi.us. In these two cases, the counties have opted not to deviate from their original domain assignments.

However, in Boulder County, Colorado, the domain bouldercounty.org is used. Since web content resides on both the bouldercounty.org site and the co.boulder.co.us sites, both will need to be searched for completeness:

site:bouldercounty.org minutes = 1,990 results on July 15, 2019

site:co.boulder.co.us minutes = 14 results on July 15, 2019

In this case, a majority of materials exist on the newer domain.

The same situation holds for city governments. Instead of "co" for county, the pattern is "ci" for city. The city of Denver has the older domain ci.denver.co.us, as well as the newer domain, denvergov.org.

site:ci.denver.co.us minutes = 4,350 results on July 15, 2019

site:denvergov.org minutes = 6,350 results on July 15, 2019

It seems that the ci.state.xx.us pattern is used much less than the co.state .xx.us pattern. It wouldn't be surprising if we see both patterns disappear in a few years, as counties, municipalities, and small places prefer to

Table 16.1   State government Internet domains (as of July 25, 2019)

State	Domains with Site-Searchable Content
Alabama	alabama.gov and state.al.us. Note: Alabama uses separate, dedicated sites in some cases; e.g., alea.gov (law enforcement); alacourt.gov (courts); alsde.edu (education); Use http://inform.alabama.gov to lookup agencies.
Alaska	alaska.gov; akleg.gov (legislature); content also under state.ak.us.
Arizona	az.gov; also uses azleg.gov (legislature); azcourts.gov (courts); azsos.gov (Secretary of State); azdor.gov (revenue); azed.gov (education); and other .gov domains; content also under state.az.us.
Arkansas	arkansas.gov; ar.gov often redirects to arkansas.gov; content also under state.ar.us.
California	ca.gov; a little content also under state.ca.us. Use Internet Archive's Wayback Machine to see content formerly under state.ca.us.
Colorado	colorado.gov; co.gov redirects to colorado.gov; coag.gov (Attorney General); content also under state.co.us.
Connecticut	ct.gov; content also under state.ct.us.
Delaware	delaware.gov; de.gov redirects to delaware.gov; content also under state.de.us.
District of Columbia	dc.gov; content also under dc.us (only for schools).
Florida	myflorida.com; florida.gov and fl.gov both redirect to myflorida.com, but much content under both .gov domains; content also under state.fl.us.
Georgia	georgia.gov; content also under ga.gov and state.ga.us.
Hawaii	hawaii.gov and ehawaii.gov; content also under state.hi.us.
Idaho	idaho.gov; id.gov mostly county sites; content also under state.id.us.
Illinois	illinois.gov; il.gov sometimes redirects to illinois.gov, but content under both domains; content also under state.il.us.
Indiana	in.gov and indiana.gov; content also under state.in.us.
Iowa	iowa.gov; ia.gov redirects to iowa.gov; content also under state.ia.us.
Kansas	kansas.gov; kslegislature.org (legislature) content also under ks.gov and state.ks.us.

(*continued*)

Table 16.1   (continued)

State	Domains with Site-Searchable Content
Kentucky	kentucky.gov; ky.gov redirects to kentucky.gov; content under both domains; content also under state.ky.us.
Louisiana	louisiana.gov and la.gov; content under both domains; content also under state.la.us.
Maine	maine.gov; content also under state.me.us.
Maryland	maryland.gov; md.gov sometimes redirects to maryland.gov; content under both domains; content also under state.md.us.
Massachusetts	mass.gov; content also under state.ma.us. Note: formerly used massachusetts.gov and ma.gov. You will find content under these old domains in the Internet Archive's Wayback Machine.
Michigan	michigan.gov; mi.gov redirects to michigan.gov; content under michigan.gov, mi.gov, and state.mi.us.
Minnesota	mn.gov and minnesota.gov; most content under state.mn.us, with some content under mn.gov and little content under minnesota.gov.
Mississippi	ms.gov, with little content under mississippi.gov; content also under state.ms.us.
Missouri	mo.gov; missouri.gov redirects to mo.gov, with content under both domains; no content under state.mo.us.
Montana	mt.gov; with little content under montana.gov and no content under state.mt.us.
Nebraska	nebraska.gov; ne.gov redirects to nebraska.gov; mostly local content under ne.gov, with content under both domains; nebraskalegislature.gov; content also under state.ne.us.
Nevada	nv.gov; content also under state.nv.us.
New Hampshire	nh.gov; content also under state.nh.us.
New Jersey	nj.gov and newjersey.gov; content also under state.nj.us.
New Mexico	newmexico.gov; content also under nm.gov and state.nm.us.
New York	ny.gov; content also under state.ny.us.
North Carolina	nc.gov; content also under state.nc.us; some government entities use different domains; e.g., Secretary of State is sosnc.gov and Motor Vehicles is ncdot.gov.
North Dakota	nd.gov; northdakota.gov redirects to nd.gov, but content only under nd.gov; limited content also under state.nd.us.

Table 16.1   (continued)

State	Domains with Site-Searchable Content
Ohio	ohio.gov; local content under oh.gov, state content under ohio.gov; content also under state.oh.us.
Oklahoma	ok.gov and oklahoma.gov, most content under ok.gov; content also under state.ok.us.
Oregon	oregon.gov; content under state.or.us.
Pennsylvania	pa.gov; content under state.pa.us; pennsylvania.gov no longer in use, but can be found in the Wayback Machine.
Puerto Rico	pr.gov, content under pr.gov only.
Rhode Island	ri.gov; rhodeisland.gov redirects to ri.gov, very little content under rhodeisland.gov (but useful for Wayback Machine searches); most content only under ri.gov and state.ri.us.
South Carolina	sc.gov; content also under state.sc.us.
South Dakota	sd.gov; content also under state.sd.us.
Tennessee	tn.gov and tennessee.gov; content also under state.tn.us.
Texas	texas.gov, some content also under tx.gov; content also under state.tx.us.
Utah	utah.gov; content also under state.ut.us.
Vermont	vermont.gov; vt.gov redirects to vermont.gov; content under vt.gov, vermont.gov, and state.vt.us.
Virgin Islands	vi.gov (don't confuse with British Virgin Islands, .vg).
Virginia	virginia.gov; content also under state.va.us. Note: va.gov is the federal Department of Veterans Affairs.
Washington	wa.gov; content also under state.wa.us; washington.gov is no longer actively used, but exists in the Wayback Machine.
West Virginia	wv.gov; content also under westvirginia.gov and state.wv.us.
Wisconsin	wisconsin.gov; wi.gov redirects to wisconsin.gov; content under wi.gov, wisconsin.gov and state.wi.us.
Wyoming	wyo.gov; wy.gov and wyoming.gov redirect to wyo.gov; content wyo.gov, wy.gov, wyoming.gov and state.wy.us.

purchase their own branding to make web access less stressful for their users.

According to the Census Bureau, in 2012, there were 3,031 counties; 19,519 municipalities; and 16,360 townships (Hogue 2013). It would not be possible to list all the possible variations of internet domains within this publication. Besides, the results would change perhaps daily. This means that the skillful searcher simply needs to apply the Google searching skills described in the book to come up with the most comprehensive results.

LEGISLATION

The easiest way to search across all state legislatures simultaneously is to use either Nexus Uni or Westlaw Campus Research. If you don't have access to those tools, you would need to search each state legislature individually for current laws, bill tracking, or session laws. Most states do not have as much documentary evidence when researching legislative histories, which can be a bit frustrating.

States tend to follow the same pattern as the federal government. Bills are introduced into either the General Assembly (sometimes called the House) or Senate, and hearings may optionally be held. States vary greatly as to the availability of legislative hearings. In Colorado, as an example, hearings are only available in audio format through the State Archives. Note that Nebraska is an exception in that it only has one legislative body (called a unicameral legislature).

Rather than providing a table with 50 sets of URLs for state legislative bodies, use Google to find current web content. Suggested search: *state of xx legislature* [where xx is the name of the state]

Many people want to do comparative legal studies between states. The single best starting point for these questions is the National Conference of State Legislatures (ncsl.org). Because of its authoritative perspective, this site is used by those drafting legislation in all states. Questions that can be researched on the site include:

• What are the marijuana laws in each state (both medical and recreational)?
• Which states offer driver's licenses to immigrants, and what are the requirements?
• What are states doing to ensure food safety?
• What are states doing to ensure social media privacy?

Think about this: It's pretty bold for a website to say what the law is in each of the 50 states on scores of topics. But lawmakers and attorneys regularly monitor this site. If anything were to be incorrect, even down to a statutory citation, it would be immediately called out and corrected. It is kind of a self-patrolled peer-review process. It's quite rare for a .org site to have that kind of authority behind it.

Although ncsl.org has a search facility on the site itself, I usually search the site via a Google domain-specific search:

- *site:ncsl.org environmental waste management*
- *site:ncsl.org amending state constitution*
- *site:ncsl.org child welfare laws*
- *site:ncsl.org landlord tenant*

In chapter 3, we brought up how difficult it is to amend the federal Constitution. However, it is a different situation with some states. To get a rather interesting and authoritative view of differences among states in terms of ease with which state constitutions can be amended, we can do a Google search: *site:ncsl.org state constitutions.*

REGULATIONS

State regulations are sometimes found in one place, and other times, they are simply posted on state agency websites. Searching for terms such as administrative code; regulations; codes, rules, and regulations; code of [state] regulations; or similar things will generally uncover a searchable database for the state. They also will be cross-searchable in tools like Nexis Uni or Westlaw Campus Research.

LOCAL ORDINANCES

The term ordinances is typically used for local governmental entities below the state level. The first place to check for this is municode.com. First browse to the state you are interested in, and then select the county or city (https://library.municode.com/). Local ordinances of over 4,100 cities and counties are hosted on the site.

If the jurisdiction you are interested in is not in municode.com, then you will need to search Google for it. In certain cases, you may want to do specific internet domain searching on the city or county level, just like we did for state materials. In some cases, cities and counties follow the originally envisioned pattern for internet addresses.

ci.[city name].xx.us—where xx is the two-letter postal code for a state

co.[county name].xx.us—where xx is the two-letter postal code for a state

Counties or cities do not always use the old pattern illustrated above. In some cases, they may use both the original pattern and a newer URL. A Google search will show you what domains they are using.

STATE GOVERNMENT INFORMATION AND COPYRIGHT

This book has emphasized the free public access to government information, so it may come as a surprise that the federal notion of public domain does not extend to the state level. State governments receive copyright protection by default. Yet many state agencies view their publications as being in the public domain and have taken on active programs of digitizing legacy documents and disseminating them to local library catalogs and digital repositories (NCSL 2014). The National Conference of State Legislatures website has many materials discussing the varying state statutes relating to who owns copyright of state statutes and codes (*site:ncsl .org state copyright*).

STATE DEPOSITORY PROGRAMS

Some states maintain active depository library programs throughout their states, distributing publications to various academic and public libraries to provide access in geographically diverse areas. Others are lacking these concepts. The GODORT State Agency Database Project is the best place to go when looking into state depository activities and databases (2019).

OLDER STATE MATERIALS

There are times when you want to look for historical state publications. This is where the Monthly Checklist of State Publications is useful. (HT 009039001, 100887904, 100076258, 102113784). This serial was published by the Library of Congress from 1921 to 1994 and is the best resource for verifying state publications of the twentieth century.

EXERCISES

1. Using Table 16.1, find all the server domains for your state. How many results are on each of these servers?
2. Now do the same for county-level and place-level governments around you. Can you see how these strategies can help you in finding local government information more efficiently?

REFERENCES

GODORT. 2019. "State Agency Databases Project: Home." Updated November 20, 2019. Accessed January 2, 2020. https://godort.libguides.com/state databases.

Hogue, Carma. 2013. "Government Organization Summary Report: 2012." United States Census Bureau. Government Divisions Briefs. Released September 26, 2013. Accessed August 12, 2019. https://www2.census.gov/govs/cog /g12_org.pdf.

NCSL (National Conference of State Legislatures). 2014. "State Government Information and the Copyright Conundrum." Accessed August 14, 2019. http://www.ncsl.org/legislators-staff/legislative-staff/research-librarians /webinar-state-government-information-and-the-copyright-conundrum .aspx.

17

Citing Government Publications

Citing government resources is usually considered onerous and frightening, but it need not be. Consider that most style manuals do not adequately deal with citing government publications in the first place, and those that do mention them generally cede authority to the Bluebook, even though the lawyer's style does not fit well with their purposes. The *Publication Manual of the American Psychological Association*, 7th edition, defers to *The Bluebook: A Uniform System of Citation* (use the most current edition). The Modern Language Association's style manual has little to say about citing government publications. The *Chicago Manual of Style*, 17th edition, has a lengthy section on citing legal and public documents. They point to either the Bluebook or the *ALWD Guide to Legal Citation*, prepared and published by the Association of Legal Writing Directors and Coleen M. Barger.

There are several reasons for this reliance on and deference to the Bluebook. (1) The Bluebook is a recognized authority that covers nearly every category of legal and government document; (2) it is unrealistic for each style manual to rehash what the Bluebook has already covered; and (3) Bluebook style is what is recognizable and accepted by the legal profession.

Let's bring a more common-sense perspective to a challenging topic. Here are some general citation principles that also apply to citing U.S. government publications.

- Consider what style manual is required for your work and adapt to it as necessary. It is likely that they will not have much to say about specific government or legal information types.

- Provide enough information to be informative and useful. That is, give the essential bibliographic elements so that other researchers and librarians can find what you are referring to. Does the context require you to state the name of the law or document, or is a number sufficient?

- Be consistent in whatever style you adopt. The important things are the inclusion of all relevant information that will assist others in locating the materials and some kind of consistency.

- Be careful in using URLs. Nothing is more inelegant in a reference list than a URL. URLs are not needed for official documents such as the *Federal Register, Congressional Record,* congressional reports and documents, and legal cases. As a general principle, consider using URLs for more volatile information, and not as much for less volatile information. If it has been cataloged by GPO, indexed in a citation database, or is a major government publication, there is no need to tell users the URL. If you include the URL you used, it only serves to make your citation list uglier. If at all possible, use GPO PURLs in citations. They are usually much shorter than the agency links. They also have a better chance of stability. Materials in databases such as Govinfo.gov will be stable, so URLs should be considered optional. They also tend to be quite long and annoying.

I consider that there are three ways to go about bibliographic citation: (1) citation by rule, (2) citation by example, and (3) citation by automation. Citation by rule is what a detailed style manual endeavors to accomplish. There are some people who actually read the manual before opening an electronic device. I am not one of those people, and I find that most students are not that way either when it comes to bibliographic citations. Citation by example simply shows citations that (hopefully) correctly follow the rules of the respective styles. That's me, and I find that most students also prefer citation by example. Citation by automation uses the strengths of modern tools such as EndNote; RefWorks; Zotero; Mendeley; and the many other software solutions, both fee-based and free, that take metadata fields (usually following MARC standards) and attempt to force them into bibliographic citation standards. Attempting to do this with government and legal publications is often disastrous. I love the technology behind citation software. It's just that you will spend more time correcting the output from these tools than if you had entered items manually in the first place. There are just too many exceptions and too many other considerations, such as congressional session, report numbers, and accepted practice that render automated processes unacceptable for government information. This brief chapter will follow the second method: citation by example.

Often personal authors are not given, but corporate authors are used instead. Even in cases where personal authors are found, it is best to cite the publication as coming from the government entity so as to convey the authority of the publications. This should be an individual call. A document may often be cited in various ways to suit the desired emphasis or the purpose of the citation.

The goal of this chapter is to focus more on essential bibliographic elements and less on slavish dependence on a particular style manual. Users may need to adapt the bibliographic elements in federal government citation to the particular style they are using. Most styles acknowledge that their rules do not address government or legal information adequately, and acquiesce to other styles for assistance in citing such sources.

The examples given here focus not so much on "citation by rule" as "citation by example." Please feel free to adapt these citations to your purpose.

This chapter will not be sufficient for many users. More detailed citations can be found in *The Complete Guide to Citing Government Information Resources*, third edition, revised edition by Debora Cheney, 2002. In addition, ProQuest also has a lot to say about citing many kinds of government information (*site:proquest.com general principles of citation*).

CITING EXECUTIVE BRANCH MATERIALS

Executive Orders, Presidential Proclamations, and Other Issuances

Bluebook style tends to just cite the bare bones facts, as shown below.

Exec. Order No. 13,559 (November 17, 2010), 3 C.F.R. 273 (2011).

Exec. Order No. 13,652, 3 C.F.R. 326 (2014), *reprinted as amended in* 5 U.S.C. app. §14 (2012).

Proclamation No. 8214 (December 27, 2007), 73 Fed. Reg. 1439 (January 8, 2008).

In many cases, however, it may be necessary or desirable to include the title of the issuance in the citation.

To Adjust the Rules of Origin under the United States-Chile Free Trade Agreement and the United States-Singapore Free Trade Agreement. Proclamation No. 8214 (December 27, 2007), 3 C.F.R. 152 (2008).

To Adjust the Rules of Origin under the United States-Chile Free Trade Agreement and the United States-Singapore Free Trade Agreement. Proclamation No. 8214 (December 27, 2007), 73 Fed. Reg. 1439 (January 8, 2008).

In some cases, it may be necessary to cite the president who authored the issuance, as below.

Trump, Donald J. "Imposing Certain Sanctions in the Event of Foreign Interference in a United States Election" (Executive Order 13848, September 12, 2018), *Compilation of Presidential Documents.* https://www.govinfo.gov/app/details/DCPD -201800593.

Trump, Donald J. "Imposing Certain Sanctions in the Event of Foreign Interference in a United States Election" (Executive Order 13848, September 12, 2018), *Federal Register,* vol. 83, p. 46843 (September 14, 2018).

Obama, Barack. "Fundamental Principles and Policymaking Criteria for Partnerships with Faith-Based and Other Neighborhood Organizations" (Executive Order 13559, November 17, 2010), *Compilation of Presidential Documents.* https://www .govinfo.gov/app/details/DCPD-201000991.

Note that in this case, since it is not citing to a print version, no volume or page numbers are given. In this case, a URL is helpful.

Obama, Barack. "Fundamental Principles and Policymaking Criteria for Partnerships with Faith-Based and Other Neighborhood Organizations" (Executive Order 13559, November 17, 2010), *Federal Register,* vol. 75, p. 71317 (November 22, 2010).

Obama, Barack. "Fundamental Principles and Policymaking Criteria for Partnerships with Faith-Based and Other Neighborhood Organizations" (Executive Order 13559, November 17, 2010), *Code of Federal Regulations,* vol. 3, 2011, 273.

Treaties

With multilateral treaties, it is important to include the date of signing and at least one formal citation.

Treaty Banning Nuclear Weapon Tests in the Atmosphere, in Outer Space and under Water, U.S.-U.K.-U.S.S.R., August 5, 1963, 14 U.S.T. 1313.

The above citation is to a multilateral treaty citing to volume 14 of the bound set *United States Treaties and Other International Agreements.* In the State Department publication *Treaties in Force,* parallel citations are given to the treaty: 14 UST 1313; TIAS 5433; 480 UNTS 43. These could also be included in the citation, since they provide additional sources where this treaty can be found.

Treaty Banning Nuclear Weapon Tests in the Atmosphere, in Outer Space and Under Water, U.S.-U.K.-U.S.S.R., August 5, 1963, 14 U.S.T. 1313; TIAS 5433; 480 UNTS 43.

For bilateral treaties, it is best to cite to the more permanent series first, and then the other sources. But since *United States Treaties and Other International Agreements* (U.S.T.) is so far behind in its publication schedule, cite to Treaties and International Acts Series (TIAS), the United Nations Treaty Series (UNTS), or Senate Treaty Documents.

Agreement concerning the program of the Peace Corps of the United States in the Republic of Moldova. Signed at Chisinau February 2, 1993. Entered into force February 2, 1993. TIAS 12485; 2364 UNTS 37.

EXECUTIVE AGENCY PUBLICATIONS

General Publications

Notice that in the citations below, I opt to include a SuDocs number and a PURL, if these are available. Arguably the PURL is more important, since most people will access materials online rather than rushing over to their nearest large depository library.

Capel, Paul D. 2018. "Agriculture—A River Runs through It: The Connections between Agriculture and Water Quality." Reston, VA: U.S. Geological Survey. (I 19.4/2:1433; https://purl.fdlp.gov/GPO/gpo106600).

Upchurch, John. "Examining Wikipedia's Value as an Information Source Using the California State University-Chico Website Evaluation Guidelines." [online submission]. ERIC Document. August 11, 2011. ED522722.

Technically, the second citation above is not a government publication. It is an independently submitted research paper indexed by the ERIC database (which is a government publication). The ERIC database notes that this is an online submission, yet many automatic citation systems interpret this as a source title, which it is not. Thus, I have placed it in brackets. It is important in the case of ERIC documents to include the ED number. Note that with EJ articles, since they are from journals, there would be no need to give the EJ number. That would not be essential to locating the article, whereas an ED number can be essential.

Annual Reports

U.S. Department of Defense. 2018. Annual Report on Civilian Casualties in Connection with United States Military Operations. (D 1.146:2018; https://purl.fdlp.gov/GPO/gpo119811).

Southwest Fisheries Science Center (U.S.). 2012. Highly migratory species annual report. La Jolla, CA: Southwest Fisheries Science Center, National Marine Fisheries Service, National Oceanic and Atmospheric Administration (C 55.331/4:2012; https://purl.fdlp.gov/GPO/gpo123857).

U.S. Department of Justice. Annual Report of the Attorney General for the Year 1903. Washington, DC: GPO. (J 1.1:).

Foreign Relations of the United States

Foreign Relations of the United States, 1969–1976, Volume XIX, Part 1, Korea, 1969–1972, eds. Daniel J. Lawler and Erin R. Mahan (Washington, DC: Government Printing Office, 2010), Document 75.

When citing FRUS, it is important to cite document numbers rather than page numbers (https://history.state.gov/historicaldocuments/citing -frus).

Topographic Map

U.S. Geological Survey. 1997. Pawnee National Grassland, Colo., and Other Forest Areas. 1:24,000. 7.5 Minute Series. Reston, VA: United States Department of the Interior, USGS. (I 19.81:P 28/997/40103-E).

Regulations

When citing the *Federal Register*, there are several options. The abbreviation FR is commonly used, but the Bluebook prefers Fed. Reg. Just pick one and go for consistency.

84 Fed. Reg. 7829.

If you want to call attention to the title, then you might do the citation this way:

"Fisheries of the Caribbean, Gulf of Mexico, and South Atlantic; Reef Fish Fishery of the Gulf of Mexico; Revisions to Red Snapper and Hogfish Management Measures." 2019. 84 Fed. Reg. 7829. Final Rule.

For the *Code of Federal Regulations*, it is important to cite the volume number, the chapter or section number or, and the year of the annual edition. Decide whether to use the abbreviation CFR or C.F.R., and be consistent.

8 CFR § 204 (2019).

Immigrant Visa Petitions, 8 CFR § 204.1-13 (2019).

Technical Reports

Gu, Hongmei, and Richard Bergman. 2018. "Life Cycle Assessment and Environmental Building Declaration for the Design Building at the University of Massachusetts." General Technical Report FPL-GTR-255. Madison, WI: United States Department of Agriculture, Forest Service, Forest Products Laboratory. (A 13.88: FPL-GTR-255; https://purl.fdlp.gov/GPO/gpo90993).

Stanford University. Dept. of Aeronautics and Astronautics. 1969. "Small scale lunar surface personnel transporter employing the hopping mode. Annual Report of NASA Grant NGR-05-020-258", March 1, 1968–February 28, 1969. NASA-CR-105966, SUDAAR-377. Available in NASA Technical Reports Server.

CITING LEGISLATIVE BRANCH MATERIALS

Congressional Record

Whenever possible, citations should be made to the permanent edition. Since the permanent edition is published three to four years after the daily edition, you should cite to the daily edition with its letter-numbered pages (S, H, E, and D). It is possible to cite an entire issue, section, specific quote, or any other specific section such as a roll call vote. Notice the options available, depending on what you want to emphasize.

161 Cong. Rec. 1626 (2015).

161 Cong. Rec. 1626 (Feb. 3, 2015) (statement of Sheila Jackson Lee).

Jackson Lee, Sheila (TX). Speech on the Value of Vaccinations. *Congressional Record*, One Hundred and Fourteenth Congress 1st Session (February 3, 2015), p. 1626.

Helpful hints on citing the permanent edition is available from ProQuest (*site:proquest.com citing congressional record permanent*).

The daily edition can be cited as follows:

161 Cong. Rec. S4335 (daily ed. June 22, 2015) (statement of Sen. Hatch).

Congressional Hearing

When just citing a hearing generally, you could follow the examples below:

U.S. Senate, Committee on Finance. *Elder Justice: Protecting Seniors from Abuse and Neglect*, Hearing, June 18, 2002 (S. Hrg. 107-734). Washington, DC: Government Printing Office, 2002. (Y 4.F 49:S.HRG.107-734).

U.S. House, Committee on Homeland Security, Subcommittee on Emergency Preparedness, Response, and Communications. *Protecting Our Future: Addressing School Security Challenges in America*, Field Hearing, Newark, NJ, July 9, 2018. Washington, DC: Government Publishing Office, 2018. https://purl.fdlp.gov/GPO/gpo114823. (Y 4.H 75:115-69).

Very often the focus is on individual testimony, and you could do something like this:

Iacocca, Lee A. Statement, July 29, 1975 to the U.S. House, Automobile Industry Task Force of the Committee on Banking, Currency and Housing. In *The Automobile Industry and Its Impact upon the Nation's Economy*, part 1. Washington, Government Printing Office, 1975, pp. 283–290. (Y 4.B 22/1:Au 8/pt.1).

Congressional Report

Seems that the Bluebook prefers the forms: H.R. Rep. and S. Rep., whereas other styles lean toward H. Rpt. and S. Rpt.

U.S. Senate. Committee on Energy and Natural Resources. *Power and Security Systems Act: Report (to accompany S. 190)*. (S. Rpt. 115-76). Washington, DC: Government Publishing Office, 2017. http://purl.fdlp.gov/GPO/gpo81266.

If your purpose was simply to cite the report and not the subject or any other details, you could follow the Bluebook format. But if you needed to focus on the corporate author or the title, then you could include fuller information.

S. Rep. No. 115-76 (2017).

S. Rpt. 115-76 (2017).

U.S. Congress. House. Permanent Select Committee on Intelligence. Report of the House Permanent Select Committee on Intelligence on Russian active measures, together with minority views. (H. Rpt. 115-1110). Washington, DC: Government Publishing Office, 2019. https://purl.fdlp.gov/GPO/gpo114379.

H.R. Rep. No. 115-1110 (2019).

U.S. House. Committee on Interstate and Foreign Commerce. *Termination of Daylight-Saving Time*. (H. Rpt. 79-945). Washington, DC: Government Printing Office, 1945.

H.R. Rep. No. 79-945 (1945).

H. Rpt. 79-945 (1945).

Congressional Document

H.R. Doc. No. 96-374 (1980).

H. Doc. 96-374 (1980).

U.S. Congress. Joint Committee on Printing. *The Capitol: A Pictorial History of the Capitol and of the Congress,* 8th ed. (H. Doc. 96-374). Washington, DC: Government Printing Office, 1980.

Wright, Carroll D. and William O. Hunt. *History and Growth of the United States Census: 1790–1890.* (S. Doc. 56-194). Washington, DC: GPO, 1900.

Public Law

You need to decide if you follow the Bluebook style (Pub. L) or not. It is quite common for "Pub. L." to be shortened to "P.L.," although this is not sanctioned by the Bluebook. Some sources even use "PL".

Bluebook style:

Pub. L. No. 93-366, § 104, 88 Stat. 409 (1974).

Deviating from the Bluebook:

TANF Extension Act of 2019, P.L. 116-4 (2019).
TANF Extension Act of 2019, PL 116-4 (2019).

If you need to draw attention to the title of the Act, then do so:

Patient Protection and Affordable Care Act, Pub. L. No. 111-148 (2010).

Laws enacted during and after 1957 are cited by public law number. Laws enacted before 1957 are cited by the date of enactment of the law and the Statutes at Large chapter number assigned to it.

CITING JUDICIAL BRANCH MATERIALS

Supreme Court Case

Miranda v. Arizona, 384 U.S. 436 (1966).
Citizens United v. Federal Election Commission, 558 U.S. 310 (2010).

It's clear in the above examples that these are Supreme Court decisions. Thus, there is no need to indicate the court as it is in the appellate section below.

Appellate Court Case

Made in the USA Foundation v. United States, 242 F.3d 1300 (11th Cir. 2001).

Hunt v. Nuclear Regulatory Com., 468 F. Supp. 817 (United States District Court for the Northern District of Oklahoma, 1979).

As you can see, I have not given an exhaustive listing of all citation possibilities, but I hope you are not as frightened by citing government resources. Just remember: cite enough information for the item to be findable (and err on the side of including more information than less information), and be consistent throughout your work.

APPENDIX A

Superintendent of Documents Classification System

Outline of Selected Superintendent of Documents Classification System (SuDocs) Stems

Stem	Agency
A	Agriculture
AE	National Archives and Records Administration
B	Broadcasting Board of Governors
C	Commerce Department
CC	Federal Communications Commission
CR	Civil Rights Commission
D	Defense Department
E	Energy Department
ED	Education Department
EP	Environmental Protection Agency
FA	Fine Arts Commission
FCA	Farm Credit Administration

(continued)

Stem	Agency
FHF	Federal Housing Financing Board
FM	Federal Mediation and Conciliation Service
FMC	Federal Maritime Commission
FR	Federal Reserve System Board of Governors
FT	Federal Trade Commission
FTZ	Foreign-Trade Zones Board
GA	Government Accountability Office
GP	Government Printing Office
GS	General Services Administration
HE	Health and Human Services Department
HH	Housing and Urban Development Department
HS	Homeland Security
I	Interior Department
IC	Interstate Commerce Commission
ID	U.S. Agency for International Development
ITC	International Trade Commission
J	Justice Department
JU	Judiciary
L	Labor Department
LC	Library of Congress
LR	National Labor Relations Board
MS	Merit Systems Protection Board
NAS	National Aeronautics and Space Administration
NC	National Capital Planning Commission
NCU	National Credit Union Administration
NF	National Foundation on the Arts and the Humanities
NMB	National Mediation Board
NS	National Science Foundation
OP	Overseas Private Investment Corporation
P	United States Postal Service
PE	Peace Corps
PM	Personnel Management Office
PR	President of the United States
PREX	Executive Office of the President
PRVP	Vice President of the United States

Stem	Agency
RR	Railroad Retirement Board
S	State Department
SBA	Small Business Administration
SE	Securities and Exchange Commission
SI	Smithsonian Institution
SSA	Social Security Administration
T	Treasury Department
TD	Transportation Department
TDA	U.S. Trade and Development Agency
VA	Veterans Affairs Department
X	Congress
Y	Congress

APPENDIX B

Congress/Year Table

Since 1934, the first session of a Congress convenes on January 3 of odd-numbered years and adjourns on January 3 on the following odd-numbered year. For ease of use, this table lists the closing date of each Congress as an even-numbered year. For exact dates of sessions, consult the Congressional Directory, Sessions of Congress table. (See: https://www.senate.gov/reference/Sessions/sessionDates.htm.)

1st	1789–1790	13th	1813–1814	25th	1837–1838
2nd	1791–1792	14th	1815–1816	26th	1839–1840
3rd	1793–1794	15th	1817–1818	27th	1841–1842
4th	1795–1796	16th	1819–1820	28th	1843–1844
5th	1797–1798	17th	1821–1822	29th	1845–1846
6th	1799–1800	18th	1823–1824	30th	1847–1848
7th	1801–1802	19th	1825–1826	31st	1849–1850
8th	1803–1804	20th	1827–1828	32nd	1851–1852
9th	1805–1806	21st	1829–1830	33rd	1853–1854
10th	1807–1808	22nd	1831–1832	34th	1855–1856
11th	1809–1810	23rd	1833–1834	35th	1857–1858
12th	1811–1812	24th	1835–1836	36th	1859–1860

(*continued*)

37th	1861–1862	65th	1917–1918	93rd	1973–1974
38th	1863–1864	66th	1919–1920	94th	1975–1976
39th	1865–1866	67th	1921–1922	95th	1977–1978
40th	1867–1868	68th	1923–1924	96th	1979–1980
41st	1869–1870	69th	1925–1926	97th	1981–1982
42nd	1871–1872	70th	1927–1928	98th	1983–1984
43rd	1873–1874	71st	1929–1930	99th	1985–1986
44th	1875–1876	72nd	1931–1932	100th	1987–1988
45th	1877–1878	73rd	1933–1934	101st	1989–1990
46th	1879–1880	74th	1935–1936	102nd	1991–1992
47th	1881–1882	75th	1937–1938	103rd	1993–1994
48th	1883–1884	76th	1939–1940	104th	1995–1996
49th	1885–1886	77th	1941–1942	105th	1997–1998
50th	1887–1888	78th	1943–1944	106th	1999–2000
51st	1889–1890	79th	1945–1946	107th	2001–2002
52nd	1891–1892	80th	1947–1948	108th	2003–2004
53rd	1893–1894	81st	1949–1950	109th	2005–2006
54th	1895–1896	82nd	1951–1952	110th	2007–2008
55th	1897–1898	83rd	1953–1954	111th	2009–2010
56th	1899–1900	84th	1955–1956	112th	2011–2012
57th	1901–1902	85th	1957–1958	113th	2013–2014
58th	1903–1904	86th	1959–1960	114th	2015–2016
59th	1905–1906	87th	1961–1962	115th	2017–2018
60th	1907–1908	88th	1963–1964	116th	2019–2020
61st	1909–1910	89th	1965–1966	117th	2021–2022
62nd	1911–1912	90th	1967–1968	118th	2023–2024
63rd	1913–1914	91st	1969–1970	119th	2025–2026
64th	1915–1916	92nd	1971–1972	120th	2027–2028

APPENDIX C

Foreign Government Internet Domains

Searching for information on foreign government sites can be a challenge. Although top-level domains (TLDs) are assigned through the Domain Name System, countries are allowed to use whatever secondary domains they choose. This guide augments chapter 9 and is intended to assist with internet site-specific searches.

Afghanistan	gov.af
Albania	gov.al
Algeria	gov.dz
Andorra	gov.ad
Angola	gov.ao
Antigua and Barbuda	gov.ag
Argentina	gov.ar
Armenia	gov.am
Australia	gov.au
Austria	gv.at; statistik.at
Azerbaijan	gov.az
Bahamas	gov.bs
Bahrain	gov.bh

(*continued*)

Bangladesh	gov.bd
Barbados	gov.bb
Belarus	gov.by
Belgium	gov.be
Belize	gov.bz
Benin	gouv.bj; presidence.bj
Bhutan	gov.bt
Bolivia	gob.bo
Bosnia and Herzegovina	gov.ba
Botswana	gov.bw
Brazil	gov.br
Brunei	gov.bn
Bulgaria	gov.bg; e-gov.bg; government.bg
Burkina Faso	gov.bf; assembleenationale.bf
Burundi	gov.bi
Cambodia	gov.kh
Cameroon	gov.cm; prc.cm
Canada	gc.ca
Cape Verde	gov.cv; governo.cv
Central African Republic	[no discernable structure]
Chad	gouv.td
Chile	gob.cl
China	gov.cn
Colombia	gov.co
Comoros	gov.km; gouv.km
Congo, Democratic Republic of the	gouv.cd; presidentrdc.cd
Congo, Republic of the	gouv.cg
Costa Rica	go.cr
Côte d'Ivoire	gouv.ci
Croatia	gov.hr
Cuba	gob.cu
Cyprus	gov.cy
Czech Republic	gov.cz
Denmark	gov.dk
Djibouti	gov.dj; gouv.dj
Dominica	gov.dm

Dominican Republic	gov.do
East Timor (Timor-Leste)	gov.tl
Ecuador	gob.ec; gov.ec
Egypt	gov.eg
El Salvador	gob.sv
Equatorial Guinea	guineaecuatorialpress.com
Eritrea	gov.er
Estonia	gov.ee
Eswatini (Swaziland)	gov.sz
Ethiopia	gov.et
Fiji	gov.fj
Finland	valtioneuvosto.fi (agencies); presidentti.fi; eduskunta.fi (parliament); um.fi (foreign affairs); vm.fi (finance); and many others
France	gouv.fr
Gabon	gouv.ga
The Gambia	gov.gm
Georgia	gov.ge
Germany	bundesregierung.de; bundestag.de (parliament)
Ghana	gov.gh
Greece	gov.gr
Grenada	gov.gd
Guatemala	gob.gt
Guinea	gov.gn
Guinea-Bissau	parlamento.gw
Guyana	gov.gy
Haiti	gouv.ht
Honduras	gob.hn; gov.hn
Hong Kong	gov.hk
Hungary	gov.hu
Iceland	go.is
India	gov.in
Indonesia	go.id
Iran	gov.ir
Iraq	gov.iq

(*continued*)

Ireland	gov.ie
Israel	gov.il
Italy	gov.it
Jamaica	gov.jm
Japan	go.jp
Jordan	gov.jo
Kazakhstan	gov.kz
Kenya	go.ke
Kiribati	gov.ki
Korea, North	gov.kp
Korea, South	go.kr
Kosovo	[TLD not yet assigned]
Kuwait	gov.kw
Kyrgyzstan	gov.kg
Laos	gov.la
Latvia	gov.lv
Lebanon	gov.lb
Lesotho	gov.ls
Liberia	gov.lr
Libya	gov.ly
Liechtenstein	liechtenstein.li
Lithuania	gov.lt
Luxembourg	gouvernement.lu
Madagascar	gov.mg
Malawi	gov.mw
Malaysia	gov.my
Maldives	gov.mv
Mali	gouv.ml; gov.ml
Malta	gov.mt
Marshall Islands	mh domain not used for government; rmiparliament.org (parliament)
Mauritania	gov.mr
Mauritius	govmu.org
Mexico	gob.mx
Micronesia, Federated States of	gov.fm
Moldova	gov.md

Monaco	gouv.mc
Mongolia	gov.mn
Montenegro	gov.me
Morocco	gov.ma
Mozambique	gov.mz
Myanmar (Burma)	gov.mm
Namibia	gov.na
Nauru	gov.nr
Nepal	gov.np
Netherlands	gov.nl
New Zealand	govt.nz
Nicaragua	gob.ni
Niger	gouv.ne
Nigeria	gov.ng
North Macedonia	gov.mk
Norway	regjeringen.no; government.no
Oman	gov.om
Pakistan	gov.pk
Palau	palaugov.pw and palaugov.org; both domains registered to commercial entities
Panama	gob.pa
Papua New Guinea	gov.pg
Paraguay	gov.py
Peru	gob.pe
Philippines	gov.ph
Poland	gov.pl
Portugal	gov.pt
Qatar	gov.qa
Romania	gov.ro
Russia	gov.ru
Rwanda	gov.rw
Saint Kitts and Nevis	gov.kn
Saint Lucia	gov.lc
Saint Vincent and the Grenadines	gov.vc
Samoa	gov.ws; samoagovt.ws
San Marino	sanmarino.sm; esteri.sm; statistica.sm

(continued)

Sao Tome and Principe	gov.st
Saudi Arabia	gov.sa
Senegal	gouv.sn; presidence.sn
Serbia	gov.rs
Seychelles	gov.sc; egov.sc
Sierra Leone	gov.sl
Singapore	gov.sg
Slovakia	gov.sk
Slovenia	gov.si
Solomon Islands	gov.sb
Somalia	gov.so
South Africa	gov.za
Spain	gob.es
Sri Lanka	gov.lk
Sudan	gov.sd
Sudan, South	gov.ss
Suriname	gov.sr
Sweden	gov.se
Switzerland	admin.ch
Syria	gov.sy; egov.sy
Taiwan	gov.tw
Tajikistan	gov.tj; president.tj; stat.tj
Tanzania	go.tz
Thailand	go.th
Togo	gouv.tg
Tonga	gov.to
Trinidad and Tobago	gov.tt
Tunisia	gov.tn
Turkey	gov.tr
Turkmenistan	gov.tm
Tuvalu	tuvalugovernment.tv
Uganda	go.ug
Ukraine	gov.ua
United Arab Emirates	government.ae
United Kingdom	gov.uk
Uruguay	gub.uy

Uzbekistan	gov.uz
Vanuatu	gov.vu
Vatican City	vaticanstate.va
Venezuela	gob.ve
Vietnam	gov.vn
Yemen	gov.ye
Zambia	gov.zm
Zimbabwe	gov.zw

APPENDIX D

Acronyms

Acronyms listed here occur frequently throughout the text. Omitted from this list are SuDocs classification stems, which appear in Appendix A.

APA   Administrative Procedure Act.

ASI   *American Statistics Index* (former Congressional Information Service publication).

ASP   *American State Papers.* The retrospective set of early documents (1789–1838) that precede the Serial Set or fill in gaps of missing documents within the Serial Set.

CBO   Congressional Budget Office.

CFR   *Code of Federal Regulations.* The codification of rules and regulations of the U.S. government.

CGP   Catalog of Government Publications. GPO's online catalog.

CIS   Congressional Information Service. Former publisher of statistical and bibliographic tools.

CONAN   *Constitution of the United States Annotated.*

CR   *Congressional Record.*

CRA   Congressional Review Act.

CRS   Congressional Research Service. The public policy research arm of the Library of Congress. Provides policy research primarily for members of Congress.

DDC   Dewey Decimal Classification.

EDGAR   Electronic Data Gathering, Analysis, and Retrieval system used by the Securities and Exchange Commission.

EPUB   [a file format for e-books].

ERIC   Education Resources Information Center.

FBIS   Foreign Broadcast Information Service. Daily reports and translations of foreign radio and press from 1941 to 2013.

FDLP   Federal Depository Library Program.

FDsys   Federal Digital System. GPO's information system that came after GPO Access and before Govinfo.gov.

FOIA   Freedom of Information Act.

FR   *Federal Register.* The official journal of the U.S. government.

FRUS   *Foreign Relations of the United States.* Department of State publication from 1861 to present covering the official documentary history of U.S. foreign policy.

GAO   Since 2005, GAO stands for the Government Accountability Office. Previously, it stood for the General Accounting Office.

GPO   Since December 2014, GPO stands for the Government Publishing Office. Previously it was the Government Printing Office.

HT   HathiTrust. Digital repository with a dedication mission of preserving U.S. government publications.

IIS   *Index to International Statistics* (former Congressional Information Service publication).

IRC   Independent Regulatory Commission.

JPRS   Joint Publications Research Service. JPRS is a sister publication series to the FBIS series.

LC   Library of Congress, or Library of Congress Classification System.

LSA   *List of Sections Affected.* Actually *List of CFR Sections Affected.* The bridge between the daily *Federal Register* and the annual *Code of Federal Regulations.*

MeSH   Medical Subject Headings. The subject system used to provide intellectual access to Medline and PubMed citations.

MOBI   Mobipocket [an e-book file extension].

NAICS	North American Industry Classification System.
NAPA	National Academy of Public Administration.
NARA	National Archives and Records Administration.
NIST	National Institute of Standards and Technology.
NPRM	Notice of Proposed Rulemaking.
NTIS	National Technical Information Service.
NTRL	National Technical Reports Library.
OCLC	Originally stood for Ohio College Library Center and later, Online Computer Library Center, but now is known just as OCLC. OCLC is a nonprofit cooperative library organization.
OMB	Office of Management and Budget.
PACER	Public Access to Court Electronic Records.
PDF	Portable Document Format. A file format created by Adobe for presenting and exchanging documents independent of software, hardware, or operating system.
PII	Personally Identifiable Information. Examples include a full name and address, social security number, and driver's license number.
PMC	PubMed Central. The free, full-text collection of medical and related journal literature maintained by the U.S. National Institutes of Health's National Library of Medicine.
PSA	Principal Statistical Agency.
PUMA	Public Use Microdata Areas.
PUMS	Public Use Microdata Sample.
PURL	Persistent Uniform Resource Locator.
SRI	*Statistical Reference Index* (former Congressional Information Service publication).
TRAIL	Technical Report Archive and Image Library.
WNC	*World News Connection*. The online version of FBIS *Daily Reports* that replaced the print and fiche issuances.

APPENDIX E

Correspondences between U.S. Code and *Code of Federal Regulations*

The table below shows current correlation between USC and CFR in terms of topic. No attempt has been made to show historic topical coverage.

Title	United States Code	*Code of Federal Regulations*
Title 1	General Provisions	General Provisions
Title 2	The Congress	Grants and Agreements
Title 3	The President	The President
Title 4	Flag and Seal, Seat of Government, and the States	Accounts
Title 5	Government Organization and Employees; 5a Federal Advisory Committee Act	Administrative Personnel
Title 6	Domestic Security	Domestic Security
Title 7	Agriculture	Agriculture
Title 8	Aliens and Nationality	Aliens and Nationality
Title 9	Arbitration	Animals and Animal Products

(*continued*)

Title	United States Code	*Code of Federal Regulations*
Title 10	Armed Forces	Energy
Title 11	Bankruptcy; 11a Bankruptcy Rules	Federal Elections
Title 12	Banks and Banking	Banks and Banking
Title 13	Census	Business Credit and Assistance
Title 14	Coast Guard	Aeronautics and Space
Title 15	Commerce and Trade	Commerce and Foreign Trade
Title 16	Conservation	Commercial Practices
Title 17	Copyrights	Commodity and Securities Exchanges
Title 18	Crimes and Criminal Procedure; 18a Unlawful Possession or Receipt of Firearms	Conservation of Power and Water Resources
Title 19	Customs Duties	Customs Duties
Title 20	Education	Employees' Benefits
Title 21	Food and Drugs	Food and Drugs
Title 22	Foreign Relations and Intercourse	Foreign Relations
Title 23	Highways	Highways
Title 24	Hospitals and Asylums	Housing and Urban Development
Title 25	Indians	Indians
Title 26	Internal Revenue Code	Internal Revenue
Title 27	Intoxicating Liquors	Alcohol, Tobacco Products, and Firearms
Title 28	Judiciary and Judicial Procedure; 28a Judicial Personnel Financial Disclosure Requirements	Judicial Administration
Title 29	Labor	Labor
Title 30	Mineral Lands and Mining	Mineral Resources
Title 31	Money and Finance	Money and Finance: Treasury
Title 32	National Guard	National Defense
Title 33	Navigation and Navigable Waters	Navigation and Navigable Waters
Title 34	Crime Control and Law Enforcement	Education

Title	United States Code	*Code of Federal Regulations*
Title 35	Patents	[Panama Canal until 1999]; now empty
Title 36	Patriotic and National Observances, Ceremonies, and Organizations	Parks, Forests, and Public Property
Title 37	Pay and Allowances of the Uniformed Services	Patents, Trademarks, and Copyrights
Title 38	Veterans' Benefits	Pensions, Bonuses, and Veterans' Relief
Title 39	Postal Service	Postal Service
Title 40	Public Buildings, Property, and Works	Protection of Environment
Title 41	Public Contracts	Public Contracts and Property Management
Title 42	The Public Health and Welfare	Public Health
Title 43	Public Lands	Public Lands: Interior
Title 44	Public Printing and Documents	Emergency Management and Assistance
Title 45	Railroads	Public Welfare
Title 46	Shipping	Shipping
Title 47	Telecommunications	Telecommunication
Title 48	Territories and Insular Possessions	Federal Acquisition Regulations System
Title 49	Transportation	Transportation
Title 50	War and National Defense	Wildlife and Fisheries
Title 51	National and Commercial Space Programs	
Title 52	Voting and Elections	
Title 53	[Reserved]	
Title 54	National Park Service and Related Programs	

APPENDIX F

Selected Major Federal Databases

Data.gov claims to have access to over 200,000 federal government data sets (https://www.data.gov/metrics). Data sets are different from databases. How many publicly accessible U.S. federal government databases actually exist is an unknown question, but it is safe to say it numbers in the thousands. We can only list selected ones here.

This list does not make reference to the many government databases that contain personally identifiable information (PII). Rather, it focuses on statistics, reports, publications, and bibliographic entries.

Database Name, URL, and Brief Description

Access to Archival Databases (AAD).
https://aad.archives.gov/aad/
National Archives
Covers 1800 to present; Ex: war casualties, passenger ship arrivals, relocated Japanese

Agricola.
https://agricola.nal.usda.gov/
National Library of Medicine Online Catalog

(continued)

Database Name, URL, and Brief Description

BEA Data
https://www.bea.gov/data
Bureau of Economic Analysis
GDP, Consumer spending, Income & saving, industries, prices & inflation

Bureau of Labor Statistics Databases.
https://www.bls.gov/data/
Producer prices, consumer prices, employment, earnings, labor force, etc.

Catalog of U.S. Government Publications (CGP)
https://catalog.gpo.gov/
Government Printing/Publishing Office's online catalog and publication list

CDC Community Health Improvement Navigator—Database of Interventions
https://wwwn.cdc.gov/chidatabase
Select a variable and view reviews and individual studies; e.g., tobacco use, BMI, cholesterol, diabetes.

CDFI Fund Searchable Award Database
https://www.cdfifund.gov/awards/state-awards/
Community Development Financial Institutions Fund searchable awards database.

Census Geocoder
https://www.census.gov/geo/maps-data/data/geocoder.html
Address look-up tool that converts your address to an approximate coordinate (longitude/latitude) and returns information about the address range that includes the address and the census geography the address is within.

Climate Data Online.
https://www.ncdc.noaa.gov/cdo-web/
National Oceanic and Atmospheric Administration. 1763–present. Links to additional databases.

Clinical Trials
https://clinicaltrials.gov/
Database of privately and publicly funded clinical studies conducted around the world.

Condominiums
https://entp.hud.gov/idapp/html/condlook.cfm
Search for FHA-approved condominium projects by location, name, or status.

Consumer Financial Protection Bureau
https://www.consumerfinance.gov/data-research/consumer-complaints/
Complaints about consumer financial products and services.

Copyright Database
https://cocatalog.loc.gov/
Search copyrights from 1978 to present.

Database Name, URL, and Brief Description

Database of Postsecondary Institutions and Programs
https://ope.ed.gov/dapip/
Information reported by recognized accrediting agencies.

Dataweb.usitc.gov
https://dataweb.usitc.gov/
Provides U.S. merchandise trade and tariff data.

Defense Technical Information Center (DTIC).
https://discover.dtic.mil/
Defense Department. Technical reports. Has a thesaurus for vocabulary control.

Development Experience Clearinghouse
https://dec.usaid.gov/
Users can view and evaluate several decades of past international development experiences.

DOE Science Cinema
https://www.osti.gov/sciencecinema/
Department of Energy. Find and watch science-related videos.

Drug Labs in the United States: National Clandestine Laboratory Register Data
https://www.dea.gov/clan-lab
Drug Enforcement Administration. Find drug labs and drug dumpsites.

Earth Explorer
 https://earthexplorer.usgs.gov/
Browse maps and search by address.

EPA Grant Awards Database
https://yosemite.epa.gov/oarm/igms_egf.nsf/Homepage?ReadForm
Summary record for all non-construction EPA grants awarded in the last 10 years.

ERIC
https://eric.ed.gov/
Dept. of Education. Index of ERIC documents (ED) and ERIC journal articles (EJ).

FCC AM Query Broadcast Station Search
https://www.fcc.gov/media/radio/am-query
Current technical data for U.S. AM radio stations.

FCC FM Query Broadcast Station Search
https://www.fcc.gov/media/radio/fm-query
Current technical data for U.S. FM radio stations.

(continued)

Database Name, URL, and Brief Description

FCC TV Query Broadcast Station Search
https://www.fcc.gov/media/television/tv-query
Current technical data for U.S. TV stations.

Federal Inmate Locator
https://www.bop.gov/inmateloc/
Bureau of Prisons. Find where prisoners are in federal prisons.

FEMA Data Visualization: Disaster Declarations for States and Counties
https://www.fema.gov/data-visualization-disaster-declarations-states-and
-counties
Historical view of disasters by state.

FRASER
https://fraser.stlouisfed.org/
Federal Reserve Bank of St. Louis. Economic statistics, current and historical.

FRED
https://fred.stlouisfed.org/
Federal Reserve Bank of St. Louis. Graphical view of economic statistics.

FS Publications
https://www.fs.fed.us/publications
Forest Service.

GAO Recommendations Database
https://www.gao.gov/reports-testimonies/recommendations-database/
Agency and policy issues that are still open and need to be addressed. Great place
for public policy research paper ideas.

GAO Reports.
https://www.gao.gov/
Government Accountability Office. Oversight reports.

GovInfo.
https://www.govinfo.gov/
Government Publishing Office. Emphasis on Congress and regulatory sources.

Grants.gov
https://www.grants.gov/
Search for government grants with facets for easy selection. Null search retrieves
entire database results.

Homeland Security Digital Library
https://www.hsdl.org/
Naval Postgraduate School. Note: Depository libraries have access to full
collection.

Database Name, URL, and Brief Description

Medline Plus
https://medlineplus.gov/
Information about diseases, conditions, and wellness issues in plain English.

MyEnvironment
https://www3.epa.gov/myem/envmap/find.html
Enter a place or address and receive air quality, water quality, energy data, cancer risk, climate data, and more.

NASA Technical Reports Server (NTRS)
https://ntrs.nasa.gov/
National Aeronautics and Space Administration technical reports.

National Environmental Publications Information System (NEPIS)
https://nepis.epa.gov/
Environmental Protection Agency. Technical reports.

National Register of Historic Places Map Search
https://bit.ly/2El0kqm
Search by name or click places on map.

National Technical Reports Library (NTRL)
https://ntrl.ntis.gov/NTRL/
National Technical Information Service (NTIS) technical reports.

NOAA Storm Events Database
https://www.ncdc.noaa.gov/stormevents/
Storm data from January 1950 to recent.

North American Industry Classification System
https://www.census.gov/eos/www/naics/
Official classification system for industries.

OSTI.gov
https://osti.gov
Office of Scientific and Technical Information. Primary search tool for technical reports, datasets, conference papers, etc.

Patents: PatFT and AppFT
https://www.uspto.gov/patent
Search patents and patent applications and view them in full text (1976 to current).

PLANTS Database
https://plants.sc.egov.usda.gov/
Look up plants by scientific or popular name.

(continued)

Database Name, URL, and Brief Description

Spending Explorer
https://www.usaspending.gov/
From the Treasury Department. Tracks federal spending.

Standard Industrial Classification (SIC) System Search
https://www.osha.gov/pls/imis/sicsearch.html
Former industrial classification system (pre-NAICS) but still in use by some today.

Standard Occupational Classification
https://www.bls.gov/soc/
Federal statistics standard for occupations from the Bureau of Labor Statistics.

Topoview—Historic USGS Maps
https://ngmdb.usgs.gov/topoview/
View or download topo maps from 1884 to 2006.

Trademarks: TESS Trademark Database
https://www.uspto.gov/trademark
Official trademark database.

Treesearch
https://www.fs.usda.gov/treesearch/
Latin name search works well.

Index

About the Author

Christopher C. Brown is reference librarian and coordinator of government documents at the University of Denver, Main Library. For more than 20 years, he has overseen the large government information collection and provided reference services to the university community and members of the general public. He is the author of *Harnessing the Power of Google: What Every Researcher Should Know* (Libraries Unlimited) and *Librarian's Guide to Online Searching* (5th edition, with Suzanne S. Bell, Libraries Unlimited). Chris has taught as an adjunct professor in the University of Denver Library School for 20 years, and dozens of students have taken his government publications course over the years.

Discarded